Instructor's Manual
with Test Item File

DATABASE PROCESSING

Eighth Edition

David M. Kroenke

David M. Kroenke
Seattle, Washington

Dr. Steven A. Morris
Middle Tennessee State University

Pearson
Education

Upper Saddle River, New Jersey 07458

Acquisitions editor: Bob Horan
Associate editor: Kyle Hannon
Production editor: Wanda Rockwell
Manufacturer: Courier, Bookmart Press, Inc.

ISBN 0-13-065552-X

10 9 8 7 6 5 4 3 2 1

Table of Contents

Instructor's Manual

Test Item File

Introduction

The database class is one of the best classes in the IT curriculum to teach. Its many elements ensure the class is always interesting. The artistic aspects of data modeling lead to the concrete process of database design. Then, those designs are implemented using any of the many DBMS products available to the instructor for classroom use. Those implemented databases can be processed using applications with either traditional or Internet technology. If desired, programming projects can be brought into this mixture either via scripting languages like VBScript or JavaScript, or via "real" languages such as Java or C++. This rich mixture can then be topped off with a discussion of data analysis using OLAP and then, finally, of object-relational databases. All in all, it's a compelling mixture of fascinating topics.

Moreover, it's important! As one CEO put it recently, "There's a database in everything." The demand for database practitioners continues to accelerate in every business discipline and industry. There are many more jobs than people to fill them, and this situation is likely to continue for some time to come.

Even the dot-com bust has not slowed the adoption of database technology. Companies are increasingly using Internet-technology within their organizations, even though the demand for e-commerce applications has not grown as expected. As reported in the *Wall Street Journal*, May 3, 2001, the General Electric Company strongly endorsed Internet-technology for e-commerce only to find that they had far more applications for it in-house than out-of-house. They are increasingly developing small internal applications (with databases) connected via email and Internet technology.

The only dark cloud on the horizon for the database class is that there is so much to teach. Unless the students have had some prior exposure to database processing, I think it will be very difficult to teach all of the material in this text in one semester. With the importance of the topic, it is time to consider creating a full-year database class. Even if this comes to pass, however, it will take time to occur, and in the near term, you will probably have to choose to omit some topics. See the Technology Alternatives section below for ideas on reducing the material to cover.

Topic Outline

I believe that teaching data modeling skills is the most important part of this class. **Once they have a design**, students can read a book on Access or SQL Server or ORACLE or *something or other for Dummies* to learn how to use a product to create a database. This course is, however, the single, most effective place for students to learn data modeling and database design skills. It may be the only place where anyone even tries!

Over the years I have found that launching immediately into data modeling confuses the students. Until they see and work with a small database, they do not understand how data modeling fits into the larger picture. Hence, I think it is important to set the stage, as is done in Chapters 1 and 2, before beginning the modeling and design topics.

Following this line of reasoning, I believe the general threads of this course are, in order:

- Establish perspective by showing what a database is, how one is used, and what the components are

- Teach data modeling and database design

- Learn how to process a database via SQL and application programs

- Learn the features and functions of DBMS products and apply that learning to Oracle, SQL Server, or both

- Teach technology and products for publishing databases using Internet technology with either ASP or JSP

- Discuss other topics as time allows and local student needs require

As stated, this is a lot of material to teach. If the students have already used Access or another personal DBMS in other courses, then you can save time by abbreviating the first item. On the other hand, if this is the students' first exposure to database processing, then the first four items will probably fill all the class time.

A Note on Data Modeling

Two different data modeling tools are taught in *Database Processing.* Chapter 3 explains the basic features and concepts of the entity-relationship model and applies that model to two small case applications. Chapter 6 then shows how to transform entity-relationship designs into normalized database designs. Chapter 4 teaches the features and concepts of the semantic object model, and Chapter 7 then teaches database design using semantic objects.

The entity-relationship model is well known and the inclusion of a large amount of material on it will be of no surprise. You may be surprised to find two chapters on the semantic object model. This model, which is an integration of the semantic data model (Hammer and McLeod) with the design philosophies of object-oriented programming, has, I believe, important advantages over the entity-relationship model. For one, it is easier for users to understand. It also leads, more naturally, to normalized database designs. Additionally, semantic objects can be used to guide database application design (as shown in Chapter 9). They also provide boundaries for logical units of work. Even more important, it is possible to better model complicated databases with the semantic object model than with the entity-relationship model. Finally, in my experience, it is far easier to learn and to teach the modeling of complicated databases with the semantic object model than with the entity-relationship model.

If time is short, you can skip the material on the semantic object model without loss of continuity. But, given the importance of data modeling, I think that presenting two different approaches is certainly appropriate and helpful to the student.
Coolstrategy.dom has developed a database modeling and design tool called Tabledesigner that uses the semantic object modeling. This product is actually a re-release of Wall Data's product Tabledesigner. If you used it in the past, Tabledesigner will seem very familiar. You can use it to generate Access and SQL Server databases as well as to create ASP pages for database processing on the Web. Your students will gain much more from this modeling technique if they use this tool in conjunction with their study. You and your students can

download a free copy of it for use in your course from www.prenhall.com/kroenke. This copy can also be placed in your lab if that is more effective for you. See Appendix B for more information about this product and its use.

Changes from the Seventh Edition

The second half of this textbook has been essentially re-written since the last edition. Chapter 11 presents some of the material from the prior edition's Chapter 12, but that material has been re-organized and modernized. The current edition Chapter 11 presents an overview of database administration and then uses that overview to introduce the features and functions of modern commercial-duty DBMS products such as Oracle and SQL Server.

Chapters 12 and 13 then present Oracle and SQL Server, respectively. The organization of the discussion in both of these chapters mirrors that of Chapter 11. Thus, Chapter 11 presents DBMS features and functions in the abstract, Chapter 12 presents those features and functions as implemented in Oracle and Chapter 13 presents them as implemented in SQL Server. The parallelism here should ease the teaching and learning of this material.

Oracle is taught using the SQL Plus Oracle utility. Because this utility is text-based, only SQL statements are used to construct relations, relationships, views, constraints, indexes, stored procedures, and triggers. This discussion of SQL DDL supplements the SQL DML presented in Chapter 9. Because SQL DDL is taught in Chapter 12, SQL Server is presented in Chapter 13 using more graphical tools. While these tools are convenient, they do hide many details from the student, and I believe that some attention should be given to the SQL DDL even if only Chapter 13 is taught.

Chapter 14 is a re-write of Chapter 11 in the 7th edition. I have removed some of the less-database oriented topics from that chapter and have introduced a substantial section on XML Schema. This topic is important not only its use today, but also because it will be a major feature of Microsoft's .Net product family. Chapter 15 is a re-write of Chapter 13 in the 7th edition. I have modernized the presentation and included discussions of accessing both Oracle and SQL Sever from ASP pages. This chapter also describes how to invoke a stored procedure from ASP.

Chapter 16 is entirely new. It presents the use of Java, JDBC, JSP, and MySQL. This chapter was written assuming the student has some knowledge of programming, but not necessarily knowledge of Java. Students who know Java will find this chapter a very easy read. Students who are not Java programmers will not understand every statement in the examples, but as stated at the start of the chapter, I do not think it is essential that they do so. Their goal should be to understand the difference in character between ASP and JSP – the close acronyms make these technologies sound more similar than they are.

Given the many short-comings of MySQL, you may wonder why it is present in this text. For one, it can be used commercially for query-only applications or for applications that do not require its missing features (and there are many such applications). Additionally, I think it is important for students to understand what is available in the open-source community for DBMS products. Finally, MySQL is free and can be a good choice for applications on a very limited budget (student clubs, for example). I also think it's a fun product with which to work – in many ways it takes me back to 1985 – and we were able to accomplish quite a bit with such products in those days. But, in no way is MySQL a legitimate competitor with Oracle or SQL Server, and I hope this comes through in this chapter.

Chapter 17 is a revision of the 7th edition's Chapter 14. The main addition to this chapter is a discussion of the OLAP star and snowflake schemas. Finally, Chapter 18 is a revision of the 7th edition's Chapter 17. The major change to it is a discussion of the object-relational features and functions of Oracle.

Of course, the normal changes that are made from edition to edition have been made as well. For example, all of the Access 2000 examples have been replaced by Access 2002 examples (the changes are more graphical in nature than in substance). Other changes have been made to make the examples more current and relevant.

Finally, a new series of short-project questions has been appended to each chapter. These projects concern, FiredUp, a small manufacturer of camping stoves. Each chapter is concluded with a set of questions that require the student to apply the ideas from the chapter to this business. Answers to these questions are provided in this Instructor's Manual.

Use of Oracle and SQL Server

You can order one of three versions of this text. One is accompanied by a version 8i of Oracle, one is accompanied by SQL Server 2000, and the third has no software at all. If you're wondering why there is no version with both Oracle and SQL Server, it is because the license agreement between Prentice-Hall and Oracle does not allow it. Therefore you have to pick a version for the students. (If you want to teach both, however, there is nothing to prevent you, as instructor, from doing so. The students can download a version of Oracle from the Oracle web site and an evaluation version of SQL Server from the Microsoft web site.) Be aware that there is a difference in the licenses, however. With SQL Server, the license for evaluation version is limited to 120 days from the date of install.

Using Oracle 8i

As stated in the text, Oracle is the world's most popular DBMS. It is also one of the world's most difficult to install software products. If you are using Oracle, and there are many good reasons to do so, plan an extra amount of time for installation. Do not give up hope, however, because once it is installed, it is quite easy to use and performs just as documented. With some time, you'll probably like it. I know I do. But, it can be a pain to install, and Prentice-Hall does not have the expertise or resources to help you. Instead, if you are having difficulties, approach a professional who has Oracle experience, maybe someone in a local chapter of DPMA or the ACM or similar organization. There may also be a local Oracle users' group that can help.

For the purposes of this text, you need only install Personal Oracle 8i. You need not install Oracle Designer (a CASE tool) nor Oracle Forms and Reports.

I like Oracle for a number of reasons. For one, using SQL Plus, the text-based editor, forces students to learn and use SQL for both DDL and DML. It also requires them to understand more about what they are doing than a pure graphical interface does. Additionally, while all stored procedures and triggers in the text are written in PL/SQL, it is possible to write them in Java as well. If your students are Java programmers, there are many opportunities to integrate Java with Oracle. Also, the concurrency control and backup and recovery mechanisms in Oracle are well designed and implemented. Finally, I believe Oracle has done a masterful job of integrating object oriented thinking with relational databases in their object-relational structures. See Chapter 18 for more information about that.

Using SQL Server 2000

SQL Server 2000 differs from Oracle in a number of ways. For one, it is a dream to install on a Windows 2000 machine; just pick directories and click![1] Also, the data definition tools are easy-to-use graphical tools similar to those in Access. While these graphical tools do ease the development process, they also hide some complexity from the student and require less SQL knowledge. You can, of course, forbid the students to use the graphical tools for creating and maintaining tables and relationships, but that is a losing battle.

As a Microsoft product, SQL Server has tight integration with Microsoft Access and also with IIS. Thus, it's easy to publish SQL Server data using Active Server Pages. (Actually, however, if you use ODBC as illustrated in Chapter 15, it's really not any harder to publish Oracle data.) Because it is easier to learn and use, students can get a lot more done with SQL Server than with Oracle. One can debate, however, whether the students have learned more about database technology in the process; they certainly will have learned less about SQL, but maybe they will have greater confidence to finish a database project.

Before the 2000 version of SQL Server, Oracle definitely provided better performance than SQL Server. With SQL Server 2000, Microsoft claims this is no longer true. Because Oracle provides more ways to tune database performance than SQL Server does, it's possible that a well-tuned Oracle applications will still outperform a SQL Server application.

I would say that, if time allows, address both products. Even if the students just work with one product, you can demonstrate the other product in class. I think it's really very difficult to say that one of these products is uniformly better than the other. Certainly, the popularity of both in the marketplace testifies to the fact that both products have a role in industry. For me, I like them both!

A Note on the ViewRidge Gallery Database

The ViewRidge Gallery schema introduced in Chapter 10 is used throughout Chapters 10-16. I chose this particular schema because it involves the processing of weak entities and an intersection table. It also has two multi-valued paths so that students will learn firsthand why

---

[1] There are two edges to this sword. When I was attempting to install Oracle on my Linux machine, I was directed to documentation that listed tests I needed to perform to determine whether or not I needed to modify the kernel. Modifying my operating system's kernel is not a task I want to take on – been there and done that – and I aborted the attempt. When I complained about that to one of my friends who likes Oracle, (Marty Murray at Portland Community College) she responded, "Hey, right, you don't have that problem with SQL Server – it just does it without asking!" And that, I think, pretty much summarizes the difference between Oracle and SQL Server. Oracle gives you great control over details and SQL Server does it for you. Microsoft will make life much easier, but you lose control of your machine.

a single SQL statement cannot represent a view and how to deal with the consequences of this fact.

The ViewRidge example is used to illustrate processing with both Oracle and SQL Server. There are slight differences in the stored procedures and triggers, due to differences in the two products, but they are nearly identical. Both Oracle and SQL Server databases are processed via ODBC in Chapter 15; in fact, as pointed out in the text, only a single statement need be changed to switch from one database to another. This surely must gladden the hearts of the ODBC designers, even as they watch Microsoft back away from it with .Net. (At least given the announcements so far, SQL Server will have many better facilities in .Net than Oracle will. I guess the only surprise is that it took them this long!)

Learning Internet Technology

While Internet technology is proving to be a great boon to database processing, it does require new knowledge on the part of the instructor. It will not be too difficult to learn what you need for this class, however, and there are many helpful resources available. If you are not already familiar with this technology, I recommend the following tasks and resources:

1. Read Chapters 14-16 to see what will be presented

2. Visit the excellent Web site that the World Wide Web Consortium (W3C) publishes at www.w3.org. Look for tutorials and links to tutorial sites for learning DHTML and XML.

3. Install a copy of Access 2002, create some tables and forms and export them to ASP. Examine the ASP code that Access generates to understand how to blend database processing with Web server processing.

4. Install a copy of NT with IIS. Publish the ASP pages from Access to a directory and use them. Make changes to the ASP pages and observe the consequences.

5. Obtain the ASP pages used in Chapter 15 from the instructor's portion of our Web site and install them on an IIS server. Make changes to the pages and observe the results.

6. Install IE 5.0 and, using Figure 11-19 as an example, write XSL for materializing XML documents.

7. Visit vendor Web sites such as www.microsoft.com, www.oracle.com, java.sun.com/products/jdbc, and www.mysql.com, and search for tutorials on DHTML, XML, OLE DB, OLAP, JDBC and other technologies.

8. Obtain the Java code from the instructor's portion of our Web site. Also obtain and install Tomcat and a Java development environment. With that, compile and run the Java programs and JSP pages.

Technology Alternatives

As explained in the preface, the text was designed with three sets of topic alternatives as follows:

Topic	Alternative One	Alternative Two
Data Modeling	Entity-relationship model Chapters 3 and 6	Semantic Object Model Chapters 4 and 7
Multi-user DBMS	Oracle Chapter 12	SQL Server Chapter 13
Web Publishing	IIS, ASP, ODBC Chapter 15	Java, JDBC, JSP Chapter 16

The text is written so that you can mix and match among these topics as necessary. The only caveat on that statement is that if you choose SQL Server and do not choose Oracle, you may want to supplement the discussion of SQL DDL in Chapter 13 with some of the examples from Chapter 12. Even that is not a requirement, however.

The choice among these alternatives really depends on the needs of your graduates. If I had to choose between the E-R model and SOM, I would certainly choose E-R because it is far more prevalent in industry. The choice between Oracle and SQL Sever depends on which is more commonly used in your community. As stated, a discussion of both is probably the best idea, if possible. As between Chapters 15 and 16, the Microsoft technology in Chapter 15 is probably more important from a pragmatic standpoint than the Java technology in Chapter 16. On the other hand, Java is such a fun language to teach and use that it's hard to give it up.

In the final analysis, if I had to abbreviate my class, I would choose E-R modeling, either of Oracle or SQL Server 2000, and omit Chapter 16. I grieve as I write that, however.

End of Chapter Exercises and Projects

Chapters include two categories of exercises and a set of projects. The purpose of the Group I questions is review. After reading the chapter, students should be able to answer all of the Group I questions without problem or hesitation. I encourage the students to use those questions when preparing for an exam. The Group II questions require the students to apply or extend the material presented in the chapter. These questions require more thought, time, and work.

Projects require application of chapter material in a problem setting. Three projects run through the first seven chapters. Two of them are introduced in Chapter 1 and concern databases that could be used for e-commerce; one uses Dell for an example and the other uses Amazon.com as an example. The third project, which is introduced at the end of Chapter 3, concerns a non-profit organization, the Metropolitan Housing Authority. These projects are used for the purpose of developing entity-relationship models and for semantic object models, as well as for transforming entity-relationship and semantic object designs into relational designs. I recommend that using one of the cases for in- class discussion of text materials and assigning the other two for student projects.

As stated, the FiredUp project runs continuously through the chapters. There are FiredUp exercises for almost every chapter. With the exception of the Oracle and SQL Server chapters, these questions and exercises should not require more than an hour or at most, two, of the student's time. The Oracle and SQL Server chapters will require more time because they involve the writing of stored procedures. I hope these exercises will be fun and useful.

Answers to all project assignments are presented in this instructor's manual. In addition, our Web site at www.prenhall.com/kroenke/ contains all Tabledesigner models of the projects. This site also has the Access 2000 and Access 2002 databases discussed in the text, as well as SQL Server databases and SQL code for constructing the Oracle databases. Code for stored procedures and triggers will be found there as well as all ASP and Java code. This site also has these same resources for Projects and FiredUp exercises.

Materials for a Course Syllabus

The following materials may be helpful for constructing a course syllabus.

Course Objectives

- Learn the role of databases and database applications in contemporary organizations

- Learn and practice data modeling using the entity-relationship and semantic object models

- Learn and practice developing database designs

- Understand the use of SQL and learn SQL syntax

- Understand the special needs of multi-user database processing and learn techniques for controlling the consequences of concurrent data access

- Know the features and functions of a commercial-duty DBMS product and understand how these are implemented in Oracle and SQL Server.

- Learn the need for both database administration and data administration

- Learn emerging Internet technology that is relevant to database processing including the use of XML, ASP, OLE DB, ADO, ODBC, JDBC, and JSP

- Understand the issues involved in enterprise data sharing and learn the nature of data warehouses

- Learn the features and functions of OLAP (OnLine Analytical Processing) and understand its relationship to database processing

- Understand the need for object database management and learn the basics of the Oracle object-relational, SQL3 and ODMG standards

Plus other objectives that relate to the projects you assign.

Sample Course Outline

The course outline shown below can be used for a class having thirty fifty-minute meetings. To cover this amount of material in thirty lessons, the course must move along very quickly. If you have many out-of-class assignments or projects, you may want to cut back discussed before. Also, this outline allows four class sessions for Oracle and SQL Server. Depending on your students' needs, you may want to devote 3 lessons to one of these products and a single lesson to the other. Also, this outline does not include either of the Appendices and you may need to make adjustments for them.

If you have a fifteen-week semester, then cases, lectures on DBMS products, and lab sessions can be added. The breakup of the chapters as shown in the outline below could still be used and the other material added around the assignments shown.

Course Outline for Thirty Fifty-minute Lectures

Class Meeting	Topic	Reading Assignment
1	Introduction	
2	Overview and History of Database Processing	Chapter 1
3	Components of a Database System	Chapter 2
4	Entity-relationship Model I	Chapter 3
5	Entity-relationship Model II	Chapter 3
6	Semantic Object Model I	Chapter 4
7	Semantic Object Model II	Chapter 4
8	Normalization	Chapter 5
9	Normalization	Chapter 5
10	Exam I	
11	Database Design with E-R I	Chapter 6
12	Database Design with E-R II	Chapter 6
13	Database Design with SOM I	Chapter 7
14	Relational Implementation and Relational Algebra	Chapter 8
15	SQL I	Chapter 9
16	SQL II	Chapter 9
17	Exam II	
18	Database Application Design	Chapter 10
19	Database Administration & DBMS Functions	Chapter 11
20	Oracle and/or SQL Server	Chapter 12/13
21	Oracle and/or SQL Server	Chapter 12/13
22	Oracle and/or SQL Server	Chapter 12/13
23	Database Processing Using Internet Technology I	Chapter 14
24	Database Processing Using Internet Technology II	Chapter 14
25	Accessing the Database Server I	Chapter 15
26	Accessing the Database Server II	Chapter 15
27	Java, JDBC, and JSP	Chapter 16
28	Sharing Enterprise Data	Chapter 17
29	Object Oriented Database Processing	Chapter 18
30	Review	

Instructor's Manual

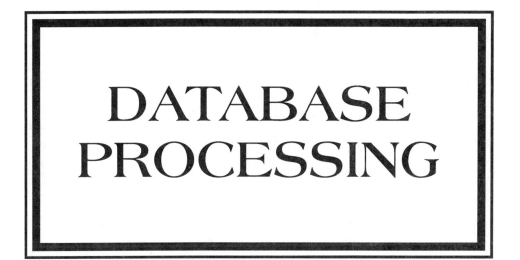

Chapter 1

Introduction to Database Processing

Objectives

- Understand different types of databases and their organizational contexts.
- Compare file processing systems and database processing systems.
- Define the term *database*.
- Learn the historical context of database processing.

Teaching Suggestions

Introduce the course by explaining that database processing is the heart of all applications today. The demand for knowledgeable people (both users and technicians) is high, but the supply is low. The knowledge gained in this course will be valuable at job-hunting time. Internet technology has tremendously amplified the need for database knowledge – that technology can be used inside organizations as well as outside for e-commerce applications. The dot com bust has not had much of a depressing effect on the demand for database expertise.

The goal of the opening sections is to teach the fact that databases vary widely in size, complexity, and organizational scope. On completing this course, the students should be able to develop personal and even some workgroup databases on their own, and they should be able to participate as productive members of a team to develop an organizational database. With some work, they should be able to develop simple Internet technology applications as well.

When discussing file processing systems, remind students that users of file processing systems are almost always at the mercy of the MIS department to write programs that manipulate stored data and produce needed information. One significant development in database processing, particularly with the more user-friendly relational DBMS products, is that users can sometimes get their own answers from the stored data.

Today, few students have had experience with file processing systems. You may need to teach them about file processing before discussing how database processing differs from file processing. The major point of all this is the need to process data by relationship.

Check to ensure the students distinguish among a database (the stored data), a DBMS (a software product that processes a database), and a database application (software that calls on a DBMS to process a database on its behalf). These terms are often misused and the differences among them are surprisingly difficult to teach.

I find the term *DBMS products* easier to pronounce than *DBMSs*.

Possibly the most interesting aspect of the history of database processing is how much it has changed in the past 25 years. With the advent of the Web, with XML, with the soon-to-be-realized emergence of fast data transmission to the home, and with HDTV, we are likely to see a continuation of this dramatic rate of change. The students should expect this; I believe that at least every five years, half of the technology they know will become obsolete. Microsoft's .Net includes a new version of ADO called ADO.Net that, if successful in the market, will cause dramatic changes in database processing during the early years of the students' careers.

Answers to Group 1 Questions

1.1 *Why is database processing an important subject?*

It is important because of the immense need for skilled database designers and implementers. Internet technology has made what was already a hot career path into one that is white hot! Without skilled people, the advantages of database technology will not be realized by organizations that need to use it.

1.2 *Describe the nature and characteristics of a single-user database application used by an individual like Mary Richards.*

See row 1 of Figure 1-8.

1.3 *Describe the nature and characteristics of a database application used by a workgroup like Treble Clef Music.*

See row 2 of Figure 1-8.

1.4 *Describe the nature and characteristics of a database application used by an organization like the state's driver's licensing and vehicle registration bureau.*

See row 3 of Figure 1-8.

1.5 *Describe the nature and characteristics of a database application used by an organization like the Calvert Island Reservation Centre.*

See row 4 of Figure 1-8. Also see Figure 1-7.

1.6 *Explain the nature and function of each of the components of Figure 1-9.*

Users have information needs that must be satisfied by forms, reports, and queries. Database applications are programs that process the database to materialize forms and reports and to process application logic. The DBMS is a program that processes the database, which is a self-describing collection of integrated records.

1.7   *How is the relationship between application programs and the DBMS changing over time?*

The DBMS is gradually taking on more and more of the application programs functions and roles.

1.8   *List the limitations of file-processing systems as described in this chapter*

    a.   Data is separated and isolated. Example: student grade records are stored separately from student extracurricular activities records, so it is difficult to check on academic eligibility.

    b.   Data is duplicated. Example: student personal data (home address, parent, health status) is duplicated between records described in (a). If a student moves, both sets of files must be updated.

    c.   Programs dependent on file formats. Example: fifteen programs exist for producing reports based on data in student grade records. Description of that file appears in every program. When file format changes, all programs must be updated.

    d.   Complex objects are difficult to represent. Example: student transcript is constructed from data belonging to student, course, and (sometimes) professor. Separate files would be kept on each of these objects, plus one for transcripts (containing duplicated data).

1.9   *Explain how database technology overcomes the limitations you listed in your answer to Question 1.8.*

In a database, data is centralized and integrated. It is not duplicated (except in the special case of distributed databases), because all applications access it through a single DBMS. Application programs do not include database file formats because all data about the structure of the database is stored in the data dictionary, which is accessed only by the DBMS, not by application programs. Complex objects are constructed by the DBMS, usually by extracting related data from various sources and combining it into a cohesive unit. This is all done without the knowledge of the user.

1.10 *Define the term database.*

A database is a self-describing collection of integrated records.

1.11 *What are metadata? What are indexes? What are application metadata?*

Metadata is data that describes the structure of the database. Indexes are data structures used to improve direct access and sequential retrieval. Application metadata is data about the structure of forms and reports, as well as other application constructs.

1.12 *Explain why a database is a model. Describe the difference between a model of reality and a model of a user's model of reality. Why is this difference important?*

A database contains records of the condition of a company or other organization. As such it is a representation of that company or organization. A database is a model of the way that the users of the database view the business. It is not a model of reality because reality is too complex (in fact, unknowable); hence a database can only be a model of a human's model. This is important because it is a waste of time for one database designer to claim "My model is a better model of the real world than yours." The real question is which model is a better model of the users' models.

1.13   *Give an example, other than one in this chapter, of a personal database application.*

A stockbroker uses a personal database application to keep track of his clients' names, telephone numbers, and addresses.

1.14   *Give an example, other than one in this chapter, of a workgroup database application.*

A political fund-raising committee uses a workgroup database to keep track of donors (and potential donors).

1.15   *Give an example, other than one in this chapter, of a large-enterprise database application.*

A construction company uses a database to keep track of project costs, labor, materials, and schedule. One database supports all of these different applications.

1.16   *What were some of the weaknesses of early organizational database applications?*

Slow and unreliable applications. DBMS developers did not know efficient ways to provide DB access; programmers did not know how to use new DB technology.

1.17   *What are the two primary advantages of the relational model?*

The relational model is readily understood by users because it stores data in tables; relationships among rows are stored in user-visible data. Relations can be processed by non-procedural programs. Especially useful in DSS applications.

1.18   *Summarize the events in the development of microcomputer DBMS products.*

Sales of generalized file processors (primarily dBase products) started micro DBMS industry. Then, true relational DBMS products were developed. Also, mainframe DBMS products were brought down to micros. Today, GUI products such as Microsoft Access and Lotus Approach give great power while being (relatively) easy to use.

1.19   *What was the major factor that gave rise to workgroup database applications?*

The development and acceptance of LAN technology and products.

1.20   *How does the client–server architecture differ from mainframe multi-user architectures?*

With client server, multiple CPUs conducting DB application processing simultaneously on the client computers.

1.21   *What is the difference between an Internet database application and a database application that uses Internet technology?*

An Internet database application uses the Internet network; a database application that uses Internet technology may or may not use the Internet network. It may use this technology in the context of an intra-net or even for a personal database application that "publishes" the application to a single individual.
The point of this question is that Internet technology can be used much more broadly than just for the Internet.

1.22   *Explain the general nature of distributed processing. What are some of the difficult problems to be faced?*

The database is spread across two or more computers. Security, control, coordination, and synchronization are difficult problems in distributed database systems.

1.23   *Describe the purpose of an object-oriented database. Why have such databases not been more accepted for information systems applications?*

To provide persistence for OOP objects. Rarely adopted (as of 2001) because the data must be converted to object format and the advantages of ODBMS aren't perceived to be great enough to justify the expense (and risk) of a conversion. Object-relational systems like that from Oracle are far more likely to see use in the near term. See the Oracle material in Chapter 18 for more information about this.

Answers to Projects

A.   *Access the web site of a computer manufacturer such as Dell (www.dell.com). Use the Web site to determine which model of laptop computer you would recommend for under $2500. Do you think one or more databases are used to support this site? If so, which features and functions of the Web site do you think would be most helped by database technology, keeping in mind both the definition of a database and the advantages of database processing?*

I used Dell's Web site and found a page that listed types of computer products. From there I found the categories of laptops and looked for those under $2500. From there I used a system configuration page that gave me options to select and then re-priced my laptop. As an aside, you can get an incredibly spiffy laptop for $2500!

But, to answer the question, all of those pages could be backed by a database application, though I doubt the top-level ones involving product categories are. I believe the system configuration page would be the one most likely to benefit a database application.

Consider what happens if the system configuration page is not driven by a database application. Whenever the options or prices on a system change, without a database application, someone will need to modify the HTML for the page to implement the new options and prices. This could be a very labor intensive process because many servers support this site. If the system configuration page is supported by a database application, and if it reads available options and prices out of a database, then to change an option or price, Dell personnel need only modify the database's data. The next time a customer accesses the page, the new data will be read from the database — very easy with low labor costs.

B. *Access the Web site of a retail bookseller such as Amazon (www.amazon.com). Use the Web site to locate the most recently published biography of William Wordsworth. Do you think one or more databases are used to support this site? If so, which features and functions of the web site do you think would be most helped by database technology, keeping in mind both the definition of a database and the advantages of database processing?*

I used Amazon's web site, and chose Book Search. There are several types of searches available. I found Search by Author, Title, and Subject; Search by ISBN; Search by Subject; Search by Publisher, Date; and Power Search. Since I wanted the most recent one, I chose to Search by Publisher and Date, entered "William Wordsworth" as subject and > 2000 as date. Three books were returned.

This searching capability has to be backed by a database application. There is no other way that Amazon could provide acceptable performance. Looking at the Power Search keywords, it appears that they have written an application that translates user-friendly terms for search criteria into predicates for SQL statements.

It is interesting to consider whether or not they have consolidated title data into one unnormalized table or whether they do joins on Title, Author, and Publisher. Because performance matters so much, and because this data is not heavily updated (a title, once it's in, doesn't change), I suspect that they have created a single (unnormalized) table and built many indexes on it for fast retrieval. Depending on the interests of your students, you might show both a normalized (three table) and unnormalized (one table) version and discuss the advantages and disadvantages of each with your students. Also discuss the use of indexes and how a lower level of update makes them more desirable.

Another interesting feature of this site appears when you select a particular book: "Customers who bought this book also bought . . ." I wonder how they generate that? Do they post-process their orders to determine correlations among book purchases and then show books that exceed some level of correlation? Or, do they just pick a book or two that happen to have keywords in common? Interestingly, when using this site, it's hard to keep in mind that Amazon has commercial interests, and while this site appears in the form of a disinterested library, it is not. They have no requirement that facilities like "customers who bought also bought" be backed by any sort of analysis. It could be book buyers in the back room saying "Let's push title XYZ." They are delivering marketing messages in the garb of a reference librarian. Or am I just being paranoid? Hard to say.

Answers to FiredUp Project Questions

FiredUp, Inc., is a small business owned by Curt and Julie Robards. Based in Brisbane, Australia, FiredUp manufacturers and sells a lightweight camping stove, called the FireNow. Curt, who previously worked as an aerospace engineer, invented and patented a burning nozzle that enables the stove to stay lit in very high wind—up to 90 miles per hour. Julie, an industrial designer by training, developed an elegant folding design that is small, lightweight, easy to set up, and very stable. The Robards manufacture the stove in their garage and they sell it directly to their customers over the Internet, by fax, and through postal mail service.

The Owners of FiredUp need to keep track of the stoves they have sold in case they should ever need to contact their users regarding product failures or other product liability matters. They also think that someday they may use their customer list for marketing additional products if and when they develop any.

A. *Do you think a database might be appropriate for FiredUp to use to keep track of their stove and customer data? Explain the circumstances for which you think a database would be appropriate and those for which it would not be appropriate. Describe the circumstances under which you think a personal database would be appropriate. Under what circumstances would a workgroup database be appropriate? What are the circumstances for which an Internet database would be appropriate for FiredUp?*

First, FiredUp can certainly use the Internet to gather customer and stove data. They probably also gather customer and stove data over the telephone, via fax and email, and via postal mail.

Whether or not a database application is needed depends on how much data they have and what they want to do with the data they gather. If they have sold less than, say, 1000 stoves or so, and if they only use the data on very exceptional occasions, then keeping manual records is probably just fine; a database is probably more trouble than it's worth. If, on the other hand, they are selling thousands of stoves, and if they actively use this data, whether for frequent product advisories or for marketing purposes, then a database is probably appropriate. A personal database would be appropriate if the data needs to be used by only one user at a time. (There could be multiple users – they just don't need to use the database simultaneously). If there is a need for simultaneous access, then a workgroup database would be appropriate.

An Internet database (meaning a database is published over the Internet) would be appropriate if they want users to be able to register online. If most of their customers are in North American, then, given their location in Australia, such a database could make a lot of sense. I think they would use this database only to gather new customer registration data and modifications to that data. There is most likely no reason to allow any external users to query or report on this data.

B. *Address the same problem for the registration of a product sold by Starbucks coffee. Say, for example, that Starbucks wants to develop the ability to track the purchasers of espresso machines from their stores. How do your answers to the questions in part A change?*

First, given the number of Starbucks stores, an organizational database will be required. Whether that database is published over the Internet depends on how they want to gather the data and disseminate the information. Most likely, registration cards are included in the packaging for the espresso machines. Customers could fill those cards out and mail or fax them to Starbucks. If Starbucks wants to enable customers to register their machines on line, then publishing a database with a data entry from via the

Web is probably a good way to do this. (If they don't want to expose this database to the Internet, they could also use a Web form to gather data, batch it into files and submit those batches for entry to the database.)

The question implies that stores want to tack purchases of espresso machines. To support this need, the organizational database will need to provide reports for consumption by the store managers or other store personnel. Given the nature of Starbucks' business – it sells commodities to unidentified customers – it's unlikely that store's need to know the name and contact information about an individual purchaser of a stove. Rather, the stores would be more interested in seeing espresso machine sales data in some summarized form, maybe comparing their sales to sales of similar stores. These reports would most likely be published over a corporate intranet using either traditional or Internet technology.

Finally, for product information and liability purposes, the database will need to be accessible by headquarters product marketing and legal personnel. A system will need to be developed to address warning, recall, and other similar letters to selected customers in the database.

Chapter 2

Introduction to Database Development

Objectives

- Learn the major elements of a database system
- Understand the functions and features of the major subsystems of a DBMS
- Describe the tasks involved in developing a database and related applications
- Learn the major elements of a database application
- Understand two strategies for developing a database and its applications

Teaching Suggestions

1.   The goal of this chapter is to present the major elements of a database and its applications. It is intended to provide a broad-brush overview of the subject before descending into the details of the technology in the next chapter.

2.   The chapter distinguishes between a database (the data, indexes, and two types of metadata) and the database applications (forms, queries, reports, menus, and application programs). For some reason, perhaps as a result of the efforts of the marketing departments of DBMS vendors, students have a hard time discriminating between the two. To the user, it's all one and the same, but to the developer, creating a database and creating an application are two different tasks, with two different skill sets required.

3.   Not all DBMS products incorporate all the features discussed in this chapter. But all DBMS products must have a DBMS engine, a definition tools subsystem (though it may be primitive), and a processing interface subsystem, and some type of data dictionary subsystem. The application development subsystem with some products is nothing more than a report writer, though with other products (Access and Approach) this subsystem is quite extensive. Quite a few DBMS products lack a data administration subsystem.

    For students who have worked with a personal DBMS like Access, you might want to install Oracle and SQL Server and show them some of the differences between personal DBMS products and commercial duty products like Oracle and SQL Server.

4.   The discussion of the general development strategies starting on page 41 is important. Major corporations that are concerned with wide-enterprise data modeling generally employ some type of top-down development -- at least to the point where a data architecture has been created. The need for such a strategy will not be apparent to the students, who will only have been exposed to relatively simple systems.

5.   The discussion of data modeling on page 42 is intended to set the stage for the discussions of E-R and SOM in Chapters 3 and 4. The goal is to help the students

understand what they're going to be doing before they get into the details of those models.

6. The terminology in the database field is often confusing. The same words often have different meanings depending on context, vendor, or even product. This is just the way it is in disciplines where the technology is fast-moving; students should get used to it. In particular, this chapter uses the words *data model* in two different ways. A *users' data model* is a representation of the users' data requirements; a *data model* is a vocabulary for creating such a representation. Thus there is the entity-relationship data model and there is the semantic object data model. Either of these data models can be used to document the users data requirements in a users' data model. All of this is very confusing, but the context usually makes the meaning clear.

7. The purpose of the FiredUp project is to start the students thinking about the role of foreign keys and how different strategies are used depending on the relationships' cardinalities. You can use this exercise to set the stage for the importance of data modeling in Chapters 3 and 4.

Answers to Group I Questions

2.1 *Name the major components of a database system, and briefly explain the function of each.*

Database has user data; metadata (describes the structure of the database); indexes (used to improve performance); and application metadata (describes the structure of the application components).

DBMS is a general-purpose product used to design, process, and administer the database.

Application programs have application logic, and enforce business rules that cannot be enforced by the DBMS.

2.2 *Give an example, other than the one in this chapter, of a relation that is likely to have problems when it is updated. Use relation R1 as an example.*

PART (PartNumber, PartDescription, VendorName, VendorPhone), where a vendor provides many parts, but a part comes from just one vendor.

2.3 *Transpose the relation in your answer to Question 2.2 into two or more relations that do not have update problems. Use relations R2 and R3 as examples.*

PART (PartNumber, PartDescription, VendorName)
VENDOR (VendorName, VendorPhone)

2.4   *Explain the roles of metadata and system tables.*

Metadata describes the structure of the database. Usually, metadata is placed in tables, so that the DBMS query and reporting facilities can be used to report on the structure of the database.

2.5   *What is the function of indexes? When are they desirable, and what is their cost?*

Indexes improve performance for sorting and direct retrieval and can be used to enforce uniqueness in a column. They are desirable when any of the benefits described above are needed in the application. The cost is that Indexes must be updated whenever the source data involved in the index is changed.

2.6   *What is the function of application metadata? How does it differ from metadata?*

Application metadata is a description of the application components such as forms, reports, menus, and queries. It differs from metadata, which is a description of the database structure.

2.7   *Explain the features and functions of the design tools subsystem of a DBMS.*

To facilitate the design and creation of the database and its applications.

2.8   *Describe the features and functions of a DBMS's run-time subsystem.*

It processes requests generated by the application. For example, it finds rows of tables based on column values and returns a set of rows to the application.

2.9   *Explain the features and functions of the DBMS engine.*

The DBMS engine is the intermediary between the design tools and the run-time subsystems and the operating system. For example, Access uses one of two different engines; the native engine used with mdb files is called Jet. SQL Server is the engine used with .adp files.

2.10   *What is a database schema? List its components.*

A schema is a description of the structure of the database's tables, relationships, domains, and business rules.

2.11   *How are relationships represented in a relational database design? Give an example of two tables with a 1:N relationship, and explain how the relationship is expressed in the data.*

Relationships are expressed by placing the key of one table into a second table. For example, for the PART and VENDOR tables in the answer to question 2.3 above, the key of VENDOR, which is VendorName, has been placed in PART.

2.12   *What is a domain, and why is it important?*

A domain is a set of values that a column may have. (Note that in Chapter 4 we will add that a domain has both a physical description and a semantic description. All Char (10) domains are not equal!

2.13   *What are business rules? Give an example of possible business rules for the relations in your answer to Question 2.11.*

Business rules are restrictions on the business' activities that must be reflected in the database and database applications. Examples: 1) A VendorName cannot exist in PART if it does not already exist in VENDOR. 2) A VendorName (in VENDOR) cannot be removed from the database unless there is no PART row that has that VendorName.

2.14   *What is a foreign key? Which column(s) in your answer to Question 2.11 is a foreign key?*

A foreign key is a key of a table that is different from the table in which the key resides. For example, in the answer to question 2.3, VendorName (in PART) is a foreign key. VendorName (in VENDOR) is not a foreign key.

2.15   *Explain the purpose of forms, reports, queries, and menus.*

A form is used to enable users to create, read, modify, and delete data. A report is a structured presentation of database data. Queries allow the users to answer questions from the data. Menus are structured presentations of allowed user actions.

2.16   *Explain the difference between query by example and query by form.*

The primary difference is that Query by Example requires the user to see and understand the structure of the tables. Query by Form, on the other hand, hides the table structure and requires the users only to fill in form fields. Query by example is a way of expressing a query by picking columns from tables and (indirectly) causing tables to be joined. There are languages that are unique to the DBMS and languages that are standardized.

2.17   *What is the first important task in developing a database and related applications?*

Build a data model that identifies the things to be stored in the database and defines their structure and the relationships among them.

2.18   *What is the role of a prototype?*

To provide a quick means of expressing requirements for users to review.

2.19   *Describe top-down development. What are its advantages and disadvantages?*

Top-down works from the general to the specific. Data models are created with a global perspective; systems have better interfaces and less repeat work is required. The danger is analysis paralysis.

2.20   *Describe bottom-up development. What are its advantages and disadvantages?*

Bottom-up works from the specific to the general. Applications are developed much faster with less initial study and investment. The danger is that systems will be inconsistent and difficult to integrate; considerable repeat work may be required.

2.21   *Explain the two different meanings of the term **data model**.*

A users' data model is a description of the users' data requirements. A data model (as in the entity-relationship data model) is a vocabulary for describing a users' data model.

Answers to Group II Questions:

2.22   *Implement a database with the relations CAPTAIN and ITEM in any DBMS to which you can gain access. Use one of the DBMS products facilities to enter data into each of these relations. Create and process a query to use the DBMS's facility to process a query that identifies those items checked out before September 1, 2001, that have not yet been checked back in. Print the name of the captain, his or her phone number, and the quantity and description of any such items.*

You can find this database in Access 2002 format in our instructor support site at www.prenhall.com/kroenke/. Look for the database named Chapter2_Example.mdb

2.23   *Interview a professional database application developer, and find out the process that this person uses to develop databases. Is this top-down development, bottom-up development, or some other strategy? How does this developer build data models and with what tools? What are the biggest problems usually encountered in developing a database?*

Answers will vary.

2.24   *Consider the statement "A database is a model of the users' model of reality." How does it differ from "A database is a model of reality?" Suppose two developers disagree about a data model, and one of them asserts, "My model is a better representation of reality." What does this person really mean? What differences are likely to result when a developer believes the first statement more than the second statement?*

This question is setting the stage for a discussion to come at the end of Chapter 3. I personally have wasted considerable time in my life arguing with other developers that "my model is a better representation of reality than your model." Unknowingly, I was simply saying, "the way I see the world is better than the way you see the world." This is sheer arrogance; what matters is how the users see their world! A database is not a model of reality; I believe Immanuel Kant was right; reality is forever unknowable by humans. All we have is our model of reality and the best we can do when building a database is to create an accurate portrayal of the users' models. This discussion will be picked up again at the end of Chapter 4.

Answers to FiredUp Project Questions

Consider the situation of FiredUp, Inc., the company introduced at the end of Chapter 1. Each of the stoves is accompanied by a product registration form that includes the following data:

PurchaserName, StreetAddress, ApartmentNumber, City, State/Province, Zip/PostalCode, Country, EmailAddress, PhoneNumber, DateOfPurchase, and SerialNumber

Assume that FiredUp decides to create a personal database with the following tables:

CUSTOMER (Name, StreetAddress, ApartmentNumber, City, State/Province, Zip/PostalCode, Country, EmailAddress, PhoneNumber)

and

PURCHASE (DateOfPurchase, SerialNumber)

A.   *Construct a table of sample data that conforms to the CUSTOMER structure. Include at least four rows in your table. For Questions A through G, just list the data using a word processor.*

Name	Street	Apt	City	State	Zip	Country	EmailAddress	Phone
Jones	123 Elm		Denver	CO	80210	US	J@abc.com	303.555.3345
Smith	123 Elm		Denver	CO	80210	US	S@abc.com	303.555.3345
Greene	44 - 5th St	5	Seattle	WA	98112	US	G@def.com	206.555.1123
Wu	22 Birch	22a	Atlanta	GA	22345	US	W@ghi.com	432.555.9987

B.   *Which of the columns of the CUSTOMER table could be used to identify a unique row of the table? Such a column is sometimes called a **primary key**, as you will learn later in this text.*

For the data that appears in this table, Email is unique. It is important to find out from the users, however, whether this will be true for all the data to be kept in this database.

C.   *Construct a table of data that conforms to the PURCHASE structure. Include at least four rows in your table.*

DateOfPurchase	SerialNumber
12/4/2001	12345
5/5/2000	44567
11/13/2001	55878
4/4/2001	66879

D.   *Which of the columns of the PURCHASE table could be used as a primary key of PURCHASE?*

From the data in this table, either DateOfPurchase or SerialNumber could be the primary key. However, unless there is something most unusual in this application, DateOfPurchase would not normally be unique. Thus, we have to look beyond the data we have to the semantics of the application to answer this question. Here, I think SerialNumber is likely to be unique for all data and would be the better choice.

E.   *Using the tables defined above, there is no way to relate a particular customer to his or her stove. One way to do that would be to add SerialNumber of PURCHASE to CUSTOMER. The CUSTOMER table would then appears as:*

CUSTOMER (Name, StreetAddress, ApartmentNumber, City, State/Province, Zip/PostalCode, Country, EmailAddress, PhoneNumber, SerialNumber)

Copy your sample CUSTOMER data and add the SerialNumber column to it. Call this new table CUSTOMER1.

CUSTOMER1

Name	Street	Apt	City	State	Zip	Country	EmailAddress	Phone	Serial Number
Jones	123 Elm		Denver	CO	80210	US	J@abc.com	303.555.3345	12345
Smith	123 Elm		Denver	CO	80210	US	S@abc.com	303.555.3345	44567
Greene	44 - 5th St	5	Seattle	WA	98112	US	G@def.com	206.555.1123	55878
Wu	22 Birch	22a	Atlanta	GA	22345	US	W@ghi.com	432.555.9987	66879

Here, I've arbitrarily assigned products to customers.

F.   *An alternative technique for representing the relationship of the two tables would be to place EmailAddress of CUSTOMER in PURCHASE. The PURCHASE table would then appear as:*

PURCHASE (DateOfPurchase, SerialNumber, EmailAddress)

Copy your sample PURCHASE data and add the EmailAddress column to it. Call this new table PURCHASE1.

PURCHASE1

DateOfPurchase	SerialNumber	EmailAddress
12/4/2001	12345	J@abc.com
5/5/2000	44567	S@abc.com
11/13/2001	55878	G@def.com
4/4/2001	66879	W@ghi.com

G. *You now have three possible database structures:*

DB1: CUSTOMER1 with PURCHASE
DB2: CUSTOMER with PURCHASE1 and
DB3: CUSTOMER1 with PURCHASE1

Under what circumstances would you recommend the structure in DB1? Under what circumstances would you recommend the structure in DB2?

DB1 will work if a customer is related to one or more purchases and a purchase is related to at most one customer.

DB2 will work if a purchase is related to one or more customers and a customer is related to at most one purchase.

H. *Under what circumstances would you recommend the structure in DB3?*

None.

Chapter 3

The Entity-Relationship Model

Objectives

- Learn the elements of the E-R model
- Show how to apply the E-R model for modeling business situations
- Practice building E-R models
- Understand why data models and databases do not represent the real world; instead, they represent a model of the users' model.

Teaching Suggestions

1.	The E-R model has many variants. A good number of those have come about because CASE vendors did not want to support the diamond relationship notation. I stress underlying concepts with the students and tell them to expect E-R diagrams in several varieties.

2.	One way to organize a lecture is to teach what entities are and then to present relationships as one of two kinds: either HAS-A or IS-A. Teach 1:1, 1:N, and N:M as varieties of HAS-A.

3.	I believe it's important for students to practice applying this model. Have them model situations on campus or businesses in which they have worked.

4.	Watch out for confusion among entities in a relationship having a minimum cardinality of 1, existence dependent entities, and ID-dependent entities. The differences are subtle — especially between the first two. For example, an ORDER must have a SALESPERSON, but need not logically require one for its existence (the ORDER could be a cash sale in which the salesperson is not recorded). The minimum cardinality of 1 arises from a business rule, not from a logical necessity. Thus ORDER requires a SALESPERSON but is not existence dependent on it. However, consider the relationship of PATIENT and PRESCRIPTION. Here, a PRESCRIPTION cannot logically exist without a PATIENT -- hence not only is the minimum cardinality 1, but also, the PRESCRIPTION is existence dependent on PATIENT. Finally, consider ASSIGNMENT, where the key of ASSIGNMENT contains the key of PROJECT. Here, not only does ASSIGNMENT have a minimum cardinality of 1, and not only is ASSIGNMENT existence dependent on PROJECT, but it is also ID-dependent on PROJECT since its key (name) includes the key (name) of another entity.

5.	This edition includes a description of the way UML employs the E-R model. Basically, UML puts an object wrapper around entities – the basic E-R methodology remains the same. UML style diagrams are becoming popular, however, and the students should know how to interpret them. Be sure to indicate that the private/protected decoration on attributes is useful for pure object-oriented applications, but have to real meaning for standard database processing. No commercial DBMS product supports those ideas – subject to DBMS security, any column of any row of any table is available. And DBMS security is independent of object hierarchies!

6. I believe that the E-R model is important primarily because it is popular and the students are likely to see it. In my opinion, the semantic object model is almost always a better model; it's more complete, users understand it, and it's easier to develop good database designs from semantic objects.

7. The E-R model is best at providing a broad overview of relationships. I try to teach that the E-R model can be used to model any kind of entities and relationships. I once used it in a meeting with salespeople when we were trying to understand the relationships of products to distributors to dealers to customers.

8. The note at the end of the chapter is most important. I think the job of designing databases became much easier when I realized it wasn't my job to model the real world; it's only my job to model the users' model. That perspective also focuses data model evaluations where they belong: on what the users think.

9. If you assign Projects A or B, encourage the students to take the hints there as suggestions, not as requirements. They should look at the web site and generate the model that they think is correct. Not all of the entities in the suggestion need be in their design, and there may be other entities not mentioned that should be in their design. At this point, they should think art, not engineering. I believe a correct answer is one that can be reasonably justified. The **correct** answer, in any case, resides in the minds of people at Dell or Amazon, not in their teacher's mind!

Answers to Group I Questions

3.1 *Define **entity** and give an example.*

An entity is something of importance to the user. Something the user wants to track. VEHICLE.

3.2 *Explain the difference between an entity class and an entity instance.*

An entity class is a group of entities of the same type, i.e. VEHICLE. An entity instance is a particular entity, i.e. VEHICLE 12345.

3.3 *Define **attribute** and give examples for the entity you described in Question 3.1.*

An item that describes a characteristic of the entity. VehicleSerialNumber, VehicleType, VehicleLicenseNumber are attributes of VEHICLE.

3.4 *Explain what a composite attribute is and give an example.*

An attribute that contains several types of sub-attributes. VehicleOwner could be the composite {FirstName, MiddleInitial, LastName}.

3.5   *Which attribute defined in your answer to Question 3.3 identifies the entity?*

VehicleSerialNumber.

3.6   *Define **relationship** and give an example.*

An association among entities. VEHICLE has a relationship with OWNER.

3.7   *Explain the difference between a relationship class and a relationship instance.*

A relationship class is an association among entity classes; a relationship instance is an association among entity instances.

3.8   *Define **degree of relationship**. Give an example, other than the one in this text, of a relationship greater than degree 2.*

Degree is the number of entities that participate in a relationship. The relationship ASSIGNMENT associates a CLIENT with an ATTORNEY with a TASK.

3.9   *List and give an example of the three types of binary relationships. Draw an E-R diagram for each.*

1:1, ATTORNEY to COMPUTER
1:N, VEHICLE to REPAIR
N:M, VEHICLE to OWNER

The diagrams look just like Figure 3-3 a, b, and c, respectively.

3.10   *Define the terms **maximum cardinality** and **minimum cardinality**.*

Maximum cardinality is the maximum number of instances of an entity that can participate in an instance of a relationship. Minimum is the least number of instances of an entity that can participate in an instance of a relationship.

3.11   *Name and sketch the symbols used in entity-relationship diagrams for (a) entity, (b) relationship, (c) weak entity and its relationship, (d) recursive relationship, and (e) subtype entity.*

(a) Rectangle, (b) diamond, (c) rounded-corner rectangle and rounded-corner diamond, (d) line with diamond back to entity, (e) entity with existence symbol.

3.12   *Give an example E-R diagram for the entities DEPARTMENT and EMPLOYEE, which have a 1:N relationship. Assume that a DEPARTMENT does not need to have any EMPLOYEE but that every EMPLOYEE does have a DEPARTMENT.*

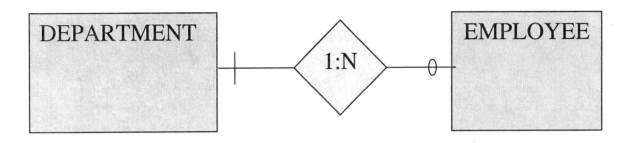

3.13 *Give an example of a recursive relationship and show it in an E-R diagram.*

Maps that refer to each other. Say, for example, a map of the world has references to a map of the continents. A map of the continents has references to maps of countries. A map of a country has references to maps of state/provinces. A map of state/provinces has references to maps of cities. This is 1:N recursion of the entity MAP.

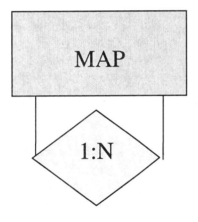

3.14 *Show example attributes for DEPARTMENT and EMPLOYEE (from Question 3.12). Use UML-style symbols.*

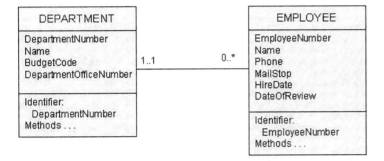

3.15 *Define the term **weak entity** and give an example other than the one in this text.*

In this text, any entity that is logically dependent on another entity. See also question. For the Audubon Society, A BIRD-OBSERVATION is a weak-entity on a BIRD.

3.16 *Explain the ambiguity in the definition of the term **weak entity**. Explain how the text interprets this term. Give examples, other than those in the text, of each type of weak entity.*

Definition depends on the source. Some say any entity whose presence depends on the presence of another entity in the database; hence any entity in a relationship having a minimum cardinality greater than or equal to one. Others say only ID-Dependent entities. The text says any entity that is logically dependent on another entity.

3.17 *Define the term **ID-dependent entity** and give an example other than one in the text.*

An ID-dependent entity is one whose identifier contains the identifier of another entity. The entity WEIGHT-MEASURE, with identifier (PersonNumber, Date), where PersonNumber is the identifier of another entity named PERSON.

3.18 *Show how to use a weak entity to represent the multi-value attribute Skill in an EMPLOYEE entity. Indicate both the maximum and minimum cardinalities on both sides of the relationship. Use traditional symbols.*

Define an entity EMPLOYEE and an entity SKILL. Let SKILL have the sole attribute SkillName. The relationship from EMPLOYEE to SKILL is 1:N; a SKILL is required to have an EMPLOYEE, and in fact is a weak entity on EMPLOYEE. An EMPLOYEE may or may not be required to have a SKILL depending on the users' requirements.

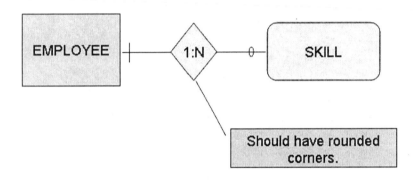

3.19 *Show how to use a weak entity to represent the multi-value composite attribute Phone that contains the single-value attributes AreaCode, PhoneNumber. Assume Phone appears in an entity called SALESPERSON. Indicate both the maximum and minimum cardinalities on both sides of the relationship. Use UML-style symbols.*

Define entities SALESPERSON and PHONE. Let PHONE have the attributes AreaCode, PhoneNumber. The relationship from SALESPERSON to PHONE is 1:N. A PHONE is required to have a SALESPERSON, but a SALESPERSON may or may not be required to have a PHONE, depending on the users' requirements.

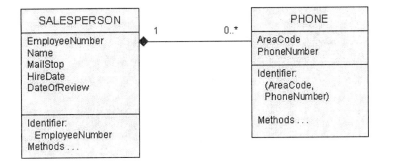

3.20   *Describe subtype entities and give an example other than those in this text.*

A subtype entity is a special variety of a supertype entity. Consider the supertype
ARTIST with properties SocialNecurityNumber, FName, LName, NetWorth and subtype
MUSICIAN with properties SocialSecurityNumber, Instrument, YearsExperience and
subtype PAINTER with properties SocialSecurityNumber, PreferredMedium,
PaintingStyle.

3.21   *Explain the term **inheritance** and show how it applies to your answer to Question 3.20.*

Subtype entities take on the properties of the supertype. In question 3.20, both
PAINTER and MUSICIAN inherit the properties of ARTIST.

3.22   *Explain the difference between a HAS-A relationship and an IS-A relationship, and give
an example of each.*

A HAS-A relationship is an association among entities of different logical types. A
DEPARTMENT HAS-A relationship(s) with EMPLOYEE. An IS-A relationships is an
association among entities of the same logical type. PAINTER IS-A ARTIST, and
MUSICIAN IS-A ARTIST.

3.23   *How are business rules treated in an E-R model?*

Business rules are limitations on data modification activity. Other than minimum and maximum cardinality, they are documented apart from entity-relationship diagrams as part of the systems requirements.

3.24   *Describe why it is important to evaluate a data model once it has been created. Summarize one technique for evaluating a data model, and explain how that technique could be used to evaluate the data model in Figure 3-21.*

Changes are much cheaper at the data model stage than at later stages. Data modeling is artistic, difficulty, and risky. Construct prototypes that show implications of data model decisions. Ask users if prototypes seem correct. Change data model (and prototype) if not, and ask again.

Answers to Group II Questions

3.25   *Change the E-R diagram in Figure 3-19 to include an entity LESSON. Let PRIVATE-LESSON and GROUP-LESSON be subtypes of LESSON. Modify the relationships as necessary. Use traditional symbols.*

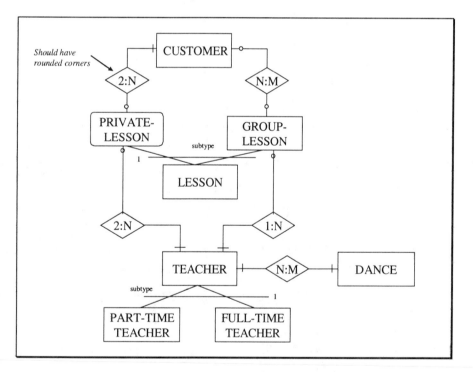

3.26   *Change the E-R diagram in Figure 3-19 to exclude TEACHER. Modify the relationships as necessary. Use UML-style symbols.*

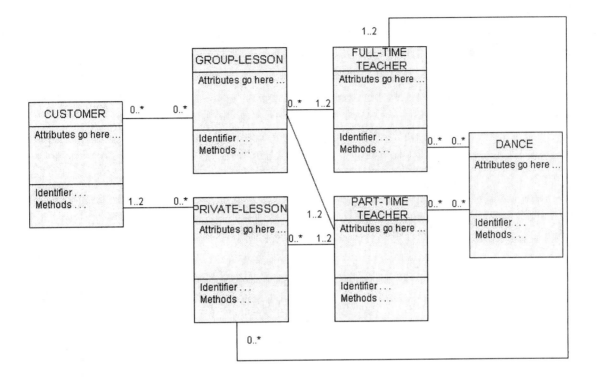

Note that there is no way to make PRIVATE-LESSON existence dependent on two entities at the same time. Hence, PRIVATE-LESSON is modeled as a strong entity.

3.27   *Which of the models in Figure 3-19 and in your answers to Questions 3.25 and 3.26 do you prefer? Explain the reason for your preference.*

I don't like either of them. In 3.25, the LESSON supertype adds nothing to the design; the relationships still must arise from the subtype because one of them is weak; also the cardinalities are different. In 3.26, all of the mandatory relationships that were out of TEACHER had to be made optional. If not, the design would imply, for example, that both a FULL-TIME and PART-TIME TEACHER are required to be at a DANCE. One of the two of them are required, but not both. Hence the model was better with the TEACHER supertype. This is a great example, by the way, of the utility of supertypes. A teacher (of some type) is required at a DANCE. Without the supertype, there is no way to show this constraint.

3.28 *Change the E-R diagram in Figure 3-21 to include subtypes of equipment. Assume that the equipment owned by San Juan Charters pertains to LEASE and that other equipment pertains to BOAT. Model the differences between the BOAT-related EQUIPMENT that is fixed on the boats and the BOAT-related EQUIPMENT that is not fixed. What benefits does the added complexity of this model bring?*

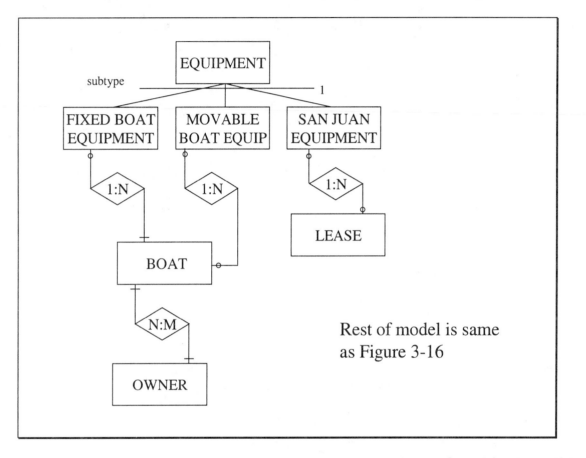

The only significant advantage of this design is that FIXED BOAT EQUIPMENT is required to have a relationship to BOAT. It is tempting to say that this design allows the users to discriminate between equipment owned by San Juan and that owned by the boat (and indirectly OWNER). This distinction could more easily be made by creating an Owner attribute in EQUIPMENT in the design in Figure 3-16. I don't think this design is worth the trouble.

Answers to Projects

In these diagrams I have omitted relationship names because they clutter the diagram and add little to the discussion.

A. *Develop an E-R diagram for a database to support the tracking needs of the following organization: The Metropolitan Housing Agency (MHA) is a nonprofit organization that advocates the development and improvement of low-income housing. The MHA operates in a metropolitan area of approximately 2.2 million people in a midwestern city.*

The MHA maintains data about the location, availability, and condition of low-income housing in 11 different census tracts in the metropolitan area. Within the boundaries of these tracts are approximately 250 different buildings that provide low-income housing. On average, each building contains 25 apartments or other units.

The MHA keeps data about each census tract, including geographic boundaries, median income of the population, elected officials, principal businesses, principal investors involved in attributes in that tract, and other demographic and economic data. It also maintains a limited amount of data about crime. For each building, the MHA stores the name, address, size, owner(s)'s name and address, mortgagor(s)'s name and address, renovations and repairs, and availability of facilities for handicapped people. In addition, the MHA keeps a list of each of the units within each building, including the type of unit, size, number of bedrooms, number of baths, kitchen and dining facilities, location in the building, and any special remarks. The MHA would like to maintain data regarding the average occupancy rates for each unit, but, to date, it has been unable to collect or store such data. The MHA does, however, keep data about whether a given unit is occupied.

The MHA serves as an information clearinghouse and offers three basic services. First, it works with politicians, lobbyists, and advocacy groups to support legislation that encourages the development of low-income housing through tax incentives, developmental zoning preferences, and other legislative inducements. To accomplish this, the MHA provides information about low-income housing to state, county, and city governments. Second, through speeches, seminars, displays at conventions, and other public relations activities, the MHA officials strive to raise the community's consciousness about the need for low-income housing. Finally, the MHA provides information about the availability of low-income housing to other agencies that work with the low-income and homeless populations.

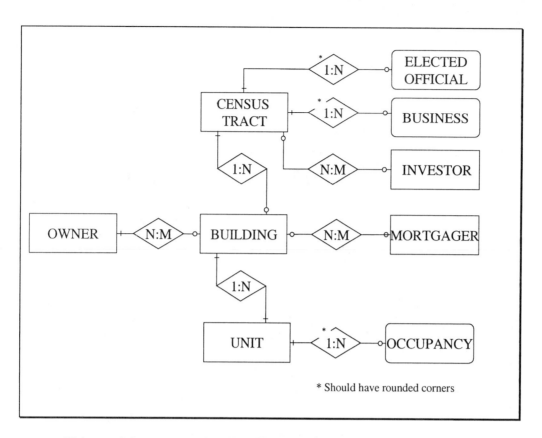

* Should have rounded corners

This model assumes that ELECTED OFFICIAL only exists in the context of a census tract. Also, it assumes that there is no need to track such officials independent of the tracks in which they have been elected. If these assumptions are not made, then ELECTED OFFICIAL should not be a weak entity and the relationship between it and CENSUS TRACT should be N:M. Similar comments pertain to BUSINESS; businesses are assumed to reside in a single census tract.

Attributes of the entities are as follows:

ENTITY	Attributes
CENSUS TRACT	TractName
	Boundary Description
	MedianIncome
	CrimeData
ELECTED OFFICIAL	Name
BUSINESS	Name
INVESTOR	Name
	AreaCode
	PhoneNumber
	FaxAreaCode
	FaxPhoneNumber
	Street
	City
	State
	Zip

BUILDING	Name
	Street
	City
	State
	Zip
	TotalSquareFootage
	Renovation/Repair Desc
	Handicap Facilities Desc

B.   Access the Web site for a computer manufacturer such as Dell (www.dell.com). Use the Web site to determine which laptop computer you would buy for a power user who has a budget of $10,000. As you use the Web site, think about the structure of a possible database of computer systems and subsystems to support this site.

Develop an E-R diagram of computer system and subsystem database for this Web site. Show all entities and relationships and at least two or three attributes per entity. Indicate minimum and maximum cardinalities for both sides of each relationship. Possible entities are BASE-SYSTEM, MEMORY-OPTION, VIDEO-CARD, and PRINTER. Of course there are many more possible entities. Model any multi-value attributes as shown in the text. Use subtypes where appropriate. To keep this project from exploding in size, constrain your design to the needs of someone who is making a purchase decision.

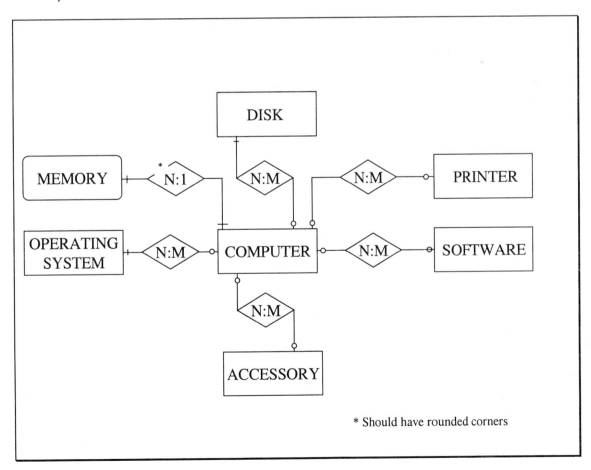

ENTITY	Attributes
BASE-SYSTEM	ProductNumber BrandName Type Description Processor BaseMemory BasePrice TotalPrice (computed on the fly, not stored?)
DISK	ProductNumber BrandName Type Description
PRINTER	ProductNumber BrandName Type Description
SOFTWARE	ProductNumber BrandName Type Description
ACCESSORY (including video cards)	ProductNumber BrandName Type Description
OPERATING SYSTEM	ProductNumber BrandName Type Description
MEMORY-OPTION	ProductNumber BrandName Type Description OptionPrice
All N:M relationships	OptionPrice

This model is straightforward except for three characteristics. The first is modeling MEMORY-OPTION as a weak entity. I did this for two reasons. First, because one can argue that various memory options logically depend on the architecture of a particular computer. This is the definition of a weak entity. On the other hand, processor boards are standardized, and so this argument may not be appropriate. This leads to the second reason: to stimulate discussion among the students about the artistic nature of data modeling and to drive home the point that the answer lies in the minds of the marketing department at Dell. No amount of arguing that my students and I do will ever generate the correct answer. The correct answer is at Dell! We need to develop a plausible data model (or several) and check it out with the users.

The second unusual characteristic is to give all N:M relationships the attribute OptionPrice. One can argue that a better design uses weak entities to represent the OptionPrice. The database design that results is the same, so perhaps it doesn't matter.

Third, I chose not to model VIDEO-CARD as a separate entity, but instead included it with ACCESSORY. This is arbitrary on my part; again, the answer depends on how Dell's marketing department wants to show their options. My guess is that if they make a good margin on video cards, they would show them as a separate category; if not, they're probably just an accessory. One message to the students is that **business needs drive database design.**

Finally, note that this model requires computers to have a disk, memory, and an operating system. This, too, may or may not be correct depending on how they view things at Dell.

As an aside, ProductNumber, BrandName, Type, and Description are shared by all entities. This suggest that they might all be subtypes of a generic entity PRODUCT. While this is true, I do not think anything is gained by modeling it that way.

C. *Access the Web site for a bookseller such as Amazon (www.amazon.com). Use the Web site to determine the three best books on XML (Extended Markup Language) for someone who is just learning that subject. As you use the Web site, think about the structure of a possible database of books, authors, subjects, and related topics.*

Develop an E-R diagram of a book database for this for this Web site. Show all entities and relationships and at least two or three attributes per entity. Indicate minimum and maximum cardinalities for both sides of each relationship. Possible entities are TITLE, AUTHOR, PUBLISHER, COPY, and SUBJECT. Of course there are many more possible entities. Model any multi-value attributes as shown in the text. Use subtypes where appropriate. To keep this project from exploding in size, assume that only books are to be tracked. Further, constrain your design to the needs of someone who is looking for books to purchase. Do not consider customer ordering, order fulfillment, purchase ordering, and other such business processes.

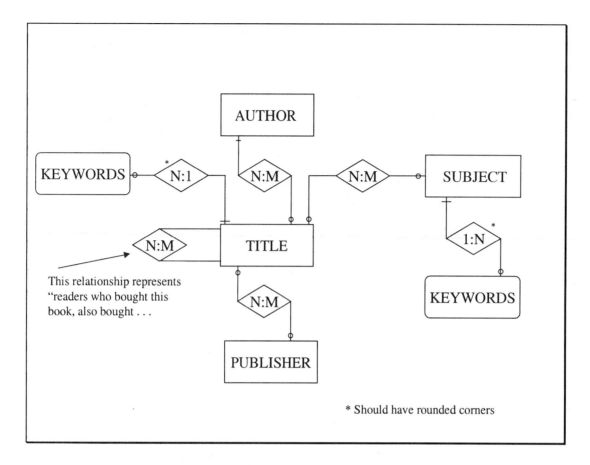

This relationship represents "readers who bought this book, also bought . . .

* Should have rounded corners

ENTITY	Attributes
TITLE	ISBN
	Title
	PublicationDate
	QuantityOnHand
	PublisherPrice
	OurPrice
AUTHOR	FirstName
	Middle Initial
	LastName
SUBJECT	Name
	Description
PUBLISHER	Name
	PhoneAreaCode
	PhoneLocalNumber
	FaxAreaCode
	FaxLocalNumber
	Street
	City
	State
	Zip
	Email
	GrossMargin

KEYWORDS	Keyword

This is a very straightforward design. For the purposes of locating a title, there is no need to include COPY; QuantityOnHand will show how many are available in stock. Name of author is separated into three parts to ease searching. The recursive relationship on TITLE is intended to support the "Readers who bought this title, also bought . . ." I omitted the reviews portion of the Amazon Web site because I didn't think it was relevant to finding a book. One could persuasively argue that this is wrong, however, because reading what others said helps to select among possibilities. If reviews are included, they would have a 1:N relationship to TITLE. I would not add another entity for REVIEWER because they are normally anonymous. REVIEW might have an optional 1:N relationship to AUTHOR and an optional 1:1 relationship to PUBLISHER, if author and publisher reviews are to be represented.

I included GrossMargin in PUBLISHER to bring up the commercial nature of this Web site. Amazon might want to sort the results of a user's query on the basis of the margin they make. This could be done in a gross way by sorting on the books from publishers that give the biggest discount or on a book-by-book basis computing the difference between cost and retail price (not shown in the model). My guess is that if they do this, they do it on publishers discount — and think of the leverage such a strategy would give the book buyers. Again, this is a dangerous Web site because it looks like the friendly, local librarian, but it is not. When I ask a used car salesperson what car I should buy, I expect that his or her answer will be conditioned by margin and inventory and other factors. There is no reason for Amazon to run its business any differently.

Answers to FiredUp Project Questions

Consider the situation of FiredUp discussed at the end of Chapters 1 and 2. Assume that FiredUp has now developed a line of three different stoves: FiredNow, FiredAlways, and FiredAtCamp. Further, assume that the owners are selling spare parts for each of their stoves and that they also are making stove repairs. Some repairs are at no charge because they are within the stove warranty period; other repairs are made at a charge for parts only; and still others are made for parts and labor. FiredUp wants to keep track of all of these data. When asked for further details, the owners made the following list:

CUSTOMER: Name, StreetAddress, ApartmentNumber, City, State/Province, Zip/PostalCode, Country, EmailAddress, PhoneNumber

STOVE: SerialNumber, Type, ManufactureDate, InspectorInitials

INVOICE: InvoiceNumber, Date, Customer, with a list of items and prices that were sold, TotalPrice

REPAIR: RepairNumber, Customer, Stove Description, with a list of items that were used in the repair and the charge for them, if any, and TotalAmount of therepair

PART: Number, Description, Cost, SalesPrice

A.   *Create an entity-relationship diagram of a database for FiredUp. Set the minimum and maximum cardinality of the relationships among entities as you think is appropriate. Explain your rationale for each cardinality value. Use weak entities as you see appropriate. Do not use subtypes. Name any ID-dependent entities, if any.*

In the following diagram, EmailAddress is used as the identifier of CUSTOMER; this is OK, but in my opinion, a surrogate key would be a better choice. This topic is addressed in Chapter 6. Also, both INV-LINE-ITEM and REP-LINE-ITEM are weak entities (as shown) and are also ID-dependent on INVOICE and REPAIR, respectively.

Note that no customer or stove attribute is necessary in INVOICE or REPAIR because that data will be obtained from CUSTOMER or STOVE entities via the relationship. Cardinality values are obvious except that both INVOICE and REPAIR are required to have a CUSTOMER. This means no cash sales, which may or may not be appropriate. Also, a REPAIR is not required to have a STOVE, which means that some repairs are non-stove repairs.

Finally, the description from the owners implies that invoices are used to sell spare parts. Is an invoice also used to sell a stove? Most likely it is, so that three of the PART entity instances will be the three models of stoves. Thus STOVE is a particular stove that has been sold and registered to a customer. The three generic types of stove are three entity instances in PART. These three entity instances are used to sell stoves using invoices.

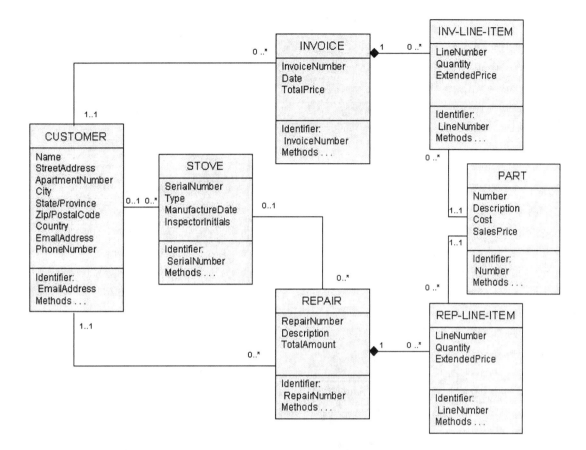

B. *Modify your entity-relationship diagram in your answer to Question A by representing INVOICE and REPAIR with appropriate subtypes. Under what circumstances is this design better than the one in your answer to question A?*

Define a supertype BILL that has attributes BillNumber and TotalDue. Then define two subtypes INVOICE and REPAIR. INVOICE has the attribute Date and no relationship to STOVE. REPAIR has the attribute Description and a relationship to STOVE.

(More realistically, REPAIR will have Date as well as INVOICE, so the subtype INVOICE will have no attributes. In that case, the INVOICE subtype could be deleted and BILL renamed to INVOICE. REPAIR would then be a subtype of INVOICE.)

These designs, while good object programming models, don't really add anything to the data model and I would not recommend them. The only reason to use subtypes in a data model is to avoid value inappropriate nulls, in this case, a value inappropriate relationship to STOVE. This just seems to hard a way to do that.

C. *Suppose that FiredUp wants to keep track of home, fax, and cell phone numbers as well as multiple e-mail addresses for each of their customers. Modify your E-R diagram to allow for multiple values of PhoneNumber and EmailAddress.*

The following diagram shows the definition of weak entities for multiple values of PhoneNumber and EmailAddress. This change has an unfortunate side consequence, however. CUSTOMER no longer has an obvious identifier. Now we really do need a surrogate key!

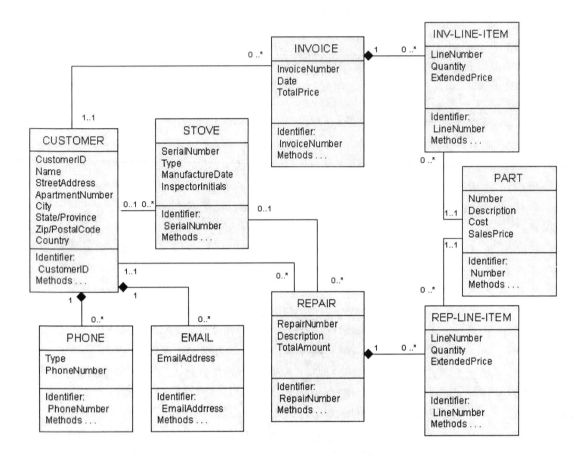

D. *Suppose that FiredUp develops different versions of the same stove product. Thus, they develop a FiredNow Version 1 and a FiredNow Version 2, and so on. Modify your entity-relationship diagram from Question A, above, as necessary to account for this situation.*

Just add a new attribute, Version, to the STOVE entity.

E. *When asking users for the data they want to track, they will not necessarily remember everything they need. Using your knowledge of small business operations, make a list of entities that they may have forgotten. Show potential relationships among these entities in an E-R diagram. How would you go about determining if any of these additional data are needed at FiredUp?*

Two additional entities that come to mind are EMPLOYEE and SUPPLIER. EMPLOYEE could have a 1:N relationship to INVOICE as SALESPERSON, and it could also have a relationship to REPAIR as repairperson. This latter relationship could be either 1:N or N:M. SUPPLIER could have an N:M relationship to PART.

The only way to determine if these are needed is to ask the owners and employees of FiredUp. Even if they say they need these changes, however, it would be a good idea to look further to see what use would be made of them. The fact that the entities and relationships are accurate portrayals of the users' model does not necessarily mean they should be in the database. The question is, will there be forms or reports or queries that necessitate these entities and relationships?

Chapter 4

The Semantic Object Model

Objectives

- Define the term *semantic object*
- Define and illustrate the use of simple, group, and object link attributes
- Demonstrate the use of *semantic object diagrams* to build a data model
- Define and illustrate the seven basic types of semantic objects
- Compare the semantic object model to the entity-relationship model

Teaching Suggestions

1. The semantic object data model is straightforward and useful. However, it is new and requires an adjustment in one's mental model. I believe it's worth the effort to learn and teach because I have found it to be much easier to teach data modeling, database design, and applications design using this model. Also, semantic objects can be shown to users; they normally have little difficulty interpreting them. Some of my end-user oriented consulting clients have developed their own semantic object models — without much assistance from me.

2. If at all possible, have the students use the version of Tabledesigner that you can obtain from www.prenhall.com/kroenke/. Appendix B has ideas of how to use it. Note that this product can both produce schemas from models and also create models from existing databases.

3. One of the key differences between semantic objects and entities is that objects show context (the boundaries of an object), they contain multi-valued attributes, and they can contain other objects. This makes the relationship among objects easier to document and to explain to the users.

4. In the context of the Web, students can think of a semantic object as the data that is to appear on a Web page. The links to other objects can be represented as URL links to other pages that show those objects. This, in fact, is done for the ASP pages that are generated by Tabledesigner.

5. Figure 4-2 shows a semantic object diagram, and Figure 4-3 shows an instance of the semantic object. Use these figures to illustrate the difference. Get the class to suggest some properties for another semantic object, say SOCCER-PLAYER (or whatever sport is popular at your school). With several properties listed (Name, Height, Weight, Birthdate, GraduationYear, Position (multi-valued), Injury (multi-valued), LifetimePointsScored) ask for a semantic object instance. Then ask the class for the name of the semantic object, and the name of the semantic object instance (it is whatever player's name they suggested).

6.   Use the same class-developed semantic object instance to discuss property domains. The physical description is, of course, very computer-oriented (data type, length, position of decimal point, value range and restrictions). But the semantic description of a property is more difficult to define, although it is an important aspect of requirements definition.

7.   **Important:** Point out that two (or more) attributes that happen to have the same physical description do not necessarily arise from the same domain. Their semantic descriptions differentiate them. Using the soccer player illustration, point out that both Weight and LifetimePointsScored may have the same physical description (positive integer, 3 digits), but they clearly describe different properties.

8.   Walk the students through the development of the semantic object diagrams on pages 86-94. Like dataflow diagrams and flowcharts, early versions are working documents, and are revised as more is learned. Some of the forms are shown with data in them and some are shown blank. This is typical of systems development; both kinds of forms are used.

9.   When semantic object diagrams are complete, we summarize all semantic objects and semantic object properties (Figure 4-13). Then we describe every domain (both physical and semantic description) as in Figure 4-14. Using the soccer player example, have the class summarize the semantic object properties and domains, as in Figure 4-14.

Answers to Group I Questions

4.1   *Explain why the E-R model and the semantic object model are like lenses.*

These models are tools for representing and expressing the views of users' data structures. They shape the image of the representation that is seen and documented.

4.2   *Define **semantic object**.*

A semantic object is a named collection of properties that sufficiently describes a distinct entity.

4.3   *Explain the difference between an object class name and an object instance name. Give an example of each.*

An object class name and an object entity name. STUDENT is an object class name; STUDENT 12345 is an object instance name.

4.4   *What is required for a set of attributes to be a sufficient description?*

The properties represent all of the characteristics that the users need to perform their work.

4.5   *Explain the words **distinct identity** as they pertain to the definition of a semantic object.*

They mean something that users recognize as independent and separate. That thing stands on its own in the users' minds. Each instance of an object is unique and identifiable in its own right. Users have names for them, such as Order-number or Employee-number. Everything about that semantic theme will be found in that object.

4.6   *Explain why a line item of an order is not a semantic object.*

Line items are not distinct entities that stand on their own. They are a piece of something that stands on its own, namely, an ORDER.

4.7   *List the three types of attributes.*

Simple attributes, group attributes, and semantic object attributes.

4.8   *Give an example of each of the following:*

In the semantic object APARTMENT:

a. *a simple, single-value attribute:*   NumberOfBedrooms

b. *a group, single-value attribute:*   ApartmentName as (BuildingName, ApartmentNumber)

c. *a simple, multi-value attribute:*   Phone jack location (one value for each phone jack in the apartment)

d. *a group, multi-value attribute:*   Occupant (FirstName, LastName), where more than one person can live in an apartment.

e. *a simple object attribute:*   BUILDING

f. *a multi-value object attribute:*   REPAIR

4.9   *What is minimum cardinality? How is it used? Which types of attributes have minimum cardinality?*

The number of values of an attribute that are required. No object will be allowed to exist for which this number is not satisfied. All types have minimum cardinality.

4.10   *What is maximum cardinality? How is it used? Which types of attributes have maximum cardinality?*

The maximum number of values an attribute can have in a semantic object. No object will be allowed to exist that has more than this number. All types have maximum cardinality.

4.11   *What are paired attributes? Why are they needed?*

Semantic object attributes are always paired. If OBJECT1 contains an attribute OBJECT2, then OBJECT2 will always contain an attribute OBJECT1. A one-way relationship is logically impossible.

4.12   *What is an object identifier? Give an example of a simple attribute object identifier and an example of a group attribute object identifier.*

An attribute that identifies instances of an object. Identifiers can be unique or non-unique. In AUTO, LicenseNumber is a simple attribute identifier. In APARTMENT, (BuildingName, ApartmentNumber) is a composite identifier.

4.13   *Define attribute domain. What are the types of attribute domain? Why is a semantic description necessary?*

An attribute domain is the set of values that an attribute may have. It has both a physical and a logical (semantic) definition. Types are simple, group, and object. The semantic description is necessary because two domains that look alike are not necessarily the same domain. Dates, for example, look alike but one domain might be ShippingDate and another might be BirthDate.

4.14   *What is a semantic object view? Give an example of an object and two views other than those in this text.*

A semantic object view is a subset of a semantic object. Consider the object APARTMENT with attributes BuildingName, ApartmentNumber, RentAmount, LastOccupiedDate. One view might have the first three attributes and another might have all four attributes.

Answers to questions 4.15 through 4.20 should be shown in semantic object diagrams.

4.15   *Give an example of a simple object other than the one discussed in this chapter.*

SOFTWARE with properties Name, Type, Price, MemoryRequired.

4.16   *Give three examples of composite objects other than those in this chapter. One of your examples should have just one multi-value simple attribute; one should have two independent multi-value groups; and the third should have nested multi-value groups.*

a. EMPLOYEE with properties Emp#, {ReviewDate, ReviewComments}$_{0.N}$.
b. EMPLOYEE with properties Emp#, {ReviewDate, ReviewComments}$_{0.N}$, and {SalaryRevisionDate, Salary}$_{0.N}$.
c. EMPLOYEE with properties Emp#, {ReviewDate, {ReviewerName, ReviewerComments}$_{0.N}$}$_{0.N}$. For this last example, there are multiple reviews on a given date.

4.17   *Give an example of four sets of compound objects other than those in this chapter. One set should have a 1:1 relationship; one set should have a 1:N relationship; one set should have an M:1 relationship; and one set should have an M:N relationship.*

  1:1   COMPUTER contains EMPLOYEE
         EMPLOYEE contains COMPUTER
  1:N   PROJECT contains COMPUTERs
         COMPUTER contains only one PROJECT
  M:1   (really same as 1:N, which is the point of this part of the question)
  N:M   COMPUTER contains SOFTWARE-PACKAGEs
         SOFTWARE-PACKAGE contains COMPUTERs

4.18   *Give an example of a hybrid object other than the one in this chapter.*

  COMPUTER contains the multi-valued group $\{$SOFTWARE-PACKAGE, Price$\}_{0.N}$, where SOFTWARE-PACKAGE is an object and Price is not.

4.19   *Give an example of one association and two compound objects other than those in this chapter.*

  JOB contains a single value of the object properties ARTIST and CUSTOMER

  CUSTOMER contains many values of JOB
  ARTIST contains many values of JOB

4.20   *Give an example of a supertype object with three subtype objects other than those in this chapter.*

  SOFTWARE contains the properties Name, Price, Vendor and the subtype objects WORD-PROCESSING-SOFTWARE, SPREADSHEET-SOFTWARE, and DBMS-SOFTWARE. WORD-PROCESSING-SOFTWARE contains the properties Name, Fonts$_{0.N}$. SPREADSHEET-SOFTWARE contains the properties Name, GraphStyles$_{0.N}$. DBMS-SOFTWARE contains the properties Name, MaxTables, MaxColumns, MaxRows.

4.21   *Give an example of archetype/version objects other than those in this chapter.*

  AUTO-TYPE has attributes Name, Description and a multi-valued object attribute AUTO-PRODUCED. AUTO-PRODUCED has the composite identifier {AUTO-TYPE, SerialNumber) and DateManufactured attribute.

4.22   *Explain the similarities between the E-R model and the semantic object model.*

  Both are tools for understanding and documenting users' data models. Both are concerned with representing the things that are important to the users and the relationships among those things.

4.23   *Explain the major differences between the E-R model and the semantic object model.*

E-R model takes entity as the basic element of interest to the user. Semantic object model takes semantic object as the basic element. Semantic objects show relationships in context of objects containing other objects. E-R model shows relationships as between entities. Usually, an entity is a different name for a table. Entities normally do not have composite attributes nor do they have multi-valued attributes. Entities do not contain other entities.

4.24   *Explain the reasoning that entities, as defined in the E-R model, do not truly exist.*

An entity is a piece of an object. In Figure 4.34, the entity SALES-ORDER is an artifact of database design. What is shown as a SALES-ORDER is only part of what the user considers a sales order. The full SALES-ORDER contains LineItem, CUSTOMER, SALESPERSON, and ITEM attributes. Entities are unnecessary; databases can be modeled and designed without them.

4.25   *Show how both the E-R model and the semantic object model would represent the data underlying the SALES-ORDER form in Figure 4-24(a), and explain the main differences.*

See Figures 4.33 and 4.34.

Answers to Group II Questions

4.26   *Modify the semantic object diagram in Figure 4-13 to include CLASS, CLASS-OFFERING, and ENROLLMENT objects. Assume ENROLLMENT is an association object that relates a STUDENT to a CLASS.*

The following model in Tabledesigner format is on www.prenhall.com/kroenke/ in the instructor supplements directory Chapter 4 as file Ques426.apm.

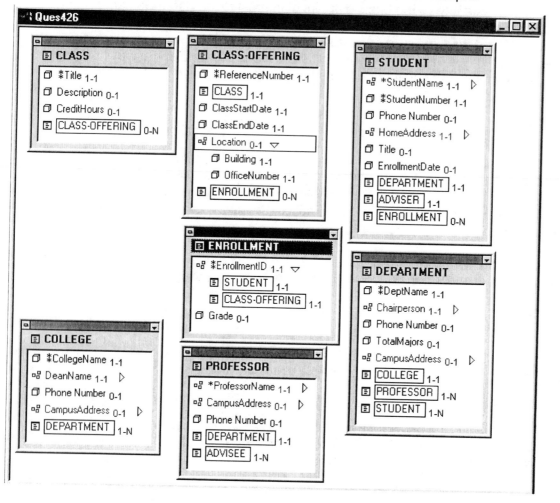

4.27 Modify the semantic object diagram in Figure 4-13 to include a COMMITTEE object. Assume that many PROFESSORs are assigned to a committee and that a COMMITTEE includes many PROFESSORs. Create a MEETING object as an archetype/version object that represents the meetings of a COMMITTEE.

The following model in Tabledesigner format is on www.prenhall.com/kroenke/ in the instructor supplements directory Chapter 4 as file Ques427.

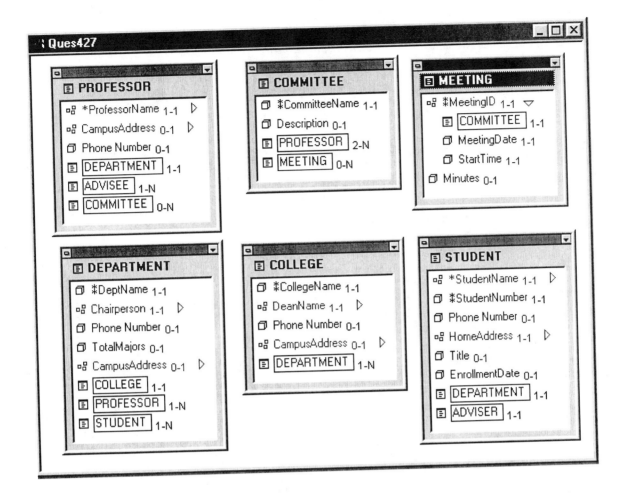

4.28 *Modify your answer to Question 4.27 to create MEETING as a multi-value group within COMMITTEE. Is this model a better model than the one in Question 4.27? Justify your answer.*

The following model in Tabledesigner format is on www.prenhall.com/kroenke/ in the instructor supplements directory Chapter 4 as file Ques428.apm .

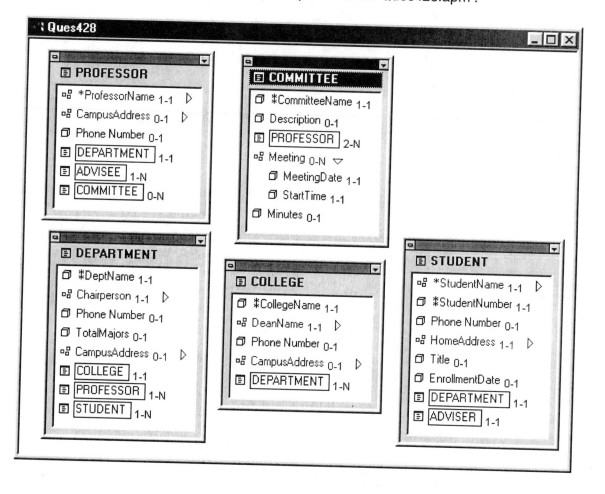

The difference is whether or not the meeting data should have an existence independent of COMMITTEE. Here, if a COMMITTEE instance is deleted, the meeting data will be deleted automatically. If meeting data is represented in MEETING, then it has an independent existence. Further, if COMMITTEE is required in MEETING, then a MEETING object can prohibit a COMMITTEE from being deleted. These matters are discussed further in Chapter 10, on the subject of deleting views.

Answers to Projects

A.   *Develop a semantic object model for the MHA case in Project A at the end of Chapter 3.*

The following model in Tabledesigner format is on www.prenhall.com/kroenke/ in the instructor supplements directory Chapter 4 as file MHA.apm.

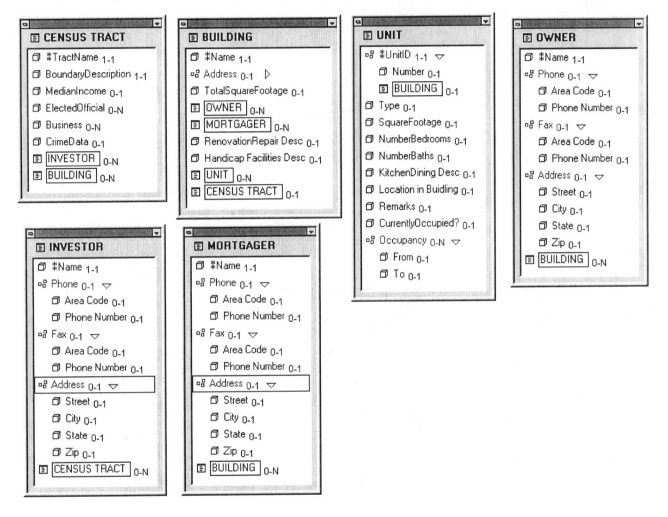

B.   *Access the Web site for a computer manufacturer such as Dell (www.dell.com). Use the Web site to determine which laptop computer you would buy for a power user who has a budget of $10,000. As you use the Web site, think about the structure of a possible database of computer systems and subsystems to support this site.*

Develop a semantic object model of computer system and subsystem database for this Web site. Possible objects are BASE-SYSTEM, MEMORY-OPTION, VIDEO CARD, and PRINTER. Show object relationships and at least two or three attributes per object. Indicate the type of each semantic object. To keep this project from exploding in size, constrain your design to the needs of someone who is making a purchase decision.

The following model in Tabledesigner format is on www.prenhall.com/kroenke/ in the instructor supplements directory Chapter 4 as file Dell.apm..

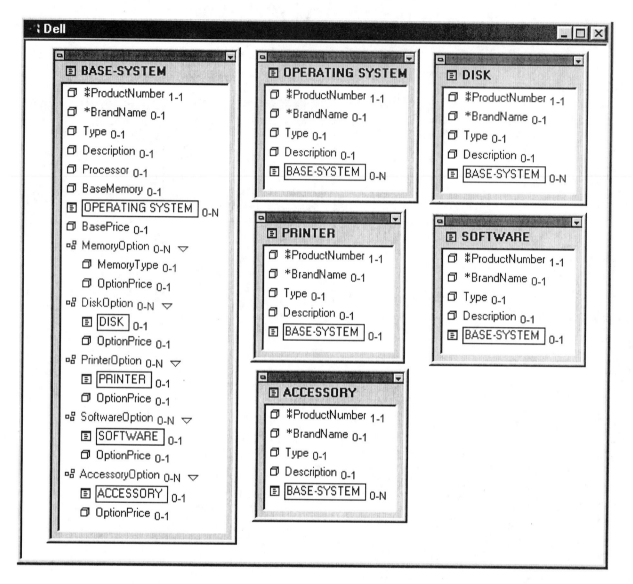

This model makes the same assumptions as the E-R model in Chapter 3. Notice how the attributes of relationships in the E-R model are carried as hybrid groups in the semantic object model. See, for example, DiskOption in BASE-SYSTEM. Also, the weak entity Memory Option is represented as a multi-value group attribute here.

C. *Access the Web site for a bookseller such as Amazon (www.amazon.com). Use the Web site to determine the three best books on XML (Extended Markup Language) for someone who is just learning that subject. As you use the Web site, think about the structure of a possible database of books, authors, subjects, and related topics. Develop a semantic object model of a book database for this Web site. Possible objects are TITLE, AUTHOR, PUBLISHER, and SUBJECT. Show object relationships and at least two or three attributes per object. Indicate the type of each semantic object. To keep this project from exploding in size, assume that only books are to be tracked. Further, constrain your design to the needs of someone who is looking for books to purchase. Do not consider customer ordering, order fulfillment, purchase ordering, and other such business processes.*

The following model in Tabledesigner format is on www.prenhall.com/kroenke/ in the instructor supplements directory Chapter 4 as file Amazon.apm.

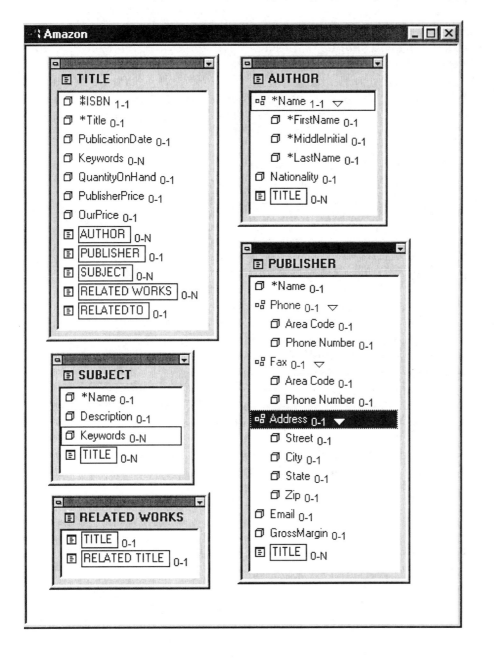

Note the recursive relationship from TITLE to RELATED WORKS. In TITLE, the object link RELATED WORKS is paired with TITLE in the RELATED WORKS object. In TITLE, the object link RELATED TO is paired with RELATED TITLE in the RELATED WORKS object. This is an example of 1:N recursion. The maximum cardinality of the RELATED WORKS object link is N. This means that many instances of the RELATED WORKS object can be connected to it. Each instance of the RELATED WORKS object points back through the RELATED TITLE link to a different title. Create sample data and work through it to make these relationships clear.

Answers to FiredUp Project Questions

Consider the situation of FiredUp discussed at the end of Chapters 1 and 2. Assume that FiredUp has now developed a line of three different stoves: FiredNow, FiredAlways, and FiredAtCamp. Further assume that the owners are selling spare parts for each of their stoves and they are also making stove repairs. Some repairs are at no charge because they are within the stove warranty period; other repairs are made at a charge for parts only; and still others are made for parts and labor. FiredUp wants to keep track of all of these data. When asked for further details, the owners made the following list:

CUSTOMER: Name, StreetAddress, ApartmentNumber, City, State/Province, Zip/PostalCode, Country, EmailAddress, PhoneNumber
STOVE: SerialNumber, Type, ManufactureDate, InspectorInitials
INVOICE: InvoiceNumber, Date, Customer, with a list of items and prices that were sold, TotalPrice
REPAIR: RepairNumber, Customer, Stove, Description, with a list of items that were used in the repair and the charge for them, if any, and TotalAmount of the repair
PART: Number, Description, Cost, SalesPrice

A. *Create a set of semantic objects for a database at FiredUp. Set the minimum and maximum cardinality of all attributes as you think is appropriate. Explain your rationale for each cardinality value. Use as many types of semantic object as you think appropriate, but do not use subtypes. (This task is easier of you download Tabledesigner, the semantic object diagramming tool described in Appendix B. Use it to define your semantic objects and print object reports to submit to your instructor. See Appendix B and ask your instructor before you do this, however.)*

The following model in Tabledesigner format is on www.prenhall.com/kroenke/ in the instructor supplements directory Chapter 4 as file FU4A.apm.

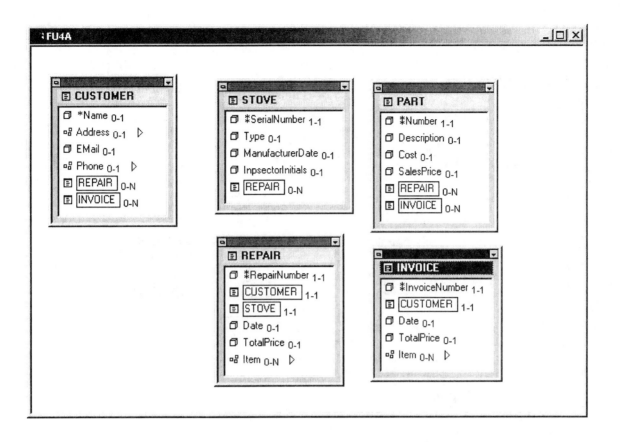

B. *Modify your object diagrams in your answer to Question A by representing INVOICE and REPAIR as subtypes. Under what circumstances is this design better than the one in your answer to Question A?*

The following model in Tabledesigner format is on www.prenhall.com/kroenke/ in the instructor supplements directory Chapter 4 as file FU4B.apm.

Because Tabledesigner does not represent subtypes (it doesn't implement all of the semantic object model), the following model simulates them by naming the appropriate object and links with the text subtype and supertype as documentation.

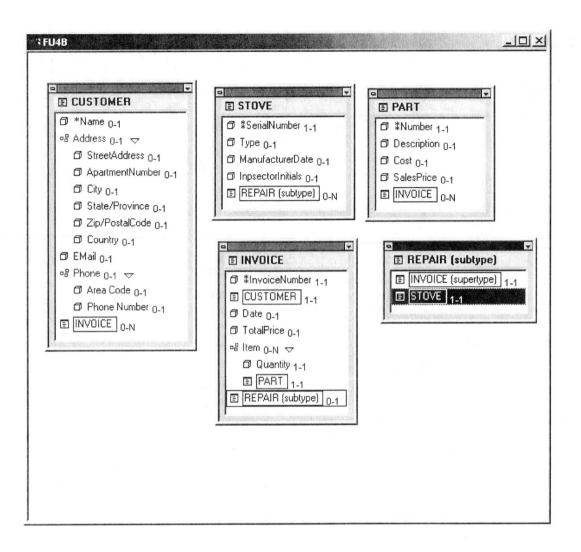

C.   *Suppose that FiredUp wants to keep track of home, fax, and cell phone numbers as well as multiple e-mail addresses for each of their customers. Modify your objects to allow for multiple values of PhoneNumber and EmailAddress.*

The following model in Tabledesigner format is on www.prenhall.com/kroenke/ in the instructor supplements directory Chapter 4 as file FU4C.apm:

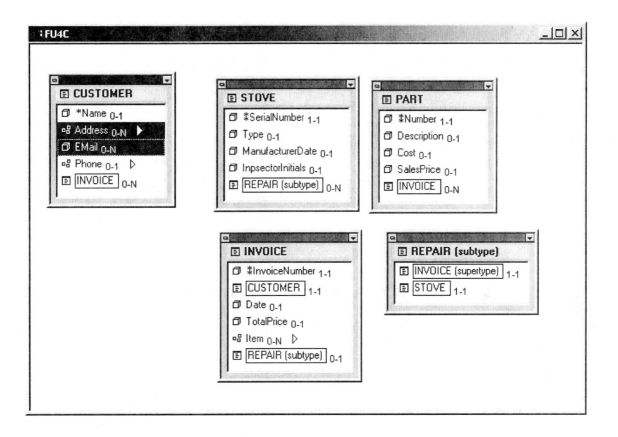

D. *Suppose that FiredUp develops different versions of the same stove product. Thus, they develop a FiredNow Version 1 and FiredNow Version 2, and so on. Modify your objects in Question A, above, as necessary to account for this situation.*

I would just add a Version attribute to the STOVE object.

E. *When asking users for the data they want to track, they will not necessarily remember everything they need. Using your knowledge of small business operations, make a list of semantic objects they may have forgotten. Be sure to show relationships among the objects. How would you go about determining if any of this additional data is needed at FiredUp?*

As in the answer to this question at the end of Chapter 3, I would think about adding EMPLOYEE and SUPPLIER as shown in the following, which can be found in Tabledesigner format on on www.prenhall.com/kroenke/ in the instructor supplements directory Chapter 4 as file FU4E.apm:

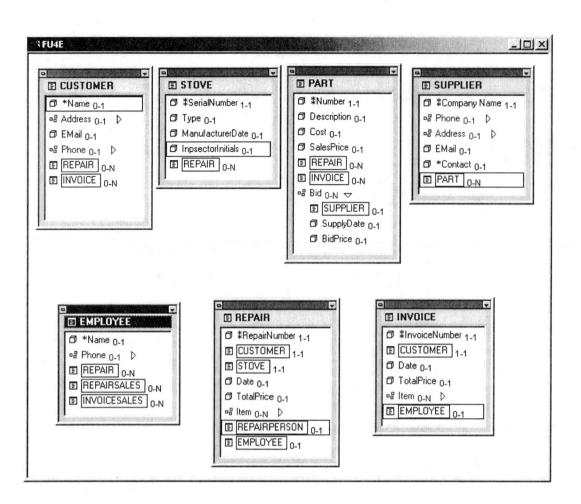

F. *If you answered the FiredUp questions at the end of Chapter 3, compare the entity-relationship model developed for that chapter with the semantic object model developed here. Which do you prefer? Which do you think the owners of FiredUp would be able to understand better?*

I believe it is much easier to work with and understand the semantic object model. For example, making Phone multi-value is a simple matter of changing a cardinality of a group when using the semantic object model. Also, I believe it is easier for business people like the owners of FiredUp to comprehend a semantic object model than an E-R model.

Chapter 5

The Relational Model and Normalization

Objectives

- Define basic relational terminology
- Understand anomalies and the need for *normalization*
- Define first, second, third, Boyce-Codd, fourth, and domain/key normal forms
- Understand the special importance of domain/key normal form
- To learn how to synthesize relations using functional dependencies

Teaching Suggestions

1. Introduce this chapter by explaining that the primary design goal is to describe the database in terms of appropriately structured relations. Such relations must be as free of modification anomalies as is practicable, given the requirements. The first part of this chapter addresses anomalies we might find in a relation as well as how to get rid of them by changing the design of the relation.

2. Relational terminology is introduced on page 122. Some people use the terms *relation, attribute,* and *tuple* for relational designs and the terms *table, column,* and *row* for relational implementations. I avoid the term *tuple* here because it is so seldom used in practice and sounds pretentious when it is used.

3. To show the students how the relational model relates to data modeling as discussed in Chapter 4, pick a simple object, say, COMPUTER with properties SerialNumber, Type, Model, AcqCost, AcqDate. Explain that, as they will learn in Chapter 7, this simple object maps into a relation COMPUTER with attributes SerialNumber, Type, Model, AcqCost, AcqDate. Thus, non-object, non-repeating properties map directly into attributes. Other mappings will be discussed in Chapter 7.

4. In my opinion, the differences in the various normal forms are not of great importance to undergraduate business students. However, the idea and means of eliminating modification anomalies, and an intuitive understanding of DK/NF and the role it plays in design is vitally important. The bottom line: just as Mrs. Gazernplatz, our eighth grade English teacher said about paragraphs, a relation should have a single theme. If it has two themes, break it up into two relations. If it has three themes, break it up into three relations. Every time we break up a relation, we create the possibility of referential integrity constraints; hence we always need to check for them.

5. Point out to students that a functional dependency means that if we know the value of one (or several) data items, then we can *find* the value of another one (or several). They can read a functional dependency such as X--->Y as "If I know the value of X, then I can look up the value of Y" (in a table somewhere).

6.   A key uniquely identifies a row. It can be one attribute or it can be a group of attributes. A relation can have several possible candidate keys. A key is always a determinant. In fact, a key functionally determines the entire row. But a determinant is not necessarily a key.

7.   In the section "The Synthesis of Relations" starting on page 139, we describe another way to design relations that will not suffer from modification anomalies. In this case, we begin with a group of attributes and figure out which ones belong together in the same relation. This approach has been used to create expert systems that construct normalized relations from lists of attributes and their functional dependencies. Such systems have never enjoyed much popularity, however, because it is non-trivial to examine all pairs of all attributes of a complicated database for possible functional dependencies.

8.   Students should be aware that many databases are poorly normalized. Sometimes that was intentional, because of design trade-offs, but sometimes it was because the designers didn't know any better. The goal for the students in this class should be to ensure if they do not normalize data, that they know that they are doing so and are prepared for the consequences. In maintenance projects, the students should expect to find many existing relations that are poorly normalized. It shouldn't be, but it is.

9.   Before assigning the FiredUp project, you may want to remind the students of the definition of foreign keys and referential integrity constraints. The term *foreign key* was introduced in Chapter 2, but we didn't focus on it. They will see lots of uses of it in the next two chapters. Referential integrity constraint was introduced in this chapter, but again, we really won't work with it until the next two chapters. This project really sets up those concepts, but the students may appreciate the reminders before starting.

     There should be lots of discussion of the normalization questions for this project. I believe the issues, problems, omissions, and need for ferreting out assumptions in these questions typify design discussions in industry. I like G in particular because it points out the usefulness for DK/NF for situations that are not considered by the five standard normal forms.

Answers to Group I Questions

5.1   *What restrictions must be placed on a table for it to be considered a relation?*

     A cell contains one and only one data value; a column must contain data of the same type; no row can be duplicated; the order of the columns is immaterial; the order of the rows is immaterial.

5.2   *Define the following terms: **relation, tuple, attribute, file, record, field, table, row, column.***

     Relation is a two-dimensional table that meets the restrictions in question 5.1; tuple is a row of a relation; attribute is a column of a relation; file is often considered the same as relation; record same as tuple; file same as attribute.

5.3   *Define **functional dependency**. Give an example of two attributes that have a functional dependency, and give an example of two attributes that do not have a functional dependency.*

A functional dependency is a relationship between attributes such that given the value of one attribute it is possible to determine the value of the other attribute. Example of functional dependency: Name--->Phone#. Example of attributes that are not functionally dependent: Age and Address.

5.4   *If SID functionally determines Activity, does this mean that only one value of SID can exist in the relation? Why or why not?*

No, a particular value of SID can occur many times in the relation. A determinant (such as SID) is not necessarily unique within a relation. However, a particular value of SID will have only one corresponding value of Activity, no matter how many rows they appear in.

5.5   *Define **determinant**.*

A determinant is an attribute whose value enables us to obtain the value(s) of other related attributes. It appears on the left side of a functional dependency. Thus, in A--->B, the determinant is A.

5.6   *Give an example of a relation having a functional dependency in which the determinant has two or more attributes.*

TOWN-RESIDENTS (Name, Age, Citizenship, Voter-eligibility) where (Age, Citizenship)--->Voter-eligibility.

5.7   *Define **key**.*

A key is a group of one or more attributes that uniquely identifies a tuple.

5.8   *If SID is a key of a relation, is it a determinant? Can a given value of SID occur more than once in the relation?*

Yes, SID is a determinant. No, multiple values of SID may not occur in a relation in which it is the key.

5.9   *What is a deletion anomaly? Give an example other than one in this text.*

A deletion anomaly occurs when facts about two themes are lost with one deletion. Example: the relation VENDOR-PART (VendorName, Phone, Part#), and assume Vendor 123 supplies only one part. When that part is deleted, information about the vendor is deleted from the database as well.

5.10   *What is an insertion anomaly? Give an example other than one in this text.*

An insertion anomaly occurs when insertion of a fact about one theme requires a fact about another theme. Example: in VENDOR-PART in the answer to question 5.9, suppose engineering is developing a product that requires a new part, but the vendor has not been selected. With an insertion anomaly you cannot add the part to the database until the vendor is also added.

5.11   *Explain the relationship of first, second, third, Boyce–Codd, fourth, fifth, and domain/key normal forms.*

Each higher normal form includes the one(s) preceding it. A relation in 3NF is also in 1NF and 2NF.

5.12   *Define **second normal form**. Give an example of a relation in 1NF but not in 2NF. Transform the relation into relations in 2NF.*

A relation is in 2NF if all nonkey attributes are dependent on all of the keys. This relation is not in 2NF:
    LINE-ITEM (OrderNumber, ItemNumber, Description).
    Key: (OrderNumber, ItemNumber).
    Dependencies: (OrderNumber, ItemNumber)--->Description.
     ItemNumber--->Description.
These equivalent relations are in 2NF:
    LINE-ITEM (OrderNumber, ItemNumber).
    STOCK (ItemNumber, Description).

5.13   *Define **third normal form**. Give an example of a relation in 2NF but not in 3NF. Transform the relation into relations in 3NF.*

A relation is in 3NF if it is in 2NF and has no transitive dependencies. This relation is not in 3NF:
DOG (Name, Breed, MaxSize)
        Key: Name
Dependencies: Name--->Breed
        Breed--->MaxSize
(transitively)Name--->MaxSize
These equivalent relations are in 3NF:
REQUIREMENT (Name, Breed)
OFFERINGS (Breed, MaxSize)

5.14   *Define **BCNF**. Give an example of a relation in 3NF but not in BCNF. Transform the relation into relations in BCNF.*

A relation is in BCNF if every determinant is a candidate key. Consider this relation: FAC-OFFICE (FID, Department, Building, Office). Assume faculty members in the same department have offices in the same building. The key is FID. FID determines Department, Building, and Office. But Department (not a candidate key) determines Building. These relations are in BCNF:

FACULTY (FID, Department, Office)
DEPARTMENT-LOCATIONS (Department, Building)

5.15   *Define **multi-value dependency**. Give an example.*

A multi-valued dependency exists if there are three attributes in a relation and an attribute is dependent on only one of the other attributes. An example is: PROF (Name, Hobby, Class-taught). Assume professors have many hobbies and teach many classes. The key of the relation is (Name, Hobby, Class-taught). When a professor takes up a new hobby, all of the class-taught values must be duplicated. This requirement makes no sense.

5.16   *Why are multi-value dependencies not a problem in relations with only two attributes?*

Multi-valued dependencies must exist in pairs because a multi-valued dependency calls for two independent attributes that can have multiple values.

5.17   *Define **fourth normal form**. Give an example of a relation in BCNF but not in 4NF. Transform the relation into relations in 4NF.*

A relation is in 4NF if it is in BCNF (every determinant is a candidate key) and it has no multi-valued dependencies. The following relation is in BCNF but not 4NF: EMPLOYEE-HISTORY (Name, Project, PublicServiceActivity). Project can be multi-valued because an employee could have worked on many projects. PublicServiceActivity can also be multi-valued. But Project and PublicServiceActivity are unrelated. These relations are in 4NF:

        EMPLOYEE-WORK-HIST (Name, Project).
        EMPLOYEE-SERVICE-HIST (Name, PublicServiceActivity)

5.18   *Define **domain/key normal form**. Why is it important?*

A relation is in DK/NF if every constraint on the relation is a logical consequence of the definition of keys and domains. DK/NF is important because if a relation is in DK/NF, then there will be NO modification anomalies.

5.19   *Transform the following relation into DK/NF. Make and state the appropriate assumptions about functional dependencies and domains.*

EQUIPMENT (Manufacturer, Model, AcquisitionDate, BuyerName, BuyerPhone, PlantLocation, City, State, ZIP)

Assumptions:
BuyerName --> BuyerPhone, PlantLocation, City, State, Zip
        Zip --> City, State
            (Manufacturer, Model, BuyerName) --> AcqDate
Relations:
BUYER (<u>BuyerName</u>, BuyerPhone, PlantLocation, City, State, Zip)
PURCHASE (<u>Manufacturer, Model, BuyerName,</u> AcqDate)

Ignore Zip functional dependency.

5.20   *Transform the following relation into DK/NF. Make and state the appropriate assumptions about functional dependencies and domains.*

INVOICE (Number, CustomerName, CustomerNumber,
CustomerAddress, ItemNumber, ItemPrice, ItemQuantity,
SalespersonNumber, SalespersonName, Subtotal, Tax, TotalDue)

Assumptions:
Number -->   CustomerNumber, ItemNumber, ItemQuantity, SalespersonNumber,
SubTotal, Tax, TotalDue
ItemNumber --> ItemPrice
CustomerNumber -- > CustomerAddress
SalespersonNumber --> SalespersonName

Relations:
INVOICE (Number, CustomerNumber, ItemNumber, ItemQuantity, SalespersonNumber,
SubTotal, Tax, TotalDue)
ITEM (ItemNumber, ItemPrice)
CUSTOMER (CustomerNumber, CustomerAddress)
SALESPERSON (SalespersonNumber, SalespersonName)

5.21   *Answer Question 5.20 again, but this time add attribute CustomerTaxStatus (0 if*
nonexempt, 1 if exempt). Also add the constraint that there will be no tax if
CustomerTaxStatus 1.

CUSTOMER becomes two relations:.
EX-CUSTOMER (CustomerNumber, CustomerName, CustomerAddress,
CustomerTaxStatus).
Constraint: CustomerTaxStatus = 1.

NOT-EX-CUSTOMER (CustomerNumber, CustomerName, CustomerAddress,
CustomerTaxStatus).
Constraint: Customer-tax-status = 0.

5.22   *Give an example, other than one in this text, in which you would judge normalization to*
not be worthwhile. Show the relations and justify your design.

BASKETBALL-PLAYER (Number, Name, Position, GameDate, PointsScored), with key
(Number, GameDate). Not normalized because Number → (Name, Position), but
(Number, GameDate) → PointsScored. People are used to looking at this data in non-
normalized format.

5.23   *Explain two situations in which database designers might intentionally choose to create*
data duplication. What is the risk of such designs?

Two reasons are de-normalization and controlled redundancy. De-normalization might
be done because people are accustomed to seeing data in a particular way – the
example of Zip → (City, State) and the answer to question 5.22 are examples.
Controlled normalization usually occurs to improve performance — creating a table that
has a subset of the data for query or high-transaction applications. The first is less risky
because people expect it — if a player changed her number, everyone would expect to
update all of her score data — or would adjust it their minds. The second is unexpected
— even unknown by the users.

Answers to Group II Questions

5.24 *Answers for relation and questions starting on page 147.*

  a.   False

  b.   False

  c.   True, but only because EmployeeName → Employee Salary. Sometimes this is stated that (ProjectID, EmployeeName) is not a minimal key.

  d.   True

  e.   False

  f.   False

  g.   (ProjectID, EmployeeName)

  h.   No. EmployeeSalary is dependent only on EmployeeName

  i.   1st but not in 2nd

  j.   Insertion: to give an employee a salary, we must first assign the employee to a project. Deletion: If project 200c is deleted we lose Parks's salary.

  k.   No

  l.   Yes

  m.   Yes

  n.   No. (Actually, for the data given, it is a determinant. This is most likely happenstance unless the organization has a rule that only one employee can have a given salary. This seems unlikely. This illustrates the dangers of inferring dependencies from sample data. Ask the users!)

  o.   No

  p.   ASSIGNMENT (ProjectID, EmployeeName)
    SALARY (EmployeeName, EmployeeSalary)

5.25 *Answers for relation and questions on page 148:*

This relation is a mess. Certainly, EmployeeName multi-determines ProjectID. From the hint "TaskID is the name of a *standard* task" it appears that EmployeeName multidetermines TaskID as well. It could be, however, that there is a transitive multidependency: EmployeeName multidetermines ProjectID and Project ID multidetermines TaskID. The answers below follow the hint and assume that ProjectID and TaskID are independent.

  a.   False

  b.   True

  c.   False

  d.   True

  e.   True

  f.   True

  g.   True, but not minimal (see answer to 5.24c)

  h.   False

  i.   False

  j.   False

  k.   Assuming there is not transitive multidependency, EmployeeName is the only determinant.

  l.   Assuming note at start, there is no transitive depedency.

m. Yes, the two unrelated attributes are ProjectID and TaskID. Note, too, that even if TaskID were not in the relation, there would still be a multivalued dependency because of the presence of Phone and TotalHours.

n. If you delete the second row, you must also delete the fourth row to preserve the multi-valued dependency.

o. Three: employees and their projects, employees and their tasks, and employees and their personal data (Phone, TotalHours). You could even say four if you split Phone and TotalHours, but that seems too fine, to me.

p. EMPLOYEE-PROJECT (EmployeeName, ProjectID)
EMPLOYEE-TASK (EmployeeName, TaskID)
EMPLOYEE-DATA (EmployeeName, Phone, TotalHours)
Three; one theme each.

5.26 *In this question, EQUIPMENT is like a machine or medical equipment or something similar.*

a. *Modify the definitions to ass this constraint: An employee may no sign up for more than one equipment appointment.*

To enforce this constraint, we need EmployeeName to determine EquipmentName. Think of this as a typical normalization problem and say that EmployeeName → EquipmentName in APPOINTMENT. In this case, we split APPOINTMENT into EQUIP-APPT and EMP-EQUIP as follows:

EQUIP-APPT (Date, Time, EquipmentName) with key (Date, Time, EquipmentName)

And

EMP-EQUIP (EmployeeName, EquipmentName) with key (EmployeeName, EquipmentName).

b. *Define nighttime to refer to the hours between 2100 and 0500. Add an attribute Employee Type whose value is 1 if the employee works during nighttime. Change this design to enforce the constraint that only employees who work at night can schedule nighttime appointments.*

Make the following changes to the design:

1. Add EmployeeType to EMPLOYEE:
EMPLOYEE (EmployeeName, PhoneNumber, EmployeeType)

2. Define new attribute NightEmp with domain in (EmployeeName of EMPLOYEE, where EmployeeType = 1)

3. Define new attribute DayTime with domain HH >05 and <21

4. Define new attribute NightTime with domain HH <=21 or <= 05

5. Replace the APPOINTMENT relation by

DAY-APPT (Date, DayTime, EquipmentName, EmployeeName)
NIGHT-APPT (Date, NightTime, EquipmentName, NightEmp)

This design effectively enforces a business rule using domain and key definitions. It probably, however, is not worth the effort because of the problems it will cause when building the rest of the application. It would most likely be a better choice to enforce the rule in application code. This does illustrate, however, a means for using DK/NF to enforce such constraints.

FiredUp Project Questions

See also note 9 at the start of the Chapter 5 discussion in the Instructor's Manual. FiredUp hired a team of database designers (who should have been fired!) who created the following elations for a database to keep track of their stove, repair, and customer data. See the projects at the end of Chapters 1 through 3 to review their needs. For each of the following relations, specify candidate keys, functional dependencies, and multi-valued dependencies (if any). Justify these specifications unless they are obvious. Given your specifications about keys and so on, what normal form does each relation have? Transform each relation into two or more relations that are in domain/key normal form. Indicate the primary key of each table, candidate keys, foreign keys, and specify any referential integrity constraints.

In answering these questions, assume the following:

➤ *Stove type and version determine tank capacity.*
➤ *A stove can be repaired many times, but never more than once on a given day.*
➤ *Each stove repair has its own repair invoice.*
➤ *A stove can be registered to different users, but never at the same time.*
➤ *A stove has many component parts and each component part can be used on many stoves. Thus, FiredUp maintains records about part types, such as burner value, and not about particular parts such as burner value number 41734 manufactured on 12 December 2001.*

In the following, keys are underlined, foreign keys are italics.

A. *PRODUCT1 (SerialNumber, Type, VersionNumber, TankCapacity, DateOfManufacture, InspectorInitials)*

Candidate Keys:

SerialNumber

Functional Dependencies:

SerialNumber → all other attributes
(Type, VersionNumber) → TankCapacity

Multi-valued dependencies:

None.

Normal form:

> 1NF but not 2nd because of the transitive dependency:

SerialNumber → (Type, VersionNumber) → TankCapacity

Domain/Key Normal Form Relations:

PRODUCT (SerialNumber, *Type, VersionNumber,* DateOfManufacture, InspectorInitials)

STOVE-TYPE(Type, VersionNumber, TankCapacity)

No candidate keys.

Referential integrity constraint:
> (Type, VersionNumber) in PRODUCT must exist in
> (Type, Version Number) in STOVE-TYPE

B. *PRODUCT2 (SerialNumber, Type, TankCapacity, RepairDate, RepairInvoiceNumber, RepairCost)*

Candidate Keys:

(RepairInvoiceNumber)
(SerialNumber, RepairDate)

Functional Dependencies:

RepairInvoiceNumber → all other attributes
(SerialNumber, RepairDate) → all other attributes
SerialNumber → (Type, TankCapacity)
> (note, without VersionNumber, Type does not determine TankCapacity)

Multi-valued dependencies:

> None.

Normal form:

> 3NF, but not BCNF because SerialNumber is not a candidate key.

Domain/Key Normal Form Relations:

> STOVE(SerialNumber, Type, TankCapacity)

> STOVE-REPAIR (RepairInvoiceNumber, RepairDate, RepairCost, *SerialNumber*)

(RepairDate, SerialNumber) is a candidate key

SerialNumber in STOVE-REPAIR must be in SerialNumber of STOVE

C.   *REPAIR1 (RepairInvoiceNumber, RepairDate, RepairCost, RepairEmployeeName, RepairEmployeePhone)*

Note: this relation has no stove attributes, so ostensibly it is for a repair of something other than a stove.

Assuming one repair person per repair:

Candidate Keys:

RepairInvoiceNumber

Functional Dependencies:

RepairInvoiceNumber → all other attributes
RepairEmployeeName → RepairEmployeePhone

Multi-valued dependencies:

None

Normal form:

1NF, but not 2NF because of transitive dependency

RepairInvoiceNumber → RepairEmployeeName → RepairEmployeePhone

Domain/Key Normal Form Relations:

REPAIR(<u>RepairInvoiceNumber</u>, RepairDate, RepairCost, *RepairEmployeeName*)

EMP-PHONE (<u>RepairEmployeeName</u>, RepairEmployeePhone)

No candidate keys.

RepairEmployeeName in REPAIR must exist in RepairEmployeeName in EMP-PHONE.

Assuming more than one repair person per repair, that employee names are unique (likely for FiredUp) and that two or more employees can share the same phone number (also likely for FiredUp). By the way, the case of more than one employee per repair is unlikely – it's here for discussion purposes, only.

Candidate Keys:

(RepairInvoiceNumber, RepairEmployeeName)

Functional Dependencies:

RepairEmployeeName → RepairEmployeePhone

Multi-valued dependencies:

None

Normal form:

3NF, but not BCNF because RepairEmployeeName is a determinant, but not a candidate key.

Domain/Key Normal Form Relations:

REPAIR (RepairInvoiceNumber, RepairDate, RepairCost)

REPAIR-EMP (*RepairInvoiceNumber, RepairEmployeeName*)

EMP-PHONE (RepairEmployeeName, RepairEmployeePhone)

No candidate keys.

RepairInvoiceNumber in REPAIR-EMP must exist in RepairInvoiceNumber in REPAIR.

RepairEmployeeName in REPAIR-EMP must exist in RepairEmployeeName in EMP-PHONE.

D.   *REPAIR2 (RepairInvoiceNumber, RepairDate, RepairCost, RepairEmployeeName, RepairEmployeePhone, SerialNumber, Type, TankCapacity)*

The following assumes one employee per repair and one or more employees per phone. The (less realistic) case of multiple employees per repair is similar to that above.

Candidate Keys:

RepairInvoiceNumber

(RepairDate, SerialNumber)

Functional Dependencies:

RepairInvoiceNumber determines all other attributes

(RepairDate, SerialNumber) determines all other attributes

SerialNumber → Type, TankCapacity

RepairEmployeeName → RepairEmployeePhone

Multi-valued dependencies:

None.

Normal form:

1NF, but not 2NF because
(RepairDate, SerialNumber) → Type, but

SerialNumber → Type

Domain/Key Normal Form Relations:

REPAIR (RepairInvoiceNumber, RepairDate, RepairCost, *RepairEmployeeName*, *SerialNumber*)

EMP-PHONE (RepairEmployeeName, RepairEmployeePhone)

STOVE (SerialNumber, Type, TankCapacity)

Candidate key: in REPAIR (RepairDate, SerialNumber)

RepairEmployeeName in REPAIR must exist in RepairEmployeeName in EMP -PHONE

SerialNumber in REPAIR must exist in SerialNumber in STOVE

E.   *REPAIR3 (RepairDate, RepairCost, SerialNumber, DateOfManufacture)*

Candidate Keys:

(RepairDate, SerialNumber)

Functional Dependencies:

(RepairDate, SerialNumber) determines all other attributes
SerialNumber → DateOfManufacture

Multi-valued dependencies:

None.

Normal form:

1NF but not 2NF because DateOfManufacture is not dependent on all of the key (RepairDate, SerialNumber)

Domain/Key Normal Form Relations:

REPAIR (<u>RepairDate</u>, *SerialNumber,* RepairCost)

STOVE (<u>SerialNumber</u>, DateOfManufacture)

No candidate keys.

SerialNumber in REPAIR must exist in SerialNumber in STOVE.

F.   *STOVE1 (SerialNumber, RepairInvoiceNumber, ComponentPartNumber)*

For this relation, we assume that the component parts are those used for a particular repair.

Candidate Keys:

(RepairInvoiceNumber, ComponentPartNumber)

Functional Dependencies:

RepairInvoiceNumber → SerialNumber

Multi-valued dependencies:

RepairInvoiceNumber →→ ComponentPartNumber (noting also that it → SerialNumber)

Normal form:

3NF but not BCNF nor 4NF

Domain/Key Normal Form Relations:

REPAIR (SerialNumber, <u>RepairInvoiceNumber</u>)

REPAIR-PART (<u>RepairInvoiceNumber</u>, <u>ComponentPartNumber</u>)

No candidate keys.

RepairInvoiceNumber in REPAIR-PART must exist in RepairInvoiceNumber in REPAIR.

G.   *STOVE2 (SerialNumber, RepairInvoiceNumber, RegisteredOwnerID)*

Assume there is a need to record the owner of a stove, even if it has never been repaired.

This example shows a good application for domain key/normal form. The assumption that every stove has a RegisteredOwnerID means that every stove will have at least one row in STOVE2. That row will have a value for SerialNumber and RegisteredOwnerID, and RepairInvoiceNumber will be null. Furthermore, because a stove may be registered to more than one owner, SerialNumber cannot determine RegisteredOwnerID. Also, because an owner may own more than one stove, RegisteredOwnerID cannot determine SerialNumber. So both SerialNumber and RegisteredOwnerID have to be in the key. However, for stoves that have been in for repair, there will be multiple rows for a given (SerialNumber, RegisteredOwnerID), so the key has to be (SerialNumber, RepairInvoiceNumber, RegisteredOwnerID).

But now we have the following constraint:

If RepairInvoiceNumber is not null, then
RepairInvoiceNumber → SerialNumber
(If RepairInvoiceNumber is null, then this is not true.)

This is a constraint within the Fagin's definition of constraint within domain key/normal form, but it is not directly discussed in any of the 5 normal forms. Thus, its current normal form is unclassifiable, but we know it is not DK/NF because of the RepairInvoiceNumber constraint that is not implied by the key definition. Hence, it will have modification anomalies.
To construct dk/nf relations, split into two as follows:

REPAIR (*SerialNumber*, RepairInvoiceNumber)

STOVE-OWNER (SerialNumber, RegisteredOwnerID)

There are no candidate keys, and there is the referential integrity constraint:

SerialNumber in REPAIR must exist in SerialNumber in STOVE-OWNER.

Chapter 6

Database Design Using Entity-Relationship Models

Objectives

- Learn how to transform E-R data models into relational, DBMS-independent designs
- Define and model three special structures: trees, networks, and bills of materials
- Understand the nature and rationale for using surrogate keys
- Learn the implications of null values

Teaching Suggestions

The goal of this chapter is to learn to transform data models in E-R form and notation into relational, DBMS-independent designs. These designs will later be implemented using a particular DBMS product.

1.   While the E-R model as defined by Chen and others included ideas like composite attributes and mutli-valued attributes, those ideas were never really developed. In practice, most people make the tacit assumption that an entity will become a single (usually normalized) relation. In fact, some people teach the idea that an entity should already be normalized. This situation presents a tough decision for us. We can teach what could have been (by assuming that an entity can be one or more normalized relations), or teach what is and will probably be the norm where your students go to work (that an entity is usually a normalized relation by a different name). In writing this chapter, except for the section on multi-value attributes, I took the latter point of view.

2.   The chapter breaks into two parts: transformation of E-R and representation of the special structures. Each part should take about one class period.

3.   The best way to teach this is with plenty of examples. Also, students seem to learn it the best if they are given plenty of homework assignments and problems to work on.

4.   Note the text encourages the student to ask you for an opinion on the use of surrogate keys. The solution in the text is a middle of the road answer– use them most of the time, but not always. This isn't very satisfying, but it's true of my practice and many other seasoned database designers as well. Still, arguments can be made that they should always be used or that they should only be used when performance considerations force their use. You may need to amplify the discussion on the problems that can occur when importing data from a database that uses data keys into a database that uses surrogate keys. Some special importing utilities will need to be used.

Answers to Group I Questions

6.1 *Explain how E-R entities are transformed into relations.*

Create a relation for each entity. Create an attribute for each property. Normalize the relation if necessary and appropriate. Represent relationships with foreign keys. 1:1, key of either as the foreign key of the other; 1:N, key of parent in child; N:M, intersection relation having keys of both.

6.2 *Why is it necessary to examine relations transformed from entities against normalization criteria? Under what conditions should the relations be altered if they are not in DK/NF? Under what conditions should they not be altered?*

An entity may contain more than one semantic theme. Normalize to eliminate modification anomalies. Don't normalize if performance considerations indicate otherwise.

6.3 *Explain how the representation of weak entities differs from the representation of strong entities.*

Referential integrity constraints will be generated. Also, if the weak entity is ID-dependent, then the key of the relation upon which it depends will need to be added to the relation.

6.4 *List the three types of binary relationships and give an example of each. Do not use the examples in this text.*

In a marina: 1:1, BOAT to SLIP; 1:N, BOAT to RENTAL-CHARGE; N:M, BOAT to OWNER.

6.5 *Define **foreign key** and give an example.*

A foreign key is an attribute that is a key of a different relation. SALES-ORDER(OrderNumber, OrderDate, SalespersonNumber, . . .) SalespersonNumber is a foreign key (assuming there is a SALESPERSON table with SalespersonNumber as its key).

6.6 *Show two different ways to represent the 1:1 relationship in your answer to Question 6.4. Use data structure diagrams.*

Assume relations: BOAT (LicenseNumber, Type, Length) and SLIP (SlipNumber, Location, Charge). Either (a) place LicenseNumber in SLIP or (b) place SlipNumber in BOAT.

6.7 *For your answers to Question 6.6, describe a method for obtaining data about one of the entities, given the key of the other. Describe a method for obtaining data about the second entity, given the key of the first. Describe answers for both of your alternatives in Question 6.6.*

To go from BOAT (using LicenseNumber) to SLIP: for (a) look up LicenseNumber in SLIP; for (b) use LicenseNumber to get row of BOAT, obtain SlipNumber from BOAT, look up row in SLIP using SlipNumber obtained. To go from SLIP (using SlipNumber) to BOAT: for (a) use SlipNumber to get row of SLIP, obtain LicenseNumber from SLIP, look up row in BOAT using LicenseNumber obtained; for (b) look up SlipNumber in BOAT.

6.8   *Why are some 1:1 relationships considered suspicious? Under what conditions should relations in a 1:1 relationship be combined into one relation?*

Because they describe the same thing. Combine if they are the same thing and are not separated for performance or security reasons and are not subtypes.

6.9   *Define the terms **parent** and **child** and give an example of each.*

A parent is a row on the one side of a 1:N relationship. A child is a row on the many side of a 1:N relationship. Say DEPARTMENT and EMPLOYEE have a 1:N relationship, a row of DEPARTMENT is a parent and rows of EMPLOYEE that pertain to that department are children.

6.10   *Show how to represent the 1:N relationship in your answer to Question 6.4. Use a data structure diagram.*

BOAT to RENTAL-CHARGE is 1:N. Assume BOAT (LicenseNumber, Type, Length) and RENTAL-CHARGE (ChargeNumber, ChargeDate, ChargeAmount). Place LicenseNumber in RENTAL-CHARGE.

6.11   *For your answer to Question 6.10, describe a method for obtaining data for all of the children, given the key of the parent. Describe a method for obtaining data for the parent, given a key of the child.*

Given a value of LicenseNumber, look up all rows in RENTAL-CHARGE having that value for LicenseNumber. Given ChargeNumber, look up row in RENTAL-CHARGE having that number; obtain the value of the LicenseNumber for the parent, use that value to look up BOAT data.

6.12   *For a 1:N relationship, explain why you must place the key of the parent in the child, rather than placing the key of the child in the parent.*

Not enough room. Can only have one value per cell in the relational model.

6.13   *Give examples of binary 1:N relationships, other than those in this text, for*

a.   *An optional-to-optional relationship.*

BOAT to SAILs

b.   *An optional-to-mandatory relationship.*

BOAT to FIRE-EXTINGUISHERs

c.   *A mandatory-to-optional relationship.*

BOAT to RENTAL-AGREEMENTs

d.   *A mandatory-to-mandatory relationship.*

BOAT to REPAIR-BILLs (assumes that every boat has at least one repair bill)

Illustrate your answer using data structure diagrams.

These are straightforward from examples in text.

6.14   *Show how to represent the N:M relationship in your answer to Question 6.4. Use a data structure diagram.*

Create an intersection table having the key of BOAT and the key of OWNER.

6.15   *For your answer to Question 6.14, describe a method for obtaining the children for one entity, given the key of the other. Also describe a method for obtaining the children for the second entity, given the key of the first.*

Assume LicenseNumber is key of BOAT and ONumber is key of OWNER. Place both keys in intersection table OB. To get all of the owners for a boat, start with LicenseNumber, look up all rows in OB having that LicenseNumber. For each row found, obtain value of ONumber. For each of these values, look up the appropriate row in OWNER. To get all of the boats for an owner, start with ONumber, look up all rows in OB having that ONumber. For each row found, obtain value of LicenseNumber. For each of these values, look up the appropriate row in BOAT.

6.16   *Why is it not possible to represent N:M relationships with the same strategy used to represent 1:N relationships?*

Because there is only room for one value per cell in a relation.

6.17   *Explain the meaning of the term **intersection relation**.*

A relation that represents the intersection of two entities having an M:N relationship. Each row of the table represents one line in a diagram connecting related entities.

6.18   *Define three types of recursive binary relationships and give an example of each.*

1:1, 1:N, N:M. Consider MEMBER, an entity representing the people who belong to an athletic club. SPOUSE is 1:1 recursive; REFERRED-BY is 1:N recursive (assuming a new member is referred by only one existing member; SPONSORED-BY is N:M recursive assuming several people are required to sponsor a new member.

6.19-6.21

6.19   *Show how to represent the 1:1 recursive relationship in your answer to Question 6.18. How does this differ from the representation of 1:1 non-recursive relationships?*

6.20   *Show how to represent the 1:N recursive relationship in your answer to Question 6.18. How does this differ from the representation of 1:N non-recursive relationships?*

6.21   *Show how to represent the M:N recursive relationship in your answer to Question 6.18. How does this differ from the representation of M:N non-recursive relationships?*

For 1:1, place a new attribute SpouseNumber in MEMBER; for 1:N, place a new attribute ReferredByNumber in MEMBER; for N:M, create a new table SPONSORED-BY with SponsoreeNumber and SponsorNumber as its attributes. It really doesn't differ – it's the same basic technique.

6.22   *Explain how to use binary relationships to represent a ternary relationship. Give an example other than the ones in this text.*

A REPAIR has a CAR, MECHANIC, and FACILITY, the relationships from each is one to many (CAR has many REPAIRs). Place the foreign key of CAR, MECHANIC, and FACILITY in REPAIR.

6.23   *In your answer to question 6.22, define a binary constraint on the ternary relationship. Explain how to represent the constraint. Since the constraint cannot be enforced in the relational model, what should be done?*

A MECHANIC works in one and only one FACILITY; a FACILITY has many mechanics. Thus, the relationship from FACILITY to MECHANIC is 1:N, and constrains REPAIR as follows: pick the FACILITY and only a set of MECHANICs are available. Pick a MECHANIC and the FACILITY is given. Represent the constraining binary relationship by placing the key of FACILITY in MECHANIC. The constraint must be enforced by application programs.

6.24   *Give examples of MUST NOT and MUST COVER binary constraints other than the ones in this text.*

In the example in question 6.22, a MUST NOT constraint would be that a given FACILITY cannot make the REPAIRS on some CARs. For MUST COVER, assume that a REPAIR has many MECHANICS. Now assume that all of the MECHANICs in a given FACILITY MUST WORK on all of the CARs that are repaired in that FACILITY.

6.25   *Give an example of a supertype and two or more subtypes, and show how to represent it using relations.*

ARTIST supertype; PAINTER, MUSICIAN, DANCER are subtypes. Create one relation for supertype and one for each subtype. All have the same key.

6.26   *Define **tree, simple network**, and **complex network**.*

A tree is a structure of nodes having 1:N relationships such that each node except the root has one parent. The root has no parent.

6.27   *Give an example of a tree structure other than one in this text, and show how to represent it by means of relations.*

BOAT has many REPAIRs; REPAIR has many PARTs. Create a relation for each entity. For each, place the key of the parent in the child.

6.28 *Give an example of a simple network other than one in this text, and show how to represent it by means of relations.*

BOAT has many REPAIRs; MECHANIC has many REPAIRs; REPAIR has only one BOAT and one MECHANIC. Create a relation for each entity. Place the keys of BOAT and MECHANIC in REPAIR.

6.29 *Give an example of a complex network other than one in this text, and show how to represent it by means of relations.*

Same as 6.28, but change so that a REPAIR has (potentially) many MECHANICs. Create a relation for BOAT, REPAIR, MECHANIC, and a new, intersection relation, REP-MECH, for the M:N relationship between REPAIR and MECHANIC. The attributes of REP-MECH are the key of REPAIR and the key of MECHANIC.

6.30 *What is a bill of materials? Give an example other than the one in this text, and show how to represent your example by means of relations.*

A bill of materials is a data structure that shows the components of sub-items and assemblies. A boat consists of hull, masts, rigging, sails, and an inner compartment. The hull consists of the body, stern, bow, and keel. The stern consists of the transom, stern walls, and stern floor assembly, etc. Use structure shown in Figure 6-25.

6.31 *Define **surrogate key** and describe two reasons for using one.*

A surrogate key is a unique, system-supplied identifier used as the primary key of a relation. The values of a surrogate key have no meaning to the users, and are normally hidden in forms and reports.

6.32 *Describe a situation other than one in this text for which there are good pragmatic reasons for using surrogate keys.*

Whenever there are large composite keys or even moderate sized ones that will appear in many different relations as foreign keys. Also, whenever there is no natural key in the data.

ORE-SAMPLE (<u>MineralName, MountainName, DistrictName, SiteName, Date</u>)

Where all of the names are Char (75) and where there is an M:N relationship between ORE-SAMPLE and PRODUCT, with 100,000 ORE-SAMPLE rows and 17,000 products.

6.33 *Explain the statement "Surrogate keys serve to maintain entity identity." Explain why this is important.*

Because surrogate key values are assigned when the row representing the entity is created and because they are never changed, they represent that entity instance regardless of changes to data values. This eases relationship maintenance and also ensures that users will not lose track of a particular entity instance, no matter how the values change.

6.34   *What are the three possible interpretations of null values?*

Value unknown, value inappropriate, value known to be blank.

6.35   *Describe three different ways to avoid null values.*

Eliminate them by giving attributes an initial value, eliminate them with subtypes, declare an initial value of blank or equivalent.

6.36   *When are null values not a problem?*

When the end users can deal with their inherent ambiguity.

Answers to Group II Questions

6.37   *Transform the entity-relationship diagram for the Jefferson Dance Club (Figure 3-19) into relations. Express your answer with a data structure diagram, and show the referential integrity constraints.*

The following page shows an SQL Server database relationship diagram.

Surrogate keys are used throughout. Column names that end with FK are foreign keys. Table names that end with _X are intersection tables. There are referential integrity constraints on all foreign keys back to the key they depend upon.

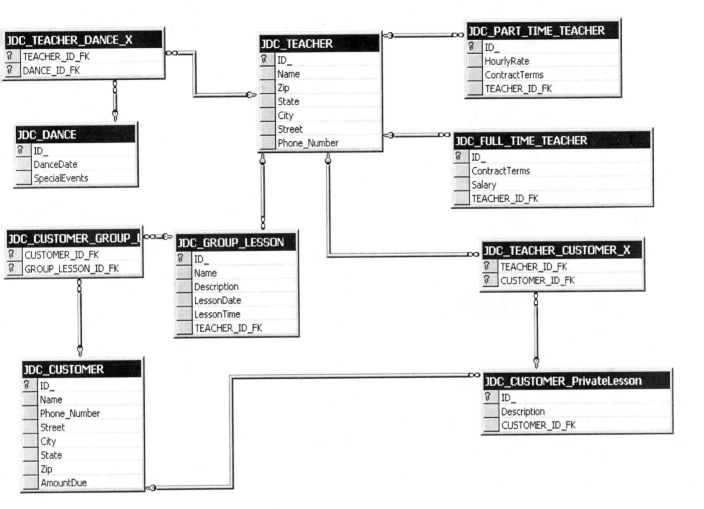

6.38 *Transform the entity-relationship diagram for San Juan Charters (Figure 3-21) into relations. Express your answer with a data structure diagram, and show the referential integrity constraints.*

The following is an SQL Server database relationship diagram.

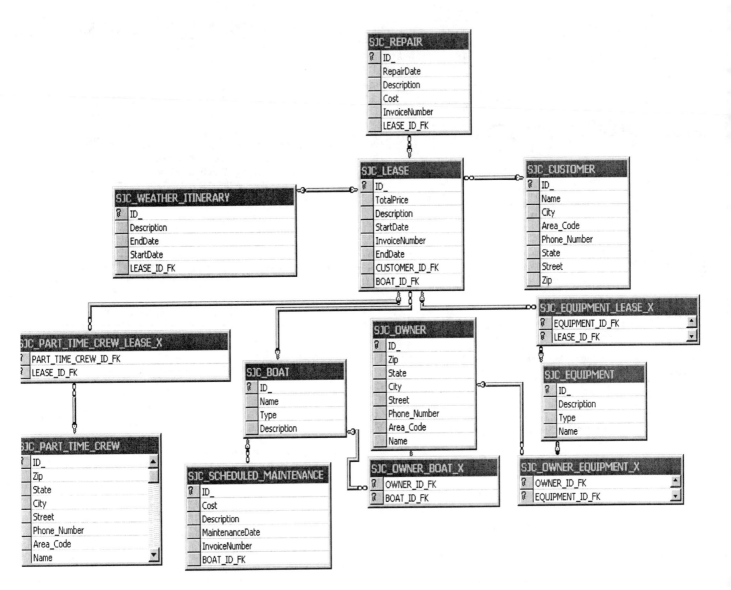

Surrogate keys are used throughout. Column names that end with FK are foreign keys. Table names that end with _X are intersection tables. All foreign keys have referential integrity constraints to the primary keys on which they depend.

6.39 *Some of the relations in Figure 6-19 are not in DK/NF. Identify them and explain why not. What normal form do they have? How can this design be justified? How else could the database application enforce the binary constraints?*

First, domain key normal form concerns the constraints that occur on a single table. So, the constraint in Figure 6-19(a) that SalespersonNumber of OrderNumber 500 must be 20 is not governed by DK/NF because it is an inter-table constraint. A similar comment pertains to Figure 6-19(b). In Figure 6-19(c), however, there are constraints that do concern just one table. In particular, InvoiceNumber multi-determines RepairNumber and RepairNumber multi-determines TaskNumber. So there are both transitive dependencies and multi-value dependencies. The result as far as normalization is concerned is to create an INVOICE-REPAIR table that has (InvoiceNumber, RepairNumber), remove TaskNumber from AUTO-REPAIR (its data is carried in TASK), and thus reduce AUTO-REPAIR to (InvoiceNumber, other nonkeydata . . .). Doing this, however, obviates the reason for creating the schema in the first place: namely, to enforce the MUST COVER constraint. In fact, reflection on the meaning of the term *must cover*, indicates that the purpose of the AUTO-REPAIR relation is to create, intentionally and by design, the insertion and deletion anomalies that DK/NF eliminates. Thus, this is a case where normalization is not only not wanted, it is undesirable! Note, too, that application programs will need to be coded to properly process the modification anomalies.

6.40 *State all referential integrity constraints for the relations in Figure 6-20(b).*

The relations are:

EMPLOYEE (EmployeeNumber, other nonkey EMPLOYEE attributes . . .)
ENGINEER (EmployeeNumber, other nonkey ENGINEER attributes . . .)
TRUCK (LicenseNumber, other nonkey TRUCK attributes, EmployeeNumber)
SERVICE (InvoiceNumber, other nonkey SERVICE attributes, EmployeeNumber)
CLIENT (ClientNumber, other nonkey CLIENT attributes, ReferredBy)
CLIENT-SERVICE (InvoiceNumber, ClientNumber, Fee)
ENGINEER-CERTIFICATION (EmployeeNumber, CertificationName, other nonkey
        ENGINEER-CERTIFICATION attributes)
CERTIFICATION (CertificationName, other nonkey CERTIFICATION attributes)

Referential Integrity Constraints are:

EmployeeNumber in TRUCK must exist in EmployeeNumber in EMPLOYEE
EmployeeNumber in SERVICE must exist in EmployeeNumber in EMPLOYEE
ReferredBy in CLIENT must exist in ClientNumber in CLIENT
ClientNumber in CLIENT-SERVICE must exist in ClientNumber in CLIENT
EmployeeNumber in ENGINEER-CERTIFICATION must exist in EmployeeNumber in
        EMPLOYEE
CertificationName in ENGINEER-CERTIFICATION must exist in CertificationName in
        CERTIFICATION

Answers to Projects

A.   *Complete Project A at the end of Chapter 3 if you have not already done so. Transform your E-R diagram into a set of relations. If any of your relations are not in DK/NF, justify your decision to create un-normalized relations.*

The following is an SQL Server relationship diagram.

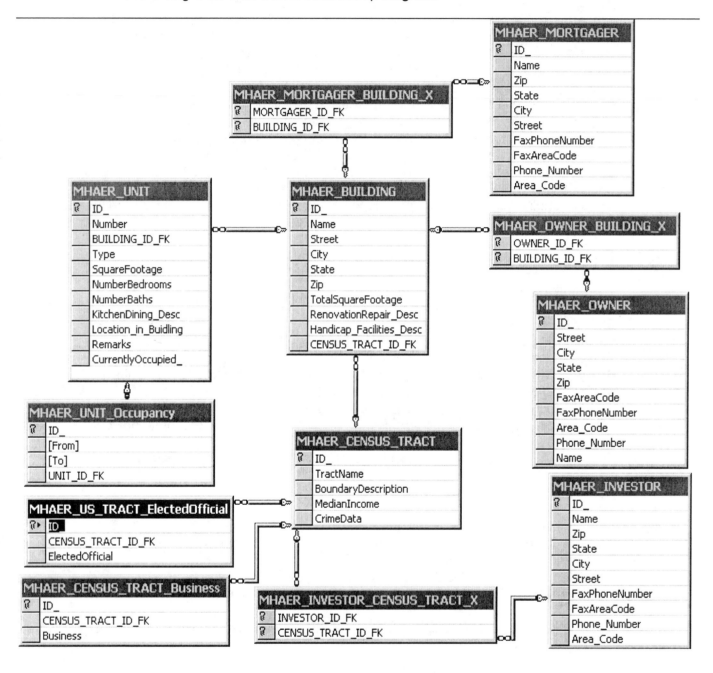

Surrogate keys are used throughout. Column names that end with FK are foreign keys. Table names that end with _X are intersection tables. Except for Zip → City, State, all tables are in DK/NF.

B. *Complete Project B at the end of Chapter 3 if you have not already done so. Transform your E-R diagram into a set of relations. If any of your relations are not in DK/NF, justify your decision to create un-normalized relations.*

The following is a SQL Server relationship diagram:

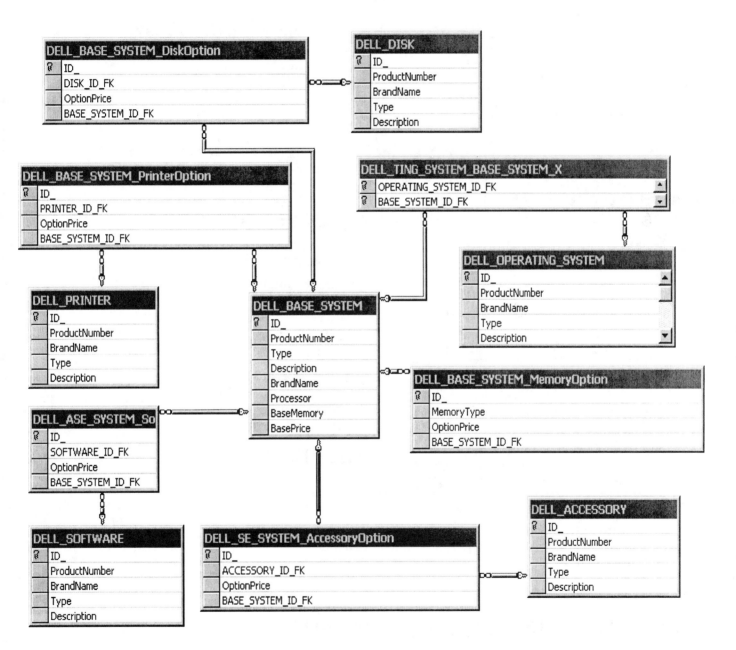

Surrogate keys are used throughout. Column names that end with FK are foreign keys. Table names that end with _X are intersection tables. Except for Zip → City, State, all tables are in DK/NF.

C.   *Complete Project C at the end of Chapter 3 if you have not already done so. Transform your E-R diagram into a set of relations. If any of your relations are not in DK/NF, justify your decision to create un-normalized relations.*

The following is an SQL Server relationship diagram:

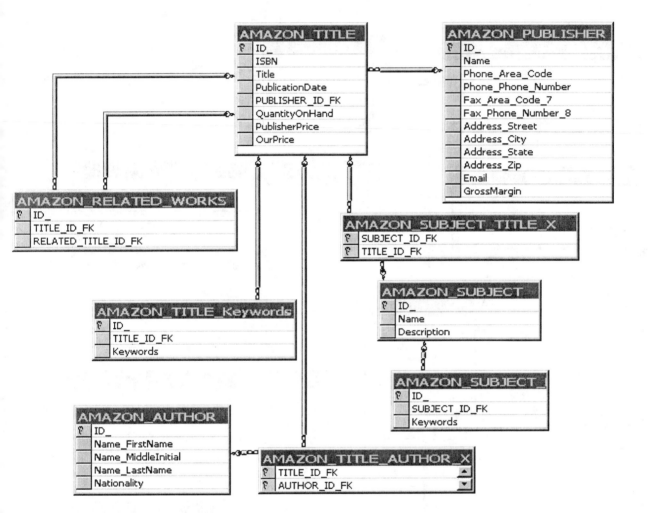

Surrogate keys are used throughout. Column names that end with FK are foreign keys. Table names that end with _X are intersection tables. Except for Zip → City, State, all tables are in DK/NF.

Answers to FiredUp Project Questions

If you have not already done so, create entity-relationship diagrams for Questions A and C in the FiredUp Project at the end of Chapter 3.

A.   *Transform the entity-relationship diagram from Question A at the end of Chapter 3 into a set of relations in domain/key normal form. For each relation, specify the primary key, candidate keys, if any, and foreign keys. Specify all interrelation constraints. If necessary, make and justify assumptions regarding the underlying semantics of the application.*

In the following, primary keys are underlined; foreign keys are in italics. Note how all relationships are replaced by the definition of foreign keys.

Relations:

CUSTOMER (<u>CustomerID</u>, Name, StreetAddress, ApartmentNumber, *Zip/PostalCode*, EmailAddress, PhoneNumber)

LOCATION-CODE (<u>Zip/PostalCode</u>, City, State/Provice, Country)

STOVE (<u>SerialNumber</u>, Type, ManufacturerDate, InspectorInitials, *CustomerID*)

INVOICE (<u>InvoiceNumber</u>, Date, TotalPrice)

INV-LINE-ITEM (<u>*InvoiceNumber*</u>, <u>LineNumber</u>, *PartNumber*, Quantity, ExtendedPrice)

REPAIR (<u>RepairNumber</u>, Date, Description, TotalAmount, SerialNumber)

REP-LINE-ITEM (<u>*RepairNumber*</u>, <u>LineNumber</u>, *PartNumber*, Quantity, ExtendedPrice)

PART (<u>Number</u>, Description, Cost, SalesPrice)

This design uses a surrogate key for CUSTOMER. EmailAddress is therefore a candidate key for CUSTOMER. There are no other candidate keys. Date has been added to REPAIR because it should be there.

Referential integrity constraints:

Zip/PostalCode in CUSTOMER must exist in Zip/PostalCode in LOCATION-CODE
CustomerID in STOVE must exist in CustomerID in CUSTOMER
InvoiceNumber in INV-LINE-ITEM must exist in InvoiceNumber in INVOICE
PartNumber in INV-LINE-ITEM must exist in Number in PART
RepairNumber in REP-LINE-ITEM must exist in RepairNumber in REPAIR
PartNumber in REP-LINE-ITEM must exist in Number in PART

B.   *Adjust your answer to Question A to allow un-normalized relations if you think just relations are appropriate. Justify any non-normalized relations you have. If necessary, make and justify assumptions regarding the underlying semantics of the application.*

Get rid of the LOCATION-CODE relation and place, City, State/Province, Country in CUSTOMER. Normalizing Zip codes adds complexity and really doesn't buy anything. Locations don't change their Zip codes very much, and when they do, the change can be handled as any other address change. Normalization is not worth the trouble.

All the rest of the normalized tables seem OK as is.

C.   *Transform the entity-relationship diagram from Question C at the end of Chapter 3 into a set of relations, preferably in domain/key normal form. If any of your relations are not in domain/key normal form, explain why not. For each relation, specify the primary key, candidate keys, if any, and foreign keys. Specify all referential integrity constraints.*

Leave Zip un-normalized with justification as in Item B.

Relations:

CUSTOMER (<u>CustomerID</u>, Name, StreetAddress, ApartmentNumber, City, State/Province, Country)

CUSTOMER-PHONE (*CustomerID*, Type, <u>PhoneNumber</u>)

CUSTOMER-EMAIL (*CustomerID*, <u>EmailAddress</u>)

STOVE (<u>SerialNumber</u>, Type, ManufacturerDate, InspectorInitials, *CustomerID*)

INVOICE (<u>InvoiceNumber</u>, Date, TotalPrice)

INV-LINE-ITEM (*<u>InvoiceNumber</u>*, <u>LineNumber</u>, *PartNumber*, Quantity, ExtendedPrice)

REPAIR (<u>RepairNumber</u>, Date, Description, TotalAmount, SerialNumber)

REP-LINE-ITEM (*<u>RepairNumber</u>*, <u>LineNumber</u>, *PartNumber*, Quantity, ExtendedPrice)

PART (<u>Number</u>, Description, Cost, SalesPrice)

This design uses a surrogate key for CUSTOMER. EmailAddress is therefore a candidate key for CUSTOMER. There are no other candidate keys. Date has been added to REPAIR because it should be there.

Referential integrity constraints:

CustomerID in CUSTOMER-PHONE must exist in CustomerID in CUSTOMER
CustomerID in CUSTOMER-EMAIL must exist in CustomerID in CUSTOMER
CustomerID in STOVE must exist in CustomerID in CUSTOMER
InvoiceNumber in INV-LINE-ITEM must exist in InvoiceNumber in INVOICE
PartNumber in INV-LINE-ITEM must exist in Number in PART
RepairNumber in REP-LINE-ITEM must exist in RepairNumber in REPAIR
PartNumber in REP-LINE-ITEM must exist in Number in PART

D.   *Adjust your answer to Question C, above, to assume that home, fax, and cell phone are to be represented by separate, single-value attributes. Is this a better design than in your answer to Question C? Explain why or why not.*

Delete CUSTOMER-PHONE. Change the CUSTOMER relation as follows:

CUSTOMER (<u>CustomerID</u>, Name, StreetAddress, ApartmentNumber, City, State/Province, Country, HomePhone, FaxPhone, CellPhone)

It may be better, depending on the use of the relation. If no other phone types are ever added and if there is no need to query on a phone number of an uncertain type, then this probably is a better design because no join will need to be made to obtain all of the CUSTOMER data. On the other hand, if other types of phone may be created and if there's a need to find out which customer has a phone number of unspecified type, then the original design may be better.

Chapter 7

Database Design with Semantic Object Models

Objectives

- Learn how to transform the seven types of semantic objects into relational, DBMS-independent designs
- Practice modeling several real-world objects

Teaching Suggestions

1. The goal of this chapter is to learn to transform data models in semantic object form and notation into relational, DBMS-independent designs. These designs will later be implemented using a particular DBMS product.

2. This is a very important chapter. An understanding of the techniques discussed here is arguably the most important learning in the course.

3. The chapter breaks into two parts: transformation of the seven types of objects and then modeling of three sample objects. Each part can take about a class period -- you might have the students bring a prepared response to question 7.26 to the second class. That is a very interesting problem.

4. You can use Figure 7-13 and the related discussion to teach encapsulation. In cases 1 and 2, an ITEM gives itself to an ORDER. How many times that ITEM appears on that ORDER is not the business of ITEM; it is purely the business of ORDER and that fact is recorded within (encapsulated) ORDER. A similar argument holds for cases 3 and 4.

5. It's worth having the students use Tabledesigner. They can create many models and let Tabledesigner generate the database structures. You can ask them to explain why the program did what it did. Also, as indicated by the projects, the easiest way to generate a SQL Server database is to use Tabledesigner. Take the SOM models in the files with suffix .apm and use them to generate the databases.

Answers to Group I Questions

7.1   *Give an example of a simple object other than one in this text. Show how to represent this object by means of a relation.*

MUSICIAN with properties Name, Instrument, SectionChairNumber. Create relation MUSICIAN (Name, Instrument, SectionChairNumber).

7.2   *Give an example of a composite object other than one in this text. Show how to represent this object by means of relations.*

MUSICIAN with properties Name, Instrument, SectionChairNumber, {ConcertDate, ConcertLocation}$_{0.N}$. Create relations MUSICIAN (<u>Name</u>, Instrument, SectionChairNumber) and MUSICIAN-CONCERT (<u>Name, ConcertDate</u>, ConcertLocation).

7.3   *Give an example of a 1:1 compound object other than one in this text. Show two ways to represent it by means of relations.*

MUSICIAN, UNIFORM
Create a relation MUSICIAN and a relation UNIFORM. Place either the key of MUSICIAN in UNIFORM or the key of UNIFORM in MUSICIAN.

7.4   *Give an example of a 1:N compound object other than one in this text. Show how to represent it by means of relations.*

MUSICIAN, INSTRUMENT-OWNED. Create a relation for each object and place the key of MUSICIAN in INSTRUMENT-OWNED.

7.5   *Give an example of an M:1 compound object other than one in this text. Show how to represent it by means of relations.*

M:1 MUSICIAN, BAND. Create a relation for each object and place the key of BAND in MUSICIAN.

7.6   *Give an example of an M:N compound object other than one in this text. Show how to represent it by means of relations.*

MUSICIAN, INSTRUMENT-PLAYED. Create a relation for each object and an intersection relation. Place the key of each of the relations in the intersection relation.

7.7   *Give an example of a Case 1 (see Figure 7-13) hybrid object. Show how to represent it by means of relations.*

See answer to question 7.24.

7.8   *Give an example of a Case 2 (see Figure 7-13) hybrid object. Show how to represent it by means of relations.*

See answer to question 7.24.

7.9   *Give an example of an association and related objects other than one in this text. Show how to represent these objects by means of relations. Assume that the association object has an identifier of its own.*

Consider the association object CONTRACT, which contains the non-object properties ContractNumber, Date, TotalPay, and Position, and the single valued object properties BAND and MUSICIAN. Suppose that BAND contains the properties <u>BandName</u>,

Conductor and a multi-value link to CONTRACT and that MUSICIAN contains the properties <u>MusicianName</u>, Phone and a multi-value link to CONTRACT. Create a relation BAND (<u>BandName</u>, Conductor), a relation MUSICIAN (<u>MusicianName</u>, Phone), and a relation CONTRACT (<u>ContractNumber,</u> Date, TotalPay, Position, BandName, MusicianName).

7.10   *Do the same as for Question 7.9, but assume that the association object does not have an identifier of its own.*

Same as 7.9 except that the key of CONTRACT is (BandName, MusicianName).

7.11   *Give an example of a parent object with at least two exclusive subtypes. Show how to represent these objects by means of relations. Use a type indicator attribute.*

ARTIST supertype object contains subtype objects PAINTER, MUSICIAN, and DANCER as subtypes. Each subtype contains properties unique to that subtype and also the supertype object as an object property. Assume an ARTIST can only be one of these types. Create a relation for each object; place ArtistNumber as the key of each relation. Add an attribute to ARTIST that indicates the type of artist; only allow one type in this attribute.

7.12   *Give an example of a parent object with at least two nonexclusive subtypes. Show how to represent these objects by means of relations. Use a type indicator attribute.*

Same as 7.11, but all the type attributes have more than one subtype; an example value of the type indicator is: PAINTER/DANCER.

7.13 - 7.19   *All of these questions involve finding forms on campus.*

Answers depend on forms that are found.

7.20   *What referential integrity constraints, if any, should be specified for the designs in Figure 7-21 (b) and (c)?*

None for 7-21(b). CustomerNumber in SUBSCRIPTION must exist in CustomerNumber in CUSTOMER for 7-21(c).

7.21   *What referential integrity constraints, if any, should be specified for the design in Figure 7-22(c)?*

Name in NUTRIENT, INGREDIENT, VIT-IRON, and USDA-RDA must exist in Name in CEREAL-PRODUCT.

7.22   *What referential integrity constraints, if any, should be specified for the design in Figure 7-23(c)?*

(DriversLicense, State) in CORRECTION-NOTICE must exist in (DriversLicense, State) in DRIVER
PersonnelNumber in CORRECTION-NOTICE must exist in PersonnelNumber in
OFFICERNumber in VIOLATION must exist in Number in CORRECTION-NOTICE
VIN in CORRECTION-NOTICE must exist in VIN in VEHICLE

7.23 *Suppose object O1 has a 1:N relationship to object O2 and that O1 has a second 1:N relationship to object O3. Further suppose that O2 is required in O1, but O3 is optional in O1. Is there a difference between the referential integrity constraint for the relationship of O1 and O2 and the referential integrity constraint for the relationship of O1 and O3? If so, what is it?*

There is a difference, but one that is not normally defined in a referential integrity constraint. The difference is that the value of the foreign key of O1 in O2 must not only exist in O1, it must also cover all key values in O1. Every value of the key of O1 must exist in at least one row of O2. The values of the foreign keys of O1 in O3 must exist in O1 but need not cover all key values in O1; there may be some values of the key of O1 that do not appear in any row in O3.

Answers to Group II Questions

7.24 *In Figure 7-13, give a different example for each of the four cases in the right-hand column. Show how each of your examples would be represented with relations.*

The following objects represent cases 1-4, respectively. They each concern the counting of fish species on a particular river. Case 1 counts a species only once on one river. Case 2 counts a fish many times on a single river. Case 3 counts many

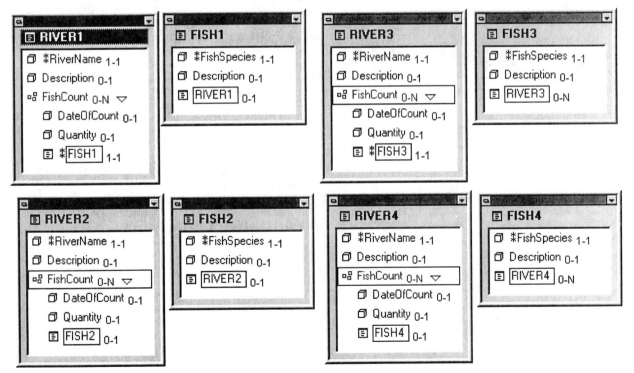

fish, but only once per river. Case 4 counts many fish and potentially many times on a river.

Cases 1, 3, and 4 would be represented with the following three tables:

RIVER (<u>RiverName</u>, Description)
FISH (<u>FishSpecies</u>, Description)
FISHCOUNT(<u>FishCountID</u>, DateOfCount, Quantity, *RiverName, FishSpecies*)

In case 1, (RiverName, FishSpecies) would be created as a unique index.
In case 3, (DateOfCount, FishSpecies) would be created as a unique index.
In case 4, no special indices would be created.

Case 2 would be presented by the tables:

RIVER (<u>RiverName</u>, Description)
FISH (<u>FishSpecies</u>, Description, *RiverName*)
FISHCOUNT(<u>FishCountID</u>, DateOfCount, Quantity, *RiverName, FishSpecies*)

Where (FishSpecies, RiverName) in FISH would be created as a unique index.

7.25 *Modify Figure 7-22(b) and (c) to add the reports shown in Figure 7-24.*

Add an INGREDIENT object and a SUPPLIER object as follows:

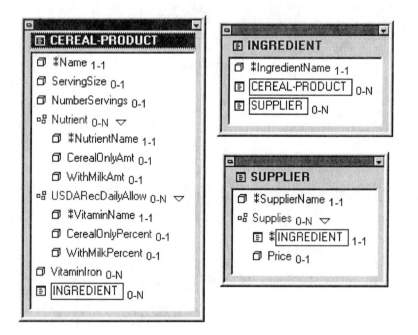

Resulting tables are (in SQL Server):

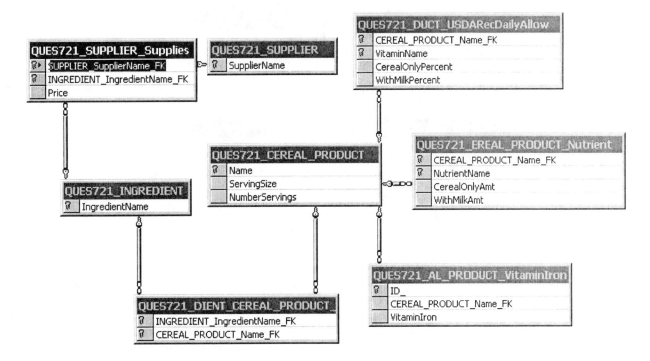

7.26   *Using the album cover shown in Figure 7-25 as a guide, perform the following tasks:*

    a.   *Draw the object diagrams for the underlying objects ARTIST, ROLE, and SONG.*

    b.   *Identify the relationships among those objects. What types of objects are they (simple, composite, and so on)?*

    c.   *Indicate for each participant in a relationship whether it is optional or mandatory.*

    d.   *Transform the object diagrams into relation diagrams. What is the key of each relation? What foreign keys appear in each relation?*

All three objects are compound objects. The other questions are answered in this model and in the SQL Server database.

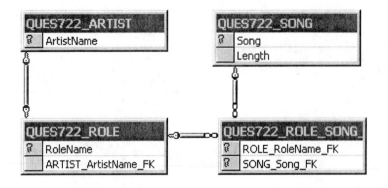

Answers to Projects

A. *Complete project A at the end of Chapter 4 if you have not already done so. Transform your semantic object model into a set of relations. If any of your relations are not in DK/NF, justify your decision to create un-normalized relations.*

The following SQL Server database was generated by Tabledesigner from the file MHA.apm in the Chapter 4 subdirectory of the Instructor Supplements section located on the www.prenhall.com/kroenke/ Web site.

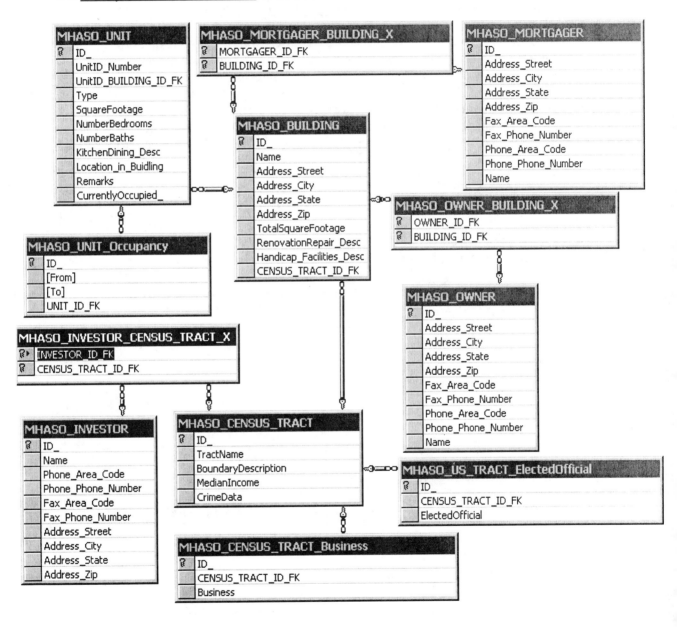

All tables use surrogate keys. Attributes ending in FK are foreign keys. Tables ending in _X are intersection tables.

This is almost the same schema as for Project A of Chapter 6. The only difference is the single valued group names, like Address, have been appended to the names of attributes they contain. See for example, MHASO_OWNER.

B. *Complete project B at the end of Chapter 4 if you have not already done so. Transform your semantic object model into a set of relations. If any of your relations are not in DK/NF, justify your decision to create un-normalized relations.*

The answer is the same as given for Project 6 B. The SQL Server database can be produced using Tabledesigner from the file Dell.apm in the Chapter 4 subdirectory of the Instructor Supplements section of www.prenhall.com/kroenke site.

C. *Complete project C at the end of Chapter 4 if you have not already done so. Transform your semantic object model into a set of relations. If any of your relations are not in DK/NF, justify your decision to create un-normalized relations.*

The answer is the same as given for Project 6 B. The SQL Server database can be produced using Tabledesigner from the file Amazon.apm in the Chapter 4 subdirectory of the Instructor Supplements section of www.prenhall.com/kroenke site.

Answers to FiredUp Project Questions

If you have not already done so, create semantic objects for Questions A and C in the FiredUp Project at the end of Chapter 4.

A. *Transform the semantic object design from Question A at the end of Chapter 4 into a set of relations in domain/key normal form. For each relation, specify the primary key, candidate keys, if any, and foreign keys. Specify all referential integrity constraints. If necessary, make and justify assumptions regarding the underlying semantics of the application.*

Relations:

CUSTOMER (CustomerID, Name, StreetAddress, ApartmentNumber, *Zip/PostalCode*, EmailAddress, PhoneNumber)

LOCATION-CODE (Zip/PostalCode, City, State/Province, Country)

STOVE (SerialNumber, Type, ManufacturerDate, InspectorInitials, *CustomerID*)

INVOICE (InvoiceNumber, Date, TotalPrice)

INV-LINE-ITEM (*InvoiceNumber*, LineNumber, *PartNumber*, Quantity, ExtendedPrice)

REPAIR (RepairNumber, Date, Description, TotalAmount, SerialNumber)

REP-LINE-ITEM (*RepairNumber*, LineNumber, *PartNumber*, Quantity, ExtendedPrice)

PART (Number, Description, Cost, SalesPrice)

This design uses a surrogate key for CUSTOMER. EmailAddress is therefore a candidate key for CUSTOMER. There are no other candidate keys. Date has been added to REPAIR because it should be there.

Referential integrity constraints:

Zip/PostalCode in CUSTOMER must exist in Zip/PostalCode in LOCATION-CODE
CustomerID in STOVE must exist in CustomerID in CUSTOMER
InvoiceNumber in INV-LINE-ITEM must exist in InvoiceNumber in INVOICE
PartNumber in INV-LINE-ITEM must exist in Number in PART
RepairNumber in REP-LINE-ITEM must exist in RepairNumber in REPAIR
PartNumber in REP-LINE-ITEM must exist in Number in PART

B. *Adjust your answer to Question A to allow un-normalized relations if you think just relations are appropriate. Justify any non-normalized relations you have. If necessary, make and justify assumptions regarding the underlying semantics of the application.*

Get rid of the LOCATION-CODE relation and place City, State/Province, Country in CUSTOMER. Normalizing Zip codes adds complexity and really doesn't buy anything. Locations don't change their Zip codes very much, and when they do, the change can be handled as any other address change. Normalization is not worth the trouble.

All the rest of the normalized tables seem OK as is.

C. *Transform the semantic objects design from Question C at the end of Chapter 4 into a set of relations, preferably in domain/key normal form. If any of your relations are not in domain/key normal form, explain why not. For each relation, specify the primary key, candidate keys, if any, and foreign keys. Specify all referential integrity constraints. Assume that home, fax, and cell phone are to be represented by a multi-value PhoneNumber attribute.*

Leave Zip un-normalized with justification as in Item B.

Relations:

CUSTOMER (CustomerID, Name, StreetAddress, ApartmentNumber, City, State/Province, Country)

CUSTOMER-PHONE (*CustomerID*, Type, PhoneNumber)

CUSTOMER-EMAIL (*CustomerID*, EmailAddress)

STOVE (SerialNumber, Type, ManufacturerDate, InspectorInitials, *CustomerID*)

INVOICE (InvoiceNumber, Date, TotalPrice)

INV-LINE-ITEM (*InvoiceNumber*, LineNumber, *PartNumber*, Quantity, ExtendedPrice)

REPAIR (RepairNumber, Date, Description, TotalAmount, SerialNumber)

REP-LINE-ITEM (*RepairNumber*, LineNumber, *PartNumber*, Quantity, ExtendedPrice)

PART (Number, Description, Cost, SalesPrice)

This design uses a surrogate key for CUSTOMER. EmailAddress is therefore a candidate key for CUSTOMER. There are no other candidate keys. Date has been added to REPAIR because it should be there.

Referential integrity constraints:

CustomerID in CUSTOMER-PHONE must exist in CustomerID in CUSTOMER
CustomerID in CUSTOMER-EMAIL must exist in CustomerID in CUSTOMER
CustomerID in STOVE must exist in CustomerID in CUSTOMER
InvoiceNumber in INV-LINE-ITEM must exist in InvoiceNumber in INVOICE
PartNumber in INV-LINE-ITEM must exist in Number in PART
RepairNumber in REP-LINE-ITEM must exist in RepairNumber in REPAIR
PartNumber in REP-LINE-ITEM must exist in Number in PART

D.   *Adjust your answer to Question C, above, to assume that home, fax and cell phone are to be represented by separate, single-value attributes. Is this a better design than in your answer to Question C? Explain why or why not.*

Delete CUSTOMER-PHONE. Change the CUSTOMER relation as follows:

CUSTOMER (CustomerID, Name, StreetAddress, ApartmentNumber, City,
           State/Province, Country, HomePhone, FaxPhone, CellPhone)

It may be better, depending on the use of the relation. If no other phone types are ever added and if there is no need to query on a phone number of an uncertain type, then this probably is a better design because no join will need to be made to obtain all of the CUSTOMER data. On the other hand, if other types of phone may be created and if there's a need to find out which customer has a phone number of unspecified type, then the original design may be better.

Note: the answers to these four questions are identical to those for the E-R model in Chapter 6.

Chapter 8

Foundations of Relational Implementation

Objectives

- Review relational terminology
- Describe the tasks to be accomplished in relational data definition
- Survey the types of tools available for relational data manipulation and describe three modes of DML interface
- Describe basic relational algebra operations and illustrate their use in expressing database queries

Teaching Suggestions

Note: The ViewRidge Gallery schema shown in Figure 10-3 will be used for examples in Chapters 11, 12, 13, 14, 15, and 16. Even if you skip this chapter or cover it quickly, be sure to introduce the students to this schema. See the note in the preface material of this manual on the rationale for using this particular schema.

1.   When discussing the relational model, emphasize the fact that relationships between tables are represented within the data that is visible to the users, not in hidden data structures (like linked lists or indexes). You may want to cover some of the material in Appendix A so that the students can get a feel for these data structures.

2.   In general, users do not want to process relations. They want to process objects composed from relations.   This means that applications need to create views of data from relations as discussed in Chapter 10. A relation, then, is a building block — akin to a brick. Just as buildings are made of bricks, database applications are constructed from rows in relations.

3.   Relational algebra is seldom used in commercial processing. Still, I think it is useful to teach it so the students understand the kind of work that the DBMS must perform. For example, the students need to know what a join is so that they understand what they are requiring the DBMS to do when they express a query in SQL that implies a join.

4.   If you're going to use Oracle or SQL Server, this chapter is a good place to introduce one of them. The discussion in the section on implementing a Relational Database can be given substance if the students are at the same time creating their own database. One good way is to create a database using one of these products in class.

5.   Note that referential integrity and inter-relation constraints are often treated as synonyms, but they may not be, depending on one's viewpoint. Some say that inter-relation constraints that are not referential integrity constraints should be considered to be business rules. Others say this is silly, they are inter-relation constraints. For example, say relation PORTFOLIO has an attribute, TotalAssets, and has a 1:N

relationship to OWNED-SECURITY. OWNED-SECURITY has an attribute Value. Now, assume there is a constraint that specifies that, for any given account, the sum of Value must equal TotalAssets. Is this a business rule or an inter-relation constraint?

I thought this issue was not worth the trouble to discuss in the text, but in my mind at least, strictly speaking, there are some inter-relation constraints that are not referential integrity constraints.

Answers to Group I Questions

8.1   *Name and describe the three tasks necessary to implement a relational database.*

Define the structure to the DBMS (text file or graphical creation facility); allocate space (done automatically for personal DBMS, can be considerable work for server or mainframe DBMS products); create data (keyed or mass input, verification important, may write verification programs).

8.2   *Define **relation, attribute, tuple,** and **domain.***

Relation: a two-dimensional table with no repeating columns and no identical rows. Attribute: column of a relation. Tuple: row of a relation. Domain: set of values an attribute can have.

8.3   *Explain the use of the terms **table, column, row, file, field,** and **record.***

Both sets: same as relation, attribute, tuple.

8.4   *Explain the difference between a relational schema and a relation.*

A relational schemata is the structure of a set of relations with constraints. A relation is the structure of the tables without constraints.

8.5   *Define **key, index, logical key,** and **physical key.***

A key is an attribute or group of attributes that identifies a unique row. A logical key is the same as a key as just defined. A physical key is an attribute that has a data structure defined (usually an index) to improve direct or sequential access. Sometimes physical keys are defined to create uniqueness constraints.

8.6   *Describe three reasons for using indexes.*

Improve performance for direct access; improve performance for sorted sequential processing. Used to implement a uniqueness constraint. (Corollary to above: can be used to improve performance in joins.)

8.7 *Under what conditions is it necessary to transform the database design during the implementation stage?*

When the database is to be implemented using a product based on a model other than the relational model. Today that would be an ODBMS, or perhaps DL/I or IMS (not discussed in text – you might want to provide a bit of background on them). No transformation is required when using a relational product because the DBMS-independent design has been expressed in terms of the relational model.

8.8 *Explain the term **data definition language**. What purpose does it serve?*

The data definition language is a means for describing the structure of a database. One can use SQL to define tables, indexes, constraints, relationships and other structures as shown in Chapter 12.

8.9 *How can a database structure be defined other than through a text file?*

Using a graphical facility, as in Access or SQL Server.

8.10 *What aspects of database design need to be defined to the DBMS?*

Name each table, define columns in that table, describe the physical format of each column. Create relationships, specify constraints, define passwords and other control facilities.

8.11 *Give an example, other than the one in this text, in which the allocation of the database to physical media is important.*

Two objects are processed concurrently. One is ORDER with ORDER and LINE-ITEM tables. The other is CUSTOMER with CUSTOMER and PAYMENT tables. The objects have no data in common. If the organization has two disk drives and channels, it may be best to put ORDER and LINE-ITEM on one and CUSTOMER and PAYMENT on the other. That way, processing of ORDER object does not interfere with the processing of the CUSTOMER object.

8.12 *Describe the best and worst extremes for loading the database with data.*

Best: data is on computer-sensible media — it is known to be consistent and free of errors. Worst: data is on hard to read paper forms that were scribbled in number 6 pencil in a rain forest by people who did not speak English. Many forms were lost when a barge overturned in the Amazon with the source documents. Documents contain the only existent data about the location of highly toxic chemicals located in industrial dump sites in areas around Philadelphia, New York, or Boston. Strangely, all of the documents pertaining to Langley, VA, survived intact.

8.13 *Name and briefly explain four categories of relational DML.*

Relational algebra manipulates relation via operators similar to arithmetic operators. The user must know what is desired and how to extract it. Relational calculus in contrast is non-procedural. Transform-oriented languages are also non-procedural, and are used to transform inputs into desired outputs. Query by Example provides the user with a picture of the structure of the relation. The user then fills in an example of the desired results.

8.14 *Describe how relational data can be manipulated by means of forms.*

Use either default form or form custom created using application tools subsystem of the DBMS.

8.15 *Explain the role of query languages in relational data manipulation. How do stored queries differ from application programs? Why are they used?*

Statement at a time by users in command mode or text processing window. Or use stored queries that were created by SQL experts and stored with the database.

8.16 *Describe the two styles of application program interface to the database. In your answer, explain the role of a precompiler.*

Call a subroutine library (more difficult) or insert SQL or other data sublanguage commands. Precompiler converts data sublanguage commands into standard language commands.

8.17 *Describe the mismatch between the orientation of the SQL and the orientation of most programming languages. How is this mismatch corrected?*

SQL is relation at a time oriented; programming languages are row at a time. Treat the result of an SQL command as a pseudofile; this is shown for Oracle and SQL Server in Chapters 12 and 13, respectively.

8.18 *How does relational algebra differ from high school algebra?*

In high school algebra, variables that are operated on represent numbers. The result is also a number. In relational algebra, the operands are relations and the end result is always another relation.

8.19 *Why is relational algebra closed?*

The result of a series of relational algebra operations is always another relation.

8.20 *Define **union compatible**. Give an example of two relations that are union compatible and two that are union incompatible.*

To be union compatible, each relation in the union must have the same number of attributes and attributes in corresponding columns must come from the same domain.

Compatible: INVENTORY (Inumber, Description, SalesPrice)
               ORDER (Partnumber, Description, Price)

or

               EMPLOYEE (Enumber, Name, Dept)
               VACATION-SCHEDULE (Number, Name, Dept-to-be-billed)

Non-compatible: INVENTORY (Pnum, Desc, Quantity-in-stock)
               ORDER (Item, Desc, Price)

and
>   INVENTORY (Part, Desc)
>   ORDER (Pnum, Desc, Supplier)

8.21-8.23

Questions 8.21 through 8.23 refer to the following two relations:

COMPANY (Name, NumberEmployees, Sales)
MANUFACTURERS (Name, PeopleCount, Revenue)

8.21   *Give an example of a union of these two relations.*

COMPANY (Name, Number-employees, Sales)
MANUFACTURER (Name, People, Revenue)

COMPANY

IBM	50000	9000000000
Univac	25000	500000000
Microsoft	35000	1500000000

MANUFACTURER

IBM	50000	9000000000
Univac	25000	500000000

Union of COMPANY and MANUFACTURER

IBM	50000	9000000000
Univac	25000	500000000
Microsoft	35000	1500000000

8.22   *Give an example of a difference of these two relations.*

Difference of COMPANY and MANUFACTURER:

Microsoft	2500	1500000000

8.23   *Give an example of an intersection of these two relations.*

Intersection of COMPANY and MANUFACTURER:

IBM	50000	9000000000
Univac	25000	500000000

8.24-8.28

Questions 8.24 through 8.28 refer to the following three relations:

SALESPERSON (Name, Salary)

ORDER (Number, CustName, SalespersonName, Amount)
CUSTOMER (Name, City, IndustryType)

An instance of these relations is shown in Figure 8-22. Use the data in those tables for the following problems:

8.24   Give an example of the product of SALESPERSON and ORDER.

The product of these two relations will contain 42 tuples.

8.25   Show an example of

SALESPERSON [Name, Salary]
SALESPERSON [Salary]

Under what conditions will SALESPERSON [Salary] have fewer rows than SALESPERSON does?

SALESPERSON[Name, Salary]

Abel	120,000
Baker	42,000
Jones	36,000
Murphy	50,000
Zenith	118,000
Kobad	34,000

SALESPERSON[Salary]

120,000
42,000
36,000
50,000
118,000
34,000

SALESPERSON[Salary] would have fewer rows than SALESPERSON if any two people have the same salary (which they do not in this example).

8.26   Show an example of a select on SALESPERSON Name, on SALESPERSON Salary, and on both SALESPERSON Name and Salary.

SELECT SALESPERSON WHERE Name = "Baker"

SELECT SALESPERSON WHERE PercentOfQuota < 30

SELECT SALESPERSON WHERE Name = "Jones" AND PercentOfQuota > 30

8.27   *Show an example of an equijoin and a natural join of SALESPERSON and ORDER in which the Name of SALESPERSON equals the SalespersonName of ORDER.*

SALESPERSON JOIN (Name = Salesperson-name) ORDER

Abel	120,000	300	Manchester Lumber	Abel	480
Abel	120,000	400	Amalgamated Housing	Abel	2500
Abel	120,000	600	Tri-City Builders	Abel	700
Jones	36,000	200	Abernathy Construction	Jones	1800
Jones	36,000	700	Manchester Lumber	Jones	150
Murphy	50,000	500	Abernathy Construction	Murphy	6000
Zenith	118,000	90	Abernathy Construction	Zenith	560

This is an equijoin. For a natural join, remove the second column of salesperson names (next to last column).

8.28   *Show relational algebra expressions for*

a.   *The names of all salespeople*

SALESPERSON[Name]

b.   *The names of all salespeople having an ORDER row*

ORDER[Salesperson-name]

c.   *The names of salespeople not having an ORDER row*

SALESPERSON[Name] - ORDER[Salesperson-name]

d.   *The names of salespeople having an order with Abernathy Construction*

ORDER WHERE Salesperson-name = 'Abernathy Construction'

e.   *The salaries of salespeople having an order with Abernathy Construction*

SALESPERSON JOIN (Name = Salesperson-name) ORDER WHERE Cust-name = 'Abernathy Construction' [Salary]

f.   *The city of all CUSTOMERS having an order with salesperson Jones*

ORDER WHERE Salesperson-name = 'Jones' JOIN [Cust-name = Name] CUSTOMER [City]

g.   *The names of all salespeople with the names of customers who have ordered from them. Include salespeople who have no orders.*

SALESPERSON LEFT OUTER JOIN (SALESPERSON.Name = SalespersonName) ORDER [SALESPERSON.Name, CustName]

Chapter 9

Structured Query Language

Objectives

- Introduce the relational data access language SQL
- Show SQL for querying a single table
- Show SQL subquery and join for querying multiple tables
- Understand the differences between subqueries and joins
- Demonstrate the use of SQL for updating data

Teaching Suggestions

1. The best way to teach SQL is with lots of examples. Show the syntax of SQL commands and then have the students answer sample queries. Use the questions at the end of the chapter as one source of examples.

2. This chapter presents SQL DML only. SQL DDL is shown in Chapters 12 and 13.

3. **Important Note to Users of the Seventh Edition:** At the request of some reviewers, I changed the attribute Age in the end of chapter questions to PercentOfQuota. The (quite valid) point was made that having an age attribute is terrible design. It should be DateOfBirth and Age, if necessary, should be computed. Rather than deal with that issue here, I just redefined Age as PercentOfQuota. If you have answers prepared to the questions, I think all you need do is search for Age and replace with PercentOfQuota.

Answers to Group I Questions

The questions in this group refer to the following three relations:

SALESPERSON (Name, PercentofQuota, Salary)
ORDER (Number, CustName, SalespersonName, Amount)
CUSTOMER (Name, City, IndustryType)

An instance of these relations is shown in Figure 9-3. Use the data in those tables and show the SQL statements to display or modify data as indicated in the following questions:

9.1   *Show the salaries of all salespeople.*

        SELECT   Salary
        FROM   SALESPERSON

9.2   *Show the salaries of all salespeople but omit duplicates.*

    SELECT   DISTINCT Salary
    FROM   SALESPERSON

9.3   *Show the names of all salespeople under 30 percent of quota.*

    SELECT   Name
    FROM   SALESPERSON
    WHERE   PercentOfQuota < 30

9.4   *Show the names of all salespeople who have an order with Abernathy Construction.*

    SELECT   SalespersonName
    FROM   ORDER
    WHERE   CustName = 'Abernathy Construction'

9.5   *Show the names of all salespeople who earn more than $49,999 and less than $100,000.*

    SELECT   Name
    FROM   SALESPERSON
    WHERE   Salary > 49999 AND Salary < 100000

9.6   *Show the names of all salespeople with PercentOfQuota greater than 49 and less than 60. Use the BETWEEN keyword.*

    SELECT   Name
    FROM   SALESPERSON
    WHERE   PercentOfQuota BETWEEN 50 AND 59

9.7   *Show the names of all salespeople with PercentofQuota greater than 49 and less than 60. Use the LIKE keyword.*

    SELECT   Name
    FROM   SALESPERSON
    WHERE   PercentOfQuota LIKE '5_'

9.8   *Show the names of customers who are located in a City ending with S.*

    SELECT   Name
    FROM   CUSTOMER
    WHERE   City LIKE '%S'

9.9   *Show the names and salary of all salespeople who do not have an order with Abernathy Construction, in ascending order of salary.*

    SELECT   Name, Salary
    FROM   SALESPERSON

```
WHERE        Name NOT IN
(SELECT      SalespersonName
FROM         ORDER
WHERE        CustName = 'Abernathy Construction')
ORDER BY     Salary
```

9.10   *Compute the number of orders.*

```
SELECT       COUNT(*)
FROM         ORDER
```

9.11   *Compute the number of different customers who have an order.*

```
SELECT       COUNT (DISTINCT CustName)
FROM         ORDER
```

9.12   *Compute the average percent of quota for salespeople.*

```
SELECT       AVG(PercentOfQuota)
FROM         SALESPERSON
```

9.13   *Show the name of the salesperson with highest percent of quota.*

```
SELECT       Name
FROM         SALESPERSON
WHERE        PercentOfQuota IN
(SELECT      MAX(PercentOfQuota)
FROM         SALESPERSON)
```

9.14   *Compute the number of orders for each salesperson.*

```
SELECT       SalespersonName, COUNT(*)
FROM         ORDER
GROUP BY     SalespersonName
```

9.15   *Compute the number of orders for each salesperson, considering only orders for an amount exceeding 500.*

```
SELECT       COUNT(*)
FROM         ORDER
WHERE        Amount > 500
GROUP BY     SalespersonName
```

9.16   *Show the names and quota percentages of salespeople who have an order with ABERNATHY CONSTRUCTION, in descending order of quota percentage (use a subquery).*

```
SELECT       Name, PercentOfQuota
FROM         SALESPERSON
WHERE        Name IN
             (SELECT         SalespersonName
```

```
                    FROM        ORDER
                    WHERE       CustName = 'Abernathy Construction')
       ORDER BY     PercentOfQuota DESC
```

9.17   *Show the names and quota percentages of salespeople who have an order with
       ABERNATHY CONSTRUCTION, in descending order of quota percentage (use a join).*

```
       SELECT       Name, PercentOfQuota
       FROM         SALESPERSON, ORDER
       WHERE        SALESPERSON.Name = ORDER.SalespersonName
           AND      ORDER.CustName = 'Abernathy Construction'
       ORDER BY     PercentOfQuota DESC
```

9.18   *Show the quota percentage of salespeople who have an order with a customer in
       MEMPHIS (use a subquery).*

```
       SELECT       PercentOfQuota
       FROM         SALESPERSON
       WHERE        Name IN
                    (SELECT      SalespersonName
                    FROM ORDER
                    WHERE        CustName IN
                                 (SELECT Name
                                 FROM CUSTOMER
                                 WHERE City = 'Memphis'))
```

9.19   *Show the quota percentage of salespeople who have an order with a customer in
       MEMPHIS (use a join).*

```
       SELECT       PercentOfQuota
       FROM         SALESPERSON, ORDER, CUSTOMER
       WHERE        SALESPERSON.Name = ORDER.SalespersonName
           AND      ORDER.CustName = CUSTOMER.Name
           AND      City = 'Memphis'
```

9.20   *Show the industry type and names of the salespeople of all orders for companies in
       MEMPHIS.*

```
       SELECT       IndustryType, PercentOfQuota
       FROM         SALESPERSON, CUSTOMER, ORDER
       WHERE        SALESPERSON.Name = ORDER.SalespersonName
           AND      ORDER.CustName = CUSTOMER.Name
           AND      CITY = 'Memphis'
```

9.21   *Show the names of salespeople along with the names of the customers which have
       ordered from them. Include salespeople who have had no orders. Use Microsoft Access
       notation.*

```
       SELECT       SALESPERSON.Name, ORDER.CustName
       FROM         SALESPERSON LEFT JOIN ORDER
           ON       SALESPERSON.Name = ORDER.SalespersonName
```

9.22　*Show the names of salespeople who have two or more orders.*

```
SELECT      SalespersonName
FROM        RDER
GROUP BY    SalespersonName
HAVING      COUNT(*) > 1
```

9.23　*Show the names and quota percentages of salespeople who have two or more orders.*

```
SELECT      SALESPERSON.Name, PercentOfQuota
FROM        SALESPERSON, ORDER
WHERE       SALESPERSON.Name = ORDER.SalespersonName
GROUP BY    SALESPERSON.Name, PercentOFQuota
HAVING      COUNT(*) > 1
```

9.24　*Show the names and quota percentages of salespeople who have an order with all customers.*

```
SELECT Name, Age
FROM SALESPERSON
WHERE Name IN
        (SELECT SalespersonName
        FROM ORDER
        GROUP BY SalespersonName
            HAVING COUNT(DISTINCT *) =
            (SELECT COUNT (*)
            FROM CUSTOMER));
```

9.25　*Show a SQL statement to insert a new row into CUSTOMER.*

```
INSERT      INTO        CUSTOMER
            VALUES      ['Wilson','Dayton','F']
```

9.26　*Show a SQL statement to insert a new name and quota percentage into SALESPERSON; assume that salary is not determined.*

```
INSERT      INTO SALESPERSON
            (Name, PercentOfQuota)
            VALUES      ['Jacob', 35]
```

9.27　*Show a SQL statement to insert rows into a new table, HIGH-ACHIEVER (Name, Salary), in which, to be included, a salesperson must have a salary of at least 100,000.*

```
INSERT      INTO HIGH-ACHIEVER
            (SELECT     Name, PercentOfQuota
            FROM        SALESPERSON
            WHERE       Salary >= 100000)
```

9.28   *Show a SQL statement to delete customer ABERNATHY CONSTRUCTION.*

    DELETE   FROM CUSTOMER
    WHERE   NAME = 'Abernathy Construction'

9.29   *Show a SQL statement to delete all orders for ABERNATHY CONSTRUCTION.*

    DELETE   FROM ORDER
    WHERE   CustName = 'Abernathy Construction')

9.30   *Show a SQL statement to change the salary of salesperson JONES to 45,000.*

    UPDATE   SALESPERSON
    SET   Salary = 45000
    WHERE   NAME = 'JONES'

9.31   *Show a SQL statement to give all salespeople a 10 percent pay increase.*

    UPDATE   SALESPERSON
    SET   Salary = Salary * 1.1

9.32   *Assume that salesperson JONES changes his name to PARKS. Show the SQL statements that make the appropriate changes.*

    UPDATE   SALESPERSON
    SET   NAME = 'Parks'
    WHERE   NAME = 'Jones'

    UPDATE   ORDER
    SET   SalespersonName = 'Parks'
    WHERE   SalespersonName = 'Jones'

Answers to Group II Questions

9.33   *Install Access 2002 and open the Northwind database. Using the query Design/SQL text tool, write SQL statements for the following queries and print them.*

a.   *List all columns of suppliers.*

    SELECT * FROM Suppliers;

b.   *List CompanyName from suppliers with CompanyName starting with "New".*

    SELECT   Suppliers.CompanyName
    FROM   Suppliers
    WHERE   Suppliers.CompanyName Like "New*";

c.   *List all columns from products from suppliers with CompanyName starting with "New".*
      Show answer using both a join and a subquery.

```
SELECT Products.*, Suppliers.CompanyName
FROM Suppliers INNER JOIN Products ON Suppliers.SupplierID = Products.SupplierID
WHERE Suppliers.CompanyName Like "New*";
```

and

```
SELECT ProductName
FROM Products
WHERE Products.SupplierID IN
        (SELECT SupplierID
         FROM Suppliers
         Where Suppliers.CompanyName LIKE "New*");
```

d.   *List the ReorderLevel and count for all products.*

```
SELECT ReorderLevel, Count(*)
FROM  Products
GROUP BY ReorderLevel;
```

e.   *List the ReorderLevel and count for all ReorderLevels having more than 1 element*

```
SELECT ReorderLevel, Count(*)
FROM  Products
GROUP BY ReorderLevel
HAVING Count(*) > 1;
```

f.   *List the ReorderLevel and count for all ReorderLevels having more than 1 element for*
      products from suppliers whose names start with "New".

```
SELECT ReorderLevel, Count(*)
FROM Products, Suppliers
WHERE Products.SupplierID = Suppliers.SupplierID
AND Suppliers.CompanyName like 'New%'
GROUP BY ReorderLevel
HAVING count(*) >1;
```

Answers to FiredUp Project Questions

Assume FiredUp has created a database with the following tables:

CUSTOMER (CustomerSK, Name, Phone, EmailAddress)
STOVE (SerialNumber, Type, Verstion, DataOfManufacture)
REGISTRATION (CustomerSK, SerialNumber, Date)
STOVE_REPAIR (RepairInvoiceNumber, SerialNumber, Data, Description, cost, CustomerSK)

Code SQL for the following; assume all dates are in the format mmddyyyy.

A.   *Show all of the data in each of the four FiredUp tables.*

    SELECT   *
    FROM CUSTOMER

    SELECT   *
    FROM STOVE

    SELECT   *
    FROM REGISTRATION

    SELECT   *
    FROM STOVE_REPAIR

B.   *List the versions of all stoves.*

    SELECT   Version
    FROM   STOVE

C.   *List the versions of all stoves of a type FiredNow.*

    SELECT   Version
    FROM   STOVE
    WHERE   Type ='FiredNow'

D.   *List the SerialNumber and Date of all registrations in the year 2000.*

    The answer to this question depends on whether or not the Date attribute is represented
    as character or date type. If the latter, the answer further depends on the DBMS in use.
    Assume here Date is of type Char and is stored in the format mmddyyyy as indicated in
    the question.

    SELECT   SerialNumber, Date
    FROM   REGISTRATION
    WHERE   Date LIKE '%2000'

E.   *List the SerialNumber and Date of all registrations in February. Use the underscore (_)*
      wildcard.

    SELECT   SerialNumber, Date
    FROM   REGISTRATION
    WHERE   Date LIKE '02_____'

    Note use of six underscores.

F. *List the SerialNumber and Date of all registrations in February. Use the percent (%) wildcard.*

SELECT	SerialNumber, Date
FROM	REGISTRATION
WHERE	Date LIKE '02&'

G. *List the names and EmailAddresses of all customers who have an e-mail address.*

SELECT	Name, EmailAddress
FROM	CUSTOMER
WHERE	EmailAddress Is Not Null

H. *List the names of all customers who do not have an EmailAddress; present the results in descending sorted order of Name.*

SELECT	Name
FROM	CUSTOMER
WHERE	EmailAddress Is Not Null
ORDER BY	Name Desc

I. *Determine the maximum cost of a stove repair.*

SELECT	Max(Cost)
FROM	STOVE_REPAIR

J. *Determine the average cost of a stove repair.*

SELECT	Avg(Cost)
FROM	STOVE_REPAIR

K. *Count all stoves.*

SELECT	Count(*)
FROM	STOVE

L. *Count all stoves of each type and display the Type and count.*

SELECT	Type, Count(*)
FROM	STOVE
GROUP BY	Type

M. *List the names and e-mail addresses of all customers who have had a stove repair that cost more than $50. Use subquery.*

SELECT	Name, EmailAddress
FROM	CUSTOMER
WHERE	CustomerSK IN
(SELECT	CustomerSK
FROM	STOVE_REPAIR
WHERE	Cost > 50)

N. *List the names and e-mail addresses of all customers who have registered a stove of type FiredNow. Use subquery.*

```
SELECT      Name, EmailAddress
FROM        CUSTOMER
WHERE       CustomerSK IN
     (SELECT      CustomerSK
      FROM        REGISTRATION
          WHERE       SerialNumber IN
          (SELECT     SerialNumber
          FROM        STOVE
          WHERE       Type ='FiredNow'))
```

O. *List the names and e-mail addresses of all customers who have had a stove repair that cost more than $50. Use join.*

```
SELECT      Name, EmailAddress
FROM        CUSTOMER, STOVE_REPAIR
WHERE       CUSTOMER.CustomerSK = STOVE_REPAIR.CustomerSK AND
            Cost > 50
```

P. *List the names, e-mail addresses of all customers who have registered a stove type FiredNow Use join.*

```
SELECT      Name, EmailAddress
FROM        CUSTOMER, REGISTRATION, STOVE
WHERE       CUSTOMER.CustomerSK = REGISTRATION.CustomerSK AND
            REGISTRATION.SerialNumber = STOVE.SerialNumber AND Type
            ='FiredNow'
```

Q. *List the names, e-mail addresses, and registration date of all customer registrations.*

```
SELECT      Name, EmailAddress, Date
FROM        CUSTOMER, REGISTRATION
WHERE       CUSTOMER.CustomerSK = REGISTRATION.CustomerSK
```

R. *Show the names and e-mail addresses of all customers who have registered a stove but who have not had that stove repaired.*

```
SELECT      Name, EmailAddress, Date
FROM        CUSTOMER, REGISTRATION
WHERE       CUSTOMER.CustomerSK = REGISTRATION.CustomerSK AND
     EXISTS
     (SELECT     *
     FROM        REGISTRATION
     WHERE       CUSTOMER.CustomerSK = REGISTRATION.CustomerSK AND
                 NOT EXISTS
                 (SELECT     *
                 FROM        STOVE_REPAIR
                 WHERE       REGISTRATION.SerialNumber =
                             STOVE_REPAIR.SerialNumber))
```

S.   *Show the names and e-mail addresses of all customers who have registered a stove but who have not had any stove repaired.*

```
SELECT      Name, EmailAddress, Date
FROM        CUSTOMER, REGISTRATION
WHERE       CUSTOMER.CustomerSK = REGISTRATION.CustomerSK AND
      NOT EXISTS
      (SELECT     *
      FROM        REGISTRATION, STOVE_REPAIR
      WHERE       CUSTOMER.CustomerSK = REGISTRATION.CustomerSK AND
                  REGISTRATION.SerialNumber =
STOVE_REPAIR.SerialNumber
```

Chapter 10

Database Application Design

Objectives

- Learn the five basic functions of a database application
- Understand database actions required to create, read, update, and delete database views
- Learn fundamental principles of database view materialization
- Understand the application's role in enforcing constraints
- Understand the application's role in control and security

Teaching Suggestions

1. The relationship of database applications and the DBMS is sometimes confusing. For a simple application using a personal DBMS, the application and the DBMS are nearly indistinguishable. If an application has only a few forms and reports, and all of these are created using DBMS facilities, then the application and the DBMS are the same. On the other hand, for an organizational database processed by say, DB2, all of the elements discussed in this chapter will be provided by application program code completely separate from the DBMS. It's easier to understand all of this by focusing on application functions that must be provided — in some cases by facilities in the DBMS and in other cases by separate application programs.

2. It is important to distinguish between a view (the logical structure of data elements) and a materialization of the view (a form or report). One view can have many materializations. While this distinction has always been important, it has become even more so in light of the three-tier architecture described in Chapter 14 where database views are constructed and processed on the Web server but are materialized on the browser.

3. A database view is a hierarchical structure of attributes from one or more entities or semantic objects. An entity or object can appear more than once in the view. Views can have more than one multi-valued path. In the View Ridge case, a CUSTOMER view has a multi-valued path to TRANSACTION and a second one to ARTIST. (See Figure 10-3e.) No single SQL statement can represent all of this view. Hence, SQL is a poor facility for describing views — even though it has been used for that purpose for years, because of the lack of anything better. XML solves this problem. It is important to make this distinction.

4. The purpose of the discussion of view CRUD is to show students how SQL relates to database applications. Too often I have found that students understand how SQL can be used for interactive query, but do not really understand its role in application processing. In fact, SQL is far more frequently used for view processing as described here than it is as an interactive query tool.

5.   The principles of form and report design in this chapter overlap those taught in a systems development class. This may be review for some students. The essential point here is to understand how the structure of the view and the nature of its contents dictate certain visual structures and controls. Forms and reports that are hard to use always have some element in which the structure of the view and the structure of the materialization fight with one another.

6.   Constraints fall in four major categories: domain, uniqueness, relationship, and business rule. In general, domain and uniqueness constraints are best enforced by the DBMS (setting aside issues involving Microsoft's Transaction Service for distributed databases, which are beyond the scope of this text).   Relationship constraints are either a) referential integrity or b) cardinality. Referential integrity constraints should be enforced by the DBMS. Some cardinality constraints are enforced by the database design and some can be enforced by making foreign keys required or unique or both. Others, like 2.3 (min of 2, max of 3) are best enforced by the application or by stored procedures. Business rule constraints can be enforced by stored procedures in the DBMS or by the application. Ensure that students understand why DBMS enforcement is usually better than application enforcement.

7.   It is important for the students to understand the limitations of user name and password security provided by most DBMS products. Such security is worthless if users are careless with their identities. In this regard, it is unfortunate that most users cannot watch professional software developers at work. They, of all people, understand the risks of user name and password and they as a class are absolutely paranoid about protecting their passwords. In fact, an etiquette and protocol has evolved in which it is considered rude not to look away when watching another person enter his or her password. When one developer is helping another at the second developer's machine, if a password is required, it is understood that the first developer will leave the computer and look away to allow the second to enter his or her password. Asking another developer for his or her password is never done and if it were, it would be considered as rude as asking for their PIN or a bank card or even for their bank balance. By the way, a good way to select a personal password is to think of the first line of a favorite song or poem and use the initial letters of the phrase. Thus, "I Left My Heart in San Francisco" would result in the password ILMHiSF. Easy to remember and very difficult to guess.

8.   Even if user identities are protected, such security is limited to vertical security. Horizontal security must be provided by application code.

Answers to Group I Questions

10.1   *List the five major functions of a database application.*

        CRUD views, materialize views, enforce constraints, provide control and security, execute application logic.

10.2   *Explain the meaning of the acronym CRUD.*

        Create, read, update, and delete.

10.3   *Define the term* **view** *as used in this chapter.*

A view is a structured list of data items from the entities or semantic objects in the data model. Note this is broader than a SQL view – something that can be constructed from a single SQL SELECT statement. We'll use SQL views in Chapters 12, 13, and 16.

10.4   *What is a view instance?*

A view instance is a view structure for a particular entity or semantic object instance.

10.5   *Explain how a view is different from a materialization.*

A view is a structure of data. A materialization is presentation of that data in some format — form, report, or API. A materialization includes labels, colors, boxes, etc. Report materializations almost always include formulas.

10.6   *Can an attribute appear more than once in a view? Why?*

An entity or object can appear more than once in a view. See ARTIST in the View Ridge Customer view. Any attribute of an entity or object that appears more than once in a view can appear more than once in a view.

10.7   *Under what conditions can a view be read with one SQL statement?*

When there is only one multi-valued path through the entities or objects. See Figure 10-3(e). Only CUSTOMER and TRANSACTION or CUSTOMER and ARTIST (via the intersection table) can appear in the view. Here's a trickier one: consider STUDENT with a 1:N relationship to GRADE, and CLASS with a 1:N relationship to GRADE. Create the view STUDENT:GRADE:CLASS. At first it appears there are two multi-valued paths — those between STUDENT and GRADE and between CLASS and GRADE. However, this view transverses from STUDENT to GRADE to CLASS, which has a max card of 1 in that direction.

10.8   *Under what conditions does reading a view require more than one SQL statement?*

When there is more than one multi-valued path.

10.9   *Explain the two paths that exist in the Customer view in Figure 10-4.*

One is via TRANSACTION; the other is via the CUSTOMER_ARTIST_INT to ARTIST.

10.10   *Define the term* **recordset**.

A record set is the result of the execution of a SQL statement that is wrapped in object structures. Recordset has methods and properties. These are discussed further in Chapter 15.

10.11   *Describe in general terms the work that is required when creating a view instance.*

Obtain the data values in memory and then store new rows of appropriate relations in the database. Set foreign key values to establish relationships within the new data rows as well as to connect the new view data with data that already exists in the database.

10.12   *How are new relationships created when creating a view instance?*

By setting foreign key values.   If surrogate keys are used, this will probably require storing new rows, reading back their surrogate keys, and then using new values to connect the new rows.

10.13   *What technique can be used to obtain the value of a surrogate key when inserting new rows into a table?*

Store the row and then read it back. Note, if there is no unique identifier other than the surrogate key, several rows may be returned. The application must check additional attribute values to find the correct one.

10.14   *List the three types of change that can occur when updating a view instance.*

Updating an attribute value; changing a relationship; adding new rows for new multi-valued attributes, such as TRANSACTION for CUSTOMER as discussed in the text.

10.15   *Explain how to change 1:N relationships. Explain how to change N:M relationships.*

Change 1:N relationships by modifying the foreign key value. Change N:M relationships by modifying the key value in the intersection table.

10.16   *What is the major difficulty when writing code to delete a view instance?*

The difficulty is in knowing how much to delete. In terms of the entity-relationship model, all weak entities are deleted. In terms of the semantic object model, all data in a given object is deleted, but no data in other objects. Deletions are also not allowed if the deletions were to cause a cardinality violation.

10.17   *How can an E-R model help determine how much to delete?*

All weak entities that depend on the base entity of the view are deleted. Also all weak entities that depend on weak entities that are being deleted.

10.18   *How can a semantic object model help determine how much to delete?*

All attributes contained within the semantic object are deleted. Objects that are pointed to by object links are not deleted, however.

10.19   *What are cascading deletions, and why are they important?*

Cascading deletions occur when the deletion of one row causes the deletion of another row. They can be used to enforce the rules in the answer to questions 10.17 and 10.18.

10.20 *Explain the statement "Form structure should reflect view structure."*

The structure of the view should be graphically evident in the structure of the form. Using the semantic object model, data from the entry point relation is presented first, followed by data in the order of the semantic object (assuming that order reflects the order of the forms and reports from which the object was derived). Multi-value data occurs in regions with column headings and possibly footings. Data from the entry point relation may need to be split on the form, but otherwise data from a relation is presented in contiguous areas on the form. The same principles can be used for report design.

10.21 *How can forms be designed to make the semantics of the data graphically evident?*

Place group boxes around groups; ensure the hierarchy of the view is expressed consistently in the hierarchical structure of the form. Keep related items together. Example: Place Address, City, State, Zip, together in a group on a form. In this way, data that is logically grouped in the user's mind is physically grouped on the form.

10.22 *How can forms be designed to encourage appropriate action?*

Buttons and other controls should be located in obvious places. Example: suppose a user is creating an order and needs to look up item data. The button for the item look up should be near the item number text field on the form. Then the form will encourage the user to look up in the correct context of the form.

10.23 *Explain the role of drop-down list boxes, option groups, and check boxes in form design.*

A drop-down list box is a box superimposed on the existing screen. It enables the user to interrupt normal processing, perform a related task, and return to the original procedure. An option group represents a group of mutually exclusive choices. Only one can be selected. A check box represents a binary selection; more than one check box can be on in a group of check boxes.

10.24 *What limitation exists for report materialization of views?*

With banded report writers, only one multi-valued path can be readily represented. If a CUSTOMER, for example, has multiple ContactPersons and multiple Payment terms, the two multi-valued groups cannot be readily presented on the report. Sub-reports, calculated values, or other artifice must be employed to show the two multi-valued attributes.

10.25 *Explain why the calculated values on reports should normally not be stored in the database.*

The values change frequently and stored values are not reliable. Either that, or some facility must be created in the application to automatically update stored computed values when the determinants of the computations change. This is costly and wasteful and is almost never done.

10.26 *Explain how the request to report objects sorted by a value changes the underlying object of the report.*

A request to sort an object refers to a set of objects and not to the named object. Show CUSTOMERs sorted by Zip is a request to create a materialization of a set of CUSTOMERs and not to a single customer. The set, in fact, is a different object.

10.27 *Why should constraints normally be enforced by the DBMS and not by a particular form, report, or application program?*

If a constraint is enforced by the DBMS, then the constraint will be invoked regardless of the source of the data change: form, application program, import program, or other. If the constraint is placed in application programs, then it must be enforced by every program — and inconsistency is likely.

10.28 *Why are constraints sometimes enforced in application programs?*

Because the DBMS lack facilities to enforce the constraint or because the constraint is particular to a given application.

10.29 *Give an example of a domain constraint and explain how it might be enforced by Access.*

InvoiceTotal must be less than 10,000. If InvoiceTotal is stored in the database, then set a rule in the table definition as shown in this chapter. If it is not stored in the database, then trap an event and write code to enforce the constraint as shown in Chapter 2.

10.30 *Describe the ambiguity that arises when values are null. Describe two ways such values can be eliminated.*

A null value can mean that the value is unknown, that a value is inappropriate, or that the value is known to be blank. Make the value required, or, in the case of value-inappropriate nulls, create subtypes, or set a default value of 'blank.'

10.31 *Why should the DBMS normally enforce uniqueness constraints?*

Because it is the central point through which all data changes are made and because it creates indexes to make such checking very fast.

10.32 *Describe the two sources of cardinality constraints.*

Non-zero settings of minimum cardinality, and maximum cardinality settings other than 1 or N.

10.33 *Name two types of relationship constraint.*

Referential integrity and cardinality.

10.34 *What is the best way to enforce constraints on foreign key values?*

Define them to the DBMS via referential integrity constraints and via required values on foreign keys, as required.

10.35 *How can a 1.1 cardinality constraint on the child side of a 1:N relationship be enforced?*

Make the foreign key required.

10.36 *Define **fragment** and **orphan**.*

A fragment is a child or parent row that does not have a required parent or child. An orphan is child row that does not have a required parent.

10.37 *Explain the entries in the first column of Figure 10-19(a).*

M-M: CUSTOMER has ORDERs (assumes no one becomes a customer until they order)
M-O: REPAIR has LABOR-CHARGEs
O-M: APPOINTMENT has DOCTORs
O-O: SALESPERSON has AUTO

10.38 *Explain why the center column of Figure 10-19(a) is unnecessary when surrogate keys are used.*

Because the surrogate key is never seen nor modified by the user.

10.39 *Explain the entries in the third column of Figure 10-19(a).*

See text discussion on pages 280-284.

10.40 *Explain the entries in the first column of Figure 10-19(b).*

See text discussion on pages 280-284.

10.41 *Explain the entries in the third column of Figure 10-19(b).*

See text discussion on pages 280-284.

10.42 *Explain why the first column of Figure 10-19(a) and the third column of Figure 10-19(b) are not enforced by the Access 2000 relationship properties shown in Figure 10-20.*

Because the only automatic relationship maintenance is cascade modify and cascade delete. These do not cover the cases shown in column one of Figure 10-19(a) nor column three of Figure 10-19(b).

10.43 *Give an example of a business rule constraint that could apply to the data model in Figure 10-3. Explain how this constraint could be enforced by trapping an event.*

No data is ever to be deleted for a CUSTOMER who purchased any work for more than $50,000. Trap the delete event in Access. Write code to find the maximum SalesPrice.

Examine that value; if it is greater than $50,000, disallow the delete. Show a message box to the user to explain why.

10.44 *Define **horizontal** and **vertical** security.*

Horizontal security allows access to all columns of the data, but restricts access to certain rows. Vertical security allows access to all rows of the data, but restricts access to certain columns.

10.45 *Which type of security is supported by user name and password?*

Vertical.

10.46 *Which type of security must be supported by application code?*

Horizontal or both.

10.47 *Explain why dynamic menus are better than static ones.*

They can be tailored to the context in which the user is operating.

10.48 *How is business logic connected to a database when using Access?*

Short answer: by trapping events and writing application code for those events. Longer answer, if Access is a cover over SQL Server, then trap events and fire stored procedures in SQL Server. (The longer answer is not discussed in the text.)

Answers to Group II Questions

Questions 10.49 through 10.52 pertain to the following Artist View, which is based on the data model in Figure 10-3.
ARTIST.Name
ARTIST.Nationality
    TRANSACTION.PurchaseDate
    TRANSACTION.SalesPrice. . .
        CUSTOMER.Name
        CUSTOMER.Phone.AreaCode
        CUSTOMER.Phone.LocalNumber
    CUSTOMER.Name. . .

The ellipses (. . .) refer to structures that can repeat.

First, note that this view contains no WORK data. This is OK, apparently the user of this view only cares about artist transactions for all of an artist's work, but it does mean that we will have to do some juggling here and there.

10.49   *Code SQL statements for reading the "Mark Tobey" instance of this view.*

    SELECT   ARTIST.Name, ARTIST.Nationality, TRANSACTION.PurchaseDate,
    TRANSACTION.SalesPrice, CUSTOMER.Name, CUSTOMER.AreaCode,
    CUSTOMER.LocalNumber,
    FROM   CUSTOMER, TRANSACTION, WORK, ARTIST
    WHERE   CUSTOMER.CustomerID = WORK.Customer_ID
         AND   WORK.WorkID = TRANSACTION.WorkID
         AND   ARTIST.Name = "Mark Tobey"

Followed by:

    SELECT   CUSTOMER.Name
    FROM   CUSTOMER, CUSTOMER_ARTIST_INT
    WHERE   CUSTOMER.CustomerID =
    CUSTOMER_ARTIST_INT.CustomerID
    AND   ARTIST.ArtistID = CUSTOMER_ARTIST_INT.ArtistID

10.50   *Code SQL statements to create a new instance of this view. Assume that you have data
    for ARTIST, one TRANSACTION, and many CUSTOMER.Name(s) for the second
    instance of CUSTOMER.Name. Assume this data is located in a structure named
    NewArtist. Use syntax similar to that in the text.*

        INSERT   INTO   ARTIST
        (ARTIST.Name,
        ARTIST.Nationality)
        VALUES   (NewArtist.ARTIST.Name, NewArtist.ARTIST.Nationality)

To get the new surrogate key value:

    SELECT   ARTIST.ArtistID, ARTIST.Nationality
    FROM   ARTIST
    WHERE   ARTIST.Name = NewArtist.Name

The question says that we have data for TRANSACTION, and that data should include
the key of the related (but missing from the view) WORK row. If it is not included in the
TRANSACTION data, then assuming that WORK.Title and WORK.Copy are given, we
can obtain the value for WorkID as follows:

    SELECT   WORK.WorkID
    FROM   WORK, ARTIST
    WHERE   WORK.ArtistID = ARTIST.ArtistID
         AND   ARTIST.Name = NewCust.WORK.ARTIST.Name
         AND   WORK.Title = NewCust.WORK.Title
         AND   WORK.Copy = NewCust.WORK.Copy

Assume that the surrogate key value, whether given as part of TRANSACTION or
obtained as above, is stored as NewCust.WORK.WorkID.

(By the way, if the WORK row is not in the database, then we should generate an error message and roll the transaction out.)

The following SQL can be executed to add the new TRANSACTION row:
```
INSERT      INTO  TRANSACTION
                    (TRANSACTION.WorkID,
                    TRANSACTION.DateAcquired,
                    TRANSACTION.AcquisitionPrice,
                    TRANSACTION.PurchaseDate,
                    TRANSACTION.CustomerID,
                    TRANSACTION.SalesPrice)
            VALUES
                    (NewArtist.WORK.WorkID,
                    NewArtist.TRANSACTION.DateAcquired,
                    NewArtist.TRANSACTION.AcquisitionPrice,
                    NewArtist.TRANSACTION.PurchaseDate,
                    NewArtist.CUSTOMER.CustomerID,
                    NewArtist.TRANSACTION.SalesPrice)
```

Now all that remains is to create rows for the intersection table.

```
For each NewArtist.CUSTOMER.Name
        SELECT      CUSTOMER.CustomerID
        FROM        CUSTOMER
        WHERE       CUSTOMER.Name = NewArtist.CUSTOMER.Name

        INSERT      INTO        CUSTOMER_ARTIST_INT
                                (ArtistID, CustomerID)
                    VALUES      (NewArtist.ARTIST.ArtistID,
                                CUSTOMER.CustomerID)
Next NewCust.ARTIST.Name
```

10.51   *Code SQL statements to update this view as follows:*

A.   *Change the spelling of Mark Tobey to Mark Toby.*

```
UPDATE ARTIST
SET         ARTIST.ArtistName = "Mark Toby"
WHERE       ARTIST.ArtistName = "Mark Tobey"
```

(Consider here the advantages of surrogate keys. Otherwise, we'd have to cascade this change through WORK and TRANSACTION.)

B.   *Create a new Transaction for Mark Toby. Assume you have the necessary transaction, work, and customer data in a structure named NewTrans.*

Assuming we have the ID of the work in NewTrans.WorkID. Otherwise, have to issue SELECT for the work specified as in the answer to question 10.50 above. Also, we have to assume that the appropriate WORK row exists; if not, write an error message and roll back.

```
INSERT       INTO  TRANSACTION
             (TRANSACTION.WorkID,
             TRANSACTION.DateAcquired,
             TRANSACTION.AcquisitionPrice,
             TRANSACTION.PurchaseDate,
             TRANSACTION.CustomerID,
             TRANSACTION.SalesPrice)
      VALUES
             (NewTrans.WorkID,
             NewTrans.TRANSACTION.DateAcquired,
             NewTrans.TRANSACTION.AcquisitionPrice,
             NewTrans.TRANSACTION.PurchaseDate,
             NewTrans.CUSTOMER.CustomerID,
             NewTrans.TRANSACTION.SalesPrice)
```

C.   *Add new interested customers for Mark Toby. Assume they are stored in a collection that you can access with the command "For Each NewCust.Name."*

```
SELECT       ArtistID
FROM         ARTIST
WHERE        ARTIST.ArtistName = "Mark Toby"
```

For each NewCust.Name
```
      SELECT       CUSTOMER.CustomerID
      FROM         CUSTOMER
      WHERE        CUSTOMER.Name = NewCust.Name

      INSERT       INTO         CUSTOMER_ARTIST_INT
                                (ArtistID, CustomerID)
                   VALUES       (ArtistID,
                                CUSTOMER.CustomerID)
```
Next NewCust.Name

10.52 *Code SQL statements to delete the row for Mark Toby and all related WORK and TRANSACTION rows.*

Execute deletions from the bottom up:

```
DELETE       TRANSACTION
WHERE        TransactionID IN
      (SELECT       WORK.TransactionID
             FROM WORK
             WHERE        WORK.ArtistID IN
                   (SELECT       ARTIST.ArtistID
                   FROM         ARTIST
                   WHERE        ARTIST.ArtistName = "Mark Toby"))
```

Then,

```
DELETE      WORK
WHERE       WORK.ArtistID IN
                (SELECT    ARTIST.ArtistID
                FROM       ARTIST
                WHERE      ARTIST.ArtistName = "Mark Toby"))
```

Next,

```
DELETE      CUSTOMER_ARTIST_INT
       WHERE       CUSTOMER_ARTIST)_INT.ArtistID IN
                (SELECT    ARTIST.ArtistID
                FROM       ARTIST
                WHERE      ARTIST.ArtistName = "Mark Toby")
```

And finally,

```
       DELETE      ARTIST
             WHERE       ARTIST.ArtistName = "Mark Toby"
```

Answers to Projects

A.   *Using Access, create the database shown in Figure 10-3. Create a form for the Artist View shown in Question 10.49. Justify the design of your form using the principles in this chapter. Hint: You can use a wizard to create one of the sub-forms, but you will need to add the second one manually. Also, add the combo boxes manually, after you have created the forms for the subform.*

See the ViewRidge.mdb database located in the subdirectory Chapter 10 of the Instructor Supplements section on www.prenhall.com/kroenke/. Both Access 2000 and Access 2002 versions are available.

B.   *Complete either Project A at the end of Chapters 3 and 4 if you have not already done so.*

1. List and describe the purpose of three views, three forms, and three reports that you think would be necessary for this application.

2. Show the structure of a GUI drop-down menu for this application. Using your model, design one of the forms for entering new housing properties. Explain which type of control (text box, drop-down list) is used for each field. Justify the structure of your form using the concepts presented in this chapter.

Here are three views from the Tabledesigner model MHA.apm located in the Chapter 4 subdirectory of the Instructore Supplements section on www.prenhall.com/kroenke.

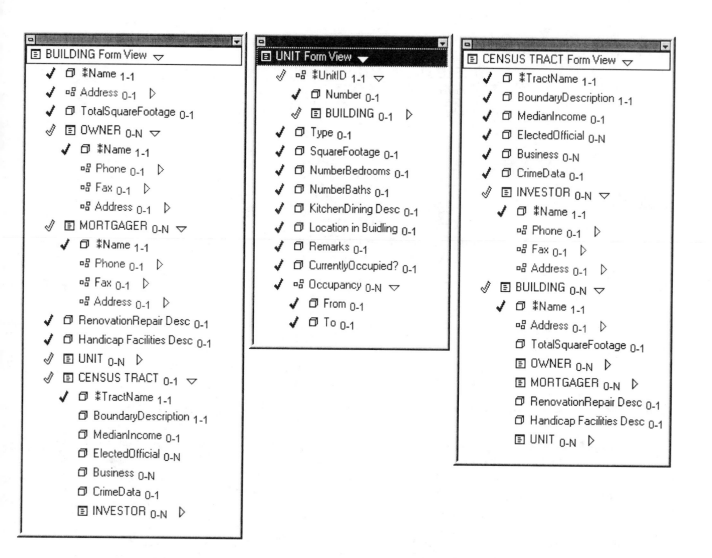

A GUI menu would present the forms and reports of the application. Most likely, the application would be divided into major functions and each of the major functions would have a set of forms and reports. Different users would see different menus. If you're using Tabledesigner, you can use it to generate a possible browser based menu for this application.

With regard to form controls, consider the UNIT view above. Here are the attributes and field types I would use:

Control	Attribute
Textbox	Number Square Footage Kitchen Dining Desc LocationInBuilding Remarks From To

Drop down list	APARTMENT Type NumberBedrooms NumberBaths
Group Box	UnitID Occupancy
Check Box	CurrentlyOccupied?

Answers to FiredUp Project Questions

Read the FiredUp Project at the end of Chapter 9. In answering the following questions, use the four tables described there.

The tables are:

CUSTOMER (<u>CustomerSK</u>, Name, Phone, EmailAddress)

STOVE (<u>SerialNumber</u>, Type, Version, DateOfManufacture)

REGISTRATION (<u>CustomerSK</u>, <u>SerialNumber</u>, <u>Date</u>)

STOVE_REPAIR (<u>RepairInvoiceNumber</u>, SerialNumber, Date, Description, Cost, CustomerSK)

A.   *Construct the following views. Use Figure 10-4 as an example.*

    1.   *Construct a view starting at STOVE and containing all tables and data. Call that view STOVE_VIEW.*

        STOVE_VIEW:

        STOVE.SerialNumber
        STOVE.Type
        STOVE.Version
        STOVE.DateOfManufacture
            REGISTRATION.CustomerSK
            REGISTRATION.SerialNumber
            REGISTRATION.Date . . .
                CUSTOMER.CustomerSK
                CUSTOMER.Name
                CUSTOMER.Phone
                CUSTOMER.EmailAddress
            STOVE_REPAIR.RepairInvoiceNumber
            STOVE_REPAIR.SerialNumber
            STOVE_REPAIR.Date
            STOVE_REPAIR.Description
            STOVE_REPAIR.Cost
            STOVE_REPAIR.CustomerSK . . .

2.   *Construct a view starting at CUSTOMER and containing all tables and data. Call that view CUSTOMER_VIEW.*

CUSTOMER_VIEW:

CUSTOMER.CustomerSK
CUSTOMER.Name
CUSTOMER.Phone
CUSTOMER.EmailAddress
    REGISTRATION.CustomerSK
    REGISTRATION.SerialNumber
    REGISTRATION.Date . . .
        STOVE.SerialNumber
        STOVE.Type
        STOVE.Version
        STOVE.DateOfManufacture
    STOVE_REPAIR.RepairInvoiceNumber
    STOVE_REPAIR.SerialNumber
    STOVE_REPAIR.Date
    STOVE_REPAIR.Description
    STOVE_REPAIR.Cost
    STOVE_REPAIR.CustomerSK . . .

3.   *Construct a view starting at REGISTRATION and containing all tables but STOVE_REPAIR. Call that view REGISTRATION_VIEW.*

REGISTRATION_VIEW:

REGISTRATION.CustomerSK
REGISTRATION.SerialNumber
REGISTRATION.Date
    CUSTOMER.CustomerSK
    CUSTOMER.Name
    CUSTOMER.Phone
    CUSTOMER.EmailAddress
    STOVE.SerialNumber
    STOVE.Type
    STOVE.Version
    STOVE.DateOfManufacture

4.   *Construct a view starting at STOVE_REPAIR and containing all tables and data. Call that view STOVE_REPAIR_VIEW.*

STOVE_REPAIR_VIEW:

STOVE_REPAIR.RepairInvoiceNumber
STOVE_REPAIR.SerialNumber
STOVE_REPAIR.Date
STOVE_REPAIR.Description

```
STOVE_REPAIR.Cost
STOVE_REPAIR.CustomerSK
        CUSTOMER.CustomerSK
        CUSTOMER.Name
        CUSTOMER.Phone
        CUSTOMER.EmailAddress
                REGISTRATION.CustomerSK
                REGISTRATION.SerialNumber
                REGISTRATION.Date . . .
        STOVE.SerialNumber
        STOVE.Type
        STOVE.Version
        STOVE.DateOfManufacture
                REGISTRATION.CustomerSK
                REGISTRATION.SerialNumber
                REGISTRATION.Date . . .
```

B. *Construct SQL statements to process views as follows. Use the SQL starting on page (262) as an example.*

Note to instructor: We assume that some program data structure is available to hold these views. Because we're not specifying a language, however, we don't know what that is. In the following, we just say place the read (or created) values into that structure. You may want to make this more particular for a particular language if all of your students share that language.

1.   *Show SQL statements necessary to read a STOVE_VIEW. Assume you start with a particular SerialNumber.*

There are two multi-valued paths through this view, so two SQL statements will be required. The first will obtain REGISTRATION and CUSTOMER data, the second will obtain STOVE_REPAIR data. Assume the given serial number is available in a variable named valueOfGivenSerialNumber.

```
SELECT      *
FROM        STOVE, REGISTRATION, CUSTOMER
WHERE       STOVE.SerialNumber = valueOfGivenSerialNumber AND
            STOVE.SerialNumber = REGISTRATION.SerialNumber AND
            REGISTRATION.CustomerSK = CUSTOMER.SK
```

Then, for STOVE_REPAIR data

```
SELECT      *
FROM        STOVE_REPAIR
WHERE       STOVE_REPAIR.SerialNumber =
            valueOfGivenSerialNumber
```

The result of these two SQL statements will be two tables of joins from which the data values can be extracted to fill out the STOVE_VIEW structure.

2. *Show SQL statements necessary to construct a new instance of REGISTRATION_VIEW. Assume the necessary stove data is already in the database, but the necessary customer data is not.*

The first task is to store the new CUSTOMER data in the database. Then, we need to read back the value of CustomerSK created by the DBMS. Finally, store a new row in REGISTRATION. It would probably be a good idea to verify that the STOVE data is actually in the database as well.

```
INSERT      INTO CUSTOMER
            (Name, Phone, EmailAddress)
            VALUES (place given values of customer attributes here)
```

Now, read back to get just stored CustomerSK

```
SELECT      CustomerSK
FROM        CUSTOMER
WHERE       CUSTOMER.EmailAddress = givenValueOfEmailAddress
```

Now, check to see if the stove data really is in the database:

```
SELECT      *
FROM        STOVE
WHERE       STOVE.SerialNumber = givenValueOfSerialNumber
```

Assuming it is, now insert registration data:

```
INSERT      INTO  REGISTRATION
            VALUES (CustomerSK, givenValueOfSerialNumber, SystemDate)
```

If a program structure exists to hold the REGISTRATION data, the results of the SQL statements can now be moved into that structure to fill out the REGISTRATION view.

3. *Show SQL statements to construct a new instance of STOVE_REPAIR. Assume the STOVE data is in the database, but the CUSTOMER data is not. Register the STOVE while recording the repair.*

To fill out the STOVE_REPAIR structure, first create the new CUSTOMER row and get the new value of CustomerSK. Save those values in the structure. Then, create the STOVE_REPAIR data and the REGISTRATION data and place them in the structure. Because the CUSTOMER is new, there will be only the new REGISTRATION row for that customer, so there is no need to check for additional REGISTRATION rows for that customer. Next, read the STOVE data and all related REGISTRATION rows for that STOVE.

```
INSERT      INTO CUSTOMER
            (Name, Phone, EmailAddress)
```

VALUES (place given values of customer attributes here)

Now, read back to get just stored CustomerSK

```
SELECT      CustomerSK
FROM        CUSTOMER
WHERE       CUSTOMER.EmailAddress = givenValueOfEmailAddress
```

Now add stove repair data:

```
INSERT      INTO STOVE_REPAIR
            VALUES (place all values, including just-read CustomerSK here)
```

Now obtain STOVE data and its registrations:

```
SELECT      *
FROM        STOVE, REGISTRATION
WHERE       STOVE.SerialNumber = givenValueOfSerialNumber
  AND       STOVE.SerialNumber = REGISTRATION.SerialNumber
```

Now all of the values are available and can be placed into a program structure for the STOVE_REPAIR view.

4. *Show SQL statements to remove all records concerning a particular stove. Use the STOVE view.*

As the text indicates, the first task is to determine how much to delete. Certainly the STOVE data and REGISTRATION data for that stove should be removed. It would be unreasonable to suppose that the customer data in one of those REGISTRATIONs should be removed, however. The situation is less obvious for STOVE_REPAIR, however. If we delete the STOVE, then to prevent orphans, we need to either a) set the SerialNumber of STOVE_REPAIR to null, or b) delete related STOVE_REPAIR rows. The advantage of the former is that it preserves records of repairs – dates, amounts, customers, even though it removes the related stove data. This might be useful for analysis of repair operations at some later date.

The choice among these alternatives depends on the business requirements. Absent an opinion from them, the most responsible thing to do is to remove any related STOVE_REPAIR data. If there are referential integrity constraints being enforced by the DBMS, we'll need to start from the bottom.

```
So,
DELETE      FROM STOVE_REPAIR
WHERE       SerialNumber = givenValueOfSerialNumber

DELETE      FROM REGISTRATION
WHERE       SerialNumber = givenValueOfSerialNumber

DELETE      FROM STOVE
WHERE       SerialNumber = givenValueOfSerialNumber
```

Chapter 11

Managing Multi-User Databases

Objectives

- Understand the purpose and importance of database administration
- Understand the need for concurrency control and learn the basic techniques used
- Learn the meaning of ACID transactions and the standard types of consistency and isolation
- Understand differences in cursor types
- Learn techniques for database security
- Understand the fundamental concepts of database backup and recovery

Teaching Suggestions

1. This chapter introduces the topic of database administration and lays out the fundamental concepts, technology, and terminology for multi-user database management. The structure of this chapter is used for the following chapters on Oracle and SQL Server.

2. In this text we distinguish between database administration and data administration. The latter is an organizational activity that typically sits high in the enterprise organization chart and may be concerned with much larger issues than the maintenance of a particular database. We address that function in Chapter 14. This chapter is concerned with database administration, a more pedestrian function that occurs at a much lower level in the organization. Every multi-user database needs a database administrator. The administrator may only have a few tasks to perform and may work on them only a few hours a week, but someone needs to be given the responsibility for ensuring that the database administration tasks are accomplished on a timely basis. This is especially true for Internet technology databases where the users may be far away or even anonymous, and where the consequences of failures and mistakes will be difficult to correct.

3. Concurrency control is important and sometimes seems obscure. The caution at the end of the concurrency control section is important: "If you do not specify the isolation level of a transaction or do not specify the type of cursors you open, the DBMS will use a default level and types. These defaults may be perfect for your application, but they also may be terrible. Thus, even though these issues can be ignored, the consequences of them cannot be avoided. Learn the capabilities of your DBMS products and use them wisely!" Specific techniques for Oracle and SQL Server are discussed in the next two chapters.

4.   Backup and recovery is an important topic and only the high-level essentials are considered in this chapter. We will follow this up with more specific discussions for Oracle and SQL Server in the next two chapters.

Answers to Group I Questions

11.1   *Briefly describe five difficult problems for organizations that create and use multi-user databases.*

Complicated to design and develop; requirements change over time; processing rights and responsibilities need to be defined; need for backup and recovery planning; manage DBMS installation. See page 295 for further discussion of these.

11.2   *Explain the difference between a database administrator and a data administrator.*

The difference is in scope; as defined in this text, a DBA has responsibility of a database and its applications. The data administrator is responsible for data organization-wide.

By the way, as distributed databases become real, this definition will need to be changed.

11.3   *List seven important tasks for a DBA.*

> Managing database structure
> Controlling concurrent processing
> Managing processing rights and responsibilities
> Developing database security
> Providing for database recovery
> Managing the DBMS
> Maintaining the data repository

11.4   *Summarize the DBA's responsibilities for managing database structure.*

See Figure 11-2.

11.5   *What is configuration control? Why is it necessary?*

Configuration control is a process by which changes to the structure of the database are coordinated and controlled. A database can be shared. Developers cannot make changes to DB for one user that may create problems for other users. Must take a community-wide view. Let need for changes be known, let people discuss impact of changes on them, etc.

11.6   *Explain the meaning of the word inappropriately in the phrase "one user's work does not inappropriately influence another user's work."*

It means that any overlap of work results is anticipated and is in accordance with the requirements. In some applications, the work of two users is supposed to be completely isolated from each other, say patient records processing for two different patients in a hospital. In other applications, two users work need not be so isolated — someone who wants the latest stock price won't mind if the price is updated as the list is being produced — as long as they know that it may happen.

11.7   *Explain the trade-off that exists in concurrency control.*

High level of control granularity means easy administration for the DBMS but poor throughput. Low level of control granularity means difficult administration for the DBMS, but better throughput.

11.8   *Define an atomic transaction and explain why atomicity is important.*

An atomic transaction is one in which either all of the database actions are committed to the database or none of them are. Without it, there is a danger that partially processed transactions will be committed to the database.

11.9   *Explain the difference between concurrent transactions and simultaneous transactions. How many CPUs are required for simultaneous transactions?*

With concurrent transactions, two or more users access the database using a single CPU on the database server. The CPU executes some instructions from one, then executes some from the other, switching back and forth between them. The actions may appear simultaneous to the two users. For transactions to be processed simultaneously, two or more CPUs are required. With modern server computers, such processing is possible.

11.10   *Give an example, other than the one in this text, of the lost update problem.*

The lost update problem occurs when two transactions attempt to update the same data resource simultaneously. Because each transaction copies the record into its work area, each can effect different changes, then rewrite the record. The problem is that all updates except the last one to be rewritten are lost. Example: at Treble Clef (from Chapter 1) two salespeople rent the same B-flat clarinet.

11.11   *Explain the difference between an explicit and an implicit lock.*

Explicit locks are set by the application program; implicit locks are set by the DBMS on behalf of the application or users.

11.12   *What is lock granularity?*

The size of the resource that is locked. Large grained locks are easy for the DBMS to administer but result in frequent conflicts; small grained locks are more difficult and expensive to administer but result in fewer conflicts.

11.13 *Explain the difference between an exclusive lock and a shared lock.*

Exclusive lock allows no other access; shared lock allows other transactions to read but not update the data.

11.14 *Explain two-phased locking.*

The two-phase locking strategy is to obtain a number of locks until the lock is released; after that, no more locks can be obtained until all are released. Thus, the transaction has a lock growing phase and then a lock shrinking phase. Most DBMS products implement a special case of this in which all locks are released when a transaction commits.

11.15 *How does releasing all locks at the end of the transaction relate to two-phase locking?*

It is a special case of two-phase locking — during the life of the transaction, locks are only acquired (the growing phase). When the transaction is committed, all locks are released. The shrinking phase occurs at one point.

11.16 *In general, how should the boundaries of a transaction be defined?*

The boundaries should be defined by the contents of a database view.

11.17 *What is deadlock? How can it be avoided? How can it be resolved once it occurs?*

Deadlock occurs when each of two transactions is waiting for a resource the other has locked. Both transactions are placed in the wait state, but neither one can get out of it. A DBMS can either prevent the deadly embrace from occurring (via control over locking) or it can allow it and then detect and break it (by aborting one of the transactions, thus releasing its locks and enabling the other transaction to continue).

11.18 *Explain the difference between optimistic and pessimistic locking.*

The assumption with optimistic locking is that conflict will not occur. No locks are placed until the transaction is completed. At that point, locks are obtained and records are updated only if they have not been changed since last read. With pessimistic locking, the assumption is made that conflict will occur. Records are locked before they're read. When the transaction is complete, all locks are released.

11.19 *Explain the benefits of marking transaction boundaries, declaring lock characteristics, and letting the DBMS place locks.*

It's more flexible and puts less demand on the application programmer. The programmer defines the boundaries of the transaction and then defines the locking behavior that is wanted. The DBMS figures out where to set locks. If the locking behavior declaration is subsequently changed, the DBMS will then place locks in accordance with the new behavior. Reduces the likelihood of programmer errors as well.

11.20 *Explain the use of BEGIN, COMMIT, and ROLLBACK TRANSACTION statements.*

Used to mark transaction boundaries. The application programmer must set these boundaries because the DBMS cannot automatically determine what DBMS operations are to be atomic.

11.21 *Explain the meaning of the expression ACID transaction.*

An ACID transaction is atomic, consistent, insolated, and durable.

11.22 *Describe statement level consistency.*

An update will apply to a set of rows as they existed at the time the statement was first executed.

11.23 *Describe transaction level consistency. What disadvantage can exist with it?*

All updates in a transaction will recreate rows as they existed at the time the transaction was begun. Depending on how this is implemented, this can mean that a transaction cannot view its own changes.

11.24 *What is the purpose of transaction isolation levels?*

They exist to provide flexibility in the degree of isolation between the work of different transactions.

11.25 *Explain read uncommitted isolation level. Give an example of its use.*

Allows dirty reads, nonrepeatable reads, and phantom reads. Making a list of web sites in response to a search for articles on a movie.

11.26 *Explain read committed isolation level. Give an example of its use.*

Disallows dirty reads. Allows nonrepeatable reads and phantom reads. Making a list of stock prices that are expected to be current only as of the time the stock price was read.

11.27 *Explain repeatable read isolation level. Give an example of its use.*

Disallows dirty reads and nonrepeatable reads. Allows phantom reads. Making a list of inventory quantities on a list of inventory items that were known to be in the database when the read began.

11.28 *Explain serializable isolation level. Give an example of its use.*

Disallows dirty reads, nonrepeatable reads, and phantom reads.   Rank ordering a list of commodities, where the ranking process requires several passes through the table.

11.29 *Explain the term **cursor**.*

A cursor is a pointer into a set of rows.

11.30 *Explain why a transaction may have many cursors. Also, how is it possible that a transaction may have more than one cursor on a given table?*

The transaction may need to process several tables at one time. A cursor can be opened on two different views of a table (these are SQL views, not application views), in which case there will be two cursors open on the same table for that transaction. Furthermore, there are some transactions in which the logic requires that two cursors process the same table – in the FiredUp example, if transaction logic requires that STOVE_REPAIR data be processed from the perspective of a STOVE and also that STOVE_REAIR data also be processed from the perspective of a CUSTOMER.

11.31 *What is the advantage of using different types of cursors?*

Conserve memory and CPU resources.

11.32 *Explain forward only cursors. Give an example of their use.*

The cursor can only move forward through the data. A single-pass report writer.

11.33 *Explain static cursors. Give an example of their use.*

A snapshot is taken of the table or query at the time it was opened. No changes appear during the processing of the cursor.   Report writing that only requires that the data be correct as of the time it was written.

11.34 *Explain keyset cursors. Give an example of their use.*

When the cursor is opened, the keys of all rows in the table or query are saved. The transaction can process those rows; if it updates a row that has been deleted by another transaction, the DBMS will create a replacement and fill that replacement with the updated data. Additions by other users will not be visible. Unless the isolation level is dirty read, changes by other users are visible only when committed to the database.

Example: Produce inventory where an item's row is deleted if the quantity on hand becomes zero. When the market runs out of lettuce, for example, the lettuce row is deleted. While this is occurring, however, another transaction could be adding lettuce. Even if the lettuce row was deleted, the second transaction will re-create it.

11.35 *Explain dynamic cursors. Give an example of their use.*

All updates, insertions, and deletions by other users are visible. Only committed changes are visible unless the isolation level is dirty read.

11.36 *What happens if you do not declare transaction isolation level and cursor type to the DBMS? Is this good or bad?*

The DBMS will pick one for you. Probably bad, unless the DBMS happens to pick choices that work well for your application.

11.37 *Explain the necessity of defining processing rights and responsibilities. How are such responsibilities enforced?*

To bring order to the processing of the database, which is a shared resource. While rights can be enforced by the DBMS and application programs, responsibilities must be documented and understood by users. The upholding of responsibilities cannot be automated. It's a matter of user training and behavior.

11.38 *Explain the relationships of USERS, GROUPS, PERMISSION, and OBJECTS for a generic database security system.*

See Figure 11-13.

11.39 *Describe the advantages and disadvantages of DBMS-provided security.*

Advantages: Easier to implement, it will be done regardless of the source of data changes and activities, probably more consistent. Disadvantages: May not suffice for particular needs. Works best for vertical security.

11.40 *Describe the advantages and disadvantages of application-provided security.*

Advantages: Can be tailored to unique requirements. Can provide horizontal security. Disadvantages: May be done poorly or inconsistently, must be programmed and maintained, may not be as robust.

11.41 *Explain how a database could be recovered via reprocessing. Why is this generally not feasible?*

Reprocessing means reapplying all transactions since the latest database save to that saved copy of the database. Because reprocessing takes as much time as original processing, reprocessing is usually infeasible. Also, asynchronous events may occur in a different order.

11.42 *Define **rollback** and **rollforward**.*

Rollback means applying before images (before changes were made) to the current database. This takes the database backwards in time. Rollforward means loading the latest database backup then applying all after images (after changes were made) to it. This brings the database forward in time.

11.43 *Why is it important to write to the log before changing the database values?*

In the event of failure, the log record is correct — otherwise the database could be behind the log and changes that were committed might not be recovered.

11.44 *Describe the rollback process. Under what conditions should it be used?*

Take current copy of DB, back out changes. Use when DB has not been lost — just some update activity needs to be removed.

11.45 *Describe the rollforward process. Under what conditions should it be used?*

Restore DB from prior save. Apply after images. Use when database has been lost.

11.46 *What is the advantage of taking frequent checkpoints of a database?*

Checkpoints are snapshots of updated parts of a database. They can be taken automatically by the DBMS. In the event of recovery, checkpoints provide a point of synchronization between the log and the database, so they can be used to perform recovery. This is faster than recovering the entire database from a backup and then applying all after images since the backup was taken.

11.47 *Summarize the DBA's responsibilities for managing the DBMS.*

See Figure 11-19 and related discussion.

11.48 *What is a data repository? A passive data repository? An active data repository?*

A collection of metadata about databases, database applications, Web pages, users, and other application components. A passive repository has to be maintained manually; an active repository is automatically updated as database or application elements are changed.

11.49 *Explain why a data repository is important. What is likely to happen if one is not available?*

A data repository is a key resource for maintaining the database and its applications and for planning changes and extensions to them. Without one, maintenance is likely to be costly, slow, and very risky.

Answers to Group II Questions

11.50 *Visit www.microsoft.com and search for information about transaction isolation levels and cursor types. For now, ignore information about RDS, ADO, ODBC, and OLE/DB and focus instead on the features and functions of SQL Server. Compare and contrast its capabilities with those described in this text.*

This question will be answered in Chapter 13.

11.51 *Visit www.oracle.com and search for information about transactions isolation levels and cursor types. Ignore information about ODBC, and focus instead on the features and functions of Oracle. Compare and contrast its capabilities with those described in this text.*

This question will be answered in Chapter 12.

11.52 *Describe the advantages and disadvantages of user name and password security. In what ways might users be careless with their identities? How can such carelessness compromise the security of the database? What steps could be taken to reduce the risk of such problems?*

It's relatively simple and straightforward to set up and for the DBMS to enforce. It provides good vertical security, but poor horizontal security. Users might give one another their passwords or otherwise make their passwords public. The chief protection is education of the users and programs that ensure users change their passwords on a regular basis.

11.53 *Search the Web for CASE tools that provide repositories and for repository products. Find what you think is the best one and list its major functions and features. Explain how those functions and features could be used to help the DBA of an e-commerce company that is adding new product lines to its business.*

Answer depends on what students find.

Answers to Project

A. Consider the Customer view in Figure 10-4.

1.   *Suppose that you are developing an application to create new instances of this view. What transaction isolation level would you use? Name the cursors involved and recommend a cursor type for each.*

Creating new instances of the Customer View necessitates creating new rows in Customer and possibly Transaction, and adding new rows to the intersection table. No data will need to be modified or deleted. Because ARTIST appears twice in the view, I would choose repeatable read to ensure that an ARTIST row does not disappear in the middle of the transaction.

Cursor	Recommended Cursor Type
CUSTOMER	KeySet
TRANSACTION	Forward Only
WORK	Forward Only
CUSTOMER_ARTIST_INT	Forward Only

2   *Suppose that you are developing an application to modify the values (only values, not relationships) in this view. What transaction isolation level would you use? Name the cursors involved and recommend a cursor type for each.*

If only modifying data values, I would choose cursor stability isolation level. I just need to know that the row I'm on won't disappear underneath me.

Cursor	Recommended Cursor Type
CUSTOMER	KeySet
TRANSACTION	Forward Only

WORK	Forward Only
CUSTOMER_ARTIST_INT	Forward Only

3. *Suppose that you are developing an application to modify both data values and relationships in this view. How does your answer to Question A.2 change?*

Answer is the same as number 1 above, for the same reasons.

4. *Suppose that you are developing an application to delete instances of inactive customers (defined as customers who have never purchased art). What transaction isolation level would you use? Name the cursors involved and recommend a cursor type for each.*

To ensure that the application doesn't delete a customer just as he or she is buying art, I would choose repeatable read. Note in the following that we need access to TRANSACTION to find out if a CUSTOMER has purchased art in the past.

Cursor	Recommended Cursor Type
CUSTOMER	Forward Only
TRANSACTION	Keyset
CUSTOMER_ARTIST_INT	Keyset

Answers to FiredUp Project Questions

A. *Assume that FiredUp, Inc., has hired you as a database consultant to develop their operational database having the four tables described at the end of Chapter 9. Assume that FiredUp personnel are the two owners, an office administrator, a repair technician, and two employees in production. The office administrator processes all registration forms. The repair technician inputs repair data, and the production employees enter stove data on stoves they have produced. Prepare a 3 to 5 page memo to FiredUp management that addresses the following issues:*

1. The need for database administration at FiredUp.

This part of the memo should summarize the issues discussed on page 294 and briefly discuss the tasks in Figure 11-1.

2. *Your recommendation for who should serve as database administrator. Assume FiredUp is not sufficiently large to need or afford a full-time database administrator.*

The database administrations tasks should probably be shared among the owners, the office administrator, and you, the consultant. The owners need to understand the importance and their vulnerability, the office admin needs to know what documentation and procedures exist and to help ensure compliance. The consultant needs to perform technical tasks.

3.   *Using Figure 11-1 as a guide, describe the nature of database administration activities at FiredUp. As an aggressive consultant, keep in mind that you can recommend yourself for performing some of the DBA functions.*

Task	Owners	Office Admin	Consultant
Managing database structure	Ensure doc exists		Design, implement, and document database structure
Controlling concurrent processing	Establish policies		Define transactions and set up DBMS concurrency
Managing processing rights and responsibilities	Set requirements Enforce responsibilities	Document rights and responsibilities	Set up security system for rights
Developing database security	Understand vulnerability	Ensure procedures are followed	Set up DBMS and application security
Providing for database recovery	Understand vulnerability	Ensure procedures are followed	Set up system and procedures, document procedures and train users
Managing the DBMS	Understand the nature of this activity		Respond to performance problems, watch for new versions of potential use to Fired Up
Maintaining the data repository	Understand the importance	Ensure documentation is kept up to date	Produce repository and other documentation

B.   *For the employees described in Question A, define users, groups, and permissions on data in the four tables described at the end of Chapter 9. Use the security scheme shown in Figure 11-13 as an example. Again, don't forget to include yourself.*

The following table identifies five groups (with the obvious personnel assigned to them) and processing rights over the four tables. This is a restrictive set of permissions and the employees may rail at it. As small as FiredUp is, there may be a need to broaden these rights. One course of action is to start restrictive and broaden from there. It's easier to give new permissions than to take existing ones away!

	STOVE	CUSTOMER	REGISTRATION	STOVE_REPAIR
Owners	Insert Change Query	Insert Change Query	Insert Change Query	Insert Change Query
Office Admin	Query	Insert Change Query	Insert Change Query	Insert Change Query
Repair Tech	Query	Query	Query	Insert Change Query
Production	Insert Change Query			
Consultant	All	All	All	All

C. Consider the REGISTRATION_VIEW and STOVE_REPAIR_VIEW defined at the end of Chapter 10.

Note: As stated in the text, the higher the level of concurrency control, the more work for the DBMS and the slower the throughput. Thus, in answering these questions, we want to declare the minimum level of concurrency control that will meet the requirements and no more.

Also note that no address data is included in the CUSTOMER table in these examples. For the real company, address data would certainly be present. We just don't need to deal with it to make the necessary points regarding concurrency control.

1. Give an example of a dirty read, a non-repeatable read, and a phantom read when processing the REGISTRATION_VIEW.

Dirty read: Suppose the office admin ran a procedure that started a transaction, created a new CUSTOMER row, started to create a new REGISTRATION row, and then rolled back. If after the insert on CUSTOMER but before the roll back, one of the owners counted the number of CUSTOMERs, a dirty read would have occurred.

Phantom read: Assume that only statement level isolation is in force. Suppose the owners were to run a stored procedure that executed the following two SQL statements:

```
UPDATE      STOVE
SET         VERSION = 'FiredNow Basic'
WHERE       VERSION = 'FiredNow'
```

And then

```
SELECT      *
FROM        STOVE
WHERE       VERSION LIKE 'FiredNow%'
```

Now suppose that after the update command executed, another transaction inserts a new STOVE row with a version = 'FiredNow' and commits that insertion to the database. The subsequent SELECT will reveal one row with the old value of 'FiredNow' even though the UPDATE ran correctly (it will also show one more row in the STOVE table than was shown when the UPDATE ran).

2.   *What concurrency control measures do you think would be appropriate for a transaction that updates the REGISTRATION_VIEW? What concurrency control measures do you think would be appropriate for a transaction that deletes REGISTRATION_VIEW data? State your assumptions.*

Update to REGISTRATION_VIEW: The answer to this question depends on how much is going to be updated. If only a single row of REGISTRATION will be updated, then a simple update statement will suffice. There is no need to worry about atomicity because there is only one SQL statement operating on a single row. No transaction will need to be declared because there is only one SQL statement and because only one row is involved. We do not want to read dirty data, but nonrepeatable reads and phantom reads will not be a problem. Read Committed isolation will thus be fine.

If more than one table is going to be updated, then for atomic behavior, all updates will need to occur within a transaction. Because only one row of CUSTOMER is connected to REGISTRATION and only one row of STOVE is connected to REGISTRATION, no more than one row of each of these tables will be updated. Hence, there is no need for cursors. Further, there is no need for more than Read Committed isolation.

Delete of REGISTRATION_VIEW data: First, as with all deletions in a view, how much is going to be deleted? Most likely, as a small retailer, FiredUp wants to keep as much customer data as it can; it's also unlikely that it will destroy the record of a stove just because someone de-registers it. Given these assumptions, then only the REGISTRATION data will be deleted in a statement like the following:

```
DELETE      REGISTRATION
WHERE       CustomerSK = 1000
    AND     SerialNumber = 20000
    AND     Date = '15/11/2001'
```

This will delete only one row (all attributes of the key are in the WHERE clause), if this is the only action, then it need not even be wrapped in a transaction for atomicity. Again, we need to prevent dirty reads, but nonrepeatable reads and phantom reads are not a problem. Set Read Committed isolation.

3.   *Answer 2 for the STOVE_REPAIR_VIEW. Justify any differences from your answer to question 2.*

Update of CUSTOMER_VIEW: As indicated in the text, the answer depends on what type of modification is involved. If only a change to the CUSTOMER table, then the answer to this portion of this question is the same as question 2. The update statement need not be in a transaction and Read Committed isolation is fine.

If changes are made to the REGISTRATION or STOVE_REPAIR tables as well (either by changing foreign keys or by adding new rows, or by deleting related rows) then a transaction will be needed. Read Committed isolation is fine. No cursors will be needed.

Delete of CUSTOMER_VIEW data: The important question is, how much is being deleted? Because both REGISTRATION and STOVE_REPAIR tables have CustomerSK as foreign keys, we cannot just delete the CUSTOMER row. We either need to delete the CUSTOMER row with all related REGISTRATION and STOVE_REPAIR rows or we need to disallow the deletion if there are related REGISTRATION and STOVE_REPAIR rows.

It might be that FiredUp has a business rule like, "Delete the CUSTOMER only if he or she has at most one REGISTRATION and no STOVE_REPAIR data." In that case, put all SQL statements inside a transaction, check to determine if there is more than one REGISTRATION and no STOVE_REPAIR, and if not, then delete the CUSTOMER and REGISTRATION row. This logic will require serializable isolation (because we read REGISTRATION once to find out how many are there and again to delete the one that is there). That's expensive. A better strategy might be to start the transaction, delete the CUSTOMER data, read related STOVE_REPAIR, if find any, roll back the transaction, delete the related REGISTRATION rows and if more than one is deleted, roll back the transaction. Otherwise commit the transaction. Which is the better strategy probably depends on the DBMS used and the workload. This a case where the developers might try both and see which is better. (In truth, for FiredUp's workload, this issue will likely never arise, but it could for a larger firm.)

On the other hand, this delete might be for the purpose of removing obsolete data from the database. If so, a transaction needs to be written to remove the CUSTOMER row and all related REGISTRATION and STOVE_REPAIR data. Because none of the attributes of REGISTRATION or STOVE_REPAIR are carried as foreign keys in other tables, there are no other relationship dependencies to worry about. So, all SQL statements need to be wrapped in a transaction for atomicity, and then three deletions coded: one for CUSTOMER, one for all REGISTRATIONs for that customer, and one for all STOVE_REPAIRs for that customer. The deletions on REGISTRATION and STOVE_REPAIR do not require cursors because they can be accomplished in a single SQL statement (the DBMS, under the covers, will, of course be running some type of cursor). If the logic regarding a deletion were required examination of the row's contents, then a cursor would be required. Given these assumptions, Read Committed isolation will be fine.

4. *What isolation level would you use for a transaction that prints a report listing all stove repairs in a given period. What cursor type would you use?*

    I would use Read Committed isolation (might even get by with Read Uncommitted if you knew that no changes could be occurring to STOVE_REPAIR for the given period). A forward only cursor should suffice.

Chapter 12

Managing Databases with Oracle

Objectives

- Learn how to install Oracle and create a database
- Learn how to use Oracle's SQL Plus text utility
- Learn SQL DDL and how to use it to create database structures with Oracle
- Understand the purpose and role of stored procedures and learn how to create simple stored procedures
- Understand the purpose and role of triggers and learn how to create simple stored procedures
- Understand how Oracle implements concurrency control
- Learn the fundamental features of Oracle backup and recovery facilities

Teaching Suggestions

1. You can spend anywhere from one to five or six class periods on this chapter. So, you need to think first about how much time you can devote to it and shape your plans accordingly.

2. For an hour's presentation, I think you can demonstrate SQL Plus, some SQL DDL, the source code of stored procedures and triggers, and the invocation of stored procedures. You might also have time to discuss briefly Oracle concurrency control.

3. Students will get much more out of this material if they install Oracle. If they do not have the version of the text that has Oracle, they can download it from the Oracle Web site. But see next item.

4. As stated in the Preface of this manual, if you haven't worked with Oracle before, plan extra time to install it. You may need outside expertise as well. Once you get it up and running, SQL Plus is easy to use and dependable.

5. All of the stored procedures, triggers, etc., are located on our Web site in the Chapter 12 subdirectory of the Instructor Supplements section on www.prenhall.com/kroenke. You can download the stored procedures and modify them for exercises.

6. The Project and the FiredUp exercises for Oracle in this chapter and those for SQL Server in the next chapter are the same. You can demonstrate how the languages of these two products are essentially the same by showing the solution to the same questions (all are shown below) for each product.

7. Another idea, if your students have access to both Oracle and SQL Server, assign some students to one product and other students to the other, and have a contest to see who can solve either the Project or the FiredUp exercises first.

Answers to Group I Questions:

12.1   *Describe the general characteristics of Oracle and the Oracle suite of products.   Explain why these characteristics mean there is considerable complexity to master.*

Oracle has many different product components that run on many different operating systems and communications protocols. It also exposes a lot of its technology to the developer – giving more control at the cost of greater complexity.

12.2   *What is SQL Plus and what is its purpose?*

SQL Plus is a text-oriented utility that works with all versions of Oracle. Used for inputting SQL and creating stored procedures and triggers.

12.3   *Name three ways of creating an Oracle database. Which is the easiest?*

Via the Configuration Assistant, via Oracle-supplied database creation procedures or via the SQL CREATE DATABASE command. Configuration Assistant is easiet.

12.4   *Explain how to change a row in the SQL Plus buffer. Assume there are three statements in the buffer, the focus is on statement 3, and you want to change the second statement from CustID 1000 to CustomerID 1000.*

List 2
Change /CustID 1000/CustomerID 1000/

12.5   *How do you set the default directory for SQL Plus to use?*

Set the Start In property of the SQL Plus icon on your desktop.

12.6   *Show the SQL statement necessary to create a table named T1 with columns C1, C2, and C3. Assume C1 is a surrogate key. Assume C2 has character data of maximum length 50 and C3 contains a date.*

```
CREATE TABLE T1 (
     C1     int     PRIMARY KEY,
     C2     varchar (50),
     C3     DATE);
```

12.7   *Show the statement necessary to create a sequence starting at 50 and incremented by 2. Name your sequence T1Seq.*

Create Sequence T1Seq Increment by 2 start with 50;

12.8   *Show how to insert a row into table T1 (Question 12.6) using the sequence created in Question 12.7.*

INSERT INTO T1 (C1, C2, C3) VALUES (T1Seq.NextVal, 'abc', '12/01/2001')

12.9   *Show an SQL statement for querying the row created in Question 12.8.*

```
SELECT *
FROM       T1
WHERE      C1 = T1Seq.CurrVal
```

12.10   *Explain the problems inherent in using sequences for surrogate key columns.*

Sequences can be used for reasons other than surrogate keys, sequences do not have to be used, developer could accidentally use the wrong sequence.

12.11   *Show SQL statements for dropping table T1 and for dropping SeqT1.*

```
DROP TABLE T1;
DROP SEQUENCE SeqT1;
```

12.12   *Show SQL statements for dropping column C3 of table T1.*

```
ALTER TABLE T1 DROP COLUMN C3;
```

12.13   *Show SQL statements for creating a relationship between table T2 and table T3. Assume that T3 has a foreign key column named FK1 that relates to T2 and that deletions in T2 should force deletions in T3.*

```
ALTER TABLE T3 ADD CONSTRAINT T3Rel
FOREIGN KEY(FK1) REFERENCES T2 ON DELETE CASCADE;
```

12.14   *Answer Question 12.13 but do not force deletions.*

```
ALTER TABLE T3 ADD CONSTRAINT T3Rel
FOREIGN KEY(FK1) REFERENCES T2;
```

12.15   *Show how to eliminate a relationship with SQL.*

```
ALTER TABLE T3 DROP CONSTRAINT T3Rel;
```

12.16   *Show SQL statements to create a unique index on columns C2 and C3 of table T1.*

```
ALTER TABLE T1 ADD CONSTRAINT T1Key PRIMARY KEY (C2, C3);
```

12.17   *Under what circumstances should indexes be used?*

When columns are to be unique, when indexes are needed for frequent sorting, or when direct access is required by selection or join.

12.18   *Show SQL statements to add a new column C4 to table T1. Assume T1 will have currency values up to $1 million.*

```
ALTER TABLE T1 ADD COLUMN C4 Numeric (9,2);
```

12.19 *Under what conditions can you drop a column in an existing table?*

Any conditions, but you will lose your data.

12.20 *Under what conditions can you add a column to an existing table?*

Only if the new column is null.

12.21 *Explain how to add a NOT NULL column to an existing table.*

Add it as null, fill the column with data, and change it to NOT NULL with an alter statement.

12.22 *Under what conditions can you change the width of a character or numeric column?*

If the column has data, then you can increase its width or increase the number of numeric characters. You can change the number of decimal places at any time. If the column has no data, you can change its width up or down and even change its data type.

12.23 *Under what conditions can you change a column's data type?*

If it has no data.

12.24 *Show how to add a constraint to specify that column C4 of table T1 cannot be less than 1,000.*

ALTER TABLE T1 ADD CONSTRAINT LCheck CHECK (C4 > 1000);

12.25 *Show how to add a constraint to specify that column C4 of table T1 cannot be less than column C5 of table T1.*

This cannot be done with a check constraint. Write a before trigger instead.

12.26 *For the View Ridge database discussed in this chapter, construct a view that contains Name, City, and State of a customer. Name your view CustView.*

CREATE VIEW CustView as
SELECT Name, City, State
FROM CUSTOMER;

12.27 *For the View Ridge database, construct a view that has customer name and artist name for all art that the customer has purchased.*

```
CREATE      VIEW CustArtistView AS
SELECT      CUSTOMER.Name CustomerName, ARTIST.NameArtistName
FROM        CUSTOMER, TRANSACTION, WORK, ARTIST
WHERE       CUSTOMER.CustomerID = TRANSACTON.CustomerID AND
            TRANSACTION.WorkID = WORK.WorkID AND
            WORK.ArtistID = ARTIST.ArtistID;
```

12.28 *For the View Ridge database, construct a view that has customer name and artist name for all artists in which the customer is interested. Explain the difference between this view and the view in Question 12.27.*

```
CREATE        VIEW CustArtistView AS
SELECT        CUSTOMER.Name CustomerName, ARTIST.Name ArtistName
FROM          CUSTOMER, CUSTOMER_ARTIST_INT
WHERE         CUSTOMER.CustomerID = CUSTOMER_ARTIST_INT.CustomerID AND
              ARTIST.ArtistID = CUSTOMER_ARTIST_INT.ArtistID;
```

12.29 *Can you combine the views in Questions 12.27 and 12.28 into one view? Why or why not?*

No, this cannot be done because these are two different multi-valued paths.

12.30 *How can you update a join view using Oracle?*

By using an instead of trigger.

12.31 *Write a PL/SQL procedure that describes the structure of the CUSTOMER, ARTIST, WORK, TRANSACTION, and CUSTOMER_ARTIST_INT tables. Store the procedure with the name VRTabs.sql and show how to invoke the PL/SQL procedure using SQL Plus.*

Create a file with the following statements and save it under the name VRTabs.sql.

```
DESCRIBE CUSTOMER;
DESCRIBE ARTIST;
DESCRIBE WORK;
DESCRIBE TRANSACTION;
DESCRIBE CUSTOMER_ARTIST_INT;
```

To invoke this file, use

Start VRTabs;

12.32 *In a PL/SQL procedure, what do the keywords IN, OUT, and IN OUT signify?*

Whether the parameters are used for input to, output from, or both.

12.33 *What must be done to be able to see output generated by the Oracle DBMS_OUTPUT package? What limits exist on such output?*

Run the command:

Set serveroutput on;

12.34 *Explain how the PL/SQL statement FOR variable IN cursorname works.*

It opens the cursor and moves the cursor down one row each time the for loop executes. Control is transferred to the statement after the loop when all rows have been processed. Note references to columns in the cursor must use the cursorname in the FOR statement and not the cursor name used when the cursor is defined.

12.35 *What statement is used to obtain errors when compiling stored procedures and triggers?*

Show errors;

12.36 *What is the syntax of the BEGIN TRANSACTION statement in PL/SQL? How is a transaction started?*

There is no such statement. Instead, a transaction is begun when the first database action occurs.

12.37 *In the stored procedure in Figure 12-16, how are the values of the variables tid and aid used if there are no suitable TRANSACTION rows in the database? How are they used if there is just one suitable TRANSACTION row in the database?*

They aren't used if there there are no suitable rows. If there is a suitable row, they are used in for the values of artist ID and transaction ID in the rest of the procedure.

12.38 *Explain the purpose of BEFORE, AFTER, and INSTEAD OF.*

Before triggers are fired before database actions occur, after triggers fire after database actions, and instead of triggers are used to update join views.

12.39 *When an update is in progress, how can the trigger code obtain the value of a column, say, C1, before the update began? How can the trigger code obtain the value that the column is being set to?*

Using the :old prefix; using the :new prefix.

12.40 *Explain why INSTEAD OF TRIGGERS are needed for join views.*

Because it is impossible to write general-purpose code for updating views. The actions to be taken depend too much on the application requirements. There's too much ambiguity as explained in the text.

12.41 *Explain what would happen if the IF statement in the trigger in Figure 12-21 was removed.*

The trigger would perform a do-nothing update.

12.42 *Show an SQL statement to obtain the tables the data dictionary contains about triggers.*

```
SELECT      Table_Name, Comments
FROM        DICT
WHERE       Table_Name LIKE ('%TRIGGERS%');
```

12.43 *What three levels of transaction isolation are supported by Oracle?*

Read committed, serializable, and read only.

12.44 *Explain how Oracle uses the system change number to read data that are current at a particular point in time.*

Oracle stores the SCN with every data change. To find data that were current at a point in time, look for all data values having an SCN less than or equal to that point in time.

12.45 *Under what circumstances will Oracle read dirty data?*

Never.

12.46 *Explain how conflicting locks are handled by Oracle when a transaction is operating in READ COMMITTED isolation mode.*

See the discussion at the top of page 355.

12.47 *Show the SQL statement necessary to set the transaction isolation level to SERIALIZABLE for an entire session.*

SET TRANSACTION ISOLATION LEVEL SERIALIZABLE;

12.48 *What happens when a transaction in serializable mode tries to update data that have been updated by a different transaction? Assume the SCN is less than the transaction's SCN. Assume the SCN is greater than the transaction's SCN.*

If the SCN is less than the transaction's SCN, the update proceeds normally. If the SCN is greater, then Oracle raises the Cannot Serialize exception and the application program must do something.

12.49 *Describe three circumstances under which a transaction could receive the "Cannot serialize" exception.*

As explained in the answer to question 12.48 and if a blocking transaction commits. Also occurs when a serializable transaction is aborted.

12.50 *Explain how Oracle processes the read only transaction isolation level.*

Oracle only reads rows having committed changes with an SCN less than the transactions SCN.

12.51 *Explain the use of user, privilege, and role in Oracle security.*

A user is an identifiable user. A privilege is a right like SELECT ANY TABLE; and a role is a set of privileges and other roles.

12.52 *What three types of files are important for Oracle backup and recovery processing?*

Data files, ReDo files, and Control files.

12.53 *What is the difference between the OnLine ReDo logs and the OffLine or Archive ReDo logs? How is each type used?*

OffLine may be on tape or media other than disk. OnLine have ReDo logs of recent activity; Offline have logs since the last backup or even further back.

12.54 *What does multiplexing mean in the context of Oracle recovery?*

Allowing Oracle to maintain duplicate copies of the control files and OnLine ReDo files.

12.55 *Explain how Oracle recovers from application failure.*

Roll back uncommitted changes.

12.56 *What is instance failure and how does Oracle recover from it?*

When the Oracle program fails. See the discussion at the bottom of page 357 and the top of page 358.

12.57 *What is media failure and how does Oracle recover from it?*

When a disk file cannot be written. See the discussion on page 358.

Answers to Projects

For the following projects, use Oracle to create the View Ridge Gallery database as described in this chapter. Consider the database view named Artist View that is shown for the Group II Questions at the end of Chapter 10.

Here is Artist View:

        ARTIST.Name
        ARTIST.Nationality
              TRANSACTION.PurchaseDate
              TRANSACTION.SalesPrice. . .
                    CUSTOMER.Name
                    CUSTOMER.Phone.AreaCode
                    CUSTOMER.Phone.LocalNumber
        CUSTOMER.Name. . .

As mentioned in Chapter 10 of this manual, no WORK data is present in this view. The users of this view apparently are only concerned with transactions for a given artist. We'll still have to process through WORK, however, to get to TRANSACTION.

A. *Write a PL/SQL procedure to read the ARTIST table portion of this view. Display the data you read using DBMS_OUTPUT as shown in the text. Accept the name of the artist as an input parameter.*

Here is the procedure:

```
CREATE OR REPLACE PROCEDURE Artist_View_A
        (
            artName                IN        char
        )
AS
        readName char (25);
        readNationality char (30);

        CURSOR        artistcursor IS
                SELECT Name, Nationality
                FROM ARTIST
                WHERE Name=artName;
BEGIN
        FOR artist IN artistcursor
                LOOP
                    readName := artist.Name;
                    readNationality := artist.Nationality;
        DBMS_OUTPUT.PUT_LINE ('Artist Name = ' || readName || 'Nationality = ' ||
            readNationality);
                END LOOP;
        DBMS_OUTPUT.PUT_LINE ('End of Artist Data');

END;
```

B.   *Write a PL/SQL procedure to read the ARTIST, TRANSACTION, and CUSTOMER
       (under TRANSACTION) table portion of this view. Display the data you read using
       DBMS_output. Accept the name of the artist as an input parameter.*

```
CREATE OR REPLACE PROCEDURE Artist_View_B
        (
            artName                IN        char
        )

AS

        readName char (25);
        readNationality char (30);
        aid      int;

        CURSOR        artistcursor IS
                SELECT ArtistID, Name, Nationality
                FROM ARTIST
                WHERE Name=artName;

        CURSOR        transcursor IS
                SELECT PurchaseDate, SalesPrice, Name, CUSTOMER.Area_Code,
                    Phone_Number
```

```
                FROM WORK, TRANSACTION, CUSTOMER
                WHERE        WORK.ArtistID = aid AND
                        WORK.WorkID = TRANSACTION.WorkID AND
                        TRANSACTION.CustomerID = CUSTOMER.CustomerID;


    BEGIN

    FOR artist IN artistcursor
            LOOP
                readName := artist.Name;
                readNationality := artist.Nationality;
                DBMS_OUTPUT.PUT_LINE ('Artist Name = ' || readName ||
                        'Nationality = ' || readNationality);
                aid := artist.ArtistID;
                For trans in transcursor
                    LOOP
                        DBMS_OUTPUT.PUT_LINE ('Purchase Date = ' || trans.PurchaseDate
                            || ' Sales Price = ' || trans.SalesPrice);
                        DBMS_OUTPUT.PUT_LINE ('Customer Name =' || trans.Name ||
    'Customer Phone =' ||
                            trans.Area_Code || ' ' || trans.Phone_Number);
                    END LOOP;

            END LOOP;

    DBMS_OUTPUT.PUT_LINE ('End of Artist Data');

    END;

    /
```

C.   *Write a PL/SQL procedure to read all of the view tables. Display the data you read using DBMS_output. Accept the name of the artist as an input parameter.*

```
    CREATE OR REPLACE PROCEDURE Artist_View_C
            (
                artName        IN      char
            )

    AS

            readName char (25);
            readNationality char (30);
            aid    int;

            CURSOR      artistcursor IS
                    SELECT ArtistID, Name, Nationality
                    FROM ARTIST
                    WHERE Name=artName;

            CURSOR      transcursor IS
```

```
        SELECT PurchaseDate, SalesPrice, Name, CUSTOMER.Area_Code,
Phone_Number
        FROM WORK, TRANSACTION, CUSTOMER
        WHERE       WORK.ArtistID = aid AND
            WORK.WorkID = TRANSACTION.WorkID AND
            TRANSACTION.CustomerID = CUSTOMER.CustomerID;

    CURSOR      interestcursor IS
        SELECT      CUSTOMER.Name
        FROM ARTIST, CUSTOMER_ARTIST_INT, CUSTOMER
        WHERE       ARTIST.Name = artName AND
            ARTIST.ArtistID = CUSTOMER_ARTIST_INT.ArtistID AND
            CUSTOMER_ARTIST_INT.CustomerID =
CUSTOMER.CustomerID;

BEGIN

FOR artist IN artistcursor
    LOOP
        readName := artist.Name;
        readNationality := artist.Nationality;
        DBMS_OUTPUT.PUT_LINE ('Artist Name = ' || readName ||
            'Nationality = ' || readNationality);

        aid := artist.ArtistID;

        DBMS_OUTPUT.PUT_LINE ('Transaction and Customer Data:');
        For trans in transcursor
            LOOP
              DBMS_OUTPUT.PUT_LINE ('Purchase Date = ' || trans.PurchaseDate
                    || ' Sales Price = ' || trans.SalesPrice);
              DBMS_OUTPUT.PUT_LINE ('Customer Name = ' || trans.Name ||
'Customer Phone =' ||
                    trans.Area_Code || ' ' || trans.Phone_Number);
            END LOOP;

        DBMS_OUTPUT.PUT_LINE ('Interested Customers:');
        For interest in interestcursor
            LOOP
              DBMS_OUTPUT.PUT_LINE ('Customer Name = ' || interest.Name);
            END LOOP;


    END LOOP;

DBMS_OUTPUT.PUT_LINE ('End of Artist Data');

END;

/
```

D.   *Write a procedure to assign a new customer interest to an artist. Assume the name of the artist and the name of the customer are input. If the customer name is not unique, display an error message. Check for duplication in the CUSTOMER_ARTIST_INT table before you insert the new row. Display an error message if there is a duplication.*

```
CREATE OR REPLACE PROCEDURE Artist_View_D
      (
              artName       IN      char,
              custName      IN      char
      )

AS

      recCount int;
      aid      int;
      cid      int;

      CURSOR      artistcursor IS
            SELECT ArtistID
            FROM ARTIST
            WHERE Name=artName;

      CURSOR      customercursor IS
            SELECT CustomerID
            FROM CUSTOMER
            WHERE Name=custName;

BEGIN

      SELECT        COUNT(*) INTO recCount
      FROM          CUSTOMER
      WHERE         CUSTOMER.Name = custName;

      If recCount = 0 Then
        DBMS_OUTPUT.PUT_LINE ('Error -- customer does not exist in database.');
        RETURN;
      ELSE  IF recCount > 1 Then
              DBMS_OUTPUT.PUT_LINE ('Error -- too many customers have this name.');
              RETURN;
           END IF;
      END IF;

      FOR artist IN artistcursor
            LOOP
              aid := artist.ArtistID;
            END LOOP;
      FOR cust IN customercursor
            LOOP
              cid := cust.CustomerID;
            END LOOP;
```

```
SELECT          COUNT(*) INTO recCount
FROM            CUSTOMER_ARTIST_INT
WHERE           CustomerID = cid AND ArtistID = aid;

If recCount > 0 Then
        DBMS_OUTPUT.PUT_LINE ('Error -- interest is already in database');
ELSE
        INSERT INTO CUSTOMER_ARTIST_INT
                (CustomerID, ArtistID)
                VALUES (cid, aid);
        DBMS_OUTPUT.PUT_LINE ('Success -- interest added correctly.');

        End If;
END;

/
```

E. *Code a BEFORE TRIGGER that checks inserts and modifications on ARTIST Nationality. If the new value is 'British' change it to 'English'.*

```
CREATE OR REPLACE TRIGGER Check_Nationality


BEFORE INSERT OR UPDATE of Nationality  ON ARTIST

FOR EACH ROW

        /* correct nationality if necessary */
BEGIN
        If :new.Nationality = 'British' Then
                :new.Nationality := 'English';  End If;
END;

/
```

Answers to FiredUp Project Questions

Use Oracle to create a database with the following four tables:

CUSTOMER (CustomerID, Name, Phone, EmailAddress)
STOVE (SerialNumber, Type, Version, DateOfManufacture)
REGISTRATION (CustomerID, SerialNumber, RDate)
STOVE-REPAIR (RepairInvoiceNumber, SerialNumber, RepairDate, Description, Cost, CustomerID)

Assume the primary keys of CUSTOMER, STOVE, and STOVE-REPAIR are surrogate keys and create sequences for each of them. Create relationships to enforce the following referential integrity constraints:

➢   CustomerID of REGISTRATION is a subset of CustomerID of CUSTOMER
➢   SerialNumber of REGISTRATION is a subset of SerialNumber of STOVE
➢   SerialNumber of STOVE-REPAIR is subset of SerialNumber of STOVE
➢   CustomerID of STOVE-REPAIR is a subset of CustomerID of CUSTOMER

Do not cascade deletions.

Here is the SQL to create these tables:

CREATE TABLE CUSTOMER(

CustomerID	int	Primary Key,
Name	varchar(50)	NOT NUll,
Phone	char (12)	Null,
EmailAddress	varchar(50)	NULL);

CREATE TABLE STOVE(

SerialNumber	int	Primary key,
Version	char(15)	NOT NULL,
Type	Char(15)	Null,
DateOfManufacture	Date	NUll);

CREATE TABLE REGISTRATION(

CustomerID	int	NOT NULL,
SerialNumber	int	NOT NULL,
RDate	Date	Not Null);

ALTER TABLE REGISTRATION ADD CONSTRAINT RegID PRIMARY KEY
(CustomerID, SerialNumber, RDate);

CREATE TABLE STOVE_REPAIR(

RepairInvoiceNumber	int	Primary Key,
SerialNumber	int	NOT NULL,
RepairDate	date	NOT Null,
Description	varchar(500)	null,
Cost	numeric(7,2)	null,
CustomerID	int	NOT NULL);

Here is the SQL to create the relationships and sequences:

ALTER TABLE REGISTRATION ADD CONSTRAINT CustomerFK

FOREIGN KEY(CustomerID) REFERENCES CUSTOMER;

ALTER TABLE REGISTRATION ADD CONSTRAINT StoveFK
FOREIGN KEY(SerialNumber) REFERENCES STOVE;

ALTER TABLE STOVE_REPAIR ADD CONSTRAINT CustomerRepairFK
FOREIGN KEY(CustomerID) REFERENCES CUSTOMER;

ALTER TABLE STOVE_REPAIR ADD CONSTRAINT StoveRepairFK
FOREIGN KEY(SerialNumber) REFERENCES STOVE;

CREATE SEQuence CustomerSEQ Increment by 1 Start with 1;
CREATE SEQuence StoveSEQ Increment by 1 Start with 10;
CREATE SEQuence RepairSEQ Increment by 1 Start with 100;

A.   *Fill your tables with sample data and display them.*

Here are sample data insertions:

INSERT INTO STOVE (SerialNumber, Version, DateOfManufacture) VALUES
        (StoveSeq.NextVal, 'FiredNow', '10-May-01');
INSERT INTO CUSTOMER (CustomerID, Name, Phone, EmailAddress) VALUES
        (CustomerSeq.NextVal, 'Bob Blessing', '206.555.3345', 'Bob@somewhere.com');
INSERT INTO REGISTRATION (CustomerID, SerialNumber, RDate) VALUES
        (CustomerSeq.CurrVal, StoveSeq.CurrVal, '22-JUN-01');

INSERT INTO STOVE (SerialNumber, Version, DateOfManufacture) VALUES
        (StoveSeq.NextVal, 'FiredAlways', '12-May-01');
INSERT INTO CUSTOMER (CustomerID, Name, Phone, EmailAddress) VALUES
        (CustomerSeq.NextVal, 'Blaire Jackson','206.555.6645',
        'Blaire@somewhere.com');
INSERT INTO REGISTRATION (CustomerID, SerialNumber, RDate) VALUES
        (CustomerSeq.CurrVal, StoveSeq.CurrVal, '22-JUL-01');
INSERT INTO STOVE_REPAIR (REPAIRINVOICENUMBER, SERIALNUMBER,
        REPAIRDATE, CUSTOMERID) VALUES
        (RepairSeq.NextVal, StoveSeq.CurrVal, '22-DEC-01', CustomerSeq.CurrVal);

INSERT INTO STOVE (SerialNumber, Version, DateOfManufacture) VALUES
        (StoveSeq.NextVal, 'FiredNow', '15-May-01');
INSERT INTO CUSTOMER (CustomerID, Name, Phone, EmailAddress) VALUES
        (CustomerSeq.NextVal, 'Richard Corneby','212.555.1145',
        'Dick@somewhere.com');
INSERT INTO REGISTRATION (CustomerID, SerialNumber, RDate) VALUES
        (CustomerSeq.CurrVal, StoveSeq.CurrVal, '05-AUG-01');

INSERT INTO STOVE (SerialNumber, Version, DateOfManufacture) VALUES
        (StoveSeq.NextVal, 'FiredNow', '15-May-01');
INSERT INTO CUSTOMER (CustomerID, Name, Phone, EmailAddress) VALUES
        (CustomerSeq.NextVal, 'Eleanore Justice',
        '209.555.0001','EJustice@somewhere.com');
INSERT INTO REGISTRATION (CustomerID, SerialNumber, RDate) VALUES
        (CustomerSeq.CurrVal, StoveSeq.CurrVal, '15-AUG-01');

INSERT INTO STOVE (SerialNumber, Version, DateOfManufacture) VALUES
        (StoveSeq.NextVal, 'FiredAlways', '20-May-00');
INSERT INTO CUSTOMER (CustomerID, Name, Phone, EmailAddress) VALUES

```
        (CustomerSeq.NextVal, 'Bob Smathers', '987.555.1109','Bob@somewhere.com');
INSERT INTO REGISTRATION (CustomerID, SerialNumber, RDate) VALUES
        (CustomerSeq.CurrVal, StoveSeq.CurrVal, '22-AUG-01');
INSERT INTO STOVE_REPAIR (REPAIRINVOICENUMBER, SERIALNUMBER,
        REPAIRDATE, CUSTOMERID) VALUES
        (RepairSeq.NextVal, StoveSeq.CurrVal, '03-JAN-02', CustomerSeq.CurrVal);
```

B. *Create a stored procedure to register a stove. The procedure receives the customer's name, phone, e-mail address, and stove serial number. If the customer already exists in the database (name, phone, and e-mail match), use that customer's CustomerID for the REGISTRATION. Otherwise, create a new CUSTOMER row for the customer. Assume a stove with the input serial number already exists in the database. If not, print an error and roll back changes to the CUSTOMER table. Code and test your procedure.*

Here is such a stored procedure. Note that it would be more efficient to check for the existence of a stove before doing any work. That would save the rollback and also enable better coding. For some reason, sequence.CurrVal can't be set to cid – that's the reason for the two INSERT statements into REGISTRATION.

This procedure probably should also check for duplicate REGISTRATION rows, or handle the exception that Oracle will generate in that case.

```
CREATE OR REPLACE PROCEDURE Register_Stove

        (
                custName        IN      char,
                custPhone       IN      char,
                custEmail       IN      char,
                stoveSerial     IN      int
        )

AS
        cid             int;
        recCount        int;

        CURSOR          custcursor IS
                SELECT          CustomerID
                FROM CUSTOMER
                WHERE           Name=custName AND
                        Phone=custPhone AND
                        EmailAddress = custEmail;
BEGIN

        cid := 0;
        FOR cust IN custcursor
                LOOP
                   cid := cust.CustomerID;
                   DBMS_OUTPUT.PUT_LINE ('Cust Found ' || cid );
                END LOOP;
        If cid = 0 Then
```

```
            DBMS_OUTPUT.PUT_LINE ('No such customer, will create new
    customer');
INSERT INTO CUSTOMER (CustomerID, Name, Phone, EmailAddress) VALUES
    (CustomerSeq.NextVal, custName, custPhone, custEmail);
    End If;

    SELECT      COUNT (*) into recCount
    FROM        STOVE
    WHERE       SerialNumber = stoveSerial;

    If recCount = 0 Then
DBMS_OUTPUT.PUT_LINE ('Stove Serial Number Invalid.  No Changes made.');
        Rollback;
        Return;
    End If;

    If cid = 0 Then
INSERT INTO REGISTRATION (CustomerID, SerialNumber, RDate)
    VALUES (CustomerSeq.CurrVal, stoveSerial, SysDate);
    Else
INSERT INTO REGISTRATION (CustomerID, SerialNumber, RDate) VALUES (cid,
    stoveSerial, SysDate);
    End IF;
END;
/
```

C. *Create a stored procedure to record a stove repair. The procedure receives customer's name, phone, e-mail address, stove serial number, repair description, and cost. Assume you are given a valid stove serial number; print an error message and make no database changes if not. Use an existing CUSTOMER row if name, phone, and e-mail match; otherwise, create a new CUSTOMER record. Assume that the STOVE-REPAIR row must be created. Register the stove, if necessary.*

```
CREATE OR REPLACE PROCEDURE Record_Stove_Repair

    (
            custName      IN    char,
            custPhone     IN    char,
            custEmail     IN    char,
            stoveSerial   IN    int,
            repairDesc    In    char,
            repairCost    IN    int
    )

AS
    cid         int;
    recCount    int;

    CURSOR      custcursor IS

            SELECT      CustomerID
```

```
                         FROM CUSTOMER
                         WHERE        Name=custName AND
                                  Phone=custPhone AND
                                  EmailAddress = custEmail;
BEGIN

              SELECT COUNT (*) into recCount
              FROM STOVE
              WHERE        SerialNumber = stoveSerial;
              If recCount = 0 Then
DBMS_OUTPUT.PUT_LINE ('Stove Serial Number Invalid.  No Changes made.');
                    Return;
              End If;

              cid := 0;
              FOR cust IN custcursor
                    LOOP
                          cid := cust.CustomerID;
                          DBMS_OUTPUT.PUT_LINE ('Cust Found ' || cid );
                    END LOOP;
              If cid = 0 Then
                    DBMS_OUTPUT.PUT_LINE ('No such customer, will create new
customer');
                    INSERT INTO CUSTOMER (CustomerID, Name, Phone, EmailAddress)
                    VALUES  (CustomerSeq.NextVal, custName, custPhone, custEmail);

                    /* Register stove here because new customer can't be registered already
*/

                    DBMS_OUTPUT.PUT_LINE ('Registering stove for new customer.');
                    INSERT INTO REGISTRATION (CustomerID, SerialNumber, RDate)
VALUES
                          (CustomerSeq.Currval, stoveSerial, SysDate);
              Else
                    /* check for registration */

                    SELECT COUNT (*) into recCount
                    FROM REGISTRATION
                    WHERE        CustomerID = cid AND
                                 SerialNumber = stoveSerial;
                    If recCount = 0 Then
INSERT INTO REGISTRATION (CustomerID, SerialNumber, RDate) VALUES (cid,
      stoveSerial, SysDate);
                          DBMS_OUTPUT.PUT_LINE ('Registering stove for existing
customer.');
                    End If;
              End If;

              If cid = 0 Then
                    INSERT INTO STOVE_REPAIR (RepairInvoiceNumber, SerialNumber,
                          RepairDate, Description, Cost, CustomerID) VALUES
```

```
                (RepairSeq.NextVal,stoveSerial,
                SysDate, repairDesc, repairCost, CustomerSeq.CurrVal);
        Else
                INSERT INTO STOVE_REPAIR (RepairInvoiceNumber, SerialNumber,
                    RepairDate, Description, Cost, CustomerID) VALUES
                    (RepairSeq.NextVal,stoveSerial,
                    SysDate, repairDesc, repairCost, cid);
        End IF;
END;
/
```

C.   *Write a PL/SQL procedure to read all of the view tables. Display the data you read using DBMS_output. Accept the name of the artist as an input parameter.*

```
CREATE OR REPLACE PROCEDURE Read_CustomerRecord

        (
            custName        IN      char
        )

AS

        cid             int;

        CURSOR custcursor IS
                SELECT      CustomerID, Phone, EmailAddress
                FROM        CUSTOMER
                WHERE       Name = custName;


        CURSOR rscursor IS
SELECT          STOVE.SerialNumber, RDate, Type, Version, DateOfManufacture
                FROM        REGISTRATION, STOVE
                WHERE       REGISTRATION.CustomerID = cid AND
                            REGISTRATION.SerialNumber = STOVE.SerialNumber;

        CURSOR stoverepaircursor IS
SELECT          RepairInvoiceNumber, SerialNumber, RepairDate, Description, Cost
                FROM        STOVE_REPAIR
                WHERE       CustomerID = cid;

BEGIN

        /* first, loop through customers */

        FOR cust IN custcursor
        LOOP
                cid := cust.CustomerID;
                DBMS_OUTPUT.PUT_LINE ('CustomerID = ' || cust.CustomerID ||
                    'Phone = ' || cust.Phone || 'email = ' || cust.EmailAddress);
```

```
        DBMS_OUTPUT.PUT_LINE ('Registration and Stove Data:');
        For rs in rscursor
          LOOP
DBMS_OUTPUT.PUT_LINE ('SerialNumber = ' ||
        rs.SerialNumber || ' RDate = ' || rs.RDate );
            DBMS_OUTPUT.PUT_LINE ('Type = ' || rs.Type || 'Version = ' ||
                    rs.Version || 'DateOfMan = ' || rs.DateOfManufacture);
          END LOOP;

        DBMS_OUTPUT.PUT_LINE ('Stove Repairs:');
        For sr in stoverepaircursor
          LOOP
            DBMS_OUTPUT.PUT_LINE ('RepairInvoiceNumber = ' ||
                    sr.RepairInvoiceNumber || 'SerialNumber = '||
                    sr.SerialNumber || 'RepairDate = ' || sr.RepairDate);
            DBMS_OUTPUT.PUT_LINE ('Description = ' || sr.Description ||
                    'Cost = '|| sr.Cost);

        END LOOP;
    END LOOP;
    DBMS_OUTPUT.PUT_LINE ('End of Customer Data');
END;
/
```

Chapter 13

Managing Databases with SQL Server 2000

Objectives

- Learn how to install SQL Server and create a database
- Learn how to use SQL Server's graphical utilities
- Learn how to submit both SQL DDL and DML via the query analyzer
- Understand the purpose and role of stored procedures and learn how to create simple stored procedures
- Understand the purpose and role of triggers and learn how to create simple stored procedures
- Understand how SQL Server implements concurrency control
- Learn the fundamental features of SQL Server backup and recovery facilities

Teaching Suggestions

1. As with Oracle, you can spend anywhere from one to five or six class periods on this chapter. So, you need to think first about how much time you can devote to it and shape your plans accordingly.

2. For an hour's presentation, I think you can demonstrate the graphical development tools, the use of Query Analyzer, the source code of stored procedures and triggers, and the invocation of triggers. You might also have time to discuss briefly SQL Server concurrency control and recovery.

3. Students will get much more out of this material if they install SQL Server. If they do not have the version of the text that has it, they can download the trial version from the Microsoft.com.

4. SQL Server is much easier to install than Oracle, and in many ways, it is easier to work with. This chapter has a different tone and orientation from Chapter 12. I didn't plan it that way; rather I think it resulted from differences in the two products and their documentation. Notice there are about 35 pages in each of the two chapters – but that is mis-leading because a lot of Chapter 13 is graphics.

5. Both the View Ridge and the FiredUp databases are located in the Chapter 13/SQL Server Databases subdirectory of the Instructor Supplements sectionf on www.prenhall.com/kroenke. You can download these files, restore them, and you will find all tables, stored procedures and triggers there. The answers given in this manual for FiredUp are present in those files.

6. The Project and the FiredUp exercises for SQL Server in this chapter and those for Oracle in the prior chapter are the same. You can demonstrate how the languages of

these two products are essentially the same by showing the solution to the same questions (all are shown in this manual) for each product.

7.   Another idea, if your student have access to both Oracle and SQL Server, assign some students to one product and other students to the other, and have a contest to see who can solve either the Project or the FiredUp exercises first.

Answers to Group I Questions

13.1   *Install SQL Server 2000 and create a database named MEDIA. Use the default settings for file sizes, names, and locations.*

As explained in text.

13.2   *Write an SQL statement to create a table named PICTURE with columns Name, Description, DateTaken, and FileName. Assume Name is char(20), Description is varchar(200), DateTaken is smalldate, and FileName is char(45). Also assume Name and DateTaken are required. Use Name is the primary key. Set the default value of Description to '(None).'*

```
CREATE TABLE PICTURE(
        Name          Char(20)       Primary Key,
        Description    Varchar(200)   NULL
                       DEFAULT        '(None)',
        DateTaken      Date           NOT NULL,
        FileName       Varchar(45)    NULL);
```

13.3   *Use the SQL Query Analyzer to submit the SQL statement in Question 13.2 to create the PICTURE table in the MEDIA database.*

Use the graphical tool Use the graphical tool as shown in text.

13.4   *Open the MEDIA database using Enterprise Manager and open the database design window for the PICTURE table. In this window, add a column PictureID and set its identity seed to 300 and identity increment to 25. Change the primary key from Name to PictureID.*

Use the graphical tool Use the graphical tool as shown in text.

13.5   *Using the graphical table design tool, set the default value of DateTaken to the system date.*

Use the graphical tool as shown in text.

13.6   *Create a User-Defined Data Type named Subject with data type char(30). Add a column to PICTURE named Topic that is based on Subject.*

Use the graphical tool as shown in text.

13.7 *Create a rule called Valid_Subjects that defines the following set of values: {'Home', 'Office', 'Family', 'Recreation', 'Sports', 'Pets'}. Bind this rule to the Subject User-Defined Data Types.*

Use the graphical tool as shown in text.

13.8 *Write ALTER statements to*
a. Change the length of Name to 50.

ALTER TABLE PICTURE ALTER COLUMN Name char(50)

b. Delete the DateTaken column.

ALTER TABLE PICTURE DROP COLUMN DateTaken

c. Add column TakenBy as char(40).

ALTER TABLE PICTURE ADD COLUMN TakenBy char(40)

13.9 *Submit your answer to Question 13.8 to SQL Server via the SQL Query Analyzer. Then open the table design window to verify that changes occurred correctly.*

Use the graphical tool as shown in text.

13.10 *Create table SLIDE-SHOW (ShowID, Name, Description, Purpose). Assume ShowID is a surrogate key. Set the data type of Name and Description however you deem appropriate. Set the data type of Purpose to Subject. Use either a CREATE statement or the graphical table design tool.*

```
CREATE TABLE SLIDE-SHOW (
        ShowID       int          Primary Key,
        Name         char(25)     NOT NULL,
        Description  Varchar(200) NULL
                     DEFAULT      '(None)',
        Purpose      Subject      NULL)
```

Create table and then use graphical tool to set the Identity seed and increment of ShowID.

13.11 *Create table SHOW-PICTURE-INT as an intersection table between PICTURE and SLIDE-SHOW.*

Use the graphical tool here because it's easier to set composite keys. Don't have to remember the syntax for the alter statement to set such a key.

13.12 *Create appropriate relationships between PICTURE and SHOW-PICTURE-INT and between SLIDE-SHOW and SHOW-PICTURE-INT. Set the referential integrity properties to disallow any deletion of a SLIDE-SHOW row that has any SHOW-PICTURE-INT rows related to it. Set the referential integrity properties to cascade deletions when a PICTURE is deleted.*

Use the graphical tool as shown in text.

13.13 *Explain why we need not set the Cascade Update properties for the relationships in MEDIA.*

Don't worry about it for SLIDE-SHOW because we're using a surrogate key. Need to set it for PICTURE's relationship, however.

13.14 *Write an SQL statement to create a view name PopularShows that has SLIDE-SHOW.Name and PICTURE Name for all slide shows that have a Purpose of either "Home" or "Pets." Execute this statement using SQL Query Analyzer.*

```
CREATE      VIEW  AS
        SELECT      SLIDE-SHOW.Name, PICTURE.Name
        FROM        SLIDE-SHOW, SHOW-PICTURE-INT, PICTURE
        WHERE       SLIDE-SHOW.ShowID = SHOW-PICTURE-INT.ShowID
        AND         PICTURE.Name = SHOW-PICTURE-INT.Name
        AND         SHOW-PICTURE.Purpose IN ['Home', 'Pets']
```

13.15 *Open the view design tool and determine that PopularShows was constructed correctly. Modify this view to include Description and FileName.*

Use the graphical tool as shown in text.

13.16 *Can the SQL DELETE statement be used with the PopularShows view? Why or why not?*

No, because no view involving more than one table can accept a delete.

13.17 *Under what circumstances can PopularShows be used for inserts and modifications?*

If they involve only a single table, or if an INSTEAD OF trigger is written for them.

13.18 *Create an index on the Purpose column. Use the Manage Index graphical design tool to do this.*

Use the graphical tool as shown in text.

13.19 *In Figure 13-21, for what purpose is the @Count variable used?*

To check to determine if the customer record already exists.

13.20 *Why is the SELECT statement that begins SELECT @Cid necessary?*

To get the surrogate key value of the new row.

13.21 *Explain how you would change the stored procedure in Figure 13-21 to connect the customer to all artists who either (a) were born before 1900 or (b) had a null value Birthdate.*

Delete the code that connects customers to artists based on nationality and then create a cursor on ARTIST. Examine each ARTIST row against the criteria and connect to the customer if the criteria are met. Loop through the entire ARTIST table this way.

13.22   *Explain the purpose of the transaction in Figure 13-24.*

The transaction exists to given atomicity to the database activity and to enable the subsequent rollback.

13.23   *What happens if an incorrect value of Copy is input to the stored procedure in Figure 13-24?*

The error message 'ArtistID not valid' will be generated and all work will be rolled back.

13.24   *Explain why the trigger in Figure 13-27 is recursive. What stops the recursion?*

The trigger is to be fired on an insert or update of TRANS. But, the trigger itself updates TRANS. The recursion stops because nothing is done if the update is not of AcquisitionPrice and the trigger updates AskingPrice.

13.25   *In Figure 13-28, explain why an @Count value of 2 or greater means that an error was made prior to the invocation of On_WORK_Insert.*

By the logic at View Ridge, there is never supposed to be more than one WORK row for a given work. It means that, somehow, two such rows are already in the database.

13.26   *In Figure 13-28, what happens if the ROLLBACK statement is executed.*

All work of the trigger and of the transaction that fired the trigger will be removed.

13.27   *What are the three primary factors that influence SQL Server locking behavior?*

Transaction isolation level, cursor concurrency, and locking hints.

13.28   *Explain the meaning of each of the four transaction isolation levels listed in Figure 13-31.*

The meaning is the same as defined in Chapter 11.

13.29   *Explain the meaning of each of the cursor concurrency settings listed in Figure 13-31.*

To provide for read-only, optimistic, pessimistic locking behavior.

13.30   *What is the purpose of Locking Hints?*

To enable the developer to influence SQL Server's locking behavior.

13.31   *What is the difference between complete and differential backups? Under what conditions are complete backups preferred? Under what conditions are differential backups preferred?*

Complete backups copy the entire database; differential just those changes since the last backup. Complete is better if they don't take too long because recovery is simpler with them. Differential are better if a complete backup would take too long.

13.32 *Explain the differences among simple, full, and bulk-logged recovery models. Under what conditions would you choose each one?*

With simple, no logging is done. With full, everything is logged and the log files can get huge. With bulk-logged, updates that involve a lot of data or changes to database structure are not logged.

13.33 *When is point in time restore necessary?*

When the database needs to be recovered to a particular time.

Answers to Projects

For the following projects, use SQL Server to create the View Ridge Gallery database as described in this chapter. Consider the database view named Artist View that is shown for the Group II Questions at the end of Chapter 10.

Here is Artist View:

```
ARTIST.Name
ARTIST.Nationality
        TRANSACTION.PurchaseDate
        TRANSACTION.SalesPrice. . .
                CUSTOMER.Name
                CUSTOMER.Phone.AreaCode
                CUSTOMER.Phone.LocalNumber
        CUSTOMER.Name. . .
```

As mentioned in Chapter 10 of this manual, no WORK data is present in this view. The users of this view apparently are only concerned with transactions for a given artist. We'll still have to process through WORK, however, to get to TRANSACTION.

A.   *Write a Transact/SQL procedure to read the ARTIST table portion of this view. Display the data you read in Query Analyzer as shown in the chapter. Accept the name of the artist as an input parameter.*

```
CREATE PROCEDURE [dbo].[Artist_View_A]
        @artName        char(25)
AS
        DECLARE        @readName as char(25)
        DECLARE        @readNationality as char(30)

        DECLARE        artistcursor CURSOR FOR
                SELECT        ArtistName, Nationality
                FROM        dbo.ARTIST
                WHERE        ArtistName=@artName
```

```
Print 'Display of Artist View '
Open artistcursor
FETCH NEXT FROM artistcursor INTO @readName, @readNationality
WHILE @@FETCH_STATUS = 0
BEGIN

        Print 'Artist Name = ' + @readName + 'Nationality = '+ @readNationality
        FETCH NEXT FROM artistcursor INTO @readName, @readNationality

END

CLOSE artistcursor
DEALLOCATE artistcursor
GO
```

B.   *Write a Transact/SQL procedure to read the ARTIST, TRANSACTION, and CUSTOMER (under TRANSACTION) table portion of this view. Display the data you read via Query Analyzer. Accept the name of the artist as an input parameter.*

```
CREATE PROCEDURE [dbo].[Artist_View_B]
        @artName        char(25)
AS
        DECLARE         @readName as char(25)
        DECLARE         @readNationality as char(30)
        DECLARE         @aid as int
        DECLARE         @pd as smalldatetime
        DECLARE         @n as char(100)
        DECLARE         @sp as money
        DECLARE         @ac as char (5)
        DECLARE         @ln as char (25)

        DECLARE         artistcursor CURSOR FOR
                SELECT          ArtistID, ArtistName, Nationality
                FROM            dbo.ARTIST
                WHERE           ArtistName=@artName

        Print 'Display of Artist Data '
        Open artistcursor
        FETCH NEXT FROM artistcursor INTO @aid, @readName, @readNationality
        WHILE @@FETCH_STATUS = 0
        BEGIN
                Print 'Artist ID = ' + Str(@aid) + ' Artist Name = ' + @readName + ' 'Nationality =
                        '+ @readNationality
                FETCH NEXT FROM artistcursor INTO @aid, @readName,
                        @readNationality
        END

        Print 'Display of Transaction and Customer Data '

        DECLARE         transcursor CURSOR FOR
                SELECT          PurchaseDate, SalesPrice, [Name], AreaCode,
                                LocalNumber
                FROM            dbo.[WORK], dbo.[TRANS], dbo.[CUSTOMER]
                WHERE           [WORK].ArtistID = @aid AND
                                [WORK].WorkID = [TRANS].WorkID AND
```

```
                          [TRANS].CustomerID = CUSTOMER.CustomerID

        Open transcursor
        FETCH NEXT FROM transcursor INTO @pd, @sp, @n, @ac, @ln
        WHILE @@FETCH_STATUS = 0
        BEGIN

                Print 'Purchase Date = ' + CAST(@pd AS varchar) + 'SalesPrice = '+
                        Str( @sp)
                Print 'Phone = ' + @ac + ' ' + @ln
                FETCH NEXT FROM transcursor INTO @pd, @sp, @n, @ac, @ln
        END

        CLOSE artistcursor
        CLOSE transcursor
        DEALLOCATE transcursor

        DEALLOCATE artistcursor
GO
```

C.   *Write a Transact/SQL procedure to read all of the view tables. Display the data you read via Query Analyzer. Accept the name of the artist as an input parameter.*

```
        CREATE PROCEDURE [dbo].[Artist_View_C]
                @artName        char(25)
        AS
                DECLARE         @readName as char(25)
                DECLARE         @readNationality as char(30)
                DECLARE         @aid as int
                DECLARE         @pd as smalldatetime
                DECLARE         @n as char(100)
                DECLARE         @sp as money
                DECLARE         @ac as char (5)
                DECLARE         @ln as char (25)

                DECLARE         artistcursor CURSOR FOR
                        SELECT          ArtistID, ArtistName, Nationality
                        FROM            dbo.ARTIST
                        WHERE           ArtistName=@artName

        Print 'Display of Artist Data '
        Open artistcursor
        FETCH NEXT FROM artistcursor INTO @aid, @readName, @readNationality
        WHILE @@FETCH_STATUS = 0
        BEGIN
                Print 'Artist ID = ' + Str(@aid) + ' Artist Name = ' + @readName + ' Nationality =
        '+ @readNationality
                FETCH NEXT FROM artistcursor INTO @aid, @readName, @readNationality

        END

        Print 'Display of Transaction and Customer Data '

        DECLARE         transcursor CURSOR FOR
                SELECT          PurchaseDate, SalesPrice, [Name], AreaCode, LocalNumber
```

```
        FROM            dbo.[WORK], dbo.[TRANS], dbo.[CUSTOMER]
        WHERE           [WORK].ArtistID = @aid AND
                        [WORK].WorkID = [TRANS].WorkID AND
                        [TRANS].CustomerID = CUSTOMER.CustomerID

Open transcursor
FETCH NEXT FROM transcursor INTO @pd, @sp, @n, @ac, @ln
WHILE @@FETCH_STATUS = 0
BEGIN

        Print 'Purchase Date = ' + CAST(@pd AS varchar) + 'SalesPrice = '+Str( @sp)
        Print 'Phone = ' + @ac + ' ' + @ln
        FETCH NEXT FROM transcursor INTO @pd, @sp, @n, @ac, @ln
END

DECLARE       intcursor CURSOR FOR
        SELECT          CUSTOMER.[Name]
        FROM            dbo.[CUSTOMER-ARTIST-INT], dbo.CUSTOMER
        WHERE           [CUSTOMER-ARTIST-INT].ArtistID = @aid and
                        [CUSTOMER-ARTIST-INT].CustomerID =
                                CUSTOMER.CustomerID


Print 'List of Customers interested in this Artist:'
Open intcursor
FETCH NEXT FROM intcursor INTO  @n
WHILE @@FETCH_STATUS = 0
BEGIN

        Print 'Customer Name = ' + @n

        FETCH NEXT FROM intcursor INTO @n
END

CLOSE artistcursor
CLOSE transcursor
CLOSE intcursor
DEALLOCATE transcursor
DEALLOCATE artistcursor
DEALLOCATE intcursor
GO
```

D.   *Write a Transact/SQL procedure to assign a new customer interest to an artist. Assume
     the name of the artist and the name of the customer are input. If the customer name is
     not unique, display an error message. Check for duplication in the
     CUSTOMER_ARTIST_INT table before you insert the new row. Display an error
     message if there is duplication.*

Here's a stored procedure that will do this. We probably should be checking for a
missing artist name as well.

```
CREATE PROCEDURE [dbo].[Record_Artist_Customer_Interest]
        @artName      char(25),
```

```
          @custName      char(100)
  AS
          DECLARE        @aid as int
          DECLARE        @cid as int
          DECLARE        @recCount as int


          SELECT         @recCount = COUNT(*)
          FROM           CUSTOMER
          WHERE          [Name] = @custName

          If @recCount = 0
            BEGIN
                Print 'Error -- customer does not exist in the database'
                Return
            END
          Else If  @recCount > 1
                Print 'Error -- too many customers have this name'

          DECLARE        artistcursor CURSOR FOR
                SELECT         ArtistID
                FROM           dbo.ARTIST
                WHERE          ArtistName=@artName

          Open artistcursor
          FETCH NEXT FROM artistcursor INTO @aid

          DECLARE        custcursor CURSOR FOR
                SELECT         CustomerID
                FROM           dbo.CUSTOMER
                WHERE          [Name]=@custName

          Open custcursor
          FETCH NEXT FROM custcursor INTO @cid

          SELECT         @recCount = Count(*)
          FROM           dbo.[CUSTOMER-ARTIST-INT]
          WHERE          [CUSTOMER-ARTIST-INT].CustomerID = @cid AND
                         [CUSTOMER-ARTIST-INT].ArtistID = @aid

          If @recCount > 0
                Print ' Error -- interest is already in the database '
          Else
                INSERT INTO dbo.[CUSTOMER-ARTIST-INT] (CustomerID, ArtistID) VALUES
                    (@cid, @aid)

          CLOSE artistcursor
          DEALLOCATE artistcursor
          CLOSE custcursor
          DEALLOCATE custcursor
  GO
```

E.   *Code an AFTER TRIGGER that checks inserts and modifications on ARTIST Nationality.
     If the new value has been assigned as 'British' change it to 'English.'*

```
CREATE TRIGGER [Nationality_Check] ON [dbo].[ARTIST]
FOR INSERT, UPDATE
AS

DECLARE @n as char (35)
DECLARE @aid as int

If NOT UPDATE (Nationality) Return

SELECT @n = Nationality, @aid = ArtistID
FROM  Inserted

If @n ! = 'British' Return

UPDATE      Artist
SET         Nationality = 'English'
WHERE       ArtistID = @aid
```

Answers to FiredUp Project Questions

Use SQL Server to create a database with the following four tables:

CUSTOMER (CustomerID, Name, Phone, EmailAddress)
STOVE (SerialNumber, Type, Version, DateOfManufacture)
REGISTRATION (*CustomerID, SerialNumber, RDate*)
STOVE_REPAIR (RepairInvoiceNumber, *SerialNumber*, RepairDate, Description, Cost, *CustomerID*)

Assume the primary keys of CUSTOMER, STOVE, and STOVE_REPAIR are surrogate keys. Create relationships to enforce the following referential integrity constraints:

➢ CustomerID of REGISTRATION is a subset of CustomerID of CUSTOMER
➢ SerialNumber of REGISTRATION is a subset of SerialNumber of STOVE
➢ SerialNumber of STOVE_REPAIR is subset of SerialNumber of STOVE
➢ CustomerID of STOVE_REPAIR is a subset of CustomerID of CUSTOMER

Do not cascade deletions.

Here is the SQL to create these tables in SQL Server

```
CREATE TABLE CUSTOMER(
    CustomerID          int             Primary Key,
    Name                varchar(50)     NOT NUll,
    Phone               char (12)       Null,
    EmailAddress        varchar(50)     NULL);

CREATE TABLE STOVE(
    SerialNumber        int             Primary key,
    Version             char(15)        NOT NULL,
    Type                char(15)        Null,
    DateOfManufacture   smalldatetime   NUll);
```

```
CREATE TABLE REGISTRATION(
        CustomerID            int              NOT NULL,
        SerialNumber          int              NOT NULL,
        RDate                 smalldatetime    Not Null);
```

ALTER TABLE REGISTRATION ADD CONSTRAINT RegID PRIMARY KEY (CustomerID, SerialNumber, RDate);

```
CREATE TABLE STOVE_REPAIR(
        RepairInvoiceNumber   int              Primary Key,
        SerialNumber          int              NOT NULL,
        RepairDate            smalldatetime    NOT Null,
        Description           varchar(500)     null,
        Cost                  money            null,
        CustomerID            int              NOT NULL);
```

Identity seeds can be set using the graphical tool design tool as shown in the text.

Here is the SQL to create relationships

ALTER TABLE REGISTRATION ADD CONSTRAINT CustomerFK

FOREIGN KEY(CustomerID) REFERENCES CUSTOMER;

ALTER TABLE REGISTRATION ADD CONSTRAINT StoveFK
FOREIGN KEY(SerialNumber) REFERENCES STOVE;

ALTER TABLE STOVE_REPAIR ADD CONSTRAINT CustomerRepairFK
FOREIGN KEY(CustomerID) REFERENCES CUSTOMER;

ALTER TABLE STOVE_REPAIR ADD CONSTRAINT StoveRepairFK
FOREIGN KEY(SerialNumber) REFERENCES STOVE;

A.   *Fill your tables with sample data and display it.*

The following will insert data into CUSTOME and STOVE:

```
INSERT INTO STOVE (Version, DateOfManufacture) VALUES
        ('FiredNow', '10-May-01');
INSERT INTO CUSTOMER ([Name], Phone, EmailAddress) VALUES
        ('Bob Blessing', '206.555.3345', 'Bob@somewhere.com');

INSERT INTO STOVE (Version, DateOfManufacture) VALUES
        ( 'FiredAlways', '12-May-01');
INSERT INTO CUSTOMER ( [Name], Phone, EmailAddress) VALUES
        ( 'Blaire Jackson','206.555.6645', 'Blaire@somewhere.com');

INSERT INTO STOVE ( Version, DateOfManufacture) VALUES
        ( 'FiredNow', '15-May-01');
INSERT INTO CUSTOMER ( [Name], Phone, EmailAddress) VALUES
        ( 'Richard Corneby','212.555.1145', 'Dick@somewhere.com');

INSERT INTO STOVE ( Version, DateOfManufacture) VALUES
```

```
                  ( 'FiredNow', '15-May-01');
INSERT INTO CUSTOMER ( [Name], Phone, EmailAddress) VALUES
         ( 'Eleanore Justice', '209.555.0001','EJustice@somewhere.com');

INSERT INTO STOVE ( Version, DateOfManufacture) VALUES
         ( 'FiredAlways', '20-May-00');
INSERT INTO CUSTOMER ([Name], Phone, EmailAddress) VALUES
         ( 'Bob Smathers', '987.555.1109','Bob@somewhere.com');Her
```

The inserts into REGISTRATION and STOVE_REPAIR depend on the values assigned by the surrogate keys. Here are the ones in the FiredUp database I created:

```
INSERT INTO REGISTRATION (CustomerID, SerialNumber, RDate) VALUES
         (1, 10, '22-JUN-01');

INSERT INTO REGISTRATION (CustomerID, SerialNumber, RDate) VALUES
         (2,11, '22-JUL-01');
INSERT INTO STOVE_REPAIR ( SERIALNUMBER, REPAIRDATE, CUSTOMERID) VALUES
         (11, '22-DEC-01', 2);

INSERT INTO REGISTRATION (CustomerID, SerialNumber, RDate) VALUES
         (3,12, '05-AUG-01');

INSERT INTO REGISTRATION (CustomerID, SerialNumber, RDate) VALUES
         (4, 13, '05-Aug-01');

INSERT INTO REGISTRATION (CustomerID, SerialNumber, RDate) VALUES
         (5, 14, '22-AUG-01');
INSERT INTO STOVE_REPAIR ( SERIALNUMBER, REPAIRDATE, CUSTOMERID) VALUES
         (14, '03-JAN-02', 5);
```

B. *Create a stored procedure to register a stove. The procedure receives the customer's name, phone, e-mail address, and stove serial number. If the customer already exists in the database (name, phone, and e-mail match), use that customer's CustomerID for the REGISTRATION. Otherwise, create a new CUSTOMER row for the customer. Assume a stove with the input serial number already exists in the database. If not, print an error and rollback changes to the CUSTOMER table. Code and test your procedure.*

```
CREATE PROCEDURE [dbo].[Register_Stove]
         @custName       char(50),
         @custPhone      char(12),
         @custEmail      char(50),
         @stoveSerial    int

AS

         DECLARE      @cid    int
         DECLARE      @recCount int


         SELECT       @recCount = COUNT(*)
         FROM         dbo.CUSTOMER
         WHERE        [Name] = @custName AND
                      Phone = @custPhone AND
                      EmailAddress = @custEmail
```

```
            BEGIN TRANSACTION
            If @recCount = 0
                  BEGIN
                        Print 'No such customer will create one now.'
                        INSERT INTO CUSTOMER ([Name], Phone, EmailAddress)
                              VALUES (@custName, @custPhone, @custEmail)
                  END
            ELSE
                  If @recCount > 1
                        BEGIN
                              Print 'Error -- too many customers have this name!'
                              Return
                        END

            SELECT        @recCount = COUNT(*)
            FROM          dbo.STOVE
            WHERE         SerialNumber = @stoveSerial


            If @recCount = 0
                  BEGIN
                        Print 'Invalid stove serial number.  No changes made.'
                        Rollback
                        Return
                  END

            SELECT        @cid = CustomerID
            FROM          dbo.CUSTOMER
            WHERE         [Name] = @custName AND
                          Phone = @custPhone AND
                          EmailAddress = @custEmail

            INSERT INTO dbo.REGISTRATION (CustomerID, SerialNumber, RDate)
                  VALUES (@cid, @stoveSerial, GetDate())

            COMMIT TRANSACTION
      GO
```

C.   *Create a stored procedure to record a stove repair. The procedure receives customer's
      name, phone, e-mail address, stove serial number, repair description, and cost. Assume
      you are given a valid stove serial number; print an error message and make no database
      changes if not. Use an existing CUSTOMER row if name, phone, and e-mail match;
      otherwise, create a new CUSTOMER record. Assume that the STOVE-REPAIR row
      must be created. Register the stove, if necessary.*

```
      CREATE PROCEDURE [dbo].[Record_Stove_Repair]
            @custName      char(50),
            @custPhone     char(12),
            @custEmail     char(50),
            @stoveSerial   int,
            @repairDesc    char(100),
            @repairCost    money

      AS
```

```
DECLARE         @cid    int
DECLARE         @recCount int

BEGIN  TRANSACTION
SELECT          @recCount = COUNT(*)
FROM            dbo.CUSTOMER
WHERE           [Name] = @custName AND
                Phone = @custPhone AND
                EmailAddress = @custEmail


If @recCount = 0
        BEGIN
                Print 'No such customer will create one now.'
                INSERT INTO CUSTOMER ([Name], Phone, EmailAddress)
                        VALUES (@custName, @custPhone, @custEmail)
        END
ELSE
        If @recCount > 1
                BEGIN
                        Print 'Error -- too many customers have this name!'
                        Return
                END


SELECT          @recCount = COUNT(*)
FROM            dbo.STOVE
WHERE           SerialNumber = @stoveSerial


If @recCount = 0
        BEGIN
                Print 'Invalid stove serial number.  No changes made.'
                Rollback
                Return
        END


SELECT          @cid = CustomerID
FROM            dbo.CUSTOMER
WHERE           [Name] = @custName AND
                Phone = @custPhone AND
                EmailAddress = @custEmail


SELECT          @recCount = COUNT(*)
FROM            REGISTRATION
WHERE           CustomerID = @cid AND
                SerialNumber = @stoveSerial
If @recCount = 0

        INSERT INTO dbo.REGISTRATION (CustomerID, SerialNumber, RDate)
                VALUES (@cid, @stoveSerial, GetDate())

INSERT INTO dbo.STOVE_REPAIR (SerialNumber, RepairDate, [Description],
        Cost, CustomerID) VALUES
                (@stoveSerial, GetDate(), @repairDesc, @repairCost, @cid)


COMMIT TRANSACTION
GO
```

D.   *Create a view that contains all of the FiredUp data for a given customer. Name this iew*
     CustomerRecord. This view must join CUSTOMER, REGISTRATION, STOVE, and
     STOVE_REPAIR data. Write a stored procedure that accepts a customer's Name and
     displays all of the data for the given customer.

```
CREATE PROCEDURE [dbo].[Read_CustomerRecord]
            @custName      char(50)
  AS

        DECLARE       @cid as int
        DECLARE       @ph as char(12)
        DECLARE       @email as char(50)
        DECLARE       @sid as int
        DECLARE       @rd as smalldatetime
        DECLARE       @type as char(15)
        DECLARE       @version as char(12)
        DECLARE       @dom as smalldatetime
        DECLARE       @rid as int
        DECLARE       @desc as varchar(250)
        DECLARE       @cost as money

        DECLARE       custcursor CURSOR FOR
            SELECT        CustomerID, Phone, EmailAddress
            FROM          dbo.[CUSTOMER]
            WHERE         Name = @custName

    OPEN custcursor
    FETCH NEXT FROM custcursor INTO @cid, @ph, @email
    WHILE @@FETCH_STATUS = 0
    BEGIN

            Print 'CustomerID = ' +Str( @cid) + ' Customer Name = ' + @custName
            Print 'Phone = ' + @ph + ' EmailAddress = ' + @email

            DECLARE       rscursor CURSOR FOR
                SELECT        STOVE.SerialNumber, RDate, Type, Version,
                              DateOfManufacture
                FROM          dbo.REGISTRATION, dbo.STOVE
                WHERE         REGISTRATION.CustomerID = @cid AND
                              REGISTRATION.SerialNumber =
                              STOVE.SerialNumber

        Open rscursor
        FETCH NEXT FROM rscursor INTO @sid, @rd, @type, @version, @dom
        WHILE @@FETCH_STATUS = 0
        BEGIN

                Print 'Stove SerialNumber = ' +Str( @sid) + ' Registration Date = '
                              + Cast (@rd as varchar)
                Print 'Type = ' + @type + ' Version = ' + @version +
                              ' DateOfManufacture = '
                              + Cast(@dom as varchar)
                FETCH NEXT FROM rscursor INTO @sid, @rd, @type,
```

```
                          @version, @dom
        END

        DECLARE      repaircursor CURSOR FOR
                SELECT      RepairInvoiceNumber, SerialNumber,
                            RepairDate, [Description], Cost
                FROM        dbo.STOVE_REPAIR
                WHERE       STOVE_REPAIR.CustomerID =  @cid

        Open   repaircursor
        FETCH NEXT FROM repaircursor INTO @rid, @sid, @rd, @desc,
                            @cost
        WHILE @@FETCH_STATUS = 0
        BEGIN

                Print 'Repair Invoice Number  = ' +Str( @rid) + ' Stove ID = ' +
                            Str(@sid)
                Print 'Repair Date = ' + Cast (@rd as varchar) + ' Description = '
                            + @desc
                Print 'Cost = ' + Cast(@cost as varchar)
                FETCH NEXT FROM repaircursor INTO @rid, @sid, @rd,
                            @desc, @cost
        END

        FETCH NEXT FROM custcursor INTO @cid, @ph, @email
        END

        CLOSE custcursor
        DEALLOCATE custcursor
        CLOSE          rscursor
        DEALLOCATE rscursor
        CLOSE repaircursor
        DEALLOCATE repaircursor
GO
```

Chapter 14

Networks, Multi-Tier Architectures, and XML

Objectives

- Understand the meaning and purpose of TCP/IP and HTTP
- Know the components of 3-tier and multi-tier architectures and the purposes of those components
- Learn the similarities and differences of DHTML and XML
- Understand the role of XSLT
- Learn the basic concepts of XML Schema and understand their important to database processing

Teaching Suggestions

1. The students need to understand the 3-tier architecture and the roles of each of the tiers. If they have a Windows NT machine and have installed either SQL Server or Oracle, they can run all three tiers on their machine. They need to know that there are clean, standardized interfaces between those three tiers, however. Thus, the functions of browser, web server, and DBMS can be split apart.

2. XML is vitally important not just for the products and technologies in use today, but also because it is the core component of .Net initiative. XML Schema will be very, very important in the next few years.

3. The XML technology discussed in this chapter, particularly for XML Schema, is rapidly developing. There will be changes and differences from what is written here. The students should learn to check out recent development on the Web.

4. Both Microsoft and Oracle are rapidly adding more and more XML to their products. I didn't cover it here because the text is already becoming too large. If you have time, however, you should discuss some of these features with your class.

5. In view of the rapid change of this technology, I don't think it's too important that students understand all of the details. Instead, they should strive to learn the components, their purposes, and how they all fit together. They should understand it to the level that they could explain to a job interviewer, for example, what XML schema is and why it's important to database processing.

Answers to Group I Questions

14.1   *Define the terms network, public network, and private network.*

A network is a collection of computers that communicate with one another using a standardized protocol. A public network can be used by anyone who pays the fee. A private network requires users to be preauthorized before they can use it.

14.2   *Define Internet.*

The Internet is a public network of computers that communicate using TCP/IP.

14.3   *What is TCP/IP and how is it used?*

Transmission Control Program / Internet Protocol, the communications protocol used by the Internet.

14.4   *Explain what it means to say that HTTP is request-oriented and stateless.*

HTTP does not poll, it waits for requests to arrive. With pure HTTP, no context is maintained for users or sessions.

14.5   *What protocol has been developed to support wireless network processing?*

WAP, the wireless application protocol.

14.6   *Name the three tiers of the three-tier architecture and describe the role of each.*

Database server processes SQL and performs multi-user database management tasks; web server is an HTTP server and CRUDs views, browser computers are HTTP clients and materialize views.

14.7   *Explain how the three-tier architecture allows for interoperability of operating systems and Web products.*

The tiers interface using standardized protocols and hence can run any operating system they want. Each tier can have a different OS, if desired.

14.8   *Explain the functions of each of the components of the Web server in Figure 14-4.*

See discussion on pages 411-412.

14.9   *Explain two uses for the extra tiers in an n-tier architecture.*

a.   Off-load application processing like views and rules onto from the web server
b.   Control distributed transactions

14.10 *Why are standards important for markup languages?*

To ensure browsers can process any Web page.

14.11 *What is W3C, and why is it important?*

W3C publishes standards and administers this process of developing them.

14.12 *Why do vendors have a love/hate relationship with standards?*

Love because they bring order to the marketplace; hate because of the double bind of adding features and functions beyond the standard,

14.13 *Summarize the disadvantages of early versions of HTML.*

Content, layout, and format of pages were confounded; lack of style-sheets, page elements not accessible from programs; no constructs to facilitate caching and manipulating of data.

14.14 *What is the difference between DHTML and HTML 4.0?*

DHTML is the Microsoft implementation of HTML 4.0; DHTML contains features and functions beyond those in the HTML 4.0 standard.

14.15 *Define DOM and explain its importance.*

It exposes all page elements as objects that can be manipulated programmatically. Note there are two uses for DOM in this chapter — this one and as an XML document parser. Meaning should be clear from context.

14.16 *Define CSS and explain its importance.*

Cascading style sheets. Enables the definitions of formats for various document elements.

14.17 *Define RDS and explain its role.*

RDS, or remote data services, is a set of ObjectX controls that allow the caching and processing of data on the client.

14.18 *Define XML and explain why it is superior to HTML and DHTML.*

XML is the extensible markup language. Where do I begin?? It's standardized, but extensible. It provides for document validation. Its robust enough to represent database views. With XML Schema, it provides a generalized solution for the processing of domains. It separates structure, content, and materialization.

14.19 *Explain why there is too much freedom with HTML.*

Because labels are used for both formatting and semantics. <H2> might be used to obtain a given formatting, or it might be used to denote a logical level in a document.

14.20 *What is a DTD, and why is it important?*

Document Type Declaration. It defines the structure of a given XML document. It can be used to determine if documents are valid instances of that structure.

14.21 *Define type-valid and not-type-valid XML documents.*

A type-valid document is an XML document that conforms to its DTD. A not-type-valid document either does not conform to its DTD, or it does not have a DTD to conform to.

14.22 *Explain how CSS is used with XML documents.*

CSS provides a way, other than XSLT, to materialize XML documents.

14.23 *Define XSLT and explain its importance.*

Extensible Style Language: Transformations. It provides facilities for materializing and transforming XML documents.

14.24 *Why is XSLT declarative? Why is it transformational?*

Declarative because it has the form of a production rule: {For this condition, Do this thing}. No procedure for transformations is defined. It is transformational because one document is transformed into a second.

14.25 *Explain the importance of context when working with XSLT.*

All rules are interpreted in the context of a particular location in a document.

14.26 *Describe the difference between DOM and SAX.*

DOM (here used in the XML parsing context) is an API that provides the content of an XML document in the form of a tree. Each node of the tree represents a piece of the document. The entire document is in memory at once.

SAX, the Simple API for XML, is an event-based parser that notifies a program when elements of an XML document have been encountered.

14.27 *What are two types of elements in XML Schema? Give an example of each.*

Simple and complex.
Simple example:
    <element name="CustomerName", type="custDomain.CustName"/>

Complex example:

    <complex Type name="Phone"/>
    <sequence>
        <element name ="AreaCode", type="custDomain.AC"/>
        <element name ="PhoneNumber", type="custDomain.LocalNumber"/>
    </sequence>

14.28   *Explain the difference between element content and element attributes.*

XML doesn't really define this as part of the specification. But, usually, element content is used for data values and element attributes are used for metadata.

14.29   *What is a target namespace and what is its function?*

The target namespace is the namespace being defined by the XML Schema document.

14.30   *What is the default namespace and how is it used?*

The default namespace is the namespace used during validation if no other namespace is indicated.

14.31   *What is the significance of giving the target namespace and the default namespace the same name?*

It means the parser should look in the schema itself for the definition of unlabeled terms.

14.32   *Give an example of a labeled namespace.*

<xmlns:music=http://www.musiccompany.com/xml/dtd>

14.33   *Explain how to use namespaces to resolve element name ambiguity.*

See the discussion of musicalInstrument and electronicDevice in Figure 14-14.

14.34   *Why do namespace names look like Internet addresses? Does the XML Schema standard require that schema documents be located at these addresses?*

According to the standard, any unique identifier can be used to define a namespace. URI's are used because they are unique, worldwide. The standard does not specify where schema documents are to be located.

14.35   *Define WAP, WML, WML Script, deck, and card.*

Wireless application protocol; wireless markup language; wireless markup language Script, a subset of JavaScript; deck, a set of cards that comprise a web page; card, a section of a web page that can be displayed on a microbrowser.

14.36   *Why is XML important to database applications?*

> Industry standards for document types
> Facility for document validity checking
> Clean separation of structure, content, and materialization
> Standard means for expressing database views
> Standard means for representing domains' *XML Characteristics*

14.37   *Why is SQL not an effective way for defining the structure of database views?*

Because SQL cannot represent views with multiple paths.

Answers to Group II Questions

14.38 *Visit www.w3.org and determine the current recommended standard for HTML. How does it differ from that described in this chapter? Is there a new standard for HTML underway? If so, what is it and what new features will it have?*

Answer depends on what happens after this manual was written.

14.39 *Visit www.w3.org and determine the current recommended standard for XSLT. How does it differ from the implementation of XSLT described in this chapter for Internet Explorer 5.0? What XSLT standards are in process?*

Answer depends on what happens after this manual was written.

14.40 *Visit www.w3.org and determine the current recommended standard for XML Schema. How does it differ from that described here?*

Answer depends on what happens after this manual was written.

14.41 *Visit either Microsoft's or Oracle's web site and investigate XML Schema products and technology that they support. How do these products differ from XML Schema described here?*

Answer depends on what happens after this manual was written.

14.42 *Visit www.xml.org, go to the registry, and find a standard for an industry type of interest to you. Describe the purpose of the standard. How useful do you believe that standard will become?*

Answer depends on what the student finds.

14.43 *Visit www.wapformum.org and determine the current recommended WAP standard. How does it differ from that described here?*

Answer depends on what happens after this manual was written.

Answers to FiredUp Project Questions

The Robards decide that they want their customers to register their stoves online. They're not sure how to go about this, so they hire you as a consultant to help them. Assume they decide to operate their own web site rather than use a service bureau.

A. *Comment on the desirability of their decision to operate their own site. What are the advantages and disadvantages?*

For a business as small as theirs, running their own web site is probably not the best idea. If they can find a hosting service that will support their needs, using it would probably be a better course of action. That service will need to support a DBMS and their applications, and they may have difficulty finding an appropriate service.

B. *Consider the three-tier architecture in the light of FiredUp's registration needs. What would be the purpose of each tier?*

The same as defined in the text. The web server would support their web site and mail service. There would be links on the web site to ASP or JSP pages that invoke database applications and/or DBMS services. The database server would run the DBMS and manage the database.

C. *Would you recommend Windows 2000 or Linux for their Web server? Explain the advantages and disadvantages of each.*

It's hard to say without knowing more about their local setting, the support available, the knowledge of their consultant, and the like. In general, it probably would be better for them to use Windows 2000 because it will be easier for them to obtain support for it and related tools. They will pay more for the software than with Linux, and the development tools will also be more expensive. The software costs, however, are probably a small portion of the total system costs. On the other hand, the up-front software costs will be more visible to FiredUp than the longer term system costs and they may not be willing to accept the fact that Windows might be cheaper in the long run.

Having said all of this, if their consultant is a knowledgeable developer with Linux, Apache, Tomcat, Java, and JSP, then there is no reason that the Linux would not be just as effective as the Windows solution. They need to be concerned about long term support, however, and they need to determine what they'll do if/when their consultant is no longer available to them.

D. *Would you recommend Access, Oracle, or SQL Server for their database server? Explain your rationale.*

While Access would probably support their workload, I would not recommend it because it is not designed for robust multi-user processing and seems to be more and more positioned by Microsoft as a desktop product. As between Oracle and SQL Server, it's a hard choice. Either will certainly provide the performance they need. I think the choice for them will depend on which of these two their consultant knows. In their shoes, I certainly wouldn't override the consultant's recommendation between the two. He or she will probably choose the DBMS produce that they know best.

As the students will see in the next chapter, when using ASP and ODBC, there is very little difference between accessing an Oracle and an SQL Server database. Both systems can work very well in this environment.

Of course, if they choose Linux, then they need to use Oracle because SQL Server doesn't run on Linux.

E. *Would it be desirable for FiredUp to combine the Web server and database server on one computer? What are the advantages and disadvantages of this?*

Yes, for their workload, it probably would. The advantages are less computing equipment to buy, maintain, and operate, less expense, and elimination of any possible communication problems between the two machines. The primary disadvantage is performance, which should not be a problem for FiredUp's workload. (Another disadvantage is potentially increased reliability if the server computers could be configured to back one another up. But that's not likely to be relevant for a small company like FiredUp.)

F.   *Create an XML DTD and sample XML registration document. Assume the database tables are:*

> CUSTOMER (CustomerID, Name, Phone, EmailAddress)
> STOVE (SerialNumber, Type, Version, DateOfManufacture)
> REGISTRATION (*CustomerID, SerialNumber,* Date)
> STOVE_REPAIR (RepairInvoiceNumber, *SerialNumber,* Date, Description, Cost, *CustomerID*)

> Assume that the registration document needs to have Name, Phone, EmailAddress, and SerialNumber, and RDate elements.

```
<!DOCTYPE registration [
    <!ELEMENT customer (name, phone, emailaddress)>
        <!ELEMENT name (#PCDATA)>
        <!ELEMENT phone (#PCDATA)>
        <!ELEMENT emailaddress (#PCDATA)>
    <!ELEMENT serialnumber (#PCDATA)>
    <!ELEMENT rdate (#PCDATA)>
]>


<registration>
    <customer>
        <name>Bob Blessing</name>
        <phone>206.555.3345</phone>
        <emailaddress>Bob@somewhere.com</emailaddress>
    </customer>
    <serialnumber>123456</serialnumber>
    <rdate>05-AUG-2001</rdate>
</registration>
```

G.   *Create an XML Schema for the registration document.*

```
<schema targetNamespace xmlns="http://www.firedup.com/registration/dtd"
        xmlns="http://www.firedup.com/xmlnames/dtd
xmlns:dt="http://www.w3.org/2000/10/XMLSchema"

<complexType name="customer">
<sequence>
        <element name="name" type ="dt:string"/>
        <element name="phone" type ="dt:string" minoccurs="0"/>
        <element name="emailaddress" type ="dt:string"/>
```

```
        </sequence>
    </complexType>

    <element name="serialnumber" type="dt:string"/>
    <element name="rdate" type="dt:date:/>

</schema>
```

Chapter 15

ODBC, OLE DB, ADO, and ASP

Objectives

- Understand the nature and characteristics of the data environment that surrounds Internet technology database applications
- Learn the purpose, features, and facilities of ODBC
- Understand the nature and goals of OLE DB
- Learn the characteristics and object model of ADO
- Learn how to access databases via ADO using ASP pages

Answers to Group I Questions

15.1   *Describe why the data environment for Web servers is complicated.*

Internet technology applications need to publish database applications that involve dozens of different data types; this includes many different types of DBMS data plus non-database data. Some data is table like, but does not conform to the definition of a relation.

15.2   *Explain the relationship of ODBC, OLE DB, and ADO.*

ODBC is an older standard for processing relational databases or flat files (including spreadsheets). OLE DB is a newer standard, based on OLE, for accessing data of any type. ADO is an object cover over OLE DB that can be used by non-object oriented programmers and in scripting languages such as VBScript and JScript.

15.3   *Explain the author's justification for describing Microsoft standards. Do you agree?*

That's a tough one — I agree or I wouldn't have written it that way, but that's not to say that I don't have misgivings about it. The rich get richer and I guess that's just a fact of life. Still, it's a well-managed company with strong technology.

15.4   *Name the components of the ODBC standard.*

Driver manager, DBMS drivers, and data source.

15.5   *What role does the driver manager serve? Who supplies it?*

The driver manager loads the correct driver for a given call. It is part of Windows (or Linux as you'll see in the next chapter).

15.6 *What role does the DBMS driver serve? Who supplies it?*

A DBMS driver is a program that translates ODBC and possibly SQL calls into commands for a particular DBMS. It is supplied by the DBMS vendor or by an independent software company.

15.7 *What is a single-tier driver?*

A single-tier driver processes both ODBC calls and SQL statements. Used with file-server oriented DBMS products.

15.8 *What is a multiple-tier driver?*

A multiple-tier driver processes ODBC calls but passes SQL statements to the server DBMS for processing.

15.9 *Do the uses of the term tier in the three-tier architecture and its use in ODBC have anything to do with each other?*

No, absolutely nothing.

15.10 *Why are conformance levels important?*

Conformance levels are important because they allow products having different levels of capability to participate in the ODBC standard. The standard need not conform to the lowest level, nor need it address only the capabilities of the highest level products.

15.11 *Summarize the three ODBC API conformance levels.*

See Figure 15-7.

15.12 *Summarize the three SQL grammar conformance levels.*

See Figure 15-8.

15.13 *Explain the difference among the three types of data sources.*

User pertains to a single user on a single machine. File holds the data source data in a file that can be shared among users – perhaps on different machines. System pertains to a particular computer.

15.14 *Which data source type is recommended for Web servers?*

System on the Web server.

15.15 *What are the two tasks to be accomplished when setting up an ODBC data source name?*

Pick the DBMS driver and a particular database.

15.16 *Why is OLE DB important?*

It is the foundation of Microsoft's data access capability. Anyone who wants to consume or provide data via Windows needs to know about OLE DB and use it in their products and programs.

15.17 *What disadvantage of ODBC does OLE DB overcome?*

Vendors can implement only a portion of their product's capabilities to provide an OLE DB interface. It's a smaller bite to take to participate.

15.18 *Define abstraction and explain how it relates to OLE DB.*

An abstraction is a generalization. When we abstract something, we lose detail, but we gain the ability to work with a broader range of types. A recordset is an abstraction of a relation.

15.19 *Give an example of abstraction involving rowset.*

A rowset is an abstraction of a recordset.

15.20 *Define object properties and methods.*

The properties of an object represent the object's characteristics. The methods of an object represent its behaviors.

15.21 *What is the difference between an object class and an object?*

An object class is the structure of an object. An object is a particular instance of the object.

15.22 *Explain the role of data consumers and data providers.*

Data consumers obtain data or services from OLE DB. Data providers deliver data or services to consumers via OLE DB.

15.23 *What is an interface?*

An interface is a packaging of objects that exposes certain properties and methods.

15.24 *What is the difference between an interface and an implementation?*

The implementation is how objects support the interface. Interfaces never change, but implementations are free to do so; no one will know.

15.25 *Explain why an implementation can be changed but an interface should not be changed.*

Because users of the object depend on the interface remaining the same. If an interface changed, users of the object would have to change their code as well.

15.26 *Summarize the goals of OLE DB.*

See Figure 15-10.

15.27 *What is MTS, and what does it do?*

A service in OLE DB for allowing transactions to process data on multiple data sources that may reside on multiple computers.

15.28 *Explain the difference between a tabular data provider and a service provider. Which type is a product that transforms OLE DB data into XML documents?*

A tabular data provider presents data in rowsets; a service provider is a transformer of data.

15.29 *In the context of OLE DB, what is the difference between a rowset and a cursor?*

In OLE DB, they are equivalent.

15.30 *What languages can use ADO?*

Basically any: JScript, VBScript, VB, Java, C#, C++, etc.

15.31 *List the objects in the ADO object model and explain their relationships.*

See Figure 15-14.

15.32 *What is the function of the Connection object?*

The connection object establishes a connection with an ODBC data source or with an OLE DB data source. It is the basis of the other objects in ADO.

15.33 *Show a snippet of VBScript for creating a Connection object.*

```
Dim objConn
Set objConn = Server.CreateObject("ADODB.connection")
objConn.IsolationLevel = adXactReadCommitted
objConn.open "ViewRidgeDSN"
```

15.33 *What is the function of the RecordSet object?*

To create an object that represents the results of a SQL statement.

15.34 *Show a snippet of VBScript for creating a RecordSet object.*

```
Dim objRecordSet, varSql
Const adoCursorType = 3 ' static cursor
Const adoLockType = 3 ' optimistic locking

varSql = "SELECT * FROM [ARTIST]"
Set objRecordSet = Server.CreateObject("ADODB.Recordset")
```

```
objRecordSet.CursorType = adoCursorType
objRecordSet.LockType = adoLockType
objRecordSet.Open varSql, objConn
```

15.36 *What does the Fields collection contain? Explain a situation in which you would use it.*

The fields collection contains the names of the columns in a recordset. Used when the program needs to process fields by name and does not already know the fields in the recordset.

15.37 *Show a snippet of VBScript for processing the Fields collection.*

```
Dim varI, varNumCols, objField
varNumCols = objRecordSet.Fields.Count

For varI = 0 to varNumCols - 1
   Set objField = objRecordSet.Fields(varI)
   '  objField.Name now has the name of the field
   '  objField.Value now has the value of the field
   '  can do something with them here
Next
```

15.38 *What does the Errors collection contain? Explain a situation in which you would use it.*

From zero to many errors that resulted during the processing of some ADO command. To interpret and display error messages.

15.39 *Show a snippet of VBScript for processing the Errors collection.*

```
Dim varErrorCount, varI, objError

On Error Resume Next
varErrorCount = objConn.Errors.Count
If varErrorCount > 0 Then
   For varI = 0 to varErrorCount - 1
      Set objError = objConn.Errors(varI)
   ' objError.Description contains
   ' a description of the error
   Next
End If
```

15.40 *What is the purpose of the Command object?*

To execute queries and stored procedures that are stored with the database.

15.41 *Show a snippet of VBScript for executing a stored parameterized query that has two parameters, A and B.*

```
objCommand.CommandText="{call Customer_Insert (?, ?, ?, ?)}" '
      setup call
```

```
' Set up four parameters with necessary values
Set objParam = objCommand.CreateParameter("NewName", adChar,
    adParamInput, 50)
objCommand.Parameters.Append objParam
objParam.Value = Request.Form("text1")

Set objParam = objCommand.CreateParameter("AreaCode", adChar,
    adParamInput, 5)
objCommand.Parameters.Append objParam
objParam.Value = Request.Form("text2")

Set objParam = objCommand.CreateParameter("PhoneNumber", adChar,
    adParamInput, 8)
objCommand.Parameters.Append objParam
objParam.Value = Request.Form("text3")

Set objParam = objCommand.CreateParameter("Nationality", adChar,
    adParamInput, 25)
objCommand.Parameters.Append objParam
objParam.Value = Request.Form("text4")

' Fire the Stored Proc

Set oRs = objCommand.Execute
```

15.42 *Explain the purpose of the <% and %> tags in ASP pages.*

They mark script that is to be executed on the ASP server rather than on the browser.

15.43 *Explain the purpose of the _conn variables in Figure 15-16.*

They save a pointer to the connection object so that the connection does not have to be recreated for a particular browser session.

15.44 *What is the reason for the code that creates varKeyName in Figure 15-18(b).*

To set the capitalization correctly for the surrogate key columns.

15.45 *Explain the purpose of the ACTION parameter of the FORM tag in Figure 15-21(a).*

Indicates whether data values are to be passed as parameters or in a Form object.

15.46 *Explain what happens when the following statement is executed in the ASP page in Figure 15-21(b).*

varTableName=Request.Form("text1")

The variable varTableName is set to the value of the control text1 that was passed to it via the Form object.

15.47 *Show a VBScript snippet for adding a new record to a recordset name objMyRecordSet. Assume the fields are A and B and their values are to be "Avalue" and "Bvalue" respectively.*

```
objMyRecordSet.AddNew
objMyRecordSet("A")= AValue
objMyRecordSet("B")= BValue
objMyRecordSet.Update
```

15.48 *What purpose is served by the Response.Write statement?*

Write something back to the browser.

Answers to Group II Questions

15.49 *Microsoft expends much effort to promulgate the OLE DB and ADO standards. It does not directly receive revenue from these standards. IIS is free with Windows NT and Windows 2000. Its web site has numerous examples of articles to help developers learn more, and all of it is free. Why do you think Microsoft does this? What goal is served?*

Everything Microsoft does has the goal of promoting the sale of Windows. Whereas Windows is the predominant operating system on the desktop, Windows NT has not had the same success on servers. Unix and Linux are serious competitors. I believe all of these efforts are made to increase the marketshare of Windows NT (and 2000) on servers.

15.50 *In the code in Figure 15-23(b), the cursor type is set to dynamic. What effect will this have on the processing of this and the Customer.asp and Artist.asp pages? Explain how you think the isolation level, cursor type, and lock type parameters should be set for an application that involves all three of these pages.*

Here is a summary of cursor types for the three pages:

Page	Isolation Level	Cursor Type	Lock Type
AddArtist.asp	Cursor Stability	Dynamic	Optimistic
Artist.asp	Cursor Stability	Static	Optimistic
Customer.asp	Cursor Stability	Static	Optimistic

Here Concurrent users of AddArtist will be able to view each other's work when that work is committed to the database.   Artist and Customer users will see data that is current when their recordset is opened, but they will not see changes that occur while they process that recordset. Since that is likely to be a short period of time, this is not too much of a problem. I think these are set correctly.

15.51 *Explain how to change the ASP page in Figure 15-16 to run with the DSN ViewRidgeOracle. Explain how to change the ASP page in Figure 15-18 to run with SQL Server. While the ease of making these changes is interesting from a technology standpoint, does this capability have any importance in the word of commerce?*

In Figure 15-16, change the DSN name to ViewRidgeOracle in the objConn open statement. Pass the account "system" with the password "manager." Can eliminate the setting of isolation level because Oracle never does dirty reads, but don't have to. May have to change parameters on record set open statements. and setting this value will fail. In Figure 15-18 change the DSN to ViewRidgeSS. Change the account to "sa" with no password. Set the cursor isolation to eliminate dirty reads. Also, make sure table names in Oracle are surrounded by quotes and table names in SQL Server are surrounded by brackets.

Well, this means the developer need only learn one way to write ASP to process a database. It's much better than having proprietary interfaces to DBMS products. In practice, however, some organizations standardize on either Oracle or SQL Server; in such an organization, this probably isn't too important.

15.52 *If you have installed Oracle, use your browser to execute the page in Figure 15-18. Now open SQL Plus and delete two rows of CUSTOMER data using the SQL DELETE command. Go back to your browser and execute the page in Figure 15-16 again. Explain the results.*

When I do this, I still see the deleted rows. I do not think that I should. Even though we are caching the connection, we are not caching the record set, so when this ASP page opens a new record set, the deleted rows should be gone. Maybe this is caused by the way SQL Plus commits changes? Perhaps there's a failure in the Oracle ODBC driver I'm using?

15.53 *If you have installed SQL Server, use your browser to execute the page in* Figures 15-16. *Now open SQL Query Analyzer and delete two rows of CUSTOMER data using the SQL DELETE command. Go back to your browser and execute the page in Figure 15-16 again. Explain the results. If you answered Question 15.52, explain the difference in results you received, if any.*

The rows are gone as they should be. I don't know why this is different for SQL Server than for Oracle.

Answers to FiredUp Project Questions

Create the YourFired database using either Oracle or SQL Server, if you have not already done so. Follow the instruction at the end of Chapters 12 or 13, respectively.

A. *Code an ASP page to display the STOVE table.*

Here is the SQL Server version of this page:

```
<HTML>
    "
<HEAD>
    "
<META HTTP-EQUIV="Content-Type" CONTENT="text/html;charset=windows-1252">
    "
```

```
<TITLE>Table Display Page</TITLE>
"

</HEAD>
"

<BODY>
"

<!--#include virtual="FiredUpSQLServer/adovbs.inc"-->
"

<%
"

     Dim objConn, objRecordSet, objField
"

     Dim varNumCols, varI, varSql
     If IsObject(Session("_conn")) Then ' if already have a connection, use
it
          Set objConn = Session("_conn")
     Else
          Set objConn = Server.CreateObject("ADODB.connection") ' get
connection

          ' open SQL Server ODBC file using system account with manager
password
          objConn.open "FiredUpInSQLServer", "sa"
          objConn.IsolationLevel = adXactReadCommitted ' avoid dirty reads
          Set Session("_conn") = objConn
     End If

   Set objRecordSet = Server.CreateObject("ADODB.Recordset")

   varSQL = "SELECT * FROM STOVE "
   objRecordSet.Open varSql, objConn, adOpenStatic, adLockReadOnly ' static
with no need to update
%>

<TABLE BORDER=1 BGCOLOR=#ffffff CELLSPACING=5><FONT FACE="Arial"
COLOR=#000000>
<CAPTION><B> FiredUp STOVE Table(in SQL Server database)</B></CAPTION></FONT>
<THEAD>
<TR>
<%
varNumCols = objRecordSet.Fields.Count
For varI = 0 to varNumCols - 1
Set objField = objRecordSet.Fields(varI)%>
<TH BGCOLOR=#c0c0c0 BORDERCOLOR=#000000 ><FONT SIZE=2 FACE="Arial"
COLOR=#000000><%=objField.Name%></FONT> </TH>
<%
Next%>
</TR>
</THEAD>
<TBODY>
<%
On Error Resume Next
objRecordSet.MoveFirst
do while Not objRecordSet.eof
%>
<TR VALIGN=TOP>
<%
```

IM - 202

```
varNumCols = objRecordSet.Fields.Count
For varI = 0 to varNumCols - 1
Set objField = objRecordSet.Fields(varI)
%>
<TD BORDERCOLOR=#c0c0c0 ><FONT SIZE=2 FACE="Arial"
COLOR=#000000><%=SERVER.HTMLEncode(objField.Value)%><BR></FONT></TD>
<%
Next%>
</TR>
<%
objRecordSet.MoveNext
loop%>
</TBODY>
<TFOOT></TFOOT>
</TABLE>
</BODY>
</HTML>
```

B.   *Code an ASP page to display any table in the FiredUp database. Use Figure 15.21 as an example.*

Here is the page to get the table name:

```
<HTML>
"
<HEAD>
"
<META HTTP-EQUIV="Content-Type" CONTENT="text/html;charset=windows-1252">
<TITLE>Table Display Form</TITLE>
</HEAD>
<BODY>

<FORM METHOD="post" ACTION="ShowFiredUpTablesSS.asp">

 <P><STRONG><FONT color=purple face="" size=5>   Table Display
Selection Form</FONT></STRONG>
<P></P>
<P> </P>

<P><FONT style="BACKGROUND-COLOR: #ffffff">
<FONT color=forestgreen face=""
style="BACKGROUND-COLOR: #ffffff">Enter
TableName:</FONT>     </FONT></P>

<P></P>

<P><FONT style="BACKGROUND-COLOR: #ffffff"></FONT> 
<INPUT id=text1 name=text1 size="20"></P>

<P><FONT style="BACKGROUND-COLOR: #ffffff">
<INPUT id=submit1 name=submit1 type=submit value="Show Table"
>   
<INPUT id=reset1 name=reset1 type=reset value="Reset Values"></FONT></P>
</FORM>
</BODY>
</HTML>
```

Here is the page to display the table (SQL Server version):

```
<HTML>
"
<HEAD>
"
<META HTTP-EQUIV="Content-Type" CONTENT="text/html;charset=windows-1252">
"
<TITLE>Table Display Page</TITLE>
"
</HEAD>
"
<BODY>
"
<!--#include virtual="FiredUpSQLServer/adovbs.inc"-->
<%

Dim objConn, objRecordSet, objField
Dim varNumCols, varI, varSql
Dim varTableName, varRecordSetName
Dim varTableNameFirst, varTableNameRest

varTablename = Request.Form("text1")


varRecordSetName = "_rs_" & varTableName ' use for saving recordset object
pointer

'If IsObject(Session("_connSS")) Then
'    Set objConn = Session("_connSS")
'Else
      Set objConn = Server.CreateObject("ADODB.connection")
      objConn.IsolationLevel = adXactReadCommitted ' avoid dirty reads
      objConn.open "FiredUpInSQLServer", "sa"
      Set Session("_connSS") = objConn
'End If

If IsObject(Session(varRecordSetName)) Then
    Set objRecordSet = Session(varRecordSetName) ' used saved recordset
object if possible
    objRecordSet.Requery
Else
      varSql = "SELECT * FROM " & "[" & varTableName & "]" ' put brackets in
case table name has spaces, etc.
      Set objRecordSet = Server.CreateObject("ADODB.Recordset")
      ' in the next statement, note use of cursor and lock types
      objRecordSet.Open varSql, objConn, adOpenDynamic,   adLockOptimistic '
allow for updates
      Set Session(varRecordSetName) = objRecordSet

End If
%>
```

```
<TABLE BORDER=1 BGCOLOR=#ffffff CELLSPACING=0><FONT FACE="Arial"
COLOR=#000000>
<CAPTION><B><%=UCase(varTableName)%> (in SQL Server
Database)</B></CAPTION></FONT>
<THEAD>
<TR>
<%
varNumCols = objRecordSet.Fields.Count
For varI = 0 to varNumCols - 1
Set objField = objRecordSet.Fields(varI)
 %>
<TH BGCOLOR=#c0c0c0 BORDERCOLOR=#000000 ><FONT SIZE=2 FACE="Arial"
COLOR=#000000><%=objField.Name%></FONT> </TH>

<%
Next%>
</TR>
</THEAD>
<TBODY>
<%
On Error Resume Next
objRecordSet.MoveFirst
do while Not objRecordSet.eof
%>
<TR VALIGN=TOP>
<%
varNumCols = objRecordSet.Fields.Count
For varI = 0 to varNumCols - 1
Set objField = objRecordSet.Fields(varI)
If objField.Name <> varKeyName Then %>
<TD BORDERCOLOR=#c0c0c0 ><FONT SIZE=2 FACE="Arial"
COLOR=#000000><%=Server.HTMLEncode(objField.Value)%><BR></FONT></TD>
<%
End If
Next%>
</TR>

<%
objRecordSet.MoveNext
loop%>
<BR><BR><A HREF="FiredUpTablesSQLServer.asp">View Another Table</A>
</TBODY>
<TFOOT></TFOOT>
</TABLE>
</BODY>
</HTML>
```

C.   *Code an ASP page to enter new STOVE data. Justify your choice of cursor isolation.*

Here is a page to gather the stove data and invoke the page to make the update:

```
<HTML>
"
<HEAD>
"
```

```
<META HTTP-EQUIV="Content-Type" CONTENT="text/html;charset=windows-1252">
"
<TITLE>New STOVE Entry Form</TITLE>
"
</HEAD>
"
<BODY>
"


"
<FORM METHOD="post" ACTION="AddStoveSS.asp">
"


"
 <P><STRONG><FONT color=purple face="" size=5>   New Stove Data
Form</FONT></STRONG>
<P></P>

<P><FONT color=forestgreen face=""
style="BACKGROUND-COLOR:
#ffffff">Version:        
             
;   
<INPUT id=text2 name=version style="HEIGHT: 22px; WIDTH: 167px"
size="20"></FONT></P>

<P><FONT style="BACKGROUND-COLOR: #ffffff"><font
color="#008000">Type:</font>        &
nbsp;            
           <INPUT id=text3
name=type style="HEIGHT: 22px; WIDTH: 164px" size="20"></FONT></P>

<P><span style="background-color: #FFFFFF"><font color="#228B22">Date of
Manufacture</font></span><FONT color=forestgreen face=""
style="BACKGROUND-COLOR:
#ffffff">:        
<INPUT id=text4 name=doman style="HEIGHT: 22px; WIDTH: 167px"
size="20"></FONT></P>

<P> </P>

 <blockquote>

<P><FONT style="BACKGROUND-COLOR: #ffffff">
<INPUT id=submit1 name=submit1 type=submit value="Save New
Stove"></FONT><FONT style="BACKGROUND-COLOR: #ffffff">   
<INPUT id=reset1 name=reset1 type=reset value="Reset Values"></FONT></P>

 </blockquote>

<P><FONT style="BACKGROUND-COLOR: #ffffff">
    </FONT></P>
</FORM>
<p><FONT style="BACKGROUND-COLOR: #ffffff">
        </FONT></p>
</BODY>
</HTML>
```

Here is the page to make the update (SQL Server Version):

```
<HTML>
"
<HEAD>
"
<META HTTP-EQUIV="Content-Type" CONTENT="text/html;charset=windows-1252">
"
<TITLE>Add ARTIST Example</TITLE>
"
</HEAD>
"
<BODY>
"
<!--#include virtual="FiredUpSQLServer/adovbs.inc"-->
<%

Dim objConn, objRecordSet, objField
Dim varNumCols, varI, varSql

Set objConn = Server.CreateObject("ADODB.connection")
objConn.open "FiredUpInSQLServer", "sa"   ' open with sa
objConn.IsolationLevel = adXactReadCommitted ' avoid dirty reads

varSql = "SELECT * FROM [STOVE]"
Set objRecordSet = Server.CreateObject("ADODB.Recordset")
' in the next statement, note use of cursor and lock types
objRecordSet.Open varSql, objConn, adOpenForwardOnly, adLockOptimistic

objRecordSet.AddNew
objRecordSet("Type")= Request.Form("type")
objRecordSet("Version")= Request.Form("version")
objRecordSet("DateOfManufacture")= Request.Form("doman")

objRecordSet.Update

On Error Resume Next
varErrorCount = objConn.Errors.Count
If varErrorCount > 0 Then
      For varI = 0 to varErrorCount - 1
            Response.Write "<BR><I>" & objConn.Errors(varI).Description &
"</I><BR>"
      Next
End If

objRecordSet.Close
objConn.Close

Response.Write "<BR>Data has been added.  Thank you!<BR>"
Response.Write "<A HREF="& """" &"FiredUpStoveSQLServer.asp" & """"& ">See
New List</A>"

%>
<BR><BR>
</BODY>
```

```
</HTML>
```

No need for more than a forward only cursor.

D. *Code an ASP page to allow customers to register their own stoves. Justify your choice of cursor isolation.*

Here is the page to gather the data:

```
<HTML>
"
<HEAD>
"
<META HTTP-EQUIV="Content-Type" CONTENT="text/html;charset=windows-1252">
"
<TITLE>Registration Entry Form</TITLE>
"
</HEAD>
"
<BODY>
"

"
<FORM METHOD="post" ACTION="AddRegistrationSS.asp">

 <P><STRONG><FONT color=purple face="" size=5>   Customer
Registration Data Form</FONT></STRONG>
<P></P>

<P><span style="background-color: #FFFFFF"><font
color="#228B22">Name</font></span><FONT color=forestgreen face=""
style="BACKGROUND-COLOR:
#ffffff">:           &
nbsp;            
  
<INPUT id=text2 name=name style="HEIGHT: 22px; WIDTH: 167px"
size="20"></FONT></P>

<P><FONT style="BACKGROUND-COLOR: #ffffff"><font
color="#008000">Phone::</font>        
;            &nbs
p;     
<INPUT id=text3 name=phone style="HEIGHT: 22px; WIDTH: 164px"
size="20"></FONT></P>

<P><FONT color=forestgreen face=""
style="BACKGROUND-COLOR: #ffffff">E-mail
Address           &nbs
p;
<INPUT id=text4 name=email style="HEIGHT: 22px; WIDTH: 167px"
size="20"></FONT></P>

<P><FONT color=forestgreen face=""
style="BACKGROUND-COLOR: #ffffff">Stove Serial Number:   
```

```
<INPUT id=text5 name=serialnum style="HEIGHT: 22px; WIDTH: 167px"
size="20"></FONT></P>

 <blockquote>

<P><FONT style="BACKGROUND-COLOR: #ffffff">
<INPUT id=submit1 name=submit1 type=submit value="Register Your
Stove"></FONT><FONT style="BACKGROUND-COLOR: #ffffff">   
<INPUT id=reset1 name=reset1 type=reset value="Reset Values"></FONT></P>

 </blockquote>

<P><FONT style="BACKGROUND-COLOR: #ffffff">
    </FONT></P>
</FORM>
<p><FONT style="BACKGROUND-COLOR: #ffffff">
        </FONT></p>
</BODY>
</HTML>
```

Here is the page to make the update (SQL Server Version):

```
<HTML>
"
<HEAD>
"
<META HTTP-EQUIV="Content-Type" CONTENT="text/html;charset=windows-1252">
"
<TITLE>Add Registration</TITLE>
"
</HEAD>
"
<BODY>
"
<!--#include virtual="FiredUpSQLServer/adovbs.inc"-->
<%

Dim objConn, objRecordSet, objField
Dim varNumCols, varI, varSql
Dim cid, cname, phone, email

cname = Request.Form("name")
phone = Request.Form("phone")
email = Request.Form("email")
snum = Request.Form("serialnum")

Set objConn = Server.CreateObject("ADODB.connection")
objConn.open "FiredUpInSQLServer", "sa"  ' open with sa
objConn.IsolationLevel = adXactReadCommitted ' avoid dirty reads

varSql = "SELECT CustomerID, Name, Phone, EmailAddress FROM [CUSTOMER] WHERE
Name = '" + cname
varSql = varSQL + "' and phone = '" + phone + "' and EmailAddress = '" +
email + "'"
Set objRecordSet = Server.CreateObject("ADODB.Recordset")
' in the next statement, note use of cursor and lock types
```

```
objRecordSet.Open varSql, objConn, adOpenDynamic, adLockOptimistic

If objRecordSet.eof then
     objRecordSet.AddNew
     objRecordSet("Name")= cname
     objRecordSet("Phone")= phone
     objRecordSet("EmailAddress")= Request.Form("email")
     objRecordSet.Update
     objRecordSet.MoveFirst
     cid = objRecordSet("CustomerID")
%><CAPTION><B>Welcome to Fired Up! <%=cname%></B></CAPTION></FONT><%

Else
%><CAPTION><B>Welcome Back! <%=cname%></B></CAPTION></FONT><%
     cid = objRecordSet("CustomerID")
End If

varSql = "SELECT SerialNumber  FROM [STOVE] WHERE SerialNumber = " + snum
Set objRecordSet = Server.CreateObject("ADODB.Recordset")
' in the next statement, note use of cursor and lock types
objRecordSet.Open varSql, objConn, adOpenDynamic, adLockOptimistic

If objRecordSet.eof Then
%><CAPTION><B>  Invalid Serial Number, But Welcome to FiredUp,
Anyway</B></CAPTION></FONT><%
Else

     varSql = "SELECT CustomerID, SerialNumber, RDate FROM [REGISTRATION]
WHERE SerialNumber = " + cstr(snum)
     varSql = varSql + " AND CustomerID = " + cstr(cid)
     Set objRecordSet = Server.CreateObject("ADODB.Recordset")
     ' in the next statement, note use of cursor and lock types
     objRecordSet.Open varSql, objConn, adForwardOnly, adLockOptimistic

     objRecordSet.AddNew
     objRecordSet("CustomerID")= cid
     objRecordSet("SerialNumber")= snum
     objRecordSet("RDate") = Date
     objRecordSet.Update
     Response.Write "<BR>Registration data has been added.  Thank you!<BR>"
End If
On Error Resume Next
varErrorCount = objConn.Errors.Count
If varErrorCount > 0 Then
     For varI = 0 to varErrorCount - 1
          Response.Write "<BR><I>" & objConn.Errors(varI).Description &
"</I><BR>"
     Next
End If

objRecordSet.Close
objConn.Close

%> </font>
<BR><BR>
</BODY>
</HTML>
```

Forward only cursor is fine. Don't need to reprocess any rows.

E. *Create a stored procedure to enter new stove repair data.*

See the stored procedure named Record_Stove_Repair_Remote in the FiredUp SQL Server database on our Web site: www.prenhall/kroenke/.

F. *Code an ASP page to invoke the stored procedure created in task E, above. Use Figure 15-25 as an example.*

Here is the page to obtain the stove repair data:

```
<HTML>
<HEAD>
<META HTTP-EQUIV="Content-Type" CONTENT="text/html;charset=windows-1252">
<TITLE>New ARTIST Entry Form</TITLE>
</HEAD>
<BODY>

<FORM METHOD="post" ACTION="AddStoveRepair.ASP">

 <P><STRONG><FONT color=purple face="" size=5>   Enter Stove Repair
Data:</FONT></STRONG><P><FONT style="BACKGROUND-COLOR: #ffffff">
 <FONT color=forestgreen face=""
style="BACKGROUND-COLOR: #ffffff">Customer
Name:</FONT>        
<INPUT id=text1 name=custName style="HEIGHT: 22px; WIDTH: 164px"
size="20"></FONT></P>

<P><span style="background-color: #FFFFFF"><font color="#228B22">Customer
Phone:</font></span><FONT color=forestgreen face=""
style="BACKGROUND-COLOR:
#ffffff">        
<INPUT id=text2 name=custPhone style="HEIGHT: 22px; WIDTH: 167px"
size="20"></FONT></P>

<P><FONT style="BACKGROUND-COLOR: #ffffff"><font color="#228B22">Customer
Email:   
</font>      
<INPUT id=text3 name=custEmail style="HEIGHT: 22px; WIDTH: 164px"
size="20"></FONT></P>

<P><FONT color=forestgreen face=""
style="BACKGROUND-COLOR: #ffffff">Stove Serial Number:  
<INPUT id=text4 name=stoveSerial style="HEIGHT: 22px; WIDTH: 167px"
size="20"></FONT></P>

<P><font color="#008000"><span style="background-color: #FFFFFF">Repair
Description:</span></font><FONT style="BACKGROUND-COLOR:
#ffffff">     
<INPUT id=text5 name=repairDescription style="HEIGHT: 22px; WIDTH: 164px"
size="20"></FONT></P>
```

```
<P><FONT color=forestgreen face=""
style="BACKGROUND-COLOR: #ffffff">Repair
Cost:            
   
<INPUT id=text6 name=repairCost style="HEIGHT: 22px; WIDTH: 167px"
size="20"></FONT></P>

<P> </P>
 <blockquote>

<P><FONT style="BACKGROUND-COLOR: #ffffff">
<INPUT id=submit1 name=submit1 type=submit value="Record
Repair">           
</FONT><FONT style="BACKGROUND-COLOR: #ffffff">
<INPUT id=reset1 name=reset1 type=reset value="Reset Values"></FONT></P>
 </blockquote>

<P> </P>
</FORM>
</BODY>
</HTML>
```

Here is the page to invoke the stored procedure:

```
<HTML>
<HEAD>
<META HTTP-EQUIV="Content-Type" CONTENT="text/html;charset=windows-1252">
<TITLE>Customer Update Display Page</TITLE>

</HEAD>
<BODY>

<P><STRONG><FONT color=purple face="" size=5>   Stove Repair Data
After Update</FONT></STRONG>
<!--#include virtual="ViewRidgeExample1/adovbs.inc"-->
<%

        Dim objConn, objCommand, objParam, oRs
        Dim objRecordSet, objField
        Dim varI, varSql, varNumCols, varValue, result

        If IsObject(Session("_conn")) Then
                Set objConn = Session("_conn") ' use current session if available
        Else
                Set objConn = Server.CreateObject("ADODB.connection")
                ' stored procedure will set its own isolation level
                objConn.open "FiredUpInSQLServer", "sa" ' use this to update via
SQL Server
        Set Session("_conn") = objConn
        End If

        Set objCommand = Server.CreateObject("ADODB.Command") ' create a
command object
        Set objCommand.ActiveConnection = objConn ' set the command objects
connection
```

```
        objCommand.CommandText="{call Record_Stove_Repair_Remote (?, ?, ?, ?,
?, ?)}" ' setup call to stored procedure

        ' Set up input parameters with necessary values
        Set objParam = objCommand.CreateParameter("custName", adChar,
adParamInput, 50)
        objCommand.Parameters.Append objParam
        objParam.Value = Request.Form("custName")

        Set objParam = objCommand.CreateParameter("custPhone", adChar,
adParamInput, 12)
        objCommand.Parameters.Append objParam
        objParam.Value = Request.Form("custPhone")

        Set objParam = objCommand.CreateParameter("custEmail", adChar,
adParamInput, 50)
        objCommand.Parameters.Append objParam
        objParam.Value = Request.Form("custEmail")

        Set objParam = objCommand.CreateParameter("stoveSerial", adInteger,
adParamInput, 4)
        objCommand.Parameters.Append objParam
        objParam.Value = Request.Form("stoveSerial")

        Set objParam = objCommand.CreateParameter("repairDescription", adChar,
adParamInput, 100)
        objCommand.Parameters.Append objParam
        objParam.Value = Request.Form("repairDescription")

        Set objParam = objCommand.CreateParameter("repairCost", adCurrency,
adParamInput, 10)
        objCommand.Parameters.Append objParam
        objParam.Value = Request.Form("repairCost")

' Fire the Stored Proc

        Set oRs = objCommand.Execute
        ' now read the data

    varSql = "SELECT RepairInvoiceNumber, SerialNumber, RepairDate,
Description, Cost, CUSTOMER.Name, CUSTOMER.Phone "
    varSql = varSql + "FROM STOVE_REPAIR, CUSTOMER WHERE CUSTOMER.CustomerID
= STOVE_REPAIR.CustomerID" ' use view that joins via the intersection table
    Set objRecordSet = Server.CreateObject("ADODB.Recordset")
    objRecordSet.Open varSql, objConn
%>

<P> <P> <P> <TABLE BORDER=1 BGCOLOR=#ffffff
CELLSPACING=5><FONT FACE="Arial" COLOR=#000000><CAPTION><B><CUSTOMERS AND
INTERESTS</B></CAPTION></FONT>
<THEAD>
<TR>
<%
varNumCols = objRecordSet.Fields.Count
For varI = 0 to varNumCols - 1
Set objField = objRecordSet.Fields(varI)
%>
```

IM - 213

```
<TH BGCOLOR=#c0c0c0 BORDERCOLOR=#000000 ><FONT SIZE=2 FACE="Arial"
COLOR=#000000><%=objField.Name%></FONT> </TH>

<%
Next%>
</TR>
</THEAD>
<TBODY>
<%
On Error Resume Next
objRecordSet.MoveFirst
do while Not objRecordSet.eof
%>
<TR VALIGN=TOP>
<%
varNumCols = objRecordSet.Fields.Count
For varI = 0 to varNumCols - 1
Set objField = objRecordSet.Fields(varI)
%>
<TD BORDERCOLOR=#c0c0c0 ><FONT SIZE=2 FACE="Arial"
COLOR=#000000><%=SERVER.HTMLEncode(objField.Value)%><BR></FONT></TD>
<%
varValue=""
Next%>
</TR>

<%
objRecordSet.MoveNext
loop%>
</TBODY>
<TFOOT></TFOOT>
</TABLE>
</BODY>
</HTML>
```

Chapter 16

JDBC, Java Server Pages, and MySQL

Objectives

Regardless of whether the students know Java, they should:

- Learn the characteristics of JDBC and the four types of JDBC drivers
- Understand the nature of JSP and know the differences between JSP and ASP
- Learn the features and functions of MySQL and be able to compare MySQL with commercial products such as Oracle and SQL Server

If the students know Java, then the following objectives are achievable:

- Learn the interface to the mm.mysql drivers and be able to write Java programs to process a MySQL database
- Know how to code a JSP to process a MySQL database
- Learn how to code a Java bean and execute it from JSP

Teaching Suggestions

1. I attempted to write this chapter so that it could be read by Java programmers and also by those who do not know how to write in Java. If the students do not program in Java, this one chapter is not going to teach them. Even still, however, they should be able to learn how JSP and ASP differ. They should also be able to appreciate, in a general way, how the tasks that were performed with ADO and VBScript are accomplished using Java.

2. No knowledge of Java is required to understand the section on MySQL.

3. As the text indicates, MySQL lacks many features and functions. It is not comparable to Oracle and SQL Server. In spite of this, I think it is worthwhile to teach for a number of reasons. For one, it is an open source DBMS and some students may want to participate in its development at some point. Also, even with its limitations, MySQL can be used for many applications, and if the students are involved in low-budget development projects, it could be used to their advantage. Also, MySQL is quite effective in query-only applications.

    On the other hand, you can skip this material if you choose because no other section in the text depends on it.

4. If the students are Java programmers then it should be easy for them to extend these Java programs and JSP pages. One thing they might do is to change the code to handle exceptions better. Excellent documentation accompanies the mm.mysql drivers.

Students can use it to learn more about the interface to the JDBC drivers; there's a lot more than is shown in this text.

5. All of the code shown in this chapter was created and run on Linux. I used the IBM Java development kit and Tomcat as both a web server and servlet processor as mentioned in the text. I had a few installation problems (mostly getting directories set up), but everything worked great! It was also a lot of fun.

6. I tried to install Oracle on my Linux machine but gave up for lack of time and motivation. I'm told that it runs well and if you have philosophical difficulty teaching a product with the limitations of MySQL, you might try the Oracle installation. There are JDBC drivers for Oracle, but I don't know of any them that are free.

Answers to Group I Questions

16.1   *What is the one major requirement for using JDBC?*

Use Java.

16.2   *What does JDBC stand for?*

It just stands for JDBC.

16.3   *What are the four JDBC driver types?*

Types 1-4; see Figure 16-1.

16.4   *Explain the purpose of Type 1 JDBC drivers.*

To enable Java programs to use ODBC.

16.5   *Explain the purpose of Types 2 through 4 JDBC drivers.*

See Figure 16-1.

16.6   *Define applet and servlet.*

An applet is Java bytecode that runs on the user's computer, usually in a Java virtual machine that is provided with the user's browser.

16.7   *Explain how Java accomplishes portability.*

Java is compiled into machine-independent bytecode. Operating system vendors (and others) write bytecode interpreters on different machine types. Thus, the compiled bytecode can run on any computer that has a bytecode interpreter.

16.8   *List the four steps in using a JDBC driver.*

Load the drivers, obtain a connection, create a statement, do something with the statement.

16.9   Show the Java statement for loading the mm.mysql drivers used in this chapter.

Class.forName("org.gjt.mm.mysql.Driver").newInstance();

16.10   Show the Java statement for connecting to a database using the mm.mysql drivers.
Assume the database is named CustData, the user is Lew, and the password is Secret.

Connection conn DriverManager.getConnection
        ("jdbc:mysql://localhost/CustData?user=Lew&password=Secret")

16.11   Show the Java statement for creating a Statement object.

Statement stmt = conn.createStatement();

16.12   Show the Java statement for creating a ResultSet object that will display the Name and
Nationality of the ARTIST table using an already created statement object named S.

ResultSet myRs = s.executeQuery("SELECT Name, Nationality FROM ARTIST")

16.13   Show Java statements for iterating the resultset created in Question 16.12.

while (myRs.next()) {

        do something with myRs
}

16.13   Show the Java statement for executing an update to change the Nationality of an artist
named "Jones" to "French." Use an already created statement object named S.

int result = s.executeUpdate("UPDATE ARTIST SET Nationality='French' WHERE
Name='Jones'");

16.14   In Question 16.14, how can you determine if the update was successful?

After the statement runs, it has the number of rows updated. If it is zero, the update was
unsuccessful.

16.16   Show a Java statement for creating an object referencing metadata for the resultset
created in Question 16.12.

ResultSetMetaData rsMeta = myRs.getMetaData();

16.17   Show the Java statements necessary to invoke a stored procedure named
Customer_Delete. Assume the procedure has three parameters: CustomerName,
CustomerAreaCode, and CustomerPhoneNumber. Assume all of these are text
parameters.

Assuming conn points to a valid connection object:

CallableStatement cs = conn.prepareCall ("{call Customer_Delete", ?, ?, ?)}");
cs.setString (1, 'Mary Orange');

```
cs.setString (2, '206');
cs.setString (1, '555-1234');
cs.execute();
```

16.18 *What is the purpose of Java Server Pages?*

To provide machine-independent web server page processing using the Java language.

16.19 *Describe the differences between ASP and JSP pages.*

Active Server Pages are files of HTML and VBScript or JScript that are interpreted and processed by IIS under Windows NT. JSP are files of HTML and Java that are complied into Java bytecode and executed as Java servlets.

16.20 *Explain how JSP pages are portable.*

Because they are written in Java they are compiled into machine-independent bytecode.

16.21 *How it is possible that small segments of Java can be coded in JSP pages? Why are not complete Java programs required?*

Because they are parsed into subclasses of the HttpServlet class. All the missing headers, etc., to make a complete program are added by the parser.

16.22 *What is the purpose of Tomcat?*

It implements the Java servlet 2.1 and JSP 1.0 specifications. It can be used as a servlet processor in conjunction with a web server such as Apache, or it can be used as a (limited) web server as well as servlet processor.

16.23 *With the standard installation of Tomcat, what actions must be taken before using JSP pages that load JDBC classes?*

Place class libraries into /usr/local/jakarta-tomcat/lib and JSP pages into /usr/local/jakarta-tomcat/webapps/ROOT/WEB-INF/classes.

16.24 *When adding new class libraries for Tomcat to use, what must you do to place the library in Tomcat's CLASSPATH?*

Restart Tomcat.

16.25 *Describe the process by which JSP pages are compiled and executed. Can a user ever access an obsolete page? Why or why not?*

No, can never access an obsolete page. See the logic in Figure 16-5.

16.26 *Why are JSP programs preferable to CGI programs?*

Because only one copy of a JSP page is in memory for all users and because pages are executed by one of Tomcat's threads and not by an independent process.

16.27 *What conditions are necessary for a Java class to be a bean?*

No public instance variables, all persistent values are accessed via getxxx and putxxx and either the class has no constructors or it has one explicitly defined zero-argument constructor.

16.28 *Show the jsp directive to access a bean named CustomerDeleteBean. Give this bean the identity custdel.*

<jsp:useBean id="custdel' class ="CustomerDeleteBean"/>

16.29 *Show the jsp directives to set a bean property named Prop1 to the value of a form parameter named Param1.*

<jsp:setProperty name="custdel"
property = "Prop1"
value = '<%=request.getParameter("Param1")%>'/>

16.30 *Why is it advantageous to give object properties and form parameters the same names? Show a jsp directive to associate properties and parameters when this is the case.*

Advantageous because can use the following:

<jsp:setProperty name ="custdel" property="*"/>

to set the values of all parameters in the bean from the same-named form properties.

16.31 *What is the difference between invoking a bean from a pure Java program and invoking a bean from Java code in a JSP?*

There isn't any difference.

16.32 *Under what conditions would you choose to use MySQL?*

If my application did not need any of the features missing in MySQL. If I wanted to participate in the open source movement. If I had a query-only application. If I needed a free DBMS for a non-commercial application and was willing to work around any problems created by MySQL's missing features.

16.33 *For what type of workload does MySQL excel?*

Query-only processing.

16.34 *List the major limitations of MySQL.*

Does not enforce referential integrity, no transaction support, no roll back or roll forward, locking only at the table level, almost no utilities for recovery.

16.35 *How does MySQL 3.0 process referential integrity constraints?*

It doesn't.

16.36 *What statement do you use for creating a new table using MySQL?*

The SQL CREATE TABLE statement.

16.37 *What issue must be addressed when connecting to MySQL using JDBC?*

Cannot give permission using localhost even if Tomcat and MySQL are on the same machine. (It turns out this is due to an error in Linux. The workaround is to give permissions using % or using the IP address of the local machine.)

16.38 *Show the MySQL command for giving the user Lew permission to access any table in the database in the CustData database. Assume the password is Secret.*

GRANT ALL ON CustData.* TO Lew@"%" IDENTIFIED BY "Secret";

16.39 *Describe transaction management facilities in MySQL 3.0.*

There aren't any. Developer has to manage own locks.

16.40 *How does MySQL use shared read locks?*

It locks at the table level. Other users can read the table data, but no other user can update it.

16.41 *How does MySQL use exclusive update locks?*

It locks at the table level. No other user can read or update the table data.

16.42 *At what level does MySQL invoke locks? What are the advantages and disadvantages of this?*

At the table level. Easy for MySQL to administer, but can result in poor throughput.

16.43 *Show how an application could provide for transaction atomicity using LOCK TABLES and UNLOCK TABLES.*

See example on the bottom of page 507 and the top of 508.

16.44 *What is the disadvantage of the strategy used in your answer to Question 16.43?*

Throughput will be zero for other users while the locks are in place.

16.45 *Why is deadlock not possible with MySQL?*

Because locks must be obtained all at one time. All locks must be freed before additional locks can be obtained.

16.46 *Under what conditions are dirty reads possible with MySQL?*

If other users are performing their own rollback.

16.47 *Describe the MySQL facilities for backup.*

Minimal. There is a log of processed commands. The log does not contain any bulk changes made using files. There is a utility for backing up a file, but it's often better just to use the operating system's file copy utility.

16.48 *What are the limits on MySQL logging?*

Not a log of before and after images; rather a log of commands and work – bulk changes are logged as commands but the bulk data is not in the log.

16.49 *According to the author, why would one choose to use MySQL?*

If you want to support the open source movement; MySQL is easy and fun to use; if can work around missing features.

Answers to Group II Questions

16.50 *Compare and contrast ASP and JSP. Describe the relative strengths and weaknesses of each. Under what circumstances would you recommend one over the other? How important is portability for Web servers? How much of a disadvantage is it to be Microsoft dependent? Some people say preferring one over the other is more a matter of personal preference and values than anything else. Do you agree or disagree?*

The drawbacks to ASP are that it requires the use of Microsoft NT and that it does not directly support a fully featured object-oriented language like Java or C#. The drawbacks to JSP are that it requires the use of Java and it is not readily supported by Microsoft. I think it is mostly a religious issue – people don't change their web server operating system very frequently. Hard to go wrong betting on Microsoft technology, even when other technology is better. ASP is probably the safer choice. Still, JSP pages are great – especially for Java programmers.

16.51 *Rewrite the Java Bean shown in Figure 16-8 to use exceptions rather than the result return parameter. Modify the JSP page to correctly process this bean. In what ways is your bean better than the one in Figure 16-8?*

It is written in accordance with Java standards, it would be easier for most Java programmers to use, it could handle more comprehensive error conditions.

Answers to Projects Questions

Please see the website www.prenhall.com/kroenke for answers and supporting material for answers to the projects and FiredUp questions.

Chapter 17

Sharing Enterprise Data

Objectives

- Learn the different system architectures that can be used to support multi-user database processing and the advantages and disadvantages of each
- Understand the benefits and problems of downloading data
- Understand the nature and problems of distributed database processing
- Learn the purpose, characteristics, and basic terminology of OnLine Analytical Processing (OLAP)
- Learn the purpose, nature, and concepts of data warehousing and data marts
- Understand that organizational data is an asset that needs not only to be protected, but also to be effectively used
- Learn the scope, role, and basic functions of data administration

Teaching Suggestions

1. The chief difference between data and database administration is scope. Data administration is organization-wide; database administration is database wide.

2. Ask the students to think about ways in which data can be made more useful to decision makers. How can data be made more relevant? Think about a continuum of ways that data can be brought closer — downloading, data warehouses, etc.

3. If every department wants to download data, the management problems become immense. Data warehousing is an attempt to centralize and specialize the skills and facilities for bringing data closer to end users.

4. OLAP is becoming important for the analysis of operational data. The SQL Server OLAP tutorial is excellent and well worth having the students work through.

Answers to Group I Questions

17.1   *List the architectures that are used to support multi-user databases.*

Teleprocessing, client-server, file-processing, distributed, and Internet-technology (three-tier).

17.2   *Sketch the architecture of a teleprocessing system. Name and identify the computer(s) and programs involved, and explain which computer processes which programs.*

See Figure 17-1. All programs reside on the centralized computer: the application programs, the communications control programs (OS communications), the DBMS and the operating system.

17.3   *Why is the users' interface on teleprocessing applications generally character oriented and primitive?*

Limited processing power in dumb terminals.

17.4   *Sketch the architecture of a client–server system. Name and identify the computer(s) and programs involved, and explain which computer processes which programs.*

See Figure 17-2. Several client computers; one server computer, usually all are microcomputers. Application programs and OS_{net} client computers, OS_{net}, OS_{dm}, DBMS on server computer.

17.5   *What types of processing hardware are used with client–server systems?*

Usually, all personal computers. Can use mainframe as server, however.

17.6   *How many servers can a client–server system have? What restrictions apply to the servers?*

There can be many servers in a client-server system. Some of them may be non-database servers. If there is more than one database server, then the servers must process different databases.

17.7   *Sketch the architecture of a file-sharing system. Name and identify the computer(s) and programs involved, and explain which computer processes which programs.*

See Figure 17-3. Multiple computers, usually micros. One file server computer and multiple user computers. OS_{net}, DBMS, applications, all on user computers. OS_{net} and OS_{dm} on file server computer.

17.8   *Explain how the processing of the following SQL query would differ in a client–server system and in a file-sharing system:*

SELECT StudentName, ClassName
FROM STUDENT, GRADE
WHERE STUDENT.StudentNumber GRADE.StudentNumber
AND GRADE.Grade 'A'
Assume that the database contains two tables:
STUDENT (StudentNumber, StudentName, StudentPhone)
GRADE (ClassNumber, StudentNumber, Grade)
Also assume that the primary and foreign keys have indexes.

In a file-sharing system, all of the data would need to be downloaded onto the user's computer and the DBMS on that computer would process the SQL. In a client-server system, the raw data would remain on the server, the DBMS on the server would process the SQL, and only the results would be returned.

17.9 *Explain why file-sharing systems are seldom used for high-volume transaction processing applications.*

Because too much data must be sent from the server to the user computer.

17.10 *Define the terms partitioned and replicated as they pertain to distributed database applications.*

Partitioned data refers to sections or pieces of the database that are distributed on different computers. Replicated refers to whether or not data is duplicated on more than one computer.

17.11 *Explain the difference between a vertical fragment and a horizontal fragment.*

A vertical fragment refers to a table that is split into two more or tables by columns; a horizontal fragment refers to a table that is split into two or more tables by rows.

17.12 *Explain the differences in the four types of distributed databases in Figure 17-5.*

See the discussion of Figures 17-5 and 17-6.

17.13 *Name and describe three techniques for supporting distributed database processing.*

Read only distributed databases where no computer can update the data.
Single update site databases where data can be updated only by specified computers.
Distributed update databases where data can be updated by many nodes.

17.14 *Describe three types of distributed update conflict.*

Loss of uniqueness, distributed lost update, update on data that is deleted by another computer.

17.15 *What is the purpose of two-phase commit?*

It allows an update to be committed only when all nodes can successfully process the update.

17.16 *Summarize the coordination problem in processing downloaded databases.*

See Figure 17-9.

17.17 *Summarize the consistency problem in processing downloaded databases.*

See Figure 17-9

17.18 *Summarize the access control problem in processing downloaded databases.*

See Figure 17-9.

17.19 *Why is computer crime a risk when processing downloaded databases?*

See Figure 17-9.

17.20 *Sketch the components of a system that uses a Web server to publish downloaded data.*

See Figure 17-10.

17.21 *What is an OLAP cube? Give an example other than the one in Figure 17-12.*

An OLAP cube is a presentation having axes on which dimensions are placed. Measures of data to be displayed are organized within the dimensions on the axes. Slices are cuts through the data made by holding certain data values constant. A cube of class data having years and quarters on the vertical axis, departments and professors on the horizontal axis, and average number of students per class as a measure. Slices could be undergraduate and graduate classes.

17.22 *Explain the difference between an OLAP axis and an OLAP dimension.*

An axis is a physical construct; a dimension is a semantic construct taken from the data.

17.23 *What is the measure of an OLAP cube?*

The measure is the item to be displayed; measures are often aggregates of data.

17.24 *What does the term slice mean in reference to OLAP cubes?*

One or more data values that are held constant in an OLAP presentation.

17.25 *What is a member of a dimension? Give examples for Time and Location dimensions.*

A member is a value of a dimension that is displayed on an axis. Members of Time are 1999, 2000, 2001, 2002; members of Location are USA, Canada, Mexico, Brazil, Chile, and Argentina.

17.26 *Explain the use of levels in Figure 17-12.*

Levels are shown for the time and the geographic dimensions. Time levels are year, quarter, month; geographic levels are state, city.

17.27 *Explain the ambiguity in the term cube.*

The term is used to refer to the construct having certain dimensions, levels, and measures and is also used to refer to a particular materialization of a cube construct.

17.28 *What is the result of the expression CROSSJOIN ({Mary, Lynda}, {Sailing, Skiing})? Of CROSSJOIN ({Sailing, Skiing}, {Mary, Lynda})?*

Mary		Lynda	
Sailing	Skiing	Sailing	Skiing

and

Sailing		Skiing	
Mary	Lynda	Mary	Lynda

17.29 *Give an SQL SELECT statement to produce a cube similar to that in Figure 17-12 except that the rows and columns are reversed and Location is presented before Category (when reading left to right).*

      SELECT   CROSSJOIN ({California.Children, Nevada}, {Existing Structure, New Structure}) ON ROWS,
                       {2000.Q1.Children, 2000.Q2, 2000.Q3, 2000.Q4, 2001.Q1.Children, 2001.Q2, 2001.Q3, 2001.Q4} ON COLUMNS
      FROM   HousingSalesCube
      WHERE   (SalesPrice, HousingType = 'SingleFamily')

17.30 *Explain the difference between the star and the snowflake schemas.*

In a star, all dimension tables are adjacent to the table containing the measure. Dimension tables may or may not be normalized. In a snowflake, some dimension tables may be two or three tables away from the measure table. Dimension tables are normally normalized in this case.

17.31 *Define ROLAP, MOLAP, and HOLAP.*

Relational OLAP, Multi-dimensional OLAP, Hybrid OLAP. Using a relational DBMS to support OLAP; using a purpose-built engine to support OLAP, using both.

17.32 *Considering the discussion in this text only, how has OLE been extended for OLAP?*

An abstraction of a cube called a *dataset* has been created on top of the rowset abstraction. Methods and properties have been defined for datasets.

17.33 *What does ADO MD stand for and what is its function?*

ADO MD is ADO for multi-dimensional (or OLAP) processing. Dataset methods and properties have been defined and exposed through ADO MD.

17.34 *Define data warehouse.*

A store of enterprise data that is designed to facilitate management decision making.

17.35 *How does having a data warehouse compare to processing downloaded data?*

Processing downloaded data must be done on a department by department basis. A data warehouse is a centralized resource for solving the problem using specialized programs, resources, and personnel.

17.36 *List and describe the components of a data warehouse.*

See Figure 17-19.

17.37 *Explain what it means to change the structure of a query or report rather than change the data in a query or report.*

When the reporting requirements change, the contents, sorting, or grouping of the report changes. This differs from printing the same report over different data.

17.38 *Give an example, other than one in this book, of a user's need to aggregate data.*

In a law firm, aggregate client billings into a client total or aggregate subject matter billings into a subject matter total.

17.39 *Give an example, other than one in this book, of a user's need to drill down data.*

In a construction company, drill down project data into building construction data, into floor construction data, into room construction data.

17.40 *Explain two sources of data inconsistencies, and give an example, other than one in this book, of each.*

Timing inconsistencies and domain inconsistencies. Timing: In a software development project, equipment costs are by week; personnel costs are by payment period. The two may differ in ways that become important when they are combined. Domain: Two sets of data may have different department name domains — one set is before a company reorganization and another is after a company reorganization.

17.41 *Summarize the problems of having tools that use different paradigms and are licensed by different vendors.*

Tools that have different paradigms will have different user interfaces that may be very difficult to reconcile. Those that are licensed by different vendors may have interfaces that do not work well together or in which it is difficult to get customer support.

17.42 *Explain which data warehouse tools must be written in-house.*

Those that cannot be purchased outside — particularly those for managing the warehouse meta-data and data from different DBMS products and from different data sources.

17.43 *Why does the ad hoc nature of data warehouse requests pose a problem?*

Information systems are structured and respond best to requests that follow a pattern.

17.44 *What is a data mart, and why would a company develop one?*

A data mart is a data warehouse for a restricted domain.

17.45 *List and briefly explain three types of data marts.*

Restricted to: particular data inputs, particular business functions, particular business units.

17.46 *Explain why data are an important organizational asset.*

Data is not only used for operational purposes, but it can be used for management decision making as well. Data characteristics of the organization; information is knowledge produced from data about those characteristics. Such information becomes more valuable all of the time.

17.47 *Describe several example uses of data besides operational systems.*

Sales trend analysis, employee effectiveness assessment, simulation of changes in organization and products.

17.48 *How is data administration similar to the job of a controller?*

Not only protect the data resource, but also invest it for maximum return to the company.

17.49 *Briefly summarize the necessity for data administration.*

Without it, data anarchy rules. What data exists, what format does it have, how is it to be protected, how should it be used, etc., are questions that go unanswered without data administration.

17.50 *List and briefly explain the challenges of data administration.*

See Figure 17-25.

17.51 *Describe data administration's marketing function.*

See Figure 17-26.

17.52 *What role does data administration take with regard to data standards?*

See Figure 17-26.

17.53 *Define data proponent.*

The department or individual that manages the official definition and format for a data item.

17.54 *What is the difference between data proponent and data owner?*

None. Data owner just sounds too possessive.

17.55 *Summarize data administration's role in regard to data policy.*

See discussion on pages 545 and 546.

17.56 *Explain what is involved in establishing a forum for conflict resolution.*

See discussion on page 546.

17.57 *How can data administration help increase the return on an organization's data asset?*

It can do this by ensuring that the organization takes steps not only to protect its data, but also to ensure that the data is effectively utilized. The analogy with finance is a good one: financial resources need to be not just accounted for and protected, but also well utilized. Use the items in Figure 17-26 as a list for potential ideas. Make sure employees and others know that organizational data administration exists, provide tools and training for using the data resources, provide a forum for the submission of needs for changes and for new information needs, develop data marts and a data warehouse as appropriate.

Answers to Group II Questions

17.58 *Consider a company that has a national sales manager and 15 regional salespeople. Each week, the salespeople download sales data from the mainframe and use it to update their sales projections for the next month. When they have done this, they connect via a modem to a server database and store their sales projections into that database. The manager then accumulates the sales data into a companywide forecast. What problems, issues, and difficulties might exist in this situation in terms of coordination, consistency, access control, and computer crime?*

This is a good question for class. Use the discussion of these problems in the text as a guideline for an answer. Here are some ideas: Assuming that IS always produces the data for download correctly, one problem is that the salespeople obtain it at different times and thus have inconsistency of different versions. They probably will not always place their projections into the database on time, and the manager needs to know this – otherwise partial projections will be a problem. Can the salespeople obtain each other's data? If so, will management problems be created? If not, what if they have a legitimate need for each other's data? Considering crime, it would be easy for a salesperson to sell data to competitors or other vendors. Here's a problem that might be new to students. Financial analysts that follow a stock closely will often call salespeople to find out how their quarter is going. Even though the salespeople are trained not to reveal this information, they often do, even unknowingly. Empowering the salespeople with tools like this increases the risk of this problem – and the attendant risk of a shareholder lawsuit or problem with the SEC.

17.59 *Consider the enterprise data that exist at your college or university. Does it seem to you that your institution makes good use of its data asset? What ways can you identify that the data asset is used for more than operational processing? Describe ways in which you think your college or university could take advantage of its data asset in the areas of*
  ➢ *Student recruitment*
  ➢ *Fund-raising*
  ➢ *Program planning*
  ➢ *Student affairs*

➢   *Alumni affairs*
➢   *Other areas.*

The answer depends on the situation at your college or university.

Chapter 18

Object-Oriented Database Processing

Objectives

- Describe the characteristics of object oriented programming and the necessity for object databases and ODBMS
- Understand the advantages and disadvantages of object persistence via traditional file processing, relational database processing, and ODBMS processing
- Learn the structures used in an Oracle object-relational database
- Learn the prominent characteristics of SQL3 and understand how objects are bound to relations
- Learn the prominent characteristics of the ODMB proposed standard

Teaching Suggestions

1. The approach that you take with this chapter depends how much object oriented programming your students know. If they have done OOP, then you can start immediately with the problems of object persistence. If not, you'll have to teach object programming ideas for the students to be able to understand the need for object persistence.

2. The SQL committee had a problem in that they needed to make the SQL3 standard upward compatible with SQL-92. This forced the committee to make objects (or ADTs) an extension of relations. SQL3 seems to me to effectively meet that requirement. Whether or not SQL3 becomes important depends, of course, on whether any vendors pay attention to it. See suggestion 4, below.

3. The ODMG Committee was able to start with a clean slate. They did not need to consider migration from the relational model, so their proposal is pure object thinking. Since today's ODBMS products are much closer to the ODMG model than to SQL3, it is likely that it will be a more important standard.

4. I wonder how important standards are today. Oracle and Microsoft are so powerful and influential that it seems that they force standards by the products and architectures they develop or endorse. There may be niches in which ODMG or SQL3 are important, but until there are viable products, it's all just talk. You might discuss this situation with your students.

5. I believe Oracle has done quite a good job of grafting object structures onto a relational DBMS. They've provided sufficient capability for industry to try out these new ideas. They can then respond to industry demand for more object-oriented facilities. As of June, 2001, Microsoft has not responded with similar capabilities in SQL Server. I would guess they must respond, however, in the next version SQL Server 2002?

Answers to Group I Questions

18.1   *Explain how object-oriented programming differs from traditional programming.*

Objects are data structures that have both data attributes and procedures (methods). Object programming differs in design in that, rather than start with programming logic, designers start first with objects, determine their interface, and then their implementation. Cohesion should be much better in OOP.

18.2   *Why are relational databases more popular than object databases today?*

They are more common, far more data is in relational format, practitioners are more familiar and comfortable with relational databases.

18.3   *Define an OOP object.*

An OOP object is an encapsulated structure having both attributes and methods.

18.4   *Define the terms encapsulated, attribute, and method.*

Encapsulated means that an object is complete in itself; programs external to the object need know nothing about the object's internal structure to interface with it. An attribute is a data element of an object; a method is a program associated with an object.

18.5   *Explain the difference between an interface and an implementation.*

The external appearance of an object is its interface — it consists of public attributes and public methods. An implementation is the encapsulated internals of the object. An object would have just one interface but could, conceivably, have many implementations.

18.6   *What is inheritance?*

Objects can be arranged in a supertype, subtype hierarchy. An object inherits the attributes and methods of its supertypes.

18.7   *What is polymorphism?*

Polymorphism occurs when the same name is used to refer to different methods in an object hierarchy. The compiler invokes the correct method depending on the type of object that is being called.

18.8   *Define the terms object class, object class library, and object instance.*

An object class is the logical structure of an object; a class library is a group of object classes; an object instance is a particular object — including particular data elements and the methods of the class.

18.9   *Explain the function of object constructors and object destructors.*

Object constructors obtain memory and create the structures necessary to instantiate a new object. Object destructors unbind object and free memory.

18.10   *Explain the difference between a transient object and a persistent object.*

A transient object exists only in transient memory and lasts only as long as a program is in execution. A persistent object is stored on disk and survives the termination of a program.

18.11   *Explain the difference in the notation CUSTOMER!Find and CUSTOMER.ZipCode.*

The first expression invokes the Find member of CUSTOMER and the second refers to the ZipCode data attribute of CUSTOMER.

18.12   *What is the function of the keyword NOTHING in Figure 18-3?*

It can be used to determine if a pointer to an object is null.

18.13   *What is the function of the keyword ME in Figure 18-3?*

It can be used to qualify references to methods or attributes or to refer to the current object instance that is running.

18.14   *What is a callback, and why is one used?*

A callback is a means by which an object registers itself with another object; callbacks are used for many purposes — one of which is to allow an object to free its reference to another object before the second object destroys itself.

18.15   *What does the term swizzling refer to?*

It refers to the process of converting an in-memory address to a permanent identifier (and sometimes to the reverse process as well).

18.16   *Briefly explain what tasks are required to use traditional file storage for object persistence.*

See Figure 18-8, column three.

18.17   *Briefly explain what tasks are required to use a relational DBMS for object persistence.*

See Figure 18-8, column two.

18.18   *Summarize the advantages and disadvantages of using an ODBMS for object persistence.*

Designed for OOP so easy to use, easy to invoke, swizzling is automatic, performance is tuned for OOP. However, not much data is in this format, few know how to use ODBMS products, lack of query and reporting facilities, performance is unknown for large-scale database transaction processing.

18.19 *Show the Oracle statements to define an object type named Pname having three attributes: FirstName, MiddleName, and LastName. Use this type as a column object in a table called PERSON.*

```
CREATE TYPE Pname AS OBJECT (
      FirstName     CHAR(25),
      MiddleName    CHAR(25),
      LastName      CHAR(50));


CREATE TABLE PERSON (
      Name          Pname);
```

18.20 *Show Oracle statements to create a variable array of up to 100 Pnames. Show statements to create a table named CLUB1 with a surrogate key, a ClubName and the variable array attribute of person names.*

```
CREATE TYPE PERSON_LIST AS VARRAY(100) OF PName;
CREATE TABLE     CLUB1 (
      ClubID          NUMBER,
      ClubName        CHAR(25),
      Members         PERSON_LIST);
```

18.21 *Show Oracle statements to create a CLUB2 table as in Question 18.20, but use a nested table of person names instead of a variable array. Name the storage table Pname_Table.*

```
CREATE PERSON_LIST2 AS TABLE OF PName;
CREATE TABLE      CLUB2          (
      ClubID                    NUMBER,
      ClubName                  CHAR(25),
      Members                   PERSON_LIST2)
      NESTED TABLE Members   STORE AS Pname_Table;
```

18.22 *Explain the differences between table CLUB1 and table CLUB2.*

UPDATE and DELETE only work with nested tables. No maximum size on the nested table; no more than 100 names in the VARRAY. VARRAY data stored with the CLUB1 data; nested table Pname_Table stored separately.

18.23 *Show Oracle statements to create a table having Pname as a row object.*

CREATE TABLE PERSONS OF Pname;

18.24 *Explain the purpose of the REF attributes in Figure 18-19. How do these attributes differ from foreign keys?*

REF is a system-supplied reference to another object. Oracle handles swizzling so it can be a memory or disk reference. Differences: REF values are hidden from users; have no user meaning. REF values can become invalid and must be tested; refs point to objects not table rows; and references are one-way.

18.25 *Explain the purposes of the following two statements:*
   a.   FOR i in 1 SELF Lineitems COUNT LOOP
   b.   UTI_REF SELECT_OBJECT (LineItems(i). Item Ref, ItemPtr)

The purpose of a. is just to iterate through all of the line items in an order. The second obtains the value of a reference and places it in the variable ItemPtr.

18.26 *What is SQL3?*

An extension to the SQL-92 standard that incorporates object persistence; it is upwardly compatible with the SQL-92 standard.

18.27 *What is an abstract data type (ADT)?*

A user-defined structure that has methods, data items, and persistent identifiers; equivalent to an object.

18.28 *Explain the difference between an object ADT and a value ADT.*

An Object ADT is an identifiable, independent data structure that can be referred to by its identifier. A value ADT has no identifier and can only be referred to via a table or a function — depending on how it was created.

18.29 *What is an OID? How can one be used?*

An OID is a pointer to an object ADT. An OID can be used to provide a reference to an object instance.

18.30 *Explain what the DBMS must do when executing the following SQL on the ADT in Figure 18-13:*

SELECT DeptName, Manager.Phone, Admin.Phone
FROM Dept

Returns DeptName by accessing the row of DEPT, returns Manager.Phone by following the OID that is stored to refer to Manager. The instance of Admin that has been stored as part of the Dept row will be used to return Admin.Phone.

18.31 *What happens when the following SQL is executed on the ADT in Figure 18-13:*

UPDATE Dept
SET Manager.Name "John Jacob Astor"

The name of the employee who is the manager of each department will be set to John Jacob Astor. The manager of every department will have this name, although the instances of the managers of the department will be unchanged.

18.32 *Code SQL that would need to be executed to change the instance of the manager of a department for the ADT in Figure 18-13.*

See UPDATE example on page 576.

18.33 *What is a row identifier in SQL3?*

A row identifier is what we have called a surrogate key in this text. It is a unique identifier for a row of a table.

18.34 *Explain the differences among a SET, MULTISET, and LIST in SQL3.*

A set is a table with no duplicate rows; a multiset is a table with duplicate rows; a list is a table that has an order defined by one or more columns.

18.35 *Explain the differences among a subtable, a supertable, and a table.*

A subtable is a subset of another table. A supertable is a table that has at least one subtable. A table is a relation that is one of the three types SET, MULTISET, LIST.

18.36 *What is ODMG-93?*

The ODMG-93 is a definition of interfaces for object data management products.

18.37 *List the five core concepts in ODMG-93.*

See Figure 18-17.

18.38 *What is the difference between a type and a class in ODMG-93?*

A class is a logical group of objects; it is an interface. A type is an implementation of a class in a particular language.

18.39 *What is the difference between a property and an attribute in ODMG-93?*

A property can be either a data attribute or a relationship; an attribute is a data value.

18.40 *What is an extent?*

The set of all instances of an object (class or type).

18.41 *What are the properties of a class in ODMG-93?*

Properties are either a data attribute or a relationship.

18.42 *In the ODMG standard, what values can properties have?*

Data values or relationships to other objects.

18.43 *In the ODMG standard, what values can attributes have?*

Data values, only.

18.44 *In the ODMG standard, what values can relationship properties have?*

Connections between objects.

18.45 *Why is method persistence important? Give an example of a problem that can occur when such persistence is not provided.*

If method persistence is not supported, two objects that were created or changed by different versions of a method would appear the same, but would not necessarily be logically the same.

18.46 *Explain how semantic objects conform to the ODMG standard and how they do not.*

Like ODMG, the properties of a semantic object are either data value or relationships. They can be either singular or plural. In SOM, relationships are always binary; in ODMG, they need not necessarily be binary. SOM has little provision for methods.

Answers to Group II Questions

18.47 *Review the requirements and relational design for View Ridge Gallery in Chapter 10. Consider the use of Oracle types and column, vararrays, nested tables, and row objects in the context of View Ridge's needs. What changes would you make to the relational design? Would you recommend replacing TRANSACTION or WORK tables with vararrays or nested tables? If so, how? If not, why not? Show how you could use Oracle REF data types to eliminate the need for the intersection table. Would you recommend this course of action?*

First, there are many possible changes to utilize Oracle's object-relational structures. It is not clear, at least from what is given about View Ridge in the text, that any of these changes are required or even desirable. And this, really, brings to light the problem DBMS vendors have. If an organization has a working database and applications, why change?

Anyway, we could replace the TRANSACTION table with either a vararray or a nested table – and such a structure could be placed in either WORK or CUSTOMER tables. I think I would choose to place it in CUSTOMER, using a REF back to the WORK row. This would mean that we would also need to put a vararray or nested table of REFs back to CUSTOMER in WORK. Again, I'm not sure this is worth it.

We can eliminate the intersection table by placing a vararray or nested table of REFs to ARTIST in CUSTOMER and a similar structure of REFs to CUSTOMER in ARTIST.

18.48 *Consider Oracle types, vararrays, and nested tables in the context of the semantic object model. Which elements of that model lend themselves to types? To vararrays? To nested tables? Show how you would use Oracle object-relational facilities to model each of the types of semantic objects described in Chapter 7.*

The fit is straightforward and easy. Any multi-value simple value or group attribute can be replaced by either a vararray or nested table. Any object link attribute can be replaced by a REF. If the object link attribute is multi-valued then it could be replaced by a vararray or nested table of REFs. A general rule is: if the maximum cardinality of an attribute is set to a specific number, such as 5 or 7, then use a vararray of that length. If, on the other hand, the max cardinality is n, then use a nested table.
Use the statement above for each of the types of semantic object. Simple is the same as shown in the text. For composite, replace multi-value attributes as above. For each of the remaining types, replace object links with REFs (on both sides of the object relationship). Subtypes do not have a direct representation using Oracle object-relation structures.

Appendix A

Data Structures for Database Processing

Answers to Selected Group I Questions

A.1   A flat file is a file in which the records have no repeating groups. Examples will vary with students, but one might be an Employee file containing no repeating groups; a non-flat file might be an Employee file containing repeating fields for employee deductions.

Flat file:

Emp#	Name	Title
107	Ahalt	Instructor
109	Wampler	Instructor
215	Meyers	Professor
350	Ko	Professor

Non-flat file:

Emp#	Name	Deductions
107	Ahalt	Insurance 35 Retirement 30 Savings 45
109	Wampler	Insurance 40 Savings 50
215	Meyers	
350	Ko	Savings 50

A.2   Two files are required, one sorted on Emp#, the other on Name:

Emp#	Name	Title
107	Ahalt	Instructor
109	Wampler	Instructor
215	Meyers	Professor
350	Ko	Professor

Emp#	Name	Title
107	Ahalt	Instructor

350	Ko	Professor
215	Meyers	Professor
109	Wampler	Instructor

A.3   Store the file in Emp# order, and use linked list to keep the file in order by name:

Emp#	Name	Title	Link
107	Ahalt	Instructor	4
109	Wampler	Instructor	Null
215	Meyers	Professor	2
350	Ko	Professor	3

Start of alphabetic list = 1

A.4   The data would be stored as in Question A.3, but there would be no link field. This would be the inverted list:

Ahalt	1
Ko	4
Meyers	3
Wampler	2

A.5   A tree is a set of records and one-to-many relationships in which a child can have at most one parent. An example is a checking account (parent) that has many deposits (children) and checks (children).

```
           ACCOUNT
   1:N                   1:N
 DEPOSIT               CHECK
```

A.6

ACCOUNT 123

DEP 188   DEP 243   CHK 455   CHK456   CHK457

A.9   A simple network is a set of records and relationships in which all relationships are one-to-many, but a child can have more than one parent if they are different record types. An example is the relationships among salesperson (parent), customer (parent), and invoice (child).

```
 SALESPERSON                    CUSTOMER
           INVOICE
```

IM - 240

A.16 A primary key is normally used to determine where a record is stored. The primary key is the key by which the record is normally accessed. Primary keys are unique. Secondary keys are other fields whose values may be used to access the record. Secondary keys can be unique or non-unique. If the secondary key is non-unique it can be used to access groups of records that contain the same value for the key.

A.17 With a unique key only one record can have a specific key value; each key value must be unique within the file. Non-unique keys do not have to have different values. Multiple records can have the same value for a non-unique key.

A.18

Note: this Student file will be used for Questions A.18, A.19, and A.20.

RRN	Number	Name	Major
1	1234	Joanie Wampler	Acct
2	2311	Jon Miley	Comp
3	3451	Jersey Eng	Acct
4	3561	Sandy Merrow	Comp
5	4566	Bob Adams	Acct

The primary key is Number. The unique secondary key is Name. The non-unique secondary key is Major. Unique secondary key represented via inverted list:

Name	RRN
Bob Adams	5
Jersey Eng	3
Sandy Merrow	4
Jon Miley	2
Joanie Wampler	1

A.19

RRN	Number	Name	Major	Major Link
1	1234	Joanie Wampler	Acct	3
2	2311	Jon Miley	Comp	4
3	3451	Jersey Eng	Acct	5
4	3561	Sandy Merrow	Comp	Null
5	4566	Bob Adams	Acct	Null

Head Acct = 1
Head Comp = 2

A.20

Major	Addr	Addr	Addr	Addr
Acct	1	3	5	Null
Comp	2	4	Null	Null

Appendix B

Working with Tabledesigner

Tabledesigner is very easy to use for creating both Access and SQL Server databases. Even if you do not have time to use the ASP generation facilities of Tabledesigner, be sure to have the students use it to create tables. They will find it much faster than using the native DBMS table generation facilities.

One of the best features of Tabledesigner is its database migration capability. You can create a database, fill it with data, and then change the model. Both the schema and the underlying data will be changed. For example, you can reverse engineer Northwind (or even better, just take the Suppliers and Products tables). Create a copy database using either Access or SQL Server. Tabledesigner will create a 1:N relationship between Suppliers and Products in the new database because that's what it will find in the key structure. You can then change the relationship to N:M and Tabledesigner will modify the underlying database to create the intersection table and fill it with data — correctly using the data that was already in the tables.

Answers to Exercises

B.1　This model is located on www.prenhall.com/kroenke/ under the name Fig413.apm. Copy it down and save under a new name. Say No to use existing databases if you are asked so that you can create new databases.

B.2　Make up your own tables or use the example in the answers to questions 4.15 to 4.19.

B.3　It is interesting to generate this model and see how many tables are created. This will illustrate the power of working with a tool from a higher-level model than working at the table level.

B.4　Even if you do not have time to assign the exercise to the students, it's well worth demonstrating it in the lab. The hardest part is setting IIS on NT. As of spring, 1999, make sure you have NT Server with Service Pack 4 installed. Using the IIS Manager to mark the root directory (or a new one you create) as Execute and enable ASP processing. If you try to run the application and the JScript shows up in the browser, that means that IIS does not think the directory is marked for executing script. Make sure when you use the Tabledesigner publishing wizard that you place your pages in a directory subordinate to the InetPub or whatever other directory you have created.

A good demonstration is to reverse the Supplier and Products tables of Northwind as described above and then do query by form. Query on products having more than UnitsInStock with a supplier name of New*. Tabledesigner will create the underlying in SQL. Then, change the max cardinality of Supplier (in Products) and regenerate the pages (if you didn't use the Exit button when you exited the browser, IIS will have a lock on the pages for 20 min (the default). So, when you regenerate, put the pages in a different directory.

B.5   Here is the model during the reverse engineering process:

Here is the revision to the model:

Here is the SQL Server database after Tabledesigner has created the new intersection table between titles and publishers:

B.6 This is straightforward. You might have to show the students how to use the generated pages to create relationships. (The browser help is pretty good — have them look there as well.)

Test Item File

DATABASE PROCESSING

CHAPTER 1

Introduction to Database Processing

True-False Questions

1.   The purpose of a database is to help people keep track of things.
     Answer: True   *Level: easy*
     Section: Four Database Examples

2.   It is the job of a program called a Data Building Model System to store and retrieve data in the database tables.
     Answer: False   *Level: moderate*
     Section: Four Database Examples
     Subsection: Mary Richards Housepainting

3.   Multi-user databases are less complicated than single-user databases because the work is distributed to many people.
     Answer: False   *Level: moderate*
     Section: Four Database Examples
     Subsection: Treble Clef Music

4.   Multi-user databases are more complicated than single-user databases because they must prevent one user's work from interfering with another's.
     Answer: True   *Level: easy*
     Section: Four Database Examples
     Subsection: Treble Clef Music

5.   Large organizational databases were the first applications of database technology.
     Answer: True   *Level: moderate*
     Section: Four Database Examples
     Subsection: State Licensing and Vehicle Registration Bureau

6.   In database application processing, business users interact directly with database applications, which directly access the database data.
     Answer: False   *Level: hard*
     Section: The Relationship of Application Programs and the DBMS

7.   In database application processing, business users interact directly with the DBMS, which directly accesses the database data.
     Answer: False   *Level: hard*
     Section: The Relationship of Application Programs and the DBMS

8.   In database application processing, business users interact directly with database applications that interact with the DBMS, which directly accesses the database data.
     Answer: True   *Level: hard*
     Section: The Relationship of Application Programs and the DBMS

9.   In most modern DBMS products, the DBMS itself can process a significant portion of the database application.
       Answer: True   *Level: moderate*
       Section: The Relationship of Application Programs and the DBMS

10.   Databases were used by the first business information systems.
       Answer: False   *Level: easy*
       Section: File-Processing Systems

11.   Business information systems that stored groups of records in separate files were called file-processing systems.
       Answer: True   *Level: easy*
       Section: File-Processing Systems

12.   One advantage of file-processing systems is that application programs are dependent on the file formats.
       Answer: False   *Level: moderate*
       Section: File-Processing Systems

13.   The most serious problem with duplicated data in a file-processing system is the massive amounts of wasted storage space.
       Answer: False   *Level: easy*
       Section: File-Processing Systems
       Subsection: Data Duplication

14.   If a collection of data is logically consistent, it is said to have "integrity".
       Answer: True   *Level: easy*
       Section: File-Processing Systems
       Subsection: Data Duplication

15.   Data integrity can be improved by increasing the number of locations in which it is duplicated.
       Answer: False   *Level: moderate*
       Section: File-Processing Systems
       Subsection: Data Duplication

16.   Data integrity is only an issue with database systems, not file-processing systems.
       Answer: False   *Level: moderate*
       Section: File-Processing Systems
       Subsection: Data Duplication

17.   In file-processing systems, the physical formats of the files and records are part of the application code.
       Answer: True   *Level: easy*
       Section: File-Processing Systems
       Subsection: Application Program Dependency

18. In file-processing systems, changes in file formats require corresponding changes in the application programs that access those files.
   Answer: True   *Level: hard*
   Section: File-Processing Systems
   Subsection: Application Program Dependency

19. One consequence of program data dependency is that file formats depend on the language or product used to generate them.
   Answer: True   *Level: easy*
   Section: File-Processing Systems
   Subsection: Incompatible Files

20. One advantage of file-processing systems is that it is easy to represent file-processing data in a form that seems natural to the users.
   Answer: False   *Level: easy*
   Section: File-Processing Systems
   Subsection: The Difficulty of Representing Data in the Users' Perspectives

21. With database processing systems, data duplication is completely eliminated.
   Answer: False   *Level: hard*
   Section: Database Processing Systems
   Subsection: Reduced Data Duplication

22. Database application programs must contain the length and data type of each of the data items they need from the database.
   Answer: True   *Level: moderate*
   Section: Database Processing Systems
   Subsection: Program / Data Independence

23. Database application programs do not need to know anything about the data items they need from the database.
   Answer: False   *Level: hard*
   Section: Database Processing Systems
   Subsection: Program / Data Independence

24. The description of a database's structure that is stored within the database itself is called the "metadata".
   Answer: True   *Level: easy*
   Section: Definition of a Database
   Subsection: A Database is Self-Describing

25. A database is called "self-describing" because it reduces data duplication.
   Answer: False   *Level: moderate*
   Section: Definition of a Database
   Subsection: A Database is Self-Describing

26.   In the standard hierarchy of data, records are aggregated into fields.
       Answer: False   *Level: moderate*
       Section: Definition of a Database
       Subsection: A Database is a Collection of Integrated Records

27.   A database is a model of reality.
       Answer: False   *Level: moderate*
       Section: Definition of a Database
       Subsection: A Database is a Model of a Model

28.   Early database applications impressed organizations with their processing speed and reliability.
       Answer: False   *Level: moderate*
       Section: The History of Database Processing
       Subsection: The Organizational Context

29.   One disadvantage of database processing systems is the vulnerability of having a single point of
       failure for multiple applications.
       Answer: True   *Level: hard*
       Section: The History of Database Processing
       Subsection: The Organizational Context

30.   According to the relational database model, an undesirable table can be changed into two or more
       desirable tables through a process called "decomposition".
       Answer: False   *Level: easy*
       Section: The History of Database Processing
       Subsection: The Relational Model

31.   The key benefit of the relational database model has turned out to be that it provides a
       standardized way for specialists to structure and process a database.
       Answer: True   *Level: easy*
       Section: The History of Database Processing
       Subsection: The Relational Model

32.   One impact of the migration of DBMS products from mainframes to microcomputers was the loss
       of an intuitive interface.
       Answer: False   *Level: moderate*
       Section: The History of Database Processing
       Subsection: Microcomputer DBMS Products

33.   In LAN-based multi-user database architecture, only one CPU is involved in database application
       processing.
       Answer: False   *Level: hard*
       Section: The History of Database Processing
       Subsection: Client-Server Database Applications

34.   File-sharing architecture is a simple mode of database processing on a LAN.
       Answer: True   *Level: easy*
       Section: The History of Database Processing
       Subsection: Client-Server Database Applications

35.   Client-server processing is a robust mode of database processing on a LAN.
       Answer: True   *Level: easy*
       Section: The History of Database Processing
       Subsection: Client-Server Database Applications

36.   Databases can be combined with Internet technologies to publish database data on the web.
       Answer: True   *Level: easy*
       Section: The History of Database Processing
       Subsection: Databases Using Internet Technology

37.   Most organizational databases today are distributed databases.
       Answer: False   *Level: moderate*
       Section: The History of Database Processing
       Subsection: Distributed Database Processing

38.   Among the most pressing problems with distributed databases are control and security.
       Answer: True   *Level: easy*
       Subsection: The History of Database Processing
       Subsection: Distributed Database Processing

Multiple Choice Questions

39.   Internet databases can store which types of data?
       a.)   pictures
       b.)   audio
       c.)   text
       d.)   video
       e.)   all of the above

Level: easy
Section: Four Database Examples

40.   A program whose job is to store and retrieve user data in the database is called the _____.
       a.)   Database Modeling System
       b.)   Database Management System
       c.)   Data Business Model System
       d.)   Relational Model Manager
       e.)   Data Business Management Service

Level: easy
Section: Four Database Examples
Subsection: Mary Richards Housepainting

41.   Multi-user databases:
    a.)   allow more than one concurrent user
    b.)   must keep one user's work from interfering with another's
    c.)   allow each user to make changes independently
    d.)   both a and b
    e.)   both a and c

Level: *moderate*
Section: *Four Database Examples*
Subsection: *Treble Clef Music*

42.   The first applications of database technology were _____.
    a.)   Internet databases
    b.)   workgroup databases
    c.)   organizational databases
    d.)   personal databases
    e.)   file-processing systems

Level: *moderate*
Section: *Four Database Examples*
Subsection: *State Licensing and Vehicle Registration Bureau*

43.   Which of the following is <u>not</u> a type of multi-user database?
    a.)   Internet databases
    b.)   workgroup databases
    c.)   organizational databases
    d.)   personal databases
    e.)   both a and d

Level: *easy*
Section: *Four Database Examples*
Subsection: *Comparison of Database Applications*

44.   For database systems needing to support approximately 15 concurrent users within an organization, which type of database would be appropriate?
    a.)   Internet database
    b.)   workgroup database
    c.)   organizational database
    d.)   personal database
    e.)   none of the above

Level: *hard*
Section: *Four Database Examples*
Subsection: *Comparison of Database Applications*

45.   Which of the following is <u>not</u> a characteristic of Internet databases?
   a.)   can support no more than 50 concurrent users
   b.)   contain structured data
   c.)   contain nonstructured data
   d.)   application content is delivered via a standard browser
   e.)   uses web-oriented technology to transfer data

Level: moderate
Section: Four Database Examples
Subsection: Calvert Island Reservations Centre

46.   Which of the following is a technology that can be used in delivering data with an Internet database?
   a.)   FTP
   b.)   SMTP
   c.)   XML
   d.)   PTL
   e.)   HTP

Level: hard
Section: Four Database Examples
Subsection: Calvert Island Reservations Centre

47.   In a database application processing system:
   a.)   the database application(s) interact with the DBMS
   b.)   the database application(s) access the database data
   c.)   the DBMS accesses the database data
   d.)   a and b
   e.)   a and c

Level: moderate
Section: The Relationship of Application Programs and the DBMS

48.   Which of the following is <u>not</u> a limitation of file-processing systems?
   a.)   Much data is duplicated.
   b.)   Data integrity is high.
   c.)   Application programs are dependent on file formats.
   d.)   Data are separated and isolated.
   e.)   All of the above are limitations of file-processing systems.

Level: moderate
Section: File-Processing Systems

49.   In a file-processing system:
        a.)   the user interacts with the application
        b.)   the user accesses the file data
        c.)   the application accesses the file data
        d.)   a and b
        e.)   a and c

Level: hard
Section: File-Processing Systems

50.   When data are duplicated, the most serious problem is:
        a.)   storage space is wasted
        b.)   data may be in different formats
        c.)   the data may not be logically consistent
        d.)   the files may be of different sizes
        e.)   difficulty in representing the users' perspectives

Level: hard
Section: File-Processing Systems
Subsection: Data Duplication

51.   In file-processing systems, the physical file formats are:
        a.)   contained in the metadata
        b.)   contained in the application code
        c.)   contained in the application metadata
        d.)   contained in the DBMS
        e.)   not needed by the application programs

Level: moderate
Section: File-Processing Systems
Subsection: Application Program Dependency

52.   In file-processing systems, the physical file formats are dependent on:
        a.)   the language or product used to generate them
        b.)   the type of data being stored
        c.)   the DBMS
        d.)   the size of the file
        e.)   the user's preference

Level: hard
Section: File-Processing Systems
Subsection: Incompatible Files

53.   As compared to file-processing systems, database processing systems:
     a.)   **make application programming easier**
     b.)   maximize the impact of data format changes on application programs
     c.)   provide users with direct access to data
     d.)   both a and c
     e.)   none of the above

Level: *moderate*
Section: *Database Processing Systems*

54.   In database processing systems:
     a.)   all record formats are stored in the database
     b.)   application programs need not include the format of the records or files they process
     c.)   application programs need to know the length and data type of the data items they need from the database
     d.)   the impact of data format changes on application programs is minimized
     e.)   **all of the above**

Level: *hard*
Section: *Database Processing Systems*
Subsection: *Program / Data Independence*

55.   A database is considered "self-describing" because:
     a.)   all the users' data is in one place
     b.)   it reduces data duplication
     c.)   **it contains a description of its own structure**
     d.)   it contains a listing of all the programs that use it
     e.)   all of the above

Level: *easy*
Section: *Definition of a Database*
Subsection: *A Database is Self-Describing*

56.   The description of the structure of a database is called:
     a.)   user data
     b.)   **data dictionary**
     c.)   indexes
     d.)   application metadata
     e.)   application data

Level: *easy*
Section: *Definition of a Database*
Subsection: *A Database is Self-Describing*

57. The standard hierarchy of data, from smallest to largest, is as follows:
    a.) bytes, characters, fields, records, files
    b.) bits, characters, fields, records, files
    c.) bits, characters, fields, files, records
    d.) bits, characters, records, databases, files
    e.) bits, characters, fields, files, databases

Level: moderate
Section: Definition of a Database
Subsection: A Database is a Collection of Integrated Records

58. A database contains:
    a.) user data
    b.) metadata
    c.) indexes
    d.) application metadata
    e.) all of the above

Level: easy
Section: Definition of a Database
Subsection: A Database is a Collection of Integrated Records

59. An index is used to:
    a.) represent relationships among the data
    b.) describe the structure of the database itself
    c.) describe the application programs that use the database
    d.) describe the structure of a data entry form or report
    e.) a and c

Level: moderate
Section: Definition of a Database
Subsection: A Database is a Collection of Integrated Records

60. An index can be used to:
    a.) document the structure of the database itself
    b.) improve the performance of the database
    c.) reduce data dependency for application programs
    d.) better represent the users' perspectives of the data
    e.) all of the above

Level: moderate
Section: Definition of a Database
Subsection: A Database is a Collection of Integrated Records

61.   When the structure of a data entry form or a report is part of a database, it is called:
      a.)   user data
      b.)   metadata
      c.)   indexes
      d.)   application metadata
      e.)   none of the above

Level: easy
Section: *Definition of a Database*
Subsection: *A Database is a Collection of Integrated Records*

62.   A database is a model of:
      a.)   the actual business
      b.)   the users' model of the business
      c.)   the programmers' view of the business
      d.)   reality as it relates to the business
      e.)   all of the above

Level: hard
Section: *Definition of a Database*
Subsection: *A Database is a Model of a Model*

63.   The principal criterion for determining the level of detail incorporated in a database is:
      a.)   the number of sample forms available during the design process
      b.)   the level of detail of the structure of the database
      c.)   the level of detail that exists in the users' minds
      d.)   the degree of detail available in the metadata
      e.)   none of the above

Level: easy
Section: *Definition of a Database*
Subsection: *A Database is a Model of a Model*

64.   Events that must be processed against the database are called _____.
      a.)   instances
      b.)   dynamics
      c.)   representations
      d.)   referrals
      e.)   transactions

Level: moderate
Section: *Definition of a Database*
Subsection: *A Database is a Model of a Model*

65.   Which of the following was <u>not</u> a factor in organizations' interest in the initial development of database technology?

    a.)   organizations were producing data at phenomenal rates
    b.)   data was difficult to manage with file-processing systems
    c.)   new systems were becoming increasingly difficult to develop
    d.)   the desire to separate and isolate data according to application programs
    e.)   the desire to integrate data from different file systems

Level: moderate
Section: The History of Database Processing
Subsection: The Organizational Context

66.   Which of the following was <u>not</u> a disadvantage of early database technologies?

    a.)   inability to integrate data
    b.)   database applications were unreliable
    c.)   database application performance was slow
    d.)   vulnerability of having a single point of failure for all data
    e.)   b and c

Level: hard
Section: The History of Database Processing
Subsection: The Organizational Context

67.   Which of the following is <u>not</u> an advantage of the relational model?

    a.)   data duplication is minimized
    b.)   many processing errors can be eliminated
    c.)   most users can obtain information from the database themselves
    d.)   provides a standard way for specialists to structure and process databases
    e.)   all of the above <u>are</u> advantages of the relational model

Level: moderate
Section: The History of Database Processing
Subsection: The Relational Model

68.   Modern microcomputer DBMS products:

    a.)   are not truly relational
    b.)   provide easy to use interfaces
    c.)   have poor response time
    d.)   are not true DBMS products
    e.)   are really just programming languages with generalized file-processing capabilities

Level: easy
Section: The History of Database Processing
Subsection: Microcomputer DBMS Products

69.   Client-server database architecture:
   a.)   has one CPU involved in the processing of database applications
   b.)   has many CPUs simultaneously involved in processing database applications
   c.)   is a simple but less robust mode of database processing on a LAN
   d.)   is the same as the multi-user architecture used on mainframe databases
   e.)   both a and d

Level: moderate
Section: The History of Database Processing
Subsection: Client-Server Database Applications

70.   The term "Internet database" refers to which of the following:
   a.)   any database joined with Internet technology to publish database data on the web
   b.)   any database that uses HTTP to publish database data to any location
   c.)   any database joined with XML to publish database data to any location
   d.)   any database joined with DHTML and XML to publish database data to any location
   e.)   all of the above

Level: hard
Section: The History of Database Processing
Subsection: Databases Using Internet Technology

71.   Which of the following is <u>not</u> true about distributed databases?
   a.)   They can combine personal, workgroup, and organizational databases.
   b.)   They are widely used by large international corporations.
   c.)   They make it appear to each user that (s)he is the only user of the organizations' data.
   d.)   They are still dealing with issues of data security.
   e.)   It is still unknown if truly distributed databases can meet the needs of day-to-day organizational processing.

Level: moderate
Section: The History of Database Processing
Subsection: Distributed Database Processing

72.   Business organizations have resisted adopting object-oriented database systems because:
   a.)   object-oriented programming uses simplified data structures that fit easily into relational databases
   b.)   the cost of purchasing ODBMS packages is prohibitively high
   c.)   the cost and risk of converting from relational databases to OBMS format is too high
   d.)   most ODBMS products lack features and functions for business information applications
   e.)   both c and d

Level: easy
Section: The History of Database Processing
Subsection: Object-Oriented DBMS (ODBMS)

Fill in the Blank Questions

73.   It is the job of a program called a(n) database management system (DBMS) to store and
        retrieve data in database tables.
Level: easy
Section: Four Database Examples
Subsection: Mary Richards Housepainting

74.   A single-user database that is used by only one person at a time is called a(n) _personal_ database.
Level: moderate
Section: Four Database Examples
Subsection: Mary Richards Housepainting

75.   A database that is used by more than one person at a time is called a(n) _multi-user_ database.
Level: moderate
Section: Four Database Examples
Subsection: Treble Clef Music

76.   _Organizational_ databases were the first applications of database technology.
Level: hard
Section: Four Database Examples
Subsection: State Licensing and Vehicle Registration Bureau

77.   A(n) _workgroup_ database is characterized by having 25 or fewer concurrent users and 100
        megabytes or less of data.
Level: hard
Section: Four Database Examples
Subsection: Comparison of Database Applications

78.   In database processing systems, the data is directly accessed only by the database management
        system (DBMS) .
Level: moderate
Section: The Relationship of Application Programs and the DBMS

79.   In database application processing systems, the user interacts directly with the database
        application programs .
Level: moderate
Section: The Relationship of Application Programs and the DBMS

80.   The first business information systems stored groups of records in separate files and were called
        file-processing systems .
Level: easy
Section: File-Processing Systems

81.   The most serious problem with data duplication concerns data integrity .
Level: moderate
Section: File-Processing Systems
Subsection: Data Duplication

82.   A collection of data has __integrity__ if it is logically consistent.
Level: *modern*
Section: *File-Processing Systems*
Subsection: *Data Duplication*

83.   In file-processing systems, the __physical format__ of files and records are part of the application code.
Level: *hard*
Section: *File-Processing Systems*
Subsection: *Application Program Dependency*

84.   A(n) __database__ is a self-describing collection of integrated records.
Level: *easy*
Section: *Definition of a Database*

85.   The description of the structure of a database is stored in the __metadata__, also known as the data dictionary or the data directory.
Level: *easy*
Section: *Definition of a Database*
Subsection: *A Database is Self-Describing*

86.   In the standard data hierarchy, a byte, or character, is composed of __bits__.
Level: *moderate*
Section: *Definition of a Database*
Subsection: *A Database is a Collection of Integrated Records*

87.   In the standard data hierarchy, a field is composed of __bytes (or characters)__.
Level: *moderate*
Section: *Definition of a Database*
Subsection: *A Database is a Collection of Integrated Records*

88.   In the standard data hierarchy, a record is composed of __fields__.
Level: *moderate*
Section: *Definition of a Database*
Subsection: *A Database is a Collection of Integrated Records*

89.   In the standard data hierarchy, a file is composed of __records__.
Level: *moderate*
Section: *Definition of a Database*
Subsection: *A Database is a Collection of Integrated Records*

90.   A(n) __index__ is used to represent relationships among the data and to improve the performance of database applications.
Level: *hard*
Section: *Definition of a Database*
Subsection: *A Database is a Collection of Integrated Records*

91.   When the structure of a form or report is part of the database it is called application metadata .
Level: hard
Section: Definition of a Database
Subsection: A Database is a Collection of Integrated Records

92.   The database is a(n) dynamic model because businesses change.
Level: hard
Section: Definition of a Database
Subsection: A Database is a Model of a Model

93.   Transactions are representations of events that must be processed against the database.
Level: easy
Section: Definition of a Database
Subsection: A Database is a Model of a Model

94.   A database is a model of the users' model or view of the business.
Level: easy
Section: Definition of a Database
Subsection: A Database is a Model of a Model

95.   The relational database model stores data as tables, with rows and columns.
Level: easy
Section: The History of Database Processing
Subsection: The Relational Model

96.   In the relational model, the process of normalization is used to change an undesirable table into two or more desirable tables.
Level: moderate
Section: The History of Database Processing
Subsection: The Relational Model

97.   Originally, it was thought that the relational model would allow users to obtain their own information from databases.
Level: easy
Section: The History of Database Processing
Subsection: The Relational Model

98.   One impact of the movement of database technology from mainframes to microcomputers was the dramatic improvement in DBMS user interfaces .
Level: moderate
Section: The History of Database Processing
Subsection: Microcomputer DBMS Products

99.   The use of multiple CPUs in processing database applications in LAN-based multi-user database architecture produced greater performance .
Level: hard
Section: The History of Database Processing
Subsection: Client-Server Database Applications

100.   Of the two types of LAN-based multi-user database processing, <u>client-server database architecture</u> is the more complex and robust.
Level: *moderate*
Section: *The History of Database Processing*
Subsection: *Client-Server Database Applications*

101.   Of the two types of LAN-based multi-user database processing, <u>file-sharing architecture</u> is the simpler and less robust.
Level: *moderate*
Section: *The History of Database Processing*
Subsection: *Client-Server Database Applications*

102.   A <u>distributed</u> database is logically integrated but physically located in more than one place.
Level: *easy*
Section: *The History of Database Processing*
Subsection: *Distributed Database Processing*

103.   Object-oriented database systems developed to handle the structures processed by <u>object-oriented programming (OOP)</u>.
Level: *easy*
Section: *The History of Database Processing*
Subsection: *Object-Oriented DBMS (ODBMS)*

Essay Questions

104.   Why is it insufficient to say that "database" is an extension of the standard data hierarchy?
With the other elements of the standard data hierarchy (bits, bytes/characters, fields, records, and files), each element is simply a collection of the previous element and no more. To say that a "database" is a collection of "files" is only a partial description of the contents of a database. While databases do contain files, they are more than the sum of the files they contain. Databases contain additional components, namely the metadata, indexes, and application metadata.
Section: *Definition of a Database*
Subsection: *A Database is a Collection of Integrated Records*

105.   Explain the problem with data duplication in a file-processing system.
In a file-processing system, a single data item can be duplicated in many files. This potentially leads to a problem with the logical consistency of the data, called data integrity. Data duplication can cause a problem with data integrity if the duplicated data item is updated in some locations but not in others. This results in two files that contain the same logical data item, but each has a different value for the item. This lack of data integrity can make it difficult to determine which file contains the correct information, and can lead to poor decision making based on obsolete data.
Section: *File-Processing Systems*
Subsection: *Data Duplication*

106.   Describe the two categories of database applications that use Internet technologies and distinguish between them.
The first category of database application that uses Internet technologies is the pure web database application. This type of database application uses Internet technologies, such as DHTML and XML, to deliver database data to internal and external constituents over the web. The second category of database application that uses Internet technologies is the classical database types (personal, workgroup, and organizational) that take advantage of Internet technologies to deliver database data to internal constituents over an internal network such as an intranet. While both categories use similar technologies, the defining characteristics that distinguish between the two are the network on which they "publish" their data, and whether their users are internal and/or external.
Section: *The History of Database Processing*
Subsection: *Databases Using Internet Technology*

107.   Why do we say a database is "self-describing" and what are the advantages associated with it?
A database is considered self-describing because it contains a description of its own structure within the database itself. This description is called the metadata, data dictionary, or data directory. The advantages gained from having metadata within the database are associated with data / program independence. Since the database contains a description of the structure of the files and records, the DBMS can use the metadata to shield the application programs from having to know the file or record formats. Further, this allows changes to be made to the structure of the records or files with a minimal impact on the application programs. Typically, only the applications that actually use the altered data items will have to be updated.
Section: *Definition of a Database*
Subsection: *A Database is Self-Describing*

108.   What are the advantages of the relational database model?
The relational database model provides several benefits. First, the relational model stores data in a way that minimizes data duplication and can eliminate some types of processing errors. Second, data is stored in tables, using rows and columns, making the data easily understandable. Third, the relationships in a relational database are viewable in the data itself through the use of columns that relate the records in one table to the records in another table. Finally, the relational model has provided a standardized way to structure and process databases.
Section: *The History of Database Processing*
Subsection: *The Relational Model*

CHAPTER 2

Introduction to Database Development

True-False Questions

1.   Users may access the DBMS directly or indirectly through application programs.
      Answer: True   *Level: moderate*
      Section: The Database

2.   The database is processed by the DBMS.
      Answer: True
      Section: The Database   *Level: easy*

3.   A database contains four main elements: user data, application programs, metadata, and indexes.
      Answer: False   *Level: moderate*
      Section: The Database

4.   Today, most databases represent user data as trees of data.
      Answer: False   *Level: easy*
      Section: The Database
      Subsection: User Data

5.   In a relation, the columns of the relation contain records for particular entities in the business environment, and the rows of the relation contain fields or attributes.
      Answer: False   *Level: moderate*
      Section: The Database
      Subsection: User Data

6.   In a relation, the columns of the relation contain fields or attributes, and the rows of the relation contain records for particular entities in the business environment.
      Answer: True   *Level: moderate*
      Section: The Database
      Subsection: User Data

7.   Most DBMS products store the metadata in the form of tables.
      Answer: True   *Level: easy*
      Section: The Database
      Subsection: Metadata

8.   System tables contain the users' data.
      Answer: False   *Level: moderate*
      Section: The Database
      Subsection: Metadata

9.   Developers have a special set of tools for querying metadata that is separate from the query tools
        for users' data.
        Answer: False   *Level: moderate*
        Section: The Database
        Subsection: Metadata

10.   Overhead data is a synonym for metadata.
        Answer: False   *Level: easy*
        Section: The Database
        Subsection: Indexes

11.   Overhead data is composed primarily of indexes.
        Answer: True   *Level: easy*
        Section: The Database
        Subsection: Indexes

12.   Indexes and linked lists are both types of overhead data.
        Answer: True   *Level: moderate*
        Section: The Database
        Subsection: Indexes

13.   Overhead data contains types of data structures that can improve the performance and
        accessibility of the database.
        Answer: True   *Level: hard*
        Section: The Database
        Subsection: Indexes

14.   Indexes are beneficial for search operations, but at the cost of slowing down sorting operations.
        Answer: False   *Level: moderate*
        Section: The Database
        Subsection: Indexes

15.   Indexes should be created for every field in a relation, even if they are not currently needed, to
        support future uses of the data.
        Answer: False   *Level: hard*
        Section: The Database
        Subsection: Indexes

16.   Application metadata is used to store the structure of some application components in the
        database.
        Answer: True   *Level: moderate*
        Section: The Database
        Subsection: Application Metadata

17.   Although all DBMS products do not support application components, all DBMS products that do
        support application components store the structure of those components in application metadata.
        Answer: False   *Level: hard*
        Section: The Database
        Subsection: Application Metadata

18.   While users can not access the application metadata directly, database developers often must directly access application metadata to create database application programs.
Answer: False   *Level: hard*
Section: The Database
Subsection: Application Metadata

19.   The design tools subsystem of the DBMS is responsible for processing the application components.
Answer: False   *Level: moderate*
Section: The DBMS
Subsection: The Design Tools Subsystem

20.   The design tools subsystem of the DBMS can facilitate the design of a database, but does not have tools to help in actually implementing the design.
Answer: False   *Level: easy*
Section: The DBMS
Subsection: The Design Tools Subsystem

21.   The design tools subsystem of the DBMS typically includes tools for creating tables, forms, queries, and reports.
Answer: True   *Level: moderate*
Section: The DBMS
Subsection: The Design Tools Subsystem

22.   If a DBMS includes a programming language or an interface to a programming language, it is considered to be part of the design tools subsystem of the DBMS.
Answer: True   *Level: moderate*
Section: The DBMS
Subsection: The Design Tools Subsystem

23.   The run-time subsystem of the DBMS processes the application components.
Answer: True   *Level: easy*
Section: The DBMS
Subsection: Run-Time Subsystem

24.   The DBMS engine acts as an intermediary between the other DBMS components and the database data.
Answer: True   *Level: easy*
Section: The DBMS
Subsection: The DBMS Engine

25.   The DBMS engine receives requests from the run-time subsystem and the design tools subsystem and translates them into commands for the operating system to read and write data on physical media.
Answer: True   *Level: moderate*
Section: The DBMS
Subsection: The DBMS Engine

26.   To retrieve data from the database, the run-time subsystem instructs the operating system to read data from the physical media.
      Answer: False   *Level: moderate*
      Section: The DBMS
      Subsection: The DBMS Engine

27.   The DBMS engine is involved in transaction management.
      Answer: True   *Level: moderate*
      Section: The DBMS
      Subsection: The DBMS Engine

28.   The run-time subsystem is responsible for locking, and backup and recovery within the database.
      Answer: False   *Level: moderate*
      Section: The DBMS
      Subsection: The DBMS Engine

29.   The database schema is a component of the DBMS engine.
      Answer: False   *Level: moderate*
      Section: Creating the Database

30.   A database schema defines a database's structure – its tables, relationships, domains, and business rules.
      Answer: True   *Level: easy*
      Section: Creating the Database

31.   A database schema is a set of values that a column can have.
      Answer: False   *Level: easy*
      Section: Creating the Database
      Subsection: An Example of a Schema

32.   A domain includes the physical format of an attribute and its uniqueness.
      Answer: True   *Level: hard*
      Section: Creating the Database
      Subsection: An Example of a Schema

33.   Business rules are restrictions on the business's activities that need to be reflected in the database and database applications.
      Answer: True   *Level: easy*
      Section: Creating the Database
      Subsection: An Example of a Schema

34.   Business rules can always be enforced in the DBMS if the database is properly designed.
      Answer: False   *Level: hard*
      Section: Creating the Database
      Subsection: An Example of a Schema

35.   Some DBMS products use "stored procedures" to enforce business rules.
      Answer: True   *Level: easy*
      Section: Creating the Database
      Subsection: An Example of a Schema

36.   Once a database schema has been designed, the next step in creating a database is to define the relationships.
      Answer: False   *Level: moderate*
      Section: Creating the Database
      Subsection: Creating Tables

37.   One disadvantage of declaring a relationship between two tables to the DBMS is that whenever those two tables are used in a form, query, or report the relationship must be declared again.
      Answer: False   *Level: moderate*
      Section: Creating the Database
      Subsection: Defining Relationships

38.   Identifiers that have no meaning to the users but are created only so that each row in a table will be uniquely identifiable to the DBMS are called foreign keys.
      Answer: False   *Level: hard*
      Section: Components of Applications
      Subsection: Forms

39.   While most DBMS products support creating queries, few actually store the query as part of the application.
      Answer: False   *Level: easy*
      Section: Components of Applications
      Subsection: Queries

40.   A criterion query is a query that has been constructed to accept criteria values at run-time.
      Answer: False   *Level: hard*
      Section: Components of Applications
      Subsection: Queries

41.   A report can be used to enter data into the database as well as display data from the database.
      Answer: False   *Level: easy*
      Section: Components of Applications
      Subsection: Reports

42.   Reports usually have a more complex structure than forms.
      Answer: True   *Level: easy*
      Section: Components of Applications
      Subsection: Reports

43.   Menus can be used to control user access to forms, reports, and programs.
      Answer: True   *Level: easy*
      Section: Components of Applications
      Subsection: Menus

44.   Menus can make application components more accessible to users, but at the cost of losing control over the users' activities.
      Answer: False   *Level: hard*
      Section: Components of Applications
      Subsection: Menus

45.   Database application programs must be written using a language that is specific to the DBMS.
      Answer: False   *Level: easy*
      Section: Components of Applications
      Subsection: Application Programs

46.   Predefined program interfaces allow database application programs written in standard
      programming languages to interact with the DBMS.
      Answer: True   *Level: moderate*
      Section: Components of Applications
      Subsection: Application Programs

47.   Top-down development proceeds from the need to develop a specific system.
      Answer: False   *Level: easy*
      Section: Database Development Processes
      Subsection: General Strategies

48.   Studying the strategic goals of the organization and the information requirements necessary to
      achieve those goals is characteristic of top-down development.
      Answer: True   *Level: easy*
      Section: Database Development Processes
      Subsection: General Strategies

49.   Top-down development tends to produce useful systems more quickly than bottom-up
      development.
      Answer: False   *Level: easy*
      Section: Database Development Processes
      Subsection: General Strategies

50.   Bottom-up development produces systems with a global perspective requiring fewer
      modifications as additional systems are built.
      Answer: False   *Level: easy*
      Section: Database Development Processes
      Subsection: General Strategies

51.   Typically, users can clearly express their needs to the database developer.
      Answer: False   *Level: easy*
      Section: Database Development Processes
      Subsection: Data Modeling

52.   Typically, database developers will start with the outputs that the users desire and work
      backward to infer the data model.
      Answer: True   *Level: moderate*
      Section: Database Development Processes
      Subsection: Data Modeling

53.   Development of multi-user databases, such as workgroup and organizational database, is simplified because the developer has more potential sources for information.
        Answer: True   *Level: easy*
        Section: Database Development Processes
        Subsection: Data Modeling

54.   Development of multi-user databases is especially difficult when the system is so large that no single user has a model of the complete structure.
        Answer: True   *Level: easy*
        Section: Database Development Processes
        Subsection: Data Modeling

Multiple Choice Questions

55.   A relation:
        a.)   is a tree containing user data
        b.)   is a table containing user data
        c.)   contains records in columns
        d.)   is always well structured
        e.)   all of the above

Level: easy
Section: The Database
Subsection: User Data

56.   A relation:
        a.)   has columns containing attributes
        b.)   has rows containing records
        c.)   should contain information on only one topic
        d.)   has columns containing fields
        e.)   all of the above

Level: moderate
Section: The Database
Subsection: User Data

57.   The process to convert a poorly structured relation into a well-structured relation is called
        _____.
        a.)   decomposition
        b.)   structuration
        c.)   transformation
        d.)   transaction
        e.)   normalization

Level: moderate
Section: The Database
Subsection: User Data

58.   Which of the following would <u>not</u> be stored in system tables?
    a.)   **user data**
    b.)   keys
    c.)   stored procedures
    d.)   lists of indexes
    e.)   length of fields

Level: moderate
Section: The Database
Subsection: Metadata

59.   Which of the following is (are) considered "overhead data"?
    a.)   metadata
    b.)   keys
    c.)   **linked lists**
    d.)   user data
    e.)   application metadata

Level: hard
Section: The Database
Subsection: Indexes

60.   An index is a type of _____.
    a.)   database
    b.)   metadata
    c.)   stored procedure
    d.)   **overhead data**
    e.)   primary key

Level: moderate
Section: The Database
Subsection: Indexes

61.   Indexes can:
    a.)   assist in search operations
    b.)   improve performance of sorting operations
    c.)   slow performance of update operations
    d.)   improve the accessibility of the database data
    e.)   **all of the above**

Level: easy
Section: The Database
Subsection: Indexes

62.   Application metadata can include the structure of all of the following <u>except</u> _____.
   - **a.)**   **indexes**
   - b.)   forms
   - c.)   queries
   - d.)   reports
   - e.)   application components

Level: *moderate*
Section: *The Database*
Subsection: *Application Metadata*

63.   The design tools subsystem of the DBMS usually provides _____.
   - a.)   tools for backup and recovery of the database
   - **b.)**   **one or more programming languages**
   - c.)   a DBMS engine
   - d.)   a component to process queries
   - e.)   a banded report

Level: *hard*
Section: *The DBMS*
Subsection: *The Design Tools Subsystem*

64.   The design tools subsystem of the DBMS typically includes tools for creating all of the following except _____.
   - a.)   forms
   - b.)   tables
   - c.)   reports
   - d.)   queries
   - **e.)**   **engine**

Level: *easy*
Section: *The DBMS*
Subsection: *The Design Tools Subsystem*

65.   Which DBMS subsystem is responsible for processing the application components?
   - a.)   DBMS engine
   - b.)   schema subsystem
   - **c.)**   **run-time subsystem**
   - d.)   design tools subsystem
   - e.)   programming interfaces.

Level: *easy*
Section: *The DBMS*
Subsection: *Run-Time Subsystem*

66.   Which DBMS subsystem is responsible for receiving requests from the other components and translating them into commands for the operating system to read or write data on the physical media?
       a.)   DBMS engine
       b.)   schema subsystem
       c.)   run-time subsystem
       d.)   design tools subsystem
       e.)   programming interfaces.

Level: easy
Section: The DBMS
Subsection: DBMS Engine

67.   The DBMS engine is directly involved in all of the following except _____.
       a.)   locking
       b.)   recovery
       c.)   domains
       d.)   backup
       e.)   transaction management

Level: moderate
Section: The DBMS
Subsection: DBMS Engine

68.   The database schema defines which of the following?
       a.)   domains
       b.)   tables
       c.)   relationships
       d.)   business rules
       e.)   all of the above

Level: moderate
Section: Creating the Database

69.   Which of the following steps in creating a database would come first?
       a.)   define relationships
       b.)   create tables
       c.)   define the schema
       d.)   generate the data entry form
       e.)   format reports

Level: moderate
Section: Creating the Database

70.   The set of values that a column can have is called the _____.
        a.)   domain
        b.)   business rules
        c.)   schema
        d.)   relation
        e.)   uniqueness

Level: moderate
Section: Creating the Database
Subsection: An Example of a Schema

71.   Business rules may be enforced by all of the following methods except _____.
        a.)   by the DBMS
        b.)   by the indexes
        c.)   by stored procedures
        d.)   by the application programs
        e.)   all of the above <u>can</u> be used to enforce business rules

Level: moderate
Section: Creating the Database
Subsection: An Example of a Schema

72.   _____ are constraints on user activities that must be enforced no matter how the data
        changes reach the DBMS.
        a.)   Domains
        b.)   Business rules
        c.)   Schema
        d.)   Relationships
        e.)   Keys

Level: moderate
Section: Creating the Database
Subsection: An Example of a Schema

73.   When the primary key of one relation is placed into a second relation to define a relationship, the
        key is called a(n) _____ in the second relation.
        a.)   primary key
        b.)   secondary key
        c.)   foreign key
        d.)   duplicate key
        e.)   surrogate key

Level: moderate
Section: Creating the Database
Subsection: Defining Relationships

74. Which of the following is not considered part of a database application?
  a.) **tables**
  b.) reports
  c.) application programs
  d.) forms
  e.) queries

Level: moderate
Section: Components of Applications

75. In a database application, data entry is typically done with a(n) _____.
  a.) report
  b.) metadata
  c.) query
  d.) **form**
  e.) table

Level: easy
Section: Components of Applications
Subsection: Forms

76. A surrogate key:
  a.) represents an attribute of an entity in the users' model
  b.) always appears as the first line of a banded report
  c.) can be used in queries, but not in tables
  d.) **has no meaning to the users**
  e.) all of the above

Level: hard
Section: Components of Applications
Subsection: Forms

77. Which of the following is <u>not</u> a means of expressing a query to a database?
  a.) **PBL**
  b.) SQL
  c.) QBE
  d.) query by form
  e.) query by example

Level: hard
Section: Components of Applications
Subsection: Queries

78.   A report:
    a.)   can be easier to design than a form since it is used only for displaying data
    b.)   can be more difficult to design than a form because it usually has a more complex structure
    c.)   is a formatted display of database data
    d.)   both a and c
    e.)   all of the above

Level: moderate
Section: Components of Applications
Subsection: Reports

79.   Menus can be used to:
    a.)   display database data
    b.)   control the users' activities
    c.)   retrieve specific data from the database
    d.)   update database data
    e.)   express a query to the database

Level: moderate
Section: Components of Applications
Subsection: Menus

80.   Application programs:
    a.)   must be written in a language specific to the DBMS being used
    b.)   can be used to enforce business rules
    c.)   can use a predefined program interface to bypass the DBMS and access data directly
    d.)   can not be written in standard programming languages
    e.)   all of the above

Level: moderate
Section: Components of Applications
Subsection: Application Programs

81.   Which of the following is <u>not</u> true of application programs?
    a.)   may be written in a language specific to the DBMS being used
    b.)   may be written in a standard programming language using a predefined program interface
    c.)   may enforce business rules
    d.)   interact with the DBMS to access database data
    e.)   are always dependent on a set of forms and reports

Level: easy
Section: Components of Applications
Subsection: Application Programs

82.   A prototype is:
       a.)   a completed database without any applications
       b.)   a completed application without any database
       c.)   created by the users to explain their model to the developers
       d.)   a sample database and applications to represent aspects of the system
       e.)   used only with top-down development

Level: *moderate*
Section: *Database Development Process*
Subsection: *General Strategies*

83.   Which of the following is <u>not</u> a characteristic of top-down development?
       a.)   involves a study of strategic goals
       b.)   creates an abstract data model
       c.)   identifies a number of systems to eventually be built
       d.)   produces systems requiring little modification to interface with new systems
       e.)   produces useful systems quickly

Level: *moderate*
Section: *Database Development Process*
Subsection: *General Strategies*

84.   Which of the following is a characteristic of bottom-up development?
       a.)   involves a study of strategic goals
       b.)   begins with the need to develop a specific system
       c.)   identifies a number of systems to eventually be built
       d.)   produces systems requiring little modification to interface with new systems
       e.)   often leads to analysis paralysis

Level: *moderate*
Section: *Database Development Process*
Subsection: *General Strategies*

85.   Capturing the users' requirements typically involves all of the following except:
       a.)   making inferences
       b.)   interviewing users
       c.)   building prototypes
       d.)   examining reports
       e.)   all of the above

Level: *moderate*
Section: *Database Development Process*
Subsection: *Data Modeling*

86.　　Data modeling in a multi-user system is complicated because:
　　　　a.)　　conflicting models must be reconciled
　　　　b.)　　no single user's model includes the complete structure
　　　　c.)　　the developers must document the logical union of different models
　　　　d.)　　users' models may be inconsistent with each other
　　　　e.)　　all of the above

Level: easy
Section: Database Development Process
Subsection: Data Modeling

Fill in the Blank Questions

87.　　The database is processed by the ＿DBMS＿ , which is used by both users and developers.
Level: easy
Section: The Database

88.　　Today, most databases represent user data in ＿relations＿ , which are tables of data.
Level: moderate
Section: The Database
Subsection: User Data

89.　　In a table of users' data, the columns contain ＿fields (attributes)＿ .
Level: easy
Section: The Database
Subsection: User Data

90.　　The process of ＿normalization＿ is used to change poorly structured tables into well-structured ones.
Level: moderate
Section: The Database
Subsection: User Data

91.　　Most DBMS products store metadata in tables, sometimes called ＿system tables＿ .
Level: moderate
Section: The Database
Subsection: Metadata

92.　　One advantage to storing metadata in tables is that ＿developers＿ can use the same tools to query the metadata as they do to query the users' data.
Level: moderate
Section: The Database
Subsection: Metadata

93.　　A type of databases data that consists primarily of indexes is called ＿overhead data＿ .
Level: moderate
Section: The Database
Subsection: Indexes

94.   Overhead data typically includes indexes and sometimes __linked lists__ .
Level: hard
Section: The Database
Subsection: Indexes

95.   Indexes are useful for __sorting__ and search operations.
Level: moderate
Section: The Database
Subsection: Indexes

96.   The structure and format of user forms, reports, and other application components are stored in the database as __application metadata__ .
Level: easy
Section: The Database
Subsection: Application Metadata

97.   The __design tools__ subsystem contains tools to facilitate the creation of the database.
Level: easy
Section: The DBMS
Subsection: The Design Tools Subsystem

98.   The __run-time__ subsystem processes the application components created using the design tools.
Level: easy
Section: The DBMS
Subsection: Run-Time Subsystem

99.   The DBMS engine is the intermediary between the other DBMS components and the __data__ .
Level: moderate
Section: The DBMS
Subsection: DBMS engine

100.   The DBMS engine receives requests from the other DBMS components and translates them into commands for the __operating system__ to read or write data from the physical media.
Level: hard
Section: The DBMS
Subsection: DBMS engine

101.   A database __schema__ defines a database's structure – its tables, relationships, domains, and business rules.
Level: moderate
Section: Creating the Database

102.   A database schema is a(n) __design__ .
Level: hard
Section: Creating the Database

103.   A __domain__ is a set of values that a column may have.
Level: *moderate*
Section: *Creating the Database*
Subsection: *An Example of a Schema*

104.   __Business rules__ are restrictions on the business's activities that need to be reflected in the database and database applications.
Level: *moderate*
Section: *Creating the Database*
Subsection: *An Example of a Schema*

105.   A primary key from one table that is placed into another table to declare a relationship is called a(n) __foreign key__ in the second table.
Level: *moderate*
Section: *Creating the Database*
Subsection: *An Example of a Schema*

106.   __Surrogate keys__ are identifiers that are created only to allow each row in a table to be uniquely identified and have no meaning to the users.
Level: *hard*
Section: *Components of Applications*
Subsection: *Forms*

107.   Queries can be expressed to the database using the data access language called __SQL__.
Level: *hard*
Section: *Components of Applications*
Subsection: *Queries*

108.   QBE, which stands for __query by example__, is a means of expressing a query to the database.
Level: *moderate*
Section: *Components of Applications*
Subsection: *Queries*

109.   Queries can be __parameterized__, meaning that they are constructed to accept a criteria value at the time they are run.
Level: *hard*
Section: *Components of Applications*
Subsection: *Queries*

110.   A means of expressing a query to the database called __query by form__ allows the user to enter query constraints on a data entry form.
Level: *easy*
Section: *Components of Applications*
Subsection: *Queries*

111.   A __report__ is a formatted display of data.
Level: *easy*
Section: *Components of Applications*
Subsection: *Reports*

112.   __Menus__ are used to organize application components to make them more accessible to the end user and to provide control over the users' activities.
Level: *easy*
Section: *Components of Applications*
Subsection: *Menus*

113.   Application programs can be written either in a language that is specific to the __DBMS__ being used or with a standard language using a predefined program interface.
Level: *moderate*
Section: *Components of Applications*
Subsection: *Application Programs*

114.   A __prototype__ is a sample database and application used to represent aspects of the system to be built.
Level: *easy*
Section: *Database Development Processes*
Subsection: *General Strategies*

115.   __Top-down__ development begins with a study of the strategic goals of the organization.
Level: *moderate*
Section: *Database Development Processes*
Subsection: *General Strategies*

116.   __Bottom-up__ development begins with the need to develop a specific system.
Level: *moderate*
Section: *Database Development Processes*
Subsection: *General Strategies*

117.   Developers generally need to use the art of __inferencing__ when determining the design for the database from information supplied by users.
Level: *hard*
Section: *Database Development Processes*
Subsection: *Data Modeling*

118.   Modeling a __multi-user__ database is complicated because many users may have different views of the data.
Level: *moderate*
Section: *Database Development Processes*
Subsection: *Data Modeling*

Essay Questions

119.   Explain the value of indexes and indicate when they should and should not be used.
Indexes can be used to improve the performance and accessibility of the database when performing certain operations, most notably sort and search operations. The data in the database is physically sorted into some order based on the values of a given field. If the data in the database needs to be sorted into an order based on the values of a different field, it is very time-consuming to extract all the records and re-sort them into the new order. An index acts as a list of records, with an abbreviated number of fields, that is sorted in order based on one of those fields. If an index exists that indicates the order the records need to be in when they are sorted by that field, then the database can use the index as a shortcut to quickly re-sort the records. Since many indexes can exist, the database can have shortcuts to sort the records in order based on any number of fields. Similarly, when searching for a subset of records that have a common value in a field, an index that is sorted on that field will have all of those records grouped together, allowing the database to more quickly access that subset of records. Since all indexes have to be updated whenever a field that they contain is updated, managing indexes adds to the overhead processing the database must perform, thereby slowing performance for update operations. For this reason, indexes should be created only for fields that the user is likely to sort by or search for.
Section: *The Database*
Subsection: *Indexes*

120.   Explain the functioning of the DBMS engine.
The DBMS engine is the only component of the DBMS that directly accesses the database data. It acts as an intermediary between the design tools and run-time components and the actual database data. The DBMS engine receives requests from the other two components and translates those requests into commands to the operating system to read or write the data on the physical media. The DBMS engine is also involved in other activities such as transaction management, locking, and backup and recovery. Its role in these activities is to ensure that when a group of actions must be completed as a group, either all actions take place or none of them are allowed to take place.
Section: *The Database*
Subsection: *The DBMS Engine*

121.   Contrast top-down and bottom-up development.
Top-down and bottom-up development differ primarily in the order in which they approach the abstraction of the data model. Top-down development begins with a highly abstract data model that represents the data needs of the entire organization. This data model is refined into less abstract models that identify a variety of systems that need to be developed. Finally, these models are refined even further into detailed models that represent the requirements of individual systems to be built. Bottom-up development starts with the detailed model of the system to be built. As new systems need to be built, existing systems' data models are modified to facilitate interfaces with the new systems.
Section: *Database Development Processes*
Subsection: *General Strategies*

122.   Explain the role of "inferencing" in data modeling.

Users have a mental model that represents their understanding of the things in their environment. This model has a structure that the developer must capture in the data model that is created to develop a database to meet the users' needs. Unfortunately, users can not articulate what the structure of that model is. Therefore, developers must infer the structure of the users' model from the things that the users can articulate, such as the information requirements for forms and reports that the users need the system to produce.
Section: *Database Development Processes*
Subsection: *Data Modeling*

123.   Why is data modeling more complicated when designing multi-user databases?

Attempting to capture one user's model of their environment for a single-user database is difficult. Multi-user databases require attempting to capture many users' models of their environment. This is further complicated by the fact that many users will have different perspectives of the environment in which they work, meaning that the users' models often are inconsistent with each other. Any inconsistencies must be resolved so that the developers can produce a comprehensive and consistent data model for the database. The situation is made even worse with large organizational databases when no single user has a model that encompasses the complete data structure. In this case, the developer must create a data model that is the logical union of all the users' models.
Section: *Database Development Processes*
Subsection: *Data Modeling*

CHAPTER 3

The Entity Relationship Model

True-False Questions

1. E-R models are expressed using a single standardized set of universally accepted symbols.
   Answer: False   *Level: easy*
   Section: Chapter Introduction

2. An entity is something in the users' work environment that the users want to track.
   Answer: True   *Level: easy*
   Section: Entities

3. Entities of a given type are grouped into entity classes.
   Answer: True   *Level: easy*
   Section: Entities

4. An entity class is described by the structure of the entities in that class.
   Answer: True   *Level: moderate*
   Section: Entities

5. An entity instance of an entity class is the representation of a particular entity and is described by the values of the attributes of the entity.
   Answer: True   *Level: hard*
   Section: Entities

6. In E-R modeling, entities within an entity class may have different attributes.
   Answer: False   *Level: easy*
   Section: Entities

7. In E-R modeling, an attribute may be either composite or multi-valued, but it cannot be both.
   Answer: False   *Level: moderate*
   Section: Attributes

8. An identifier of an entity instance must consist of one and only one attribute.
   Answer: False   *Level: easy*
   Section: Identifiers

9. A "composite identifier" is defined as a composite attribute that is an identifier.
   Answer: False   *Level: hard*
   Section: Identifiers

10. An identifier may be either unique or nonunique.
    Answer: True   *Level: moderate*
    Section: Identifiers

11.   E-R modeling recognizes both relationship classes and relationship instances.
       Answer: True   *Level: easy*
       Section: Relationships

12.   Relationships do not have attributes.
       Answer: False   *Level: moderate*
       Section: Relationships

13.   A single relationship class involves only one entity class.
       Answer: False   *Level: hard*
       Section: Relationships

14.   A binary relationship is a relationship based on numerical entity instance identifiers.
       Answer: False   *Level: moderate*
       Section: Relationships

15.   The degree of a relationship is expressed as the relationship's maximum cardinality.
       Answer: False   *Level: hard*
       Section: Relationships

16.   A relationship's minimum cardinality indicates whether or not an entity <u>must</u> be involved in the
       relationship.
       Answer: True   *Level: easy*
       Section: Entity-Relationship Diagrams

17.   Relationships among instances of a single entity class are called redundant relationships.
       Answer: False   *Level: moderate*
       Section: Entity-Relationship Diagrams

18.   A weak entity is an entity that cannot exist in the database without (and is logically dependent
       upon) another type of entity also existing in the database.
       Answer: True   *Level: hard*
       Section: Weak Entities

19.   ID-dependent entities are a common type of weak entity.
       Answer: True   *Level: moderate*
       Section: Weak Entities

20.   All weak entities must have a minimum cardinality of 1 on the entity on which it depends.
       Answer: True   *Level: hard*
       Section: Weak Entities

21.   Multi-valued attributes are represented in E-R diagrams by creating a new weak entity to
       represent the multi-valued attribute and creating a 1:N relationship.
       Answer: True   *Level: moderate*
       Section: Representing Multi-Value Attributes

22.   Subtype entities are used to produce a closer-fitting model when an entity has sets of optional
       attributes.
       Answer: True   *Level: easy*
       Section: Subtype Entities

23.   Entities with an IS-A relationship should have the same identifier.
       Answer: True   *Level: easy*
       Section: Subtype Entities

24.   Inheritance in a generalization hierarchy means that the supertype entity inherits all the attributes
       of the subtype entity.
       Answer: False   *Level: moderate*
       Section: Subtype Entities

25.   It is not important to document business rules during data modeling since they will be enforced
       by the application programs.
       Answer: False   *Level: easy*
       Section: Documentation of Business Rules

26.   UML is intended for modeling and designing object oriented programs and applications.
       Answer: True   *Level: easy*
       Section: UML-Style Entity-Relationship Diagrams

27.   For database design, UML style E-R diagrams must be treated very differently from traditional E-
       R diagrams because of their object oriented background.
       Answer: True   *Level: moderate*
       Section: UML-Style Entity-Relationship Diagrams

28.   Maximum cardinalities are represented in UML style E-R diagrams with the same notation (1:1,
       1:N, N:M) as in traditional E-R diagrams.
       Answer: False   *Level: moderate*
       Section: UML-Style Entity-Relationship Diagrams

29.   In UML style E-R diagrams, a weak entity is shown by placing a filled-in diamond on the parent
       of the weak entity.
       Answer: True   *Level: moderate*
       Section: Representation of Weak Entities

30.   One weakness of UML style E-R diagrams is that there is no means of distinguishing between a
       weak entity that is ID-dependent and a weak entity that is not ID-dependent.
       Answer: False   *Level: hard*
       Section: Representation of Weak Entities

31.   UML style E-R diagrams allow for the existence of class attributes, which are attributes that
       pertain to the collection of all entities within that class not to the individual entity instances
       themselves.
       Answer: True   *Level: hard*
       Section: Constructs Introduced by UML

32.   UML style E-R diagrams allow for three different levels of visibility of attributes.
        Answer: True   *Level: easy*
        Section: Constructs Introduced by UML

33.   UML style E-R diagrams introduce object oriented notation that is of limited practical value in
        traditional, relational database design.
        Answer: True   *Level: easy*
        Section: The Role of UML in Database Processing Today

34.   The goal of data models is to strive to produce the most accurate model of the real world as
        possible.
        Answer: False   *Level: hard*
        Section: Databases as Models of Models

Multiple Choice Questions

35.   Which of the following is not a key element of E-R models?
        a.)   identifiers
        b.)   entities
        c.)   objects
        d.)   attributes
        e.)   relationships

Level: easy
Section: Elements of the Entity-Relationship Model

36.   The representation of a particular entity is called a(n) _____.
        a.)   entity class
        b.)   entity relationship
        c.)   entity instance
        d.)   entity attribute
        e.)   none of the above

Level: easy
Section: Entities

37.   An equivalent term for "attributes" is _____.
        a.)   identifiers
        b.)   properties
        c.)   entities
        d.)   instances
        e.)   composites

Level: easy
Section: Attributes

38.   Attributes may be _____ attributes:
    a.)   composite
    b.)   element
    c.)   multi-valued
    d.)   both a and c
    e.)   both b and c

Level: moderate
Section: Attributes

39.   An identifier may be:
    a.)   composite
    b.)   unique
    c.)   a single attribute
    d.)   nonunique
    e.)   all of the above

Level: moderate
Section: Identifiers

40.   Which type of identifier is used to identify a set of instances of a given entity?
    a.)   class
    b.)   attribute
    c.)   unique
    d.)   instance
    e.)   nonunique

Level: moderate
Section: Identifiers

41.   A composite attribute is an attribute that:
    a.)   is multi-valued
    b.)   describes a characteristic of the relationship
    c.)   consists of a group of attributes
    d.)   is calculated at run-time
    f.)   is an identifer

Level: easy
Section: Attributes

42.   For a relationship to be considered a binary relationship it must satisfy which of the following conditions?
    a.)   it must involve exactly two entity classes
    b.)   it must have a maximum cardinality of 1:1
    c.)   it must have a maximum cardinality of 1:N
    d.)   both a and b
    e.)   both a and c

Level: hard
Section: Relationships

43.   Minimum cardinality refers to
    a.)   The most instances of one entity class that can be involved in a relationship with one instance of another entity class.
    b.)   The minimum number of entity classes involved in a relationship.
    c.)   Whether or not an instance of one entity class is required to be related to an instance of another entity class.
    d.)   Whether or not an entity is a weak entity.
    e.)   none of the above.

Level: moderate
Section: Entity-Relationship Diagrams

44.   A hash mark across the relationship line near an entity indicates:
    a.)   a maximum cardinality of "one"
    b.)   a unique identifier
    c.)   a minimum cardinality of "zero"
    d.)   a maximum cardinality of "many"
    e.)   none of the above

Level: moderate
Section: Entity-Relationship Diagrams

45.   To represent a multi-valued attribute in an E-R model, _____ .
    a.)   create a new weak entity with a 1:N relationship
    b.)   create a new subtype entity with a 1:1 relationship
    c.)   create a new strong entity with a 1:1 relationship
    d.)   create a new weak entity with a 1:1 relationship
    e.)   create a new subtype entity with a 1:N relationship

Level: hard
Section: Representing Multi-Value Attributes

46.   Supertype / subtype entities are said to have a(n) _____ relationship.
    a.)   HAS-A
    b.)   IS-A
    c.)   recursive
    d.)   redundant
    e.)   multi-valued

Level: easy
Section: Subtype Entities

47.   Which of the following is not true about subtype entities?
       a.)   Subtypes may be exclusive.
       b.)   The supertype and subtypes will have the same identifier.
       c.)   Subtypes are used to avoid a situation in which some attributes are required to be null.
       d.)   Subtypes have attributes that are required by the supertype.
       e.)   Subtypes can produce a closer-fitting data model.

Level: moderate
Section: Subtype Entities

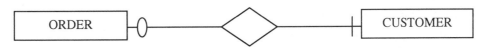

48.   If a given customer can place a maximum of many orders and a given order can be placed by at most one customer, which of the following should be placed inside the relationship in the figure shown above?
       a.)   0:1
       b.)   1:1
       c.)   1:N
       d.)   N:1
       e.)   N:M

Level: moderate
Section: Relationships

49.   In terms of generalization hierarchies, the characteristic of "inheritance" means that:
       a.)   the attributes of an instance of the supertype include the attributes of the subtype
       b.)   an instance of the supertype must belong to one of the subtypes
       c.)   the attributes of an instance of the subtype include the attributes of the supertype
       d.)   there is a redundant relationship among instances of the subtype
       e.)   the attributes of different subtypes must not overlap with each other

Level: hard
Section: Subtype Entities

50.   Which of the following is not true about business rules?
       a.)   Business rules are captured in an E-R diagram. (page DOCUMENTATION OF BUSINESS RULES, easy)
       b.)   Business rules may restrict the processing against entities.
       c.)   Business rules may be enforced by the DBMS.
       d.)   Business rules may be enforced by application programs.
       f.)   Business rules may be written manual procedures.

Level: easy
Section: Documentation of Business Rules

51.   Which of the following is true about UML?
       a.)   UML is a methodology for developing OOP systems.
       b.)   UML is a set of tools to support the development OOP systems.
       c.)   UML is primarily focused database development.
       d.)   Both a and b are correct.
       e.)   All of the above are correct.

Level: hard
Section: UML-Style Entity-Relationship Diagrams

52.   In UML style E-R diagrams, the second segment of an entity class contains _____.
       a.)   the name of the entity
       b.)   the cardinalities of the entity
       c.)   constraints and methods
       d.)   relationships
       e.)   entity attributes

Level: easy
Section: UML-Style Entity-Relationship Diagrams

53.   Which of following would indicate a minimum cardinality of 1 and a maximum cardinality of many in UML notation?
       a.)   1:N
       b.)   1 .. N
       c.)   1 / *
       d.)   1 .. *
       e.)   1: *

Level: moderate
Section: UML Entities and Relationship

54.   In UML style E-R diagrams, the third segment of an entity class contain _____.
       a.)   the name of the entity
       b.)   the cardinalities of the entity
       c.)   constraints and methods
       d.)   relationships
       e.)   entity attributes

Level: easy
Section: UML Entities and Relationship

55.   Which of the following is not a true statement about the current version of UML?
    a.)   UML places a filled-in diamond on the parent of a weak entity.
    b.)   UML does not provide a means to document exclusivity among subtypes.
    c.)   UML uses the label <identifying> to document an ID-dependent relationship
    d.)   UML does not provide a means of identifying a recursive relationship.
    e.)   UML shows the cardinality on the parent entity of a weak entity as simple "1".

Level: hard
Section: Representation of Weak Entities

56.   In UML style E-R diagrams, which of the following would be considered a class attribute of the entity class CUSTOMER?
    a.)   Customer Name (meaning, the first and last name of the customer)
    b.)   Customer Address (meaning, the street, city, state, and zip code of the customer's residence)
    c.)   Customer Count (meaning, the count of the number of customers)
    d.)   Customer Number (meaning, a assigned number to uniquely identify a customer)
    e.)   both a and b

Level: hard
Section: Constructs Introduced by UML

57.   Which of the following is <u>not</u> a characteristic that was introduced to E-R diagramming by UML?
    a.)   class attributes
    b.)   relationship attributes
    c.)   visibility of attributes
    d.)   methods
    e.)   constraints

Level: hard
Section: Relationships

58.   In UML, an attribute preceded by a _____ is "protected".
    a.)   !
    b.)   #
    c.)   -
    d.)   +
    e.)   <Persistent>

Level: moderate
Section: Constructs Introduced by UML

59.   In UML, an attribute that is accessible only by methods of its entity class or of its subclasses is
       said to be _____.
       a.)   private
       b.)   exclusive
       c.)   protected
       d.)   public
       e.)   persistent

Level: easy
Section: *Constructs Introduced by UML*

60.   In UML, an attribute that is accessible only methods of its entity class is said to be _____.
       a.)   private
       b.)   exclusive
       c.)   protected
       d.)   public
       e.)   persistent

Level: easy
Section: *Constructs Introduced by UML*

61.   In UML, an attribute that is accessible and can be changed by any method of any object is said to
       be _____.
       a.)   private
       b.)   exclusive
       c.)   protected
       d.)   public
       e.)   persistent

Level: easy
Section: *Constructs Introduced by UML*

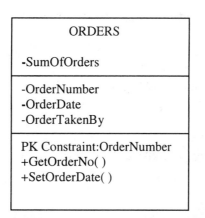

62.   In the UML style entity class ORDERS shown above, "SumOfOrders" is _____.
       a.)   an entity attribute
       b.)   method
       c.)   constraint
       d.)   class attribute
       e.)   none of the above

Level: easy
Section: *Constructs Introduced by UML*

63.   In the UML style entity class ORDERS shown above, "GetOrderNo( )" is a _____.
       a.)   private method
       b.)   protected constraint
       c.)   public constraint
       d.)   public method
       e.)   protected method

Level: moderate
Section: *Constructs Introduced by UML*

64.   One technique that is useful in evaluating an E-R data model before designing it is to
_____.
   a.)   generate forms from a prototype
   b.)   pose potential queries against the design
   c.)   create sample tables
   d.)   generate sample reports from a prototype
   e.)   none of the above

Level: hard
Section: Evaluating the E-R Data Model

Fill in the Blank Questions

65.   A(n) _entity_ is something that the users want to track in their environment.
Level: easy
Section: Entities

66.   Entities of a given type are grouped into _entity classes_.
Level: easy
Section: Entities

67.   A(n) _instance_ is the representation of a particular entity.
Level: easy
Section: Entities

68.   A(n) _composite_ attribute consists of a group of attributes.
Level: easy
Section: Attributes

69.   If an identifier is a(n) _unique_ identifier, it will one, and only one, entity instance.
Level: easy
Section: Identifies

70.   Entities can be associated with one another in _relationships_.
Level: easy
Section: Relationships

71.   The number of entity classes in a relationship is the _degree_ of the relationship.
Level: moderate
Section: Relationships

72.   Relationships of degree 2 are referred to as _binary_ relationships.
Level: moderate
Section: Relationships

73.   To show a minimum cardinality of "one", a(n) _hash mark_ is placed across the relationship line.
Level: *moderate*
Section: *Entity-Relationship Diagrams*

74.   To show a minimum cardinality of "zero", a(n) _oval_ is placed across the relationship line.
Level: *moderate*
Section: *Entity-Relationship Diagrams*

75.   Relationships among entities of a single class are sometimes called _recursive_ relationships.
Level: *moderate*
Section: *Entity-Relationship Diagrams*

76.   In some versions of E-R diagrams, attributes are shown in _ellipses_ attached to the entity to which they belong.
Level: *hard*
Section: *Showing Attributes in....*

77.   An entity that is not weak is called a(n) _strong_ entity.
Level: *easy*
Section: *Weak Entities*

78.   A special type of weak entity in which the identifier of the entity includes the identifier of another entity is called a(n) _ID-dependent_ entity.
Level: *moderate*
Section: *Weak Entities*

79.   Entities containing optional sets of attributes are often represented using _subtypes_.
Level: *moderate*
Section: *Subtype Entities*

80.   In a generalization hierarchy, the _supertype_ entity contains the attributes that are common to all subtypes.
Level: *moderate*
Section: *Subtype Entities*

81.   Generalization hierarchies have a characteristic called _inheritance_, which means that entities in the subtypes have all the attributes of the supertype.
Level: *hard*
Section: *Subtype Entities*

82.   _Business rules_ may or may not be enforced by the DBMS or by application programs, but it is important that they become a part of the system's requirements.
Level: *hard*
Section: *Documentation of Business Rules*

83.   Computer-based tools for building E-R diagrams are showing up in popular _CASE_ products.
Level: *moderate*
Section: *....and Case Tools*

84.   UML is a set of structures and techniques for designing _object-oriented_ programs and
        applications.
Level: easy
Section: UML-Style Entity-Relationship Diagrams

85.   In UML style E-R diagrams, a(n) _asterisk_ means a maximum cardinality of "many". (
Level: moderate
Section: UML Entities and Relationships

86.   In UML style E-R diagrams, a filled-in diamond is placed on the _parent_ of a weak entity.
Level: moderate
Section: Representation of Weak Entities

87.   When modeling a weak entity in UML style E-R diagrams, the cardinality on the parent entity is
        always shown as _1_. (page Representation of Weak Entities, hard)
Level: hard
Section: Representation of Weak Entities

88.   In UML style E-R diagrams, the fact that a weak entity is not ID-dependent is indicated by
        putting the label _<non-identifying>_ on the relationship.
Level: hard
Section: Representation of Weak Entities

89.   In UML style E-R diagrams, the classes of all entities that are to be stored in the database are
        labeled with the keyword _<Persistent>_.
Level: hard
Section: Constructs Introduced by UML

90.   In UML style E-R diagrams, an attribute that is preceded by a "+" has a visibility of _public_.
Level: hard
Section: Constructs Introduced by UML

91.   In UML style E-R diagrams, an attribute that is preceded by a "#" has a visibility of _protected_.
Level: hard
Section: Constructs Introduced by UML

92.   In UML style E-R diagrams, an attribute that is preceded by a "-" has a visibility of _private_.
Level: hard
Section: Constructs Introduced by UML

93.   One technique to evaluate the E-R data model is to pose _queries_ against the design.
Level: hard
Section: Evaluating the E-R Data Model

94.   The objective of data modeling is not to model reality, but rather the _users' perceptions_ of
        reality.
Level: hard
Section: Databases as Models of Modesl

Essay Questions

95. What new contributions to data modeling do UML style E-R diagrams introduce? How valuable are these from a practical perspective?
     UML style diagrams are a relatively new technique that focuses on object-oriented application design. UML style diagrams introduce new, object-oriented, concepts to data modeling, such as persistence, class attributes, visibility of attributes, and methods. All of these concepts are of limited practical value to actual database design since they cannot be easily or effectively represented in a relational database.
     Section: *Constructs Introduced by UML*

96. Explain the ambiguity in the definition of a weak entity.
     The traditional definition of a weak entity is an entity that cannot exist in the database unless another entity exists in the database. Taken literally, this would include any entity that has a minimum cardinality of "1" to another entity since it could not be placed into the database without the existence of the second entity. Many people feel that this definition is too broad. Therefore, an alternative definition of a weak entity that would require an entity to logically depend on another entity in order to be considered weak has been presented. Under this more narrow definition, all entities that have a minimum cardinality of "1" to another entity would not be considered weak.
     Section: *Weak Entities*

97. Explain the concept of a generalization hierarchy and how it is represented in a traditional E-R diagram.
     A generalization hierarchy is when instances of an entity can be categorized into different types with each type sharing some common characteristics while having certain characteristics that are unique to each type. This is represented in E-R diagrams through the use of supertype and subtype entities. The supertype entity class contains the attributes that are common to all of the subtypes. The subtype entity classes represent the different types, or categories, of the supertype. Only the attributes that are unique to a given subtype tend to be listed as the attributes of that subtype. However, generalization hierarchies have a characteristic called "inheritance", which indicates that all subtypes include, or inherit, all the attributes of the supertype. Each subtype has a relationship with the supertype. All subtypes should have the same identifier as the supertype since they represent different perspectives of the same thing.
     Section: *Subtype Entities*

98. What are "business rules"? What is their role in database design? How are they enforced?
     Business rules are policies that constrain the processing of the entities by an information system. These rules often surface during requirements analysis for database design, however, they typically cannot be captured in an E-R diagram. They are an important part of the overall system design, and should be documented with the data requirements. These policies may eventually be enforced by the DBMS, the application program, or through manual procedures for the users.
     Section: *Documentation of Business Rules*

99.   Is it the objective of database design to model the real world? Why, or why not?
       No, it is not the objective of database design to model the real world. Reality is too complex, contains too much data, and contains too many relationships that are extraneous to the needs of the users. The objective of database design is to model the users' perception of their business environment. This produces a more parsimonious model that effectively supports the intended use by the business users.
       Section: Databases

CHAPTER 4

The Semantic Object Model

True-False Questions

1. Whether a developer uses an E-R model or a semantic object model, the eventual database design that is created should be exactly the same.
    Answer: False   *Level: moderate*
    Section: Chapter Introduction

2. The semantic object model is different from object-oriented database processing.
    Answer: True   *Level: easy*
    Section: Chapter Introduction

3. Semantic objects represent the users' perceptions more closely than the E-R model.
    Answer: True   *Level: moderate*
    Section: Semantic Objects

4. Unlike entities, semantic objects are not grouped into classes.
    Answer: False   *Level: easy*
    Section: Semantic Objects
    Subsection: Defining Semantic Objects

5. An "identifier" is a named collection of attributes that sufficiently describes a distinct identity.
    Answer: False   *Level: hard*
    Section: Semantic Objects
    Subsection: Defining Semantic Objects

6. Semantic objects represent distinct identities.
    Answer: True   *Level: easy*
    Section: Semantic Objects
    Subsection: Defining Semantic Objects

7. A semantic object must represent something with a physical existence.
    Answer: False   *Level: hard*
    Section: Semantic Objects
    Subsection: Defining Semantic Objects

8. Attributes of a semantic object that contain only a single element are called link attributes.
    Answer: False   *Level: moderate*
    Section: Semantic Objects
    Subsection: Attributes

9.   A simple attribute has only one element.
        Answer: True   *Level: easy*
        Section: Semantic Objects
        Subsection: Attributes

10.   An attribute that contains a group of other attributes is called a composite attribute.
        Answer: False   *Level: moderate*
        Section: Semantic Objects
        Subsection: Attributes

11.   Semantic object attributes are used to establish a relationship between one semantic object and another.
        Answer: True   *Level: easy*
        Section: Semantic Objects
        Subsection: Attributes

12.   All attributes of a semantic object are collectively referred to as "semantic object attributes".
        Answer: False   *Level: hard*
        Section: Semantic Objects
        Subsection: Attributes

13.   For simple attributes in a semantic object model, only the maximum cardinality needs to be indicated.
        Answer: False   *Level: moderate*
        Section: Semantic Objects
        Subsection: Attributes

14.   The cardinality of a group attribute is inherited by all the attributes in that group.
        Answer: False   *Level: moderate*
        Section: Semantic Objects
        Subsection: Attributes

15.   The cardinalities of an attribute operate only between the attribute and the container of the attribute.
        Answer: True   *Level: moderate*
        Section: Semantic Objects
        Subsection: Attributes

16.   Object attributes are always paired attributes.
        Answer: True   *Level: hard*
        Section: Semantic Objects
        Subsection: Attributes

17.   An object identifier is an attribute or group of attributes that always uniquely identifies object instances.
        Answer: False   *Level: hard*
        Section: Semantic Objects
        Subsection: Object Identifiers

18.   Object identifiers may or may not be unique.
        Answer: True   *Level: moderate*
        Section: Semantic Objects
        Subsection: Object Identifiers

19.   The cardinality of an object identifier is almost always 1.1.
        Answer: True   *Level: hard*
        Section: Semantic Objects
        Subsection: Object Identifiers

20.   The domain of simple and group attributes include both a physical description and a semantic
        description.
        Answer: True   *Level: easy*
        Section: Semantic Objects
        Subsection: Attribute Domains

21.   The domain of an object attribute is a dynamically enumerated list containing all object instances
        of a particular type.
        Answer: True   *Level: moderate*
        Section: Semantic Objects
        Subsection: Attribute Domains

22.   The portion of a semantic object that is visible to a particular application is called the "application
        object".
        Answer: False   *Level: moderate*
        Section: Semantic Objects
        Subsection: Semantic Object Views

23.   An attribute that is computed from other values has a "formula domain".
        Answer: True   *Level: hard*
        Section: Creating Data Models with Semantic Objects
        Subsection: Specifying Objects

24.   A "simple object" is a semantic object that contains only single-value object attributes.
        Answer: False   *Level: easy*
        Section: Types of Objects
        Subsection: Simple Objects

25.   A "simple object" can contain only simple attributes.
        Answer: False   *Level: easy*
        Section: Types of Objects
        Subsection: Simple Objects

26.   A "composite object" is exactly like a "simple object" except that it contains at least one attribute
        with a maximum cardinality greater than 1.
        Answer: True   *Level: moderate*
        Section: Types of Objects
        Subsection: Composite Objects

27.   A "composite object" can not contain more than one multi-valued attribute.
      Answer: False   *Level: moderate*
      Section: Types of Objects
      Subsection: Composite Objects

28.   It is possible to include a multi-valued simple attribute within a multi-valued group attribute.
      Answer: True   *Level: easy*
      Section: Types of Objects
      Subsection: Composite Objects

29.   A "compound object" contains at least one multi-value, simple or group attribute but no object attributes.
      Answer: False   *Level: easy*
      Section: Types of Objects
      Subsection: Compound Objects

30.   A "compound object" can contain no multi-value attributes.
      Answer: False   *Level: moderate*
      Section: Types of Objects
      Subsection: Compound Objects

31.   A semantic object that has a multi-value group attribute containing an object attribute is called a "hybrid object".
      Answer: True   *Level: moderate*
      Section: Types of Objects
      Subsection: Hybrid Objects

32.   A "hybrid object" is a semantic object that relates two or more objects and stores data that are peculiar to that relationship.
      Answer: False   *Level: moderate*
      Section: Types of Objects
      Subsection: Association Objects

33.   Parent attributes appear as the first attribute of a subtype object and are always required.
      Answer: True   *Level: easy*
      Section: Types of Objects
      Subsection: Parent / Subtype Objects

34.   Subtype attributes in the parent object always have a minimum cardinality of 1.
      Answer: False   *Level: hard*
      Section: Types of Objects
      Subsection: Parent / Subtype Objects

35.   The parent object inherits all of the attributes of the subtype object.
      Answer: False   *Level: easy*
      Section: Types of Objects
      Subsection: Parent / Subtype Objects

36.   A semantic object can not have more than one subtype attribute.
        Answer: False   *Level: moderate*
        Section: Types of Objects
        Subsection: Parent / Subtype Objects

37.   From a semantic object perspective, an entity in an E-R model represents only a portion of the
        data in the users' model of that entity in their environment.
        Answer: True   *Level: moderate*
        Section: Comparing the Semantic Object and the E-R Model

Multiple Choice Questions

38.   The term "semantic" means:
        a.)   data
        b.)   meaning
        c.)   attribute
        d.)   detailed
        e.)   true

Level: easy
Section: Semantic Objects

39.   Which of the following is not true of semantic objects?
        a.)   always represent physical entities
        b.)   always provide a sufficient description
        c.)   are always named
        d.)   always describe a distinct identity
        e.)   always contain a collection of attributes

Level: moderate
Section: Semantic Objects
Subsection: Defining Semantic Objects

40.   Semantic objects are grouped into _____.
        a.)   composites
        b.)   entities
        c.)   objects
        d.)   classes
        e.)   associations

Level: easy
Section: Semantic Objects
Subsection: Defining Semantic Objects

41.   When we say a collection of attributes is a "sufficient description", that means it:
    a.)   contains all possible attributes of that object
    b.)   contains enough attributes that users can distinguish between instances
    c.)   contains all the attributes necessary for users to do their work
    d.)   contains enough attributes that the developer can implement a table
    e.)   contains domain specifications for each attribute

Level: hard
Section: Semantic Objects
Subsection: Defining Semantic Objects

42.   Which type of attribute has a single element?
    a.)   single
    b.)   simple
    c.)   link
    d.)   compound
    e.)   semantic

Level: hard
Section: Semantic Objects
Subsection: Attributes

43.   Which type of attribute is composed of other attributes?
    a.)   simple
    b.)   meta
    c.)   group
    d.)   compound
    e.)   composite

Level: easy
Section: Semantic Objects
Subsection: Attributes

44.   Which of the following refers to an attribute that establishes a relationship between semantic objects?
    a.)   semantic object attribute
    b.)   object attribute
    c.)   object link
    d.)   both a and b
    e.)   all of the above

Level: easy
Section: Semantic Objects
Subsection: Attributes

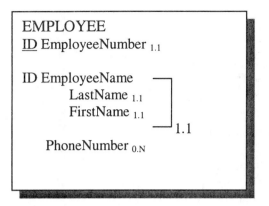

45.   In the EMPLOYEE semantic object above, what is the minimum cardinality of the attribute
        PhoneNumber?
        a.)   one
        b.)   zero
        c.)   two
        d.)   many
        e.)   insufficient information to determine

Level: easy
Section: Semantic Objects
Subsection: Attributes

46.   Because the semantic object model has no one-way object relationships, object attributes are
        sometimes called _____.
        a.)   binary attributes
        b.)   dual attributes
        c.)   paired attributes
        d.)   set attributes
        e.)   relational attributes

Level: moderate
Section: Semantic Objects
Subsection: Attributes

47.   A group identifier:
        a.   has more than one attribute
        b.   identifies a group of instances
        c.   identifies a group of attributes in an object
        d.   is the identifier for a group of semantic objects
        e.   links two objects

Level: moderate
Section: Semantic Objects
Subsection: Object Identifiers

```
┌─────────────────────────────────┐
│ STUDENT                         │
│ ID StudentID 1.1                │
│                                 │
│ ID StudentName  ─┐              │
│        LastName 1.1  │          │
│        FirstName 1.1 ┘          │
│                        1.1      │
│     PhoneNumber 0.N             │
│                                 │
│     StudentAddress ─┐           │
│        Street 1.1   │           │
│        City 1.1     │           │
│        State 1.1    │           │
│        ZipCode 1.1 ─┘           │
│                        0.N      │
└─────────────────────────────────┘
```

48.   In terms of the STUDENT semantic object above, which of the following is true?
      a.)   a student may have at most one phone number
      b.)   a student may or may not have a value for zip code
      c.)   a student must have at least one phone number
      d.)   a student can have at most one Street
      e.)   a student may or may not have a Student ID

Level: hard
Section: Semantic Objects
Subsection: Attributes

49.   If a non-identifying simple attribute has a cardinality of _____, the cardinality does not have
      to be shown in the semantic object diagram.
      a.)   N.M
      b.)   0.1
      c.)   0.N
      d.)   1.1
      e.)   1.N

Level: easy
Section: Semantic Objects
Subsection: Object Identifiers

```
┌─────────────────────────────────┐
│ STUDENT                         │
│ ID StudentID 1.1                │
│                                 │
│ ID StudentName    ┐             │
│       LastName 1.1 │            │
│       FirstName 1.1 ┘           │
│                     └ 1.1       │
│   PhoneNumber 0.N               │
│                                 │
│   StudentAddress  ┐             │
│       Street 1.1   │            │
│       City 1.1     │            │
│       State 1.1    │            │
│       ZipCode 1.1  ┘            │
│                     0.N         │
└─────────────────────────────────┘
```

50.   In terms of the STUDENT semantic object above, which of the following is <u>not</u> true?
   a.)   a student must have a student ID
   b.)   a student must have exactly one last name
   c.)   a student must have exactly one city
   d.)   a student may not have a phone number
   e.)   a student may have many phone numbers

Level: moderate
Section: Semantic Objects
Subsection: Attributes

51.   Which of the following is not true about object identifiers?
   a.)   must be unique
   b.)   usually have a cardinality of 1.1
   c.)   are used by the users to identify object instances
   d.)   may be a group attribute
   e.)   are denoted by "ID" on the semantic object diagram

Level: moderate
Section: Semantic Objects·
Subsection: Object Identifiers

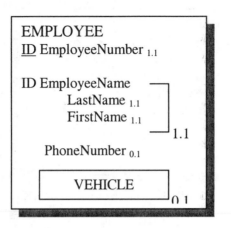

52.   In terms of the EMPLOYEE semantic object above, what is the maximum number of employees
       that a vehicle can be associated with?
       a.)   one
       b.)   zero
       c.)   two
       d.)   many
       e.)   insufficient information to determine

Level: hard
Section: Semantic Objects
Subsection: Attributes

EMPLOYEE
ID EmployeeNumber $_{1.1}$

ID EmployeeName
     LastName $_{1.1}$
     FirstName $_{1.1}$
                      1.1
PhoneNumber $_{0.1}$

VEHICLE
                      0.1

53.   In the EMPLOYEE semantic object above, which attributes are unique object identifiers?
       a.)   EmployeeNumber only
       b.)   Vehicle only
       c.)   EmployeeNumber and EmployeeName
       d.)   EmployeeNumber and Vehicle
       e.)   EmployeeNumber, EmployeeName, and Vehicle

Level: moderate
Section: Semantic Objects
Subsection: Object Identifiers

54.   Which of the following is not true about attribute domains?
       a.)   includes a physical description
       b.)   may include an enumerated list
       c.)   includes a semantic description
       d.)   may include a set of object instances
       e.)   is not needed for group attributes

Level: moderate
Section: Semantic Objects
Subsection: Attribute Domains

55.   The portion of a semantic object that is visible to a particular application is called a(n)
       _____.
       a.)   semantic object subset
       b.)   subtype semantic object
       c.)   semantic object view
       d.)   application semantic object
       e.)   program object

Level: moderate
Section: Semantic Objects
Subsection: Semantic Object Views

56.   Views can be used to:
       a.)   help develop the data model from existing reports
       b.)   help users articulate their data needs
       c.)   relate data model requirements to management
       d.)   normalize a relation
       e.)   express a semantic description of an attribute

Level: hard
Section: Semantic Objects
Subsection: Semantic Object Views

57.   When the value of an attribute is computed from other values, it is said to have a _____.
       a.)   computed domain
       b.)   application view
       c.)   formula domain
       d.)   semantic description
       e.)   enumerated list

Level: hard
Section: Creating a Data Model with Semantic Objects
Subsection: Specifying Objects

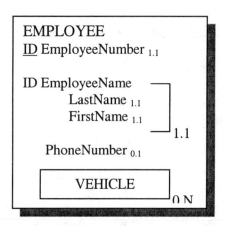

58.   The EMPLOYEE semantic object above is an example of what type of semantic object?
   a.)   hybrid
   b.)   complex
   c.)   compound
   d.)   composite
   e.)   simple

Level: *easy*
Section: *Types of Objects*
Subsection: *Compound Objects*

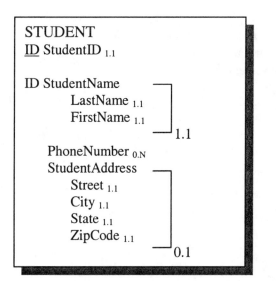

59.   The STUDENT semantic object above is an example of what type of semantic object?
   a.)   hybrid
   b.)   complex
   c.)   compound
   d.)   composite
   e.)   simple

Level: *easy*
Section: *Types of Objects*
Subsection: *Simple Objects*

60.   A *simple object* is a semantic object that contains only _____.
     a.)   single-value, simple or group attributes
     b.)   single-value, object attributes
     c.)   multi-value, simple or group attributes
     d.)   single-value, simple attributes
     e.)   simple attributes

Level: easy
Section: Types of Objects
Subsection: Simple Objects

```
STUDENT
ID StudentID 1.1

ID StudentName    ⌐
      LastName 1.1 |
      FirstName 1.1 |
                  ⌐ 1.1
PhoneNumber 0.N
StudentAddress    ⌐
      Street 1.1   |
      City 1.1     |
      State 1.1    |
      ZipCode 1.1  |
                  ⌐ 0.N
```

61.   The STUDENT semantic object above is an example of what type of semantic object?
     a.)   hybrid
     b.)   complex
     c.)   compound
     d.)   composite
     e.)   simple

Level: easy
Section: Types of Objects
Subsection: Composite Objects

62.   A *composite object* is a semantic object that contains _____.
     a.)   single-value, simple or group attributes but no object attributes
     b.)   at least one object attribute
     c.)   at least one multi-value, simple or group attribute but no object attributes
     d.)   at least one multi-value, object attribute
     e.)   at least one group attribute but no object attributes

Level: moderate
Section: Types of Objects
Subsection: Composite Objects

63.   A *compound object* is a semantic object that contains at least one _____.
      a.)   single-value, group attribute
      b.)   multi-value, simple or group attribute
      c.)   object
      d.)   multi-value
      e.)   group

Level: moderate
Section: Types of Objects
Subsection: Compound Objects

64.   A *hybrid object* is a semantic object that contains at least one _____.
      a.)   single-value group attribute that includes a multi-value semantic object attribute
      b.)   single-value group attribute that includes a any semantic object attribute
      c.)   multi-value group attribute and at least one multi-value semantic object attribute
      d.)   multi-value group attribute that includes any semantic object attribute
      e.)   a group attribute and a semantic object attribute

Level: hard
Section: Types of Objects
Subsection: Hybrid Objects

65.   Which of the following is <u>not</u> true about association objects?
      a.)   used to relate two or more objects
      b.)   can store data that is peculiar to the relationship between objects
      c.)   must have two or more object attributes
      d.)   may not have a unique identifier of its own
      e.)   can not contain multi-value attributes

Level: moderate
Section: Types of Objects
Subsection: Association Objects

66.   Regarding a subtype object:
      a.)   the first attribute must be the parent attribute
      b.)   it inherits all of the attributes of its parent
      c.)   it has a paired attribute in its parent
      d.)   it can be nested
      e.)   all of the above

Level: easy
Section: Types of Objects
Subsection: Parent / Subtype Objects

67.   A version object:
a.)   may be a composite object
b.)   typically contains the archetype object in its identifier
c.)   typically is a simple object
d.)   produces archetype objects
e.)   all of the above

Level: *moderate*
Section: *Types of Objects*
Subsection: *Archetype / Version Objects*

Fill in the Blank Questions

68.   The word semantic means __meaning__ .
Level: *easy*
Section: *Semantic Objects*

69.   A semantic object is a named collection of attributes that sufficiently describes a(n) __distinct identity__ .
Level: *moderate*
Section: *Semantic Objects*
Subsection: *Defining Semantic Objects*

70.   Semantic objects are grouped into __classes__ .
Level: *easy*
Section: *Semantic Objects*
Subsection: *Defining Semantic Objects*

71.   Objects represent __distinct identities__ ; that is, they are something that users recognize as independent and separate.
Level: *moderate*
Section: *Semantic Objects*
Subsection: *Defining Semantic Objects*

72.   Simple attributes have a single __element__ .
Level: *easy*
Section: *Semantic Objects*
Subsection: *Attributes*

73.   __Group__ attributes are composites of other attributes.
Level: *easy*
Section: *Semantic Objects*
Subsection: *Attributes*

74.   Semantic object attributes are attributes that establish a(n) __relationship__ between one semantic object and another.
Level: easy
Section: Semantic Objects
Subsection: Attributes

75.   Object attributes, or paired attributes, are also sometimes called __object links__ .
Level: hard
Section: Semantic Objects
Subsection: Attributes

76.   Cardinalities only operate between an attribute and the __container__ of that attribute.
Level: hard
Section: Semantic Objects
Subsection: Attributes

77.   The __minimum cardinality__ indicates the number of instances of the attribute that must exist in order for the object to be valid.
Level: easy
Section: Semantic Objects
Subsection: Attributes

78.   An object __identifier__ is one or more attributes that the users employ to identify object instances.
Level: easy
Section: Semantic Objects
Subsection: Object Identifiers

79.   A(n) __group identifier__ is an identifier that has more than one attribute.
Level: easy
Section: Semantic Objects
Subsection: Object Identifiers

80.   The __domain__ of an attribute is a description of an attribute's possible values.
Level: easy
Section: Semantic Objects
Subsection: Attribute Domains

81.   The __physical__ description of a domain indicates the type of data and length of the data.
Level: moderate
Section: Semantic Objects
Subsection: Attribute Domains

82.   The __semantic__ description of a domain indicates the function or purpose of the attribute.
Level: moderate
Section: Semantic Objects
Subsection: Attribute Domains

83.   A(n) __enumerated list__ specifies the physical description of a domain when it consists of a set of specific values.
Level: hard
Section: Semantic Objects
Subsection: Attribute Domains

84.   The domain of a(n) __object attribute__ is the set of object instances of that type.
Level: moderate
Section: Semantic Objects
Subsection: Attribute Domains

85.   The domain of a(n) __object attribute__ is a dynamically enumerated list containing all of the object instances of a particular type.
Level: hard
Section: Semantic Objects
Subsection: Attribute Domains

86.   The portion of an object that is visible to a particular application is called the __semantic object view__ .
Level: easy
Section: Semantic Objects
Subsection: Semantic Object Views

87.   When the value of an attribute is computed from other values, the attribute has a(n) __formula__ domain.
Level: hard
Section: Creating Data Models with Semantic Objects
Subsection: Specifying Objects

88.   A(n) __single-value attribute__ is an attribute whose maximum cardinality is one.
Level: easy
Section: Types of Objects

89.   A(n) __multi-value attribute__ is an attribute whose maximum cardinality is greater than one.
Level: easy
Section: Types of Objects

90.   A simple object is a semantic object that contains only __single-value__ , simple or group attributes.
Level: moderate
Section: Types of Objects
Subsection: Simple Objects

91.   A(n) __composite object__ is a semantic object that contains at least one multi-value, simple or group attribute but no object attributes.
Level: moderate
Section: Types of Objects
Subsection: Composite Objects

92.   A(n) __compound__ object contains at least one object attribute.
Level: *moderate*
Section: *Types of Objects*
Subsection: *Compound Objects*

93.   A(n) __hybrid__ object is a semantic object with at least one multi-valued group attribute that contains a semantic object attribute.
Level: *moderate*
Section: *Types of Objects*
Subsection: *Hybrid Objects*

94.   A(n) __association__ object relates two (or more) objects and stores data that are peculiar to that relationship.
Level: *easy*
Section: *Types of Objects*
Subsection: *Association Objects*

95.   The first attribute of a subtype object is the __parent attribute__.
Level: *moderate*
Section: *Types of Objects*
Subsection: *Parent / Subtype Objects*

96.   A subtype __inherits__ all of the attributes of its parent.
Level: *moderate*
Section: *Types of Objects*
Subsection: *Parent / Subtype Objects*

97.   A(n) __archetype__ object is a semantic object that produces other semantic objects that represent versions
Level: *moderate*
Section: *Types of Objects*
Subsection: *Archetype / Version Objects*

Essay Questions

98.   Explain the concept of semantic objects as being a "sufficient description".
       A semantic object is said to be a sufficient description in two ways. First, it is a sufficient description in that it contains all the attributes necessary for the users to do their work. Second, it is considered sufficient because it is self-contained. All of the data required about a given object is contained in that object; a user need not look anywhere else to find data about that object.
       Section: *Semantic Objects*
       Subsection: *Defining Semantic Objects*

99.   Explain why semantic object attributes are called paired attributes.
       Semantic object attributes are the mechanism for indicating a relationship between two semantic
       objects. When there is a relationship between two objects, the objects are placed as object
       attributes within each other. They are called paired attributes because relationships are by
       definition two-way relationships. Therefore, when a semantic object is placed in another
       semantic object as an object attribute, a corresponding object attribute representing the second
       semantic object is required in the first semantic object.
       Section: *Semantic Objects*
       Subsection: *Attributes*

100.   Describe the two ways that semantic object views can be used.
       A semantic object view can be used in two ways. First, it can be used during database design to
       reverse-engineer a data model. Since the view an application has of an object is represented in
       the reports, forms, and queries of that application, a developer can study the reports and forms
       that the users need and integrate those views into the data model. Second, once the database
       structure has been created, views can be used to develop new forms and reports from the existing
       database.
       Section: *Semantic Objects*
       Subsection: *Semantic Object Views*

101.   Distinguish between the physical description and the semantic description of an attribute domain.
       The physical description of an attribute defines the data type, length of the data, and other
       constraints that exist on the values the attribute can have. The physical description indicates
       specifications for the storage and processing of the attribute. The semantic description of the
       attribute indicates the logical meaning of the attribute in the users' environment. The semantic
       description differentiates between attributes that have the same physical description.
       Section: *Semantic Objects*
       Subsection: *Attribute Domains*

102.   Explain the differences between the E-R model and the semantic object model.
       The primary differences between the E-R model and the semantic object model come from the
       difference in orientation. The E-R model considers entities and relationships to be the basic
       building blocks of a data model. The semantic object model considered semantic objects to be
       the basic build block of a data model. The E-R model tends to be less detailed, thereby producing
       less metadata, than the semantic object model. Semantic objects, the basic building block of
       semantic object modeling, are self-contained from the users perspective. Everything that a user
       thinks of as being a characteristic of a given identity in their environment is captured within a
       single semantic object. With E-R models, all the data that a user thinks of as being a
       characteristic of a given identity is spread across multiple entities, requiring relationships to
       reconstruct the user's perspective. Semantic object models, therefore, tend to produce a data
       model that more closely resembles the users' model.
       Section: *Comparing the Semantic Object and E-R Model*

CHAPTER 5

The Relational Model and Normalization

True-False Questions

1.   A relation is a three-dimensional table.
        Answer: False   *Level: moderate*
        Section: The Relational Model

2.   The columns of a relation are sometimes called "tuples".
        Answer: False   *Level: easy*
        Section: The Relational Model

3.   Attribute Y is functionally dependent on attribute X if the value of attribute X determines the value of Y.
        Answer: True   *Level: moderate*
        Section: The Relational Model
        Subsection: Functional Dependencies

4.   The functional dependency noted as A → B, means that if the value of A can be determined from the value of B.
        Answer: False   *Level: easy*
        Section: The Relational Model
        Subsection: Functional Dependencies

5.   In the functional dependency shown as A → B, B is the determinant.
        Answer: False   *Level: moderate*
        Section: The Relational Model
        Subsection: Functional Dependencies

6.   Functional dependencies can involve groups of attributes.
        Answer: True   *Level: easy*
        Section: The Relational Model
        Subsection: Functional Dependencies

7.   A tuple is a group of one or more attributes that uniquely identifies a row.
        Answer: False   *Level: easy*
        Section: The Relational Model
        Subsection: Keys

8.   A row is uniquely identified by a key.
        Answer: True   *Level: easy*
        Section: The Relational Model
        Subsection: Keys

9.   A key can be composed of a group of attributes taken together.
        Answer: True   *Level: easy*
        Section: The Relational Model
        Subsection: Keys

10.   Keys and functional dependencies are the result of the underlying semantics of the users' mental models.
        Answer: True   *Level: hard*
        Section: The Relational Model
        Subsection: Keys

11.   It is possible to have a relation that does not have a key.
        Answer: False   *Level: moderate*
        Section: The Relational Model
        Subsection: Keys

12.   A determinant of a functional dependency may or may not be unique in a relation.
        Answer: True   *Level: moderate*
        Section: The Relational Model
        Subsection: Functional Dependencies, Keys, and Uniqueness

13.   Keys are always unique.
        Answer: True   *Level: easy*
        Section: The Relational Model
        Subsection: Functional Dependencies, Keys, and Uniqueness

14.   A key functionally determines an entire row.
        Answer: True   *Level: easy*
        Section: The Relational Model
        Subsection: Functional Dependencies, Keys, and Uniqueness

15.   If a table meets the minimum definition of a relation, it has an effective or appropriate structure.
        Answer: False   *Level: moderate*
        Section: Normalization

16.   Undesirable consequences of changing the data in a relation are called "modification anomalies".
        Answer: True   *Level: moderate*
        Section: Normalization

17.   A deletion anomaly exists when deleting data about one entity results in the loss of data about another entity.
        Answer: True   *Level: easy*
        Section: Normalization
        Subsection: Modification Anomalies

18.   A constraint, based on a business rule, that requires an instance of an entity to exist in one relation before it can be referenced in another relation is called an insertion anomaly.
        Answer: False   *Level: hard*
        Section: Normalization
        Subsection: Modification Anomalies

19.   A referential integrity constraint is based on a business rule.
       Answer: True   *Level: moderate*
       Section: Normalization
       Subsection: Modification Anomalies

20.   The essence of normalization is taking a relation that has more than one theme and breaking it
       into multiple relations that each has only one theme.
       Answer: True   *Level: easy*
       Section: Normalization
       Subsection: Essence of Normalization

21.   Breaking a relation into two or more relations may create the need for a referential integrity
       constraint to be defined.
       Answer: True   *Level: moderate*
       Section: Normalization
       Subsection: Essence of Normalization

22.   Relations are classified into "normal forms" based on the types of modification anomalies that
       they are vulnerable to.
       Answer: True   *Level: moderate*
       Section: Normalization
       Subsection: Classes of Relations

23.   The only normal form that guarantees that a relation is free from every possible type of anomaly
       is 5NF.
       Answer: False   *Level: hard*
       Section: Normalization
       Subsection: Classes of Relations

24.   Any table that meets the definition of a relation is in 2NF.
       Answer: False   *Level: easy*
       Section: First through Fifth Normal Forms

25.   A relation is in *first normal form* if all of its non-key attributes are dependent on part of the key.
       Answer: False   *Level: moderate*
       Section: First through Fifth Normal Forms

26.   To be in second normal form, a relation must contain no partial dependencies.
       Answer: True   *Level: moderate*
       Section: First through Fifth Normal Forms
       Subsection: Second Normal Form

27.   A relation is in second normal form if it is in first normal form and all of its non-key attributes are
       dependent on the entire key.
       Answer: True   *Level: moderate*
       Section: First through Fifth Normal Forms
       Subsection: Second Normal Form

28.   Relations that have a composite key and are in 1NF are automatically in 2NF.
       Answer: False   *Level: easy*
       Section: First through Fifth Normal Forms
       Subsection: Second Normal Form

29.   A transitive dependency exists when a non-key attribute is determined by only part of the key.
       Answer: False   *Level: moderate*
       Section: First through Fifth Normal Forms
       Subsection: Third Normal Form

30.   A relation is in 3NF if it is in 2NF and contains no transitive dependencies.
       Answer: True   *Level: easy*
       Section: First through Fifth Normal Forms
       Subsection: Third Normal Form

31.   A relation can have only one candidate key.
       Answer: False   *Level: moderate*
       Section: First through Fifth Normal Forms
       Subsection: Boyce-Codd Normal Form

32.   A relation is in Boyce-Codd Normal Form if it is in 3NF and every determinant is a candidate key.
       Answer: True   *Level: easy*
       Section: First through Fifth Normal Forms
       Subsection: Boyce-Codd Normal Form

33.   A multi-value dependency exists when a relation has at least three attributes, two of which are multi-value and their values depend only on the third attribute.
       Answer: True   *Level: moderate*
       Section: First through Fifth Normal Forms
       Subsection: Fourth Normal Form

34.   A relation is in 4NF if it is in 3NF and contains no multi-value dependencies.
       Answer: True   *Level: moderate*
       Section: First through Fifth Normal Forms
       Subsection: Fourth Normal Form

35.   Fifth normal form deals with obscure problems with transitive dependencies.
       Answer: False   *Level: easy*
       Section: First through Fifth Normal Forms
       Subsection: Fifth Normal Form

36.   A relation is in DK/NF if every domain is the logical consequence of the definition of constraints and keys.
       Answer: False   *Level: hard*
       Section: Domain Key Normal Form
       Subsection: Definition

37. In considering DK/NF, a constraint includes any rule governing static values in the relation except constraints that are time-based.
    Answer: True   *Level: moderate*
    Section: Domain Key Normal Form
    Subsection: Definition

38. There is no known algorithm for converting a relation into DK/NF.
    Answer: True   *Level: moderate*
    Section: Domain Key Normal Form
    Subsection: Definition

39. If A → B and B → A, then A and B have a many-to-many attribute relationship.
    Answer: False   *Level: moderate*
    Section: The Synthesis of Relations

40. Attributes that have a one-to-one attribute relationship must occur together in at least one relation.
    Answer: True   *Level: moderate*
    Section: The Synthesis of Relations
    Subsection: One-to-One Attribute Relationships

41. It is generally undesirable to have attributes that have a one-to-one attribute relationship appear in more than one relation together.
    Answer: True   *Level: moderate*
    Section: The Synthesis of Relations
    Subsection: One-to-One Attribute Relationships

42. In general, a row of a relation should have all of the data about one instance of the relation's theme.
    Answer: True   *Level: moderate*
    Section: Multi-Value Dependencies, Iteration 2

43. De-normalization is the process of constructing relations by synthesis of attribute relationships.
    Answer: False   *Level: moderate*
    Section: Optimization
    Subsection: De-Normalization

44. Relations may be unnormalized or de-normalized to improve database performance.
    Answer: True   *Level: easy*
    Section: Optimization
    Subsection: De-Normalization

Multiple Choice Questions

45.   A *relation* is also known as:
   a.)   a table
   b.)   a tuple
   c.)   a relationship
   d.)   an attribute
   e.)   a field

Level: easy
Section: The Relational Model

46.   A tuple is also known as a:
   a.)   table
   b.)   relation
   c.)   row
   d.)   field
   e.)   column

Level: moderate
Section: The Relational Model

47.   A functional dependency in a relation:
   a.)   usually involves a formula
   b.)   always involves a key
   c.)   exists among tuples
   d.)   must always be removed through normalization
   e.)   none of the above

Level: easy
Section: The Relational Model
Subsection: Functional Dependencies

48.   Which of the following is known to be true from the functional dependency shown as (A, B) →
        (C, D)?
   a.)   A is the determinant of C
   b.)   A and B together are determined by C and D together
   c.)   A and B together determine D
   d.)   C and D together determine A
   e.)   A determines B

Level: moderate
Section: The Relational Model
Subsection: Functional Dependencies

49.   Which of the following is known to be true from the functional dependency shown as
       A → (X, Y)?
       a.)   X is functionally dependent on A
       b.)   A determines Y
       c.)   A is a determinant
       d.)   X and Y are functionally dependent on A
       e.)   all of the above

Level: moderate
Section: The Relational Model
Subsection: Functional Dependencies

50.   Which of the following, if any, is <u>not</u> true about keys?
       a.)   can be a group of attributes taken together
       b.)   must uniquely identify a row
       c.)   are determined by users' mental models and business rules
       d.)   must be functionally determined by another attribute
       e.)   all of the above <u>are</u> true

Level: moderate
Section: The Relational Model
Subsection: Keys

51.   If the removal of facts about one entity results in the unintentional lose of data about another
       entity, this is referred to an a(n) _____.
       a.)   normalization anomaly
       b.)   insertion anomaly
       c.)   entity anomaly
       d.)   deletion anomaly
       e.)   removal anomaly

Level: moderate
Section: Normalization
Subsection: Modification Anomalies

52.   The notation CUST-CAR[License] ⊆ CAR-RENT[License] indicates:
       a.)   License in CAR-RENT is a subset of License in CUST-CAR.
       b.)   Before a value can be entered in the License field of the CAR-RENT relation, it must
              have a matching value in the License field of the CUST-CAR relation.
       c.)   License in CUST-CAR is functionally dependent on License in CAR-RENT.
       d.)   Before a value can be entered in the License field of the CUST-CAR relation, it must
              have a matching value in the License field of the CAR-RENT relation.
       e.)   CUST-CAR and CAR-RENT are functionally dependent on the License field.

Level: hard
Section: Normalization
Subsection: Modification Anomalies

53.   Which of the following is <u>not</u> true about normalization?
        a.)   produces relations with a single theme
        b.)   may create referential integrity constraints
        c.)   reduces the number of functional dependencies in the schema
        d.)   reduces anomalies
        e.)   splits a poorly structured relation into two or more well-structured relations

Level: *easy*
Section: *Normalization*
Subsection: *Essence of Normalization*

54.   A table that meets the definition of a relation is in:
        a.)   First Normal Form
        b.)   Second Normal Form
        c.)   Third Normal Form
        d.)   Boyce-Codd Normal Form
        e.)   Fourth Normal Form

Level: *easy*
Section: *First through Fifth Normal Forms*

55.   Which of the following is <u>not</u> a requirement for 1NF?
        a.)   cells must contain single values
        b.)   all entries in a column must be of the same kind
        c.)   no two rows may be identical
        d.)   rows must be ordered by the value of the key
        e.)   the order of the columns is insignificant

Level: *easy*
Section: *First through Fifth Normal Forms*

56.   A relation is in 2NF if it is in 1NF and all its non-key attributes are:
        a.)   dependent on part of the key
        b.)   dependent on all of the key
        c.)   independent of the key
        d.)   independent of each other
        e.)   independent of any other relation

Level: *moderate*
Section: *First through Fifth Normal Forms*
Subsection: *Second Normal Form*

57.   Which of the following is a requirement of 2NF?
        a.)   must contain a partial dependency
        b.)   must contain a composite key
        c.)   must contain no partial dependencies
        d.)   must contain no transitive dependencies
        e.)   must contain a multi-valued dependency

Level: moderate
Section: First through Fifth Normal Forms
Subsection: Second Normal Form

58.   A relation is in third normal form if it is in second normal form and all its non-key attributes are:
        a.)   dependent on part of the key
        b.)   dependent on all of the key
        c.)   independent of the key
        d.)   independent of each other
        e.)   independent of any other relation

Level: moderate
Section: First through Fifth Normal Forms
Subsection: Third Normal Form

59.   Which of the following is a requirement of 3NF?
        a.)   must contain a partial dependency
        b.)   must contain a composite key
        c.)   must contain no partial dependencies
        d.)   must contain no transitive dependencies
        e.)   must contain a multi-valued dependency

Level: moderate
Section: First through Fifth Normal Forms
Subsection: Third Normal Form

EMPLOYEE (SSN, SupervisorID, Department)
Key: SSN
Functional Dependencies: SSN → SupervisorID
                         SupervisorID → Department

SSN	Supervisor	Department
123-45-6789	100	Engineering
234-56-7890	200	Marketing
345-67-8901	100	Engineering
456-78-9012	300	Production
567-89-0123	100	Engineering
678-90-1234	200	Marketing

60.   Which type of dependency is present in the EMPLOYEE relation above?
   a.)   partial dependency
   b.)   transitive dependency
   c.)   determinant dependency
   d.)   multi-valued dependency
   e.)   deletion dependency

Level: hard
Section: First through Fifth Normal Forms
Subsection: Third Normal Form

61.   A relation is in Boyce-Codd normal form if it is in 3NF and:
   a.)   every determinant is a candidate key
   b.)   every determinant is a primary key
   c.)   every attribute is a candidate key
   d.)   there is more than one candidate key
   e.)   there is more than one primary key

Level: moderate
Section: First through Fifth Normal Forms
Subsection: Boyce-Codd Normal Form

62.   A "candidate key" is:
   a.)   a primary key.
   b.)   any group of attributes that are a determinant
   c.)   functionally dependent on the non-key attributes
   d.)   an attribute or group of attributes that can be the key
   e.)   the primary key selected to be the key of a relation

Level: easy
Section: First through Fifth Normal Forms
Subsection: Boyce-Codd Normal Form

63.   A *multi-value dependency* exists when a relation has:
   a.)   at least two attributes, both of them are multi-value, and their values depend on each other
   b.)   at least two attributes, one of them is multi-value, and its value depends on the other
   c.)   at least three attributes, two of them are multi-value, and their values depend on only the third attribute
   d.)   at least three attributes, one of them is multi-value, and its value depends on the other two attributes
   e.)   at least three attributes, all of them are multi-value, and their values depend on each other

Level: hard
Section: First through Fifth Normal Forms
Subsection: Fourth Normal Form

64.   A relation is in fourth normal form if it is in BCNF and it has no:
   a.)   transitive dependencies
   b.)   multi-value dependencies
   c.)   partial dependencies
   d.)   deletion dependencies
   e.)   referential integrity conflicts

Level: easy
Section: First through Fifth Normal Forms
Subsection: Fourth Normal Form

65.   The anomalies addressed by moving from BCNF to 4NF generally deal with:
   a.)   excessive updates and redundancy of data for each entity
   b.)   inability to uniquely identify an entity
   c.)   inability to reconstruct relations once they have been decomposed
   d.)   creation of identical rows in a relation
   e.)   functional dependencies

Level: hard
Section: First through Fifth Normal Forms
Subsection: Fourth Normal Form

66.   Fifth normal form deals with:
   a.)   excessive updates and redundancy of data for each entity
   b.)   inability to uniquely identify an entity
   c.)   inability to reconstruct relations once they have been decomposed
   d.)   creation of identical rows in a relation
   e.)   dependencies between referential integrity constraints

Level: moderate
Section: First through Fifth Normal Forms
Subsection: Fifth Normal Form

67.   A relation is in domain/key normal form if:
    a.)   every key of the relation is a logical consequence of the definition of constraints and determinants
    b.)   every key of the relation is a logical consequence of the definition of constraints and domains
    c.)   every constraint on the relation is a logical consequence of the definition of keys and determinants
    d.)   every constraint on the relation is a logical consequence of the definition of keys and domains
    e.)   every domain of the relation is a logical consequence of the definition of keys and constraints

Level: *moderate*
Section: *Domain / Key Normal Form*
Subsection: *Definition*

68.   In the definition of DK/NF, which of the following is a type of constraint that is <u>excluded</u> from consideration?
    a.)   edit rules
    b.)   intra-relation constraints
    c.)   functional dependencies
    d.)   time-based constraints
    e.)   inter-relation constraints

Level: *moderate*
Section: *Domain / Key Normal Form*
Subsection: *Definition*

69.   The advantage of having a relation in domain/key normal form is that:
    a.)   it takes less storage space than other normal forms
    b.)   it is easily obtained from Boyce-Codd normal form
    c.)   there is a relatively simple algorithm for obtaining DK/NF
    d.)   it is obtained by enforcing referential integrity constraints
    e.)   it is guaranteed to have no modification anomalies

Level: *easy*
Section: *Domain / Key Normal Form*
Subsection: *Definition*

70.   Synthesizing relations means that the developers start with a:
    a.)   relation containing functional dependencies
    b.)   relation without any functional dependencies
    c.)   set of attributes with certain functional dependencies
    d.)   set of domains and their constraints
    e.)   set of anomalies based on dependencies

Level: *easy*
Section: *The Synthesis of Relations*

71.   If two attributes *A* and *B* have a one-to-one attribute relationship, it is shown as:
        a.)   A → B and B → A
        b.)   A → B, but B not → A
        c.)   B → A, but A not → B
        d.)   A not → B and B not → A
        e.)   A → B

Level: *moderate*
Section: *The Synthesis of Relations*

72.   If two attributes *A* and *B* have a many-to-one attribute relationship, it is shown as:
        a.)   A → B and B → A
        b.)   A → B, but B not → A
        c.)   B → A, and A ← B
        d.)   A not → B and B not → A
        e.)   A → B

Level: *moderate*
Section: *The Synthesis of Relations*

73.   If two attributes *A* and *B* have a many-to-many attribute relationship, it is shown as:
        a.)   A → B and B → A
        b.)   A → B, but B not → A
        c.)   B → A, and A ← B
        d.)   A not → B and B not → A
        e.)   A → B

Level: *moderate*
Section: *The Synthesis of Relations*

74.   When creating a database with attributes that have a one-to-one attribute relationship:
        a.)   the two attributes must appear in a relation together
        b.)   usually only appear in one relation together
        c.)   other attributes that are functionally dependent on either of them may appear in a relation with them.
        d.)   either of the attributes can appear in relations without the other
        e.)   all of the above

Level: *moderate*
Section: *The Synthesis of Relations*
Subsection: *One-to-One Relationships*

75.   When a relation has a key consisting of multiple attributes, you can add a new attribute to the
relation:
a.)   without any restriction
b.)   so long as it is functionally dependent on part of the key
c.)   so long as it is functionally dependent on all of the key
d.)   so long as it is functionally dependent on a non-key attribute
e.)   so long as it is a candidate key

Level: *moderate*
Section: *The Synthesis of Relations*
Subsection: *Many-to-Many Relationships*

76.   Database performance can be improved through appropriate use of:
a.)   controlled redundancy
b.)   de-normalization
c.)   data integrity violations
d.)   synchronous dependencies
e.)   both a and b

Level: *moderate*
Section: *Optimization*

Fill in the Blank Questions

77.   A(n) relation   is a two-dimensional table.
Level: *easy*
Section: *The Relational Model*

78.   In relational terms, a row is called a(n) tuple .
Level: *easy*
Section: *The Relational Model*

79.   A functional dependency   is a relationship between attributes such that if we know the value of
one attribute, we can determine the value of the other attribute.
Level: *easy*
Section: *The Relational Model*
Subsection: *Functional Dependencies*

80.   If by knowing the value of A, we can find the value of B, then we would say that B is
functionally   dependent on A.
Level: *moderate*
Section: *The Relational Model*
Subsection: *Functional Dependencies*

81.   In functional dependencies, the attribute whose value is known or given is referred to as the <u>determinant</u> .
Level: moderate
Section: The Relational Model
Subsection: Functional Dependencies

82.   A(n) <u>key</u> is a group of one or more attributes that uniquely identifies a row.
Level: easy
Section: The Relational Model
Subsection: Keys

83.   Unlike determinants, <u>keys</u> are always unique.
Level: easy
Section: The Relational Model
Subsection: Functional Dependencies, Keys, and Uniqueness

84.   A key functionally determines the entire <u>row</u> .
Level: easy
Section: The Relational Model
Subsection: Functional Dependencies, Keys, and Uniqueness

85.   For some relations, changing the data can have undesirable consequences called <u>modification anomalies</u> .
Level: moderate
Section: Normalization

86.   Every time we break up a relation during the normalization process, we may create <u>referential integrity</u> constraints.
Level: moderate
Section: Normalization
Subsection: Essence of Normalization

87.   Normal forms are <u>nested</u> so that if a relation is in 2NF, it is also in 1NF.
Level: easy
Section: Normalization
Subsection: Classes of Relations

88.   A relation that is in <u>domain / key</u> normal form is assured to be free from all anomalies.
Level: moderate
Section: Normalization
Subsection: Classes of Relations

89.   Any table that meets the definition of a(n) <u>relation</u> is said to be in first normal form.
Level: easy
Section: First through Fifth Normal Form

90.   If a table is a relation then it is in <u>1NF</u> .
Level: easy
Section: First through Fifth Normal Form

91.   To be in 1NF, the cells of a table must contain a(n) __single__ value.
Level: *moderate*
Section: *First through Fifth Normal Form*

92.   A relation is in 2NF if it is in 1NF and all of its non-key attributes are dependent on __all of the key__ .
Level: *moderate*
Section: *First through Fifth Normal Form*
Subsection: *Second Normal Form*

93.   A relation is in __second normal form__ if all its non-key attributes are dependent on the entire key.
Level: *easy*
Section: *First through Fifth Normal Form*
Subsection: *Second Normal Form*

94.   A relation is in 2NF if it is in 1NF and has no __partial dependencies__ .
Level: *easy*
Section: *First through Fifth Normal Form*
Subsection: *Second Normal Form*

95.   A relation is in third normal form if it is in second normal form and has no __transitive dependencies__ .
Level: *moderate*
Section: *First through Fifth Normal Form*
Subsection: *Third Normal Form*

96.   Two or more attributes or attribute collections that can be a key are called __candidate keys__ .
Level: *moderate*
Section: *First through Fifth Normal Form*
Subsection: *Boyce-Codd Normal Form*

97.   A defining requirement for __Boyce-Codd__ normal form is that every determinant must be a candidate key.
Level: *moderate*
Section: *First through Fifth Normal Form*
Subsection: *Boyce-Codd Normal Form*

98.   A relation is in BCNF if it is in 3NF and every __determinant__ is a candidate key.
Level: *moderate*
Section: *First through Fifth Normal Form*
Subsection: *Boyce-Codd Normal Form*

99.   A relation is in BCNF if it is in 3NF and every determinant is a __candidate key__ .
Level: *moderate*
Section: *First through Fifth Normal Form*
Subsection: *Boyce-Codd Normal Form*

100.   Relations in BCNF have no anomalies in regard to functional dependencies .
Level: hard
Section: First through Fifth Normal Form
Subsection: Boyce-Codd Normal Form

101.   A multi-value dependency exists when a relation has at least three attributes, two of them are multi-value, and their values depend on only the third attribute.
Level: easy
Section: First through Fifth Normal Form
Subsection: Fourth Normal Form

102.   A relation is in 4NF if it is in BCNF and it has no multi-value dependencies .
Level: moderate
Section: First through Fifth Normal Form
Subsection: Fourth Normal Form

103.   Fifth normal form deals with obscure dependencies that may not have any practical consequences.
Level: moderate
Section: First through Fifth Normal Form
Subsection: Fifth Normal Form

104.   Domain / key normal form requires that every constraint be a logical consequence of the definition of domains and keys.
Level: moderate
Section: Domain / Key Normal Form
Subsection: Definition

105.   In regard to DK/NF, a constraint is broadly defined to include all types of constraints except time-based constraints.
Level: hard
Section: Domain / Key Normal Form
Subsection: Definition

106.   If the functional dependencies between two attributes is A → B and B → A, then they have a(n) one-to-one attribute relationship.
Level: easy
Section: Synthesis of Relations

107.   If the functional dependencies between two attributes is A → B, but B not → A, then they have a(n) many-to-one attribute relationship.
Level: moderate
Section: Synthesis of Relations

108.   If the functional dependencies between two attributes is A not → B and B not → A, then they have a(n) many-to-many attribute relationship.
Level: moderate
Section: Synthesis of Relations

109.   When synthesizing relations, if two attributes have the relationship A → B, but B not → A, then create a relation with __A__ as the key.
Level: easy
Section: Synthesis of Relations
Subsection: Many-to-One Attribute Relationships

110.   When synthesizing relations, if attributes have the dependencies (A, B) → C, then create a relation with __(A, B)__ as the key.
Level: moderate
Section: Synthesis of Relations
Subsection: Many-to-One Attribute Relationships

111.   Relations are sometimes left unnormalized to improve __performance__ .
Level: easy
Section: Optimization
Subsection: De-Normalization

Essay Questions

112.   Describe the requirements that a table must meet to qualify as a relation.
In order for a table to meet the requirements of a relation, it must satisfy certain conditions. First, the cells must contain single values – no group or array values are allowed. Second, the rows must be unique. Third, each column must contain the same kind of data for all rows. Fourth, the order of the columns and the rows is insignificant. Finally, each column must have a unique name.
Section: The Relational Model

113.   Explain the relationships among keys, functional dependencies, and uniqueness.
All keys represent a functional dependency, since each key functionally determines the entire row. Since the key determines the entire row, if a key were duplicated in a relation, then the entire row would have to be duplicated. Since a relation can contain no duplicate rows, the key must be unique. All functional dependencies are not represented through keys. Therefore, the determinant of a functional dependency may or may not be unique.
Section: The Relational Model
Subsection: Functional Dependencies, Keys, and Uniqueness

114.   Explain the essence of normalization that is implemented through the use of normal forms.
The essence of normalization is to create relations that contain data on a single theme, and for each row in a relation to contain all the data about that theme for a given entity. This essence is implemented in the normal forms by taking a relation that contains data on more than one theme and splitting it into multiple relations that each contain data on a single theme.
Section: Normalization
Subsection: Essence of Normalization

115.   Explain the concept of a transitive dependency and give an example not included in the book.
        A transitive dependency is evidenced through a functional dependency among non-key attributes. If the key of a relation determines the value of one attribute because it can determine the value of another attribute, then a transitive dependency exists. For example, if an employee is assigned a computer to work on and the computer has an assigned IP address for the corporate network, the relation EMPLOYEE (EmployeeID, ComputerID, IPaddress) with EmployeeID as the key, contains a transitive dependency. The IP address is not really determined by the EmployeeID, but rather by the ComputerID, such that EmployeeID determines IPaddress only because EmployeeID determines ComputerID which in turn determines IPaddress. The functional dependencies can be shown as:
        EmployeeID → ComputerID
        ComputerID → IPaddress
        Therefore EmployeeID → ComputerID → IPaddress
        Section: *First through Fifth Normal Forms*
        Subsection: *Third Normal Form*

116.   Explain the practical value that DK/NF has in the real world, and why that practical value is limited.
        Domain key normal form has practice value as a database design objective. Since a relation in domain key normal form is guaranteed to contain no anomalies, it is the preferred normalization goal. Many relations can achieve DK/NF while others cannot. The fact that many relations cannot be placed in DK/NF, and there is no method for determining which can and which cannot, limits the practical value of DK/NF as a design goal. Further, there is no algorithm for achieving DK/NF even for relations that can reach this ultimate level of normalization.
        Section: *Domain / Key Normal Form*
        Subsection: *Definition*

117.   Contrast the analytic and synthetic perspectives of relational design.
        The analytic perspective of relational design starts from a relation and attempts to identify the anomalies to which it is vulnerable in order to determine which normal form it is in. The synthetic perspective starts with a collection of attributes and their functional dependencies. It then attempts to determine which relations should be formed from these attributes based on their attribute relationships.
        Section: *The Synthesis of Relations*

118.   Explain what it means to de-normalize, and why that may be appropriate.
        De-normalization is the process of taking a normalized set of relations and converting them into a smaller set of relations that is in a lower normal form and thus vulnerable to a greater number of anomalies. While the fully normalized set of relations is more desirable from a theoretical perspective, it does have some disadvantages. The greater the number of relations in the database, the more work that is required by the database whenever data must be retrieved from multiple relations to re-construct the users' view of the data. In some circumstances, the anomalies introduced by de-normalizing a data model may be considered an acceptable cost for the performance improvement from reducing the overhead work performed by the database.
        Section: *Optimization*
        Subsection: *De-Normalization*

CHAPTER 6

Database Design Using Entity-Relationship Models

True-False Questions

1. When creating a relational model from E-R diagrams, first create a relation for each relationship.
   Answer: False   *Level: moderate*
   Section: Transformation of Entity-Relationship Models into Relational Database Designs
   Subsection: Representing Entities with the Relational Model

2. Each entity in the E-R model is represented as a relation in the relational model.
   Answer: True   *Level: easy*
   Section: Transformation of Entity-Relationship Models into Relational Database Designs
   Subsection: Representing Entities with the Relational Model

3. An entity needs to be examined according to normalization criteria before creating a relation from it in the relational model.
   Answer: False   *Level: moderate*
   Section: Transformation of Entity-Relationship Models into Relational Database Designs
   Subsection: Representing Entities with the Relational Model

4. When creating a relation in the relational model from an entity in the E-R model, the attributes of the entity become the rows of the relation.
   Answer: False   *Level: easy*
   Section: Transformation of Entity-Relationship Models into Relational Database Designs
   Subsection: Representing Entities with the Relational Model

5. Weak entities require special treatment when creating a relational model from an E-R model.
   Answer: True   *Level: easy*
   Section: Transformation of Entity-Relationship Models into Relational Database Designs
   Subsection: Representing Entities with the Relational Model

6. A weak entity that is existence dependent but not ID-dependent can be represented in the relational model just as a strong entity is, except that constraints noting the existence dependency need to be enforced.
   Answer: True   *Level: hard*
   Section: Transformation of Entity-Relationship Models into Relational Database Designs
   Subsection: Representing Entities with the Relational Model

7. A weak entity that is existence dependent and ID-dependent can be represented in the relational model just as is a strong entity.
   Answer: False   *Level: easy*
   Section: Transformation of Entity-Relationship Models into Relational Database Designs
   Subsection: Representing Entities with the Relational Model

8.   For an ID-dependent weak entity, it is necessary to add the key of the parent entity to the weak entity's relation.
      Answer: True   *Level: easy*
      Section: Transformation of Entity-Relationship Models into Relational Database Designs
      Subsection: Representing Entities with the Relational Model

9.   To represent a 1:1 binary relationship in a relational model, the key of one relation is placed into the second relation.
      Answer: True   *Level: easy*
      Section: Transformation of Entity-Relationship Models into Relational Database Designs
      Subsection: Representing Has-A Relationships

10.   When the key of one relation is placed into a second relation to represent a relationship, the key is called a "relational key" in the second relation.
      Answer: False   *Level: moderate*
      Section: Transformation of Entity-Relationship Models into Relational Database Designs
      Subsection: Representing Has-A Relationships

11.   A foreign key is a key that does not belong in any relation.
      Answer: False   *Level: moderate*
      Section: Transformation of Entity-Relationship Models into Relational Database Designs
      Subsection: Representing Has-A Relationships

12.   When placing a foreign key for a 1:1 relationship, the key of either table can be used as the foreign key in the other relation.
      Answer: True   *Level: moderate*
      Section: Transformation of Entity-Relationship Models into Relational Database Designs
      Subsection: Representing Has-A Relationships

13.   Entities that participate in a 1:1 relationship that is mandatory for both entities should often be combined into a single entity if they have the same key.
      Answer: True   *Level: moderate*
      Section: Transformation of Entity-Relationship Models into Relational Database Designs
      Subsection: Representing Has-A Relationships

14.   One reason for representing a single logical entity as two relations is for security reasons.
      Answer: True   *Level: easy*
      Section: Transformation of Entity-Relationship Models into Relational Database Designs
      Subsection: Representing Has-A Relationships

15.   One reason for representing a single logical entity as two relations is to simplify application programming.
      Answer: False   *Level: moderate*
      Section: Transformation of Entity-Relationship Models into Relational Database Designs
      Subsection: Representing Has-A Relationships

16.   In a 1:N relationship, the term "parent" refers to the relation on the "many" side of the
         relationship.
         Answer: False   *Level: easy*
         Section: Transformation of Entity-Relationship Models into Relational Database Designs
         Subsection: Representing Has-A Relationships

17.   In representing a 1:N relationship in a relational model, the key of the relation representing the
         parent entity is placed as a foreign key in the relation representing the child entity.
         Answer: True   *Level: moderate*
         Section: Transformation of Entity-Relationship Models into Relational Database Designs
         Subsection: Representing Has-A Relationships

18.   In representing a 1:N relationship in a relational model, the key of the relation representing the
         entity on the "many" side is placed as a foreign key in the relation representing the entity on the
         "one" side of the relationship.
         Answer: False   *Level: hard*
         Section: Transformation of Entity-Relationship Models into Relational Database Designs
         Subsection: Representing Has-A Relationships

19.   To represent a 1:N relationship in a relational model, an intersection relation is created.
         Answer: False   *Level: moderate*
         Section: Transformation of Entity-Relationship Models into Relational Database Designs
         Subsection: Representing Has-A Relationships

20.   To represent a M:N relationship in a relational model, a relation is created to represent the
         relationship itself.
         Answer: True   *Level: moderate*
         Section: Transformation of Entity-Relationship Models into Relational Database Designs
         Subsection: Representing Has-A Relationships

21.   To represent a M:N relationship in a relational model, an intersection relation is created.
         Answer: True   *Level: easy*
         Section: Transformation of Entity-Relationship Models into Relational Database Designs
         Subsection: Representing Has-A Relationships

22.   The key of an intersection relation is always the combination of the keys of both parents.
         Answer: True   *Level: moderate*
         Section: Transformation of Entity-Relationship Models into Relational Database Designs
         Subsection: Representing HAS-A Relationships

23.   When transforming an E-R model into a relational model, recursive relationships are treated
         fundamentally the same as other HAS-A relationships.
         Answer: True   *Level: hard*
         Section: Transformation of Entity-Relationship Models into Relational Database Designs
         Subsection: Representing Recursive Relationships

24.   Recursive M:N relationships are represented with an intersection relation that shows pairs of
        related rows from a single relation.
        Answer: True   *Level: hard*
        Section: Transformation of Entity-Relationship Models into Relational Database Designs
        Subsection: Representing Recursive Relationships

25.   Ternary relationships are handled just like binary relationships except that special considerations
        may have to be documented as business rules.
        Answer: True   *Level: hard*
        Section: Transformation of Entity-Relationship Models into Relational Database Designs
        Subsection: Representing Ternary and Higher-Order Relationships

26.   When transforming a ternary relationship into a relational model, a MUST NOT constraint means
        the binary relationship indicates all combinations that must appear in the ternary relationship.
        Answer: False   *Level: moderate*
        Section: Transformation of Entity-Relationship Models into Relational Database Designs
        Subsection: Representing Ternary and Higher-Order Relationships

27.   To represent an IS-A relationship in a relational model, the IS-A relationship must be converted
        into a HAS-A relationship.
        Answer: False   *Level: easy*
        Section: Transformation of Entity-Relationship Models into Relational Database Designs
        Subsection: Representing IS-A Relationships (Subtypes)

28.   When transforming supertype / subtype entities into a relational model, an entity is created for the
        supertype only.
        Answer: False   *Level: easy*
        Section: Transformation of Entity-Relationship Models into Relational Database Designs
        Subsection: Representing Is-A Relationships (Subtypes)

29.   When transforming supertype / subtype entities into a relational model, all of the attributes for the
        supertype relation are placed into the subtype relations.
        Answer: False   *Level: hard*
        Section: Transformation of Entity-Relationship Models into Relational Database Designs
        Subsection: Representing Is-A Relationships (Subtypes)

30.   When transforming supertype / subtype entities into a relational model, the key of the supertype
        relation is placed into the subtype relation typically as the key.
        Answer: True   *Level: moderate*
        Section: Transformation of Entity-Relationship Models into Relational Database Designs
        Subsection: Representing Is-A Relationships (Subtypes)

31.   A "tree" is a pattern of relationships such that the elements of the data structure have only one-to-
        many relationships with one another.
        Answer: True   *Level: easy*
        Section: Trees, Networks, and Bills of Materials
        Subsection: Trees

32. All the elements of a "tree" data structure are called parents.
    Answer: False   *Level: moderate*
    Section: Trees, Networks, and Bills of Materials
    Subsection: Trees

33. The relationships between elements in a tree data structure are called roots.
    Answer: False   *Level: easy*
    Section: Trees, Networks, and Bills of Materials
    Subsection: Trees

34. The element at the top of a "tree" data structure is called the root.
    Answer: True   *Level: easy*
    Section: Trees, Networks, and Bills of Materials
    Subsection: Trees

35. The difference between a "tree" data structure and a "simple network" data structure is that elements in a tree can have only one parent.
    Answer: True   *Level: hard*
    Section: Trees, Networks, and Bills of Materials
    Subsection: Simple Networks

36. A "complex network" data structure is like a "simple network" except all the relationships are many-to-many.
    Answer: False   *Level: hard*
    Section: Trees, Networks, and Bills of Materials
    Subsection: Complex Networks

37. A "complex network" data structure must contain at least one many-to-many relationship.
    Answer: True   *Level: moderate*
    Section: Trees, Networks, and Bills of Materials
    Subsection: Complex Networks

38. "Complex network" data structures require at least one intersection relation.
    Answer: True   *Level: hard*
    Section: Trees, Networks, and Bills of Materials
    Subsection: Complex Networks

39. A "bill of materials" data structure is generally regarded as a ternary IS-A relationship.
    Answer: False   *Level: hard*
    Section: Trees, Networks, and Bills of Materials
    Subsection: Bills of Materials

40. A surrogate key is appropriate when the primary key of a relation contains a lengthy text field.
    Answer: True   *Level: easy*
    Section: Trees, Networks, and Bills of Materials
    Subsection: Surrogate Keys

41.   Surrogate keys usually slow performance but are better representations of the users' model.
           Answer: False   *Level: moderate*
           Section: Trees, Networks, and Bills of Materials
           Subsection: Surrogate Keys

42.   Surrogate keys are normally not shown on forms or reports.
           Answer: True   *Level: easy*
           Section: Trees, Networks, and Bills of Materials
           Subsection: Surrogate Keys

43.   A null value is an attribute value that has been set to zero.
           Answer: False   *Level: moderate*
           Section: Trees, Networks, and Bills of Materials
           Subsection: Null Values

44.   A null value may mean that an attribute is not appropriate for a given entity instance.
           Answer: True   *Level: moderate*
           Section: Trees, Networks, and Bills of Materials
           Subsection: Null Values

Multiple Choice Questions

45.   The first step in transforming an E-R model into a relational model is to:
           a.)   create a relation for each relationship
           b.)   evaluate the entities against the normalization criteria
           c.)   create a relation for each entity
           d.)   remove any recursive relationships
           e.)   document referential integrity constraints

Level: moderate
Section: Transformation of Entity-Relationship Models into Relational Database Designs
Subsection: Representing Entities with the Relational Model

46.   When transforming an E-R model into a relational model, the key of the strong entity should be placed as a key into the weak entity:
           a.)   when the weak entity is existence dependent
           b.)   when there is a recursive relationship between the strong and weak entities
           c.)   when the weak entity is existence dependent and ID-dependent
           d.)   when the weak entity has a 1:N relationship with the strong entity
           e.)   all of the above

Level: hard
Section: Transformation of Entity-Relationship Models into Relational Database Designs
Subsection: Representing Entities with the Relational Model

47.   When transforming an E-R model into a relational model and creating a relation for a weak entity that is not ID-dependent:
    a.)   The dependency needs to be noted so that an application does not create a weak entity without its proper strong entity.
    b.)   The key of the strong entity must be placed as part of the key in the weak entity.
    c.)   A business rule needs to be implemented so that when the strong entity is deleted, the corresponding weak entities are also deleted.
    d.)   A composite key must be created for the weak entity.
    e.)   Both a and c

Level: moderate
Section: Transformation of Entity-Relationship Models into Relational Database Designs
Subsection: Representing Entities with the Relational Model

48.   The simplest form of binary relationship is:
    a.)   ternary
    b.)   1:1
    c.)   1:N
    d.)   0:1
    e.)   recursive

Level: easy
Section: Transformation of Entity-Relationship Models into Relational Database Designs
Subsection: Representing Has-A Relationships

49.   When representing a 1:1 relationship in a relational model:
    a.)   the key of each relation must be placed as foreign keys into the other
    b.)   the key of either relation may be placed as a foreign key into the other
    c.)   the key of both relations must be the same
    d.)   the intersection relation gets the key from both relations
    e.)   both b and c

Level: easy
Section: Transformation of Entity-Relationship Models into Relational Database Designs
Subsection: Representing Has-A Relationships

50.   If two entities are both mandatory in a 1:1 relationship, consider
    a.)   joining them into a single relation if they have the same key
    b.)   joining them into a single relation if they have different keys
    c.)   creating a surrogate key
    d.)   making one a weak entity
    e.)   converting them to an IS-A relationship

Level: hard
Section: Transformation of Entity-Relationship Models into Relational Database Designs
Subsection: Representing Has-A Relationships

51.   A single entity may be separated into two relations:
    a.)   if it has a recursive relationship
    b.)   if it participates in two or more 1:1 relationships
    c.)   if it participates in two or more 1:N relationships
    d.)   it improves performance or security
    e.)   all of the above

Level: *hard*
Section: *Transformation of Entity-Relationship Models into Relational Database Designs*
Subsection: *Representing Has-A Relationships*

52.   To represent a one-to-many relationship in a relational model:
    a.)   the key of the child is placed as a foreign key into the parent
    b.)   the key of the parent is placed as a foreign key into the child
    c.)   an intersection relation must be created
    d.)   the key of the relation on the "many" side is placed in the relation on the "one" side
    e.)   the keys of both relations are joined into a composite key

Level: *moderate*
Section: *Transformation of Entity-Relationship Models into Relational Database Designs*
Subsection: *Representing Has-A Relationships*

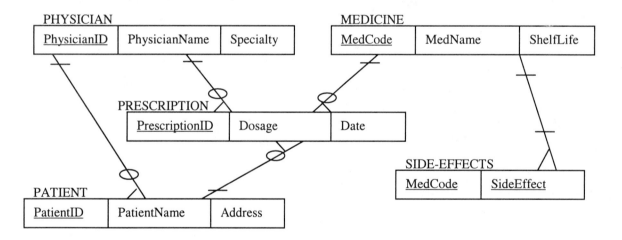

53.   Based on the data structure diagram above, which of the following is true?
    a.)   PrescriptionID must be placed as a foreign key in PHYSICIAN
    b.)   MedCode must be placed as a foreign key in PATIENT
    c.)   MEDICINE and SIDE-EFFECTS should be combined into a single relation
    d.)   PatientID must be placed as a foreign key in PRESCRIPTION
    e.)   PrescriptionID must be placed as a foreign key in PATIENT

Level: *hard*
Section: *Transformation of Entity-Relationship Models into Relational Database Designs*
Subsection: *Representing Has-A Relationships*

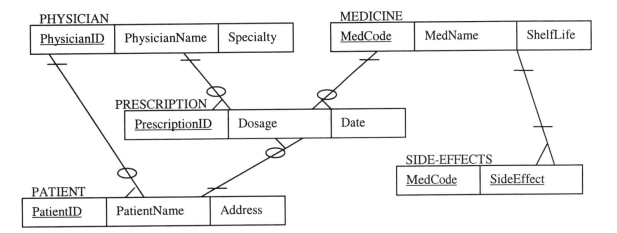

54. In the data structure diagram shown above, what would be the structure of the PATIENT relation after all foreign keys had been appropriately placed?
     a.) PATIENT (<u>PatientID</u>, PatientName, Address, PrescriptionID)
     b.) PATIENT (<u>PatientID</u>, <u>PrescriptionID</u>, PatientName, Address)
     c.) PATIENT (<u>PatientID</u>, PatientName, Address, PrescriptionID, PhysicianID)
     d.) PATIENT (<u>PatientID</u>, PatientName, Address, PhysicianID)
     e.) PATIENT (<u>PatientID</u>, <u>PhysicianID</u>, PatientName, Address)

Level: moderate
Section: Transformation of Entity-Relationship Models into Relational Database Designs
Subsection: Representing Has-A Relationships

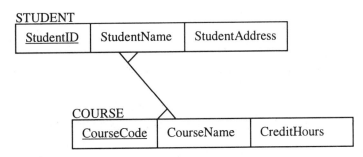

55. Which of the following would be used to represent the relationship above between a STUDENT and a COURSE?
     a.) Place StudentID in the COURSE relation.
     b.) Place CourseCode in the STUDENT relation.
     c.) Create an intersection relation with StudentID as the key
     d.) Create an intersection relation with CourseCode as the key
     e.) Create an intersection relation with both StudentID and CourseCode as the key

Level: moderate
Section: Transformation of Entity-Relationship Models into Relational Database Designs
Subsection: Representing Has-A Relationships

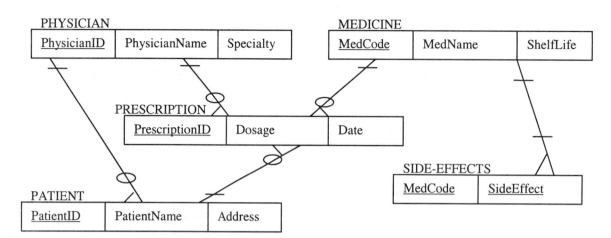

56.   In the data structure diagram shown above, what would be the structure of the PRESCRIPTION
relation after all foreign keys had been appropriately placed?
a.)   PRESCRIPTION (PrescriptionID, Dosage, Date)
b.)   PRESCRIPTION (PrescriptionID, PhysicianID, MedCode, Dosage, Date)
c.)   PRESCRIPTION (PrescriptionID, Dosage, Date, PhysicianID, PatientID, MedCode)
d.)   PRESCRIPTION (PrescriptionID, Dosage, Date, PhysicianID, PatientID, MedCode,
SideEffect)
e.)   none of the above

Level: hard
Section: Transformation of Entity-Relationship Models into Relational Database Designs
Subsection: Representing Has-A Relationships

57.   Many-to-many relationships are represented by:
a.)   two relations with an M:N relationship
b.)   two relations with a 1:N relationship
c.)   by an intersection relation which has M:N relationships with the two relations
d.)   by an intersection relation which has 1:N relationships with the two relations
e.)   by two intersection relations which each have 1:N relationships with the two relations

Level: hard
Section: Transformation of Entity-Relationship Models into Relational Database Designs
Subsection: Representing Has-A Relationships

58.   In representing a recursive relationship in a relational model:
a.)   the parent rows and child rows are in different relations
b.)   the child rows and the parent rows are in the same relation
c.)   the child rows are eliminated when they have the same key as the parent rows
d.)   the relationship must be reduced to a 1:1 relationship
e.)   the relationship must be converted into an IS-A relationship

Level: moderate
Section: Transformation of Entity-Relationship Models into Relational Database Designs
Subsection: Representing Recursive Relationships

59.   A relationship between two instances of the same entity is called a _____ relationship.
    a.)   binary
    b.)   reclusive
    c.)   recursive
    d.)   ternary
    e.)   weak

Level: easy
Section: Transformation of Entity-Relationship Models into Relational Database Designs
Subsection: Representing Recursive Relationships

60.   Which of the following is <u>not</u> true of recursive relationships?
    a.)   When the recursive relationship is M:N, an intersection relation is created.
    b.)   The rows of a single relation can play two different roles.
    c.)   The techniques for representing the relationships are the same as for non-recursive relationships except the rows are in the same relation.
    d.)   Recursive relationships can be 1:1, 1:N, or M:N relationships.
    e.)   Even when the relationship is 1:N, a new relation must be defined to represent the relationship.

Level: moderate
Section: Transformation of Entity-Relationship Models into Relational Database Designs
Subsection: Representing Recursive Relationships

61.   Which of the following is <u>not</u> true of ternary relationships?
    a.)   can be treated as a collection of binary relationships
    b.)   are represented in the same way as binary relationships
    c.)   must involve at least one M:N relationship
    d.)   involve three entities of different logical types
    e.)   often require documentation of special considerations as business rules

Level: hard
Section: Transformation of Entity-Relationship Models into Relational Database Designs
Subsection: Representing Ternary and Higher-Order Relationships

62.   Which of the following is <u>not</u> true about representing subtypes in a relational model?
    a.)   One relation is created for the supertype and one for each subtype
    b.)   All of the attributes of the supertype are added to the subtype relations
    c.)   The key of the supertype is typically made the key of the subtypes
    d.)   A 1:1 relationship is represented between the supertype and each subtype
    e.)   An instance of the supertype may be related to one instance each of several subtypes

Level: moderate
Section: Transformation of Entity-Relationship Models into Relational Database Designs
Subsection: Representing Is-A Relationships (Subtypes)

63.   In a supertype-subtype structure, the relationship between an instance in the supertype and an instance in one of the subtypes is:
       a.)   1:1
       b.)   1:N
       c.)   N:1
       d.)   M:N
       e.)   recursive

Level: easy
Section: Transformation of Entity-Relationship Models into Relational Database Designs
Subsection: Representing Is-A Relationships (Subtypes)

64.   A tree is a data structure in which the elements of the structure have _____ relationship(s).
       a.   only 1:1
       b.   only 1:N
       c.   only N:1
       d.   at least one M:N
       e.   only M:N

Level: moderate
Section: Tree Networks and Bills of Materials
Subsection: Trees

65.   Every element in a "tree" data structure has a parent except the _____.
       a.)   node
       b.)   parent
       c.)   child
       d.)   root
       e.)   branch

Level: easy
Section: Trees, Networks, and Bills of Materials
Subsection: Trees

66.   Elements in a "tree" data structure that have the same parent are called _____.
       a.)   twins
       b.)   roots
       c.)   nodes
       d.)   branches
       e.)   hierarchies

Level: easy
Section: Trees, Networks, and Bills of Materials
Subsection: Trees

67.   A "simple network" data structure differs from a "tree" data structure in that:
    a.)   a simple network includes at least one M:N relationship
    b.)   a tree includes at least one 1:1 relationship
    c.)   a child in a tree can have only one sibling
    d.)   a child in a simple network can have more than one parent
    e.)   a simple network has at least one 1:1 relationship

Level: moderate
Section: Trees, Networks, and Bills of Materials
Subsection: Simple Networks

68.   When representing a simple network data structure in a relational model:
    a.)   at least one intersection relation must be created
    b.)   at least one child will have two or more parents
    c.)   all relationships are IS-A relationships
    d.)   the root is a supertype relation
    e.)   each parent will have two or more children

Level: moderate
Section: Trees, Networks, and Bills of Materials
Subsection: Simple Networks

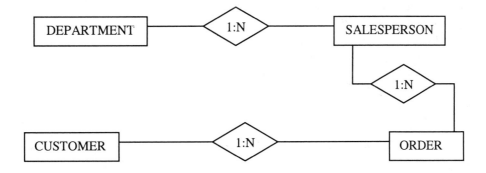

69.   The entities shown above describe what type of data structure?
    a.)   a tree data structure
    b.)   a complex network data structure
    c.)   a hybrid data structure
    d.)   a simple network data structure
    e.)   a bill of materials data structure

Level: moderate
Section: Trees, Networks, and Bills of Materials
Subsection: Simple Networks

70.   A "complex network" is a data structure in which the elements of the structure have
_____ relationship(s).

    a.   only 1:1
    b.   only 1:N
    c.   only N:1
    d.   at least one M:N
    e.   only M:N

Level: hard
Section: Trees, Networks, and Bills of Materials
Subsection: Complex Networks

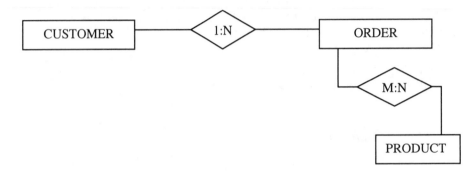

71.   The entities shown above describe what type of data structure?

    a.)   a tree data structure
    b.)   a complex network data structure
    c.)   a hybrid data structure
    d.)   a simple network data structure
    e.)   a bill of materials data structure

Level: moderate
Section: Trees, Networks, and Bills of Materials
Subsection: Complex Networks

72.   The "bill of materials" data structure:

    a.)   contains only 1:N relationships
    b.)   is a theoretical construct that does not appear in the real world
    c.)   usually concerns a M:N recursive relationship
    d.)   must contain at least one 1:1 relationship
    e.)   both a and b

Level: hard
Section: Trees, Networks, and Bills of Materials
Subsection: Bills of Materials

73.   Which of the following is <u>not</u> true about surrogate keys?
    a.)   They are identifiers that are supplied by the system, not the users.
    b.)   They have no meaning to the users.
    c.)   They tend to slow database performance.
    d.)   They are hidden on forms and reports.
    e.)   The DBMS will not allow their values to be changed.

Level: *moderate*
Section: *Trees, Networks, and Bills of Materials*
Subsection: *Surrogate Keys*

74.   A surrogate key should be considered when:
    a.)   a relationship is M:N
    b.)   a composite key is required
    c.)   the key contains a lengthy text field
    d.)   the key contains a number
    e.)   an index needs to be created

Level: *moderate*
Section: *Trees, Networks, and Bills of Materials*
Subsection: *Surrogate Keys*

75.   A null value can mean:
    a.)   the attribute is inappropriate for a given instance
    b.)   the user has deleted an entity instance from the relation
    c.)   the value of the attribute is unknown
    d.)   the attribute has a formula domain
    e.)   both a and c

Level: *moderate*
Section: *Trees, Networks, and Bills of Materials*
Subsection: *Null Values*

Fill in the Blank Questions

76.   When transforming an E-R model into a relational model, first create a(n) __relation__ for each entity.
Level: *easy*
Section: *Transformation of Entity-Relationship Models into Relational Database Designs*
Subsection: *Representing Entities with the Relational Model*

77.   Once a relation has been defined for an entity, it should be examined according to the __normalization__ criteria.
Level: *moderate*
Section: *Transformation of Entity-Relationship Models into Relational Database Designs*
Subsection: *Representing Entities with the Relational Model*

78.   If a weak entity is existence dependent but not __ID dependent__, it can be represented using the same techniques as strong entities.
Level: hard
Section: *Transformation of Entity-Relationship Models into Relational Database Designs*
Subsection: *Representing Entities with the Relational Model*

79.   When creating a relation for an ID dependent entity, both the key of the __parent__ and the key of the entity itself must appear in the relation.
Level: moderate
Section: *Transformation of Entity-Relationship Models into Relational Database Designs*
Subsection: *Representing Entities with the Relational Model*

80.   The simplest form of a binary relationship is a(n) __1:1__ relationship.
Level: easy
Section: *Transformation of Entity-Relationship Models into Relational Database Designs*
Subsection: *Representing Has-A Relationships*

81.   When the key of one relation is stored in another relation, it is called a(n) __foreign key__.
Level: easy
Section: *Transformation of Entity-Relationship Models into Relational Database Designs*
Subsection: *Representing Has-A Relationships*

82.   In 1:N relationships, the relation on the "one" side is called the __parent__.
Level: easy
Section: *Transformation of Entity-Relationship Models into Relational Database Designs*
Subsection: *Representing Has-A Relationships*

83.   In 1:N relationships, the relation on the "many" side is called the __child__.
Level: easy
Section: *Transformation of Entity-Relationship Models into Relational Database Designs*
Subsection: *Representing Has-A Relationships*

84.   In 1:N relationships, the foreign key is placed inside the __child__ relation.
Level: moderate
Section: *Transformation of Entity-Relationship Models into Relational Database Designs*
Subsection: *Representing Has-A Relationships*

85.   To represent a M:N relationship in a relational model, create a relation for the __relationship__ itself.
Level: moderate
Section: *Transformation of Entity-Relationship Models into Relational Database Designs*
Subsection: *Representing Has-A Relationships*

86.   In representing a M:N relationship in a relational model, a(n) __intersection__ relation is created.
Level: hard
Section: *Transformation of Entity-Relationship Models into Relational Database Designs*
Subsection: *Representing Has-A Relationships*

87.   To represent a M:N relationship in a relational model, in essence it is reduced to two __1:N__
        relationships.
Level: *hard*
Section: *Transformation of Entity-Relationship Models into Relational Database Designs*
Subsection: *Representing Has-A Relationships*

88.   In a 1:N recursive relationship, both the parent and child rows reside in the same __relation__ .
Level: *moderate*
Section: *Transformation of Entity-Relationship Models into Relational Database Designs*
Subsection: *Representing Recursive Relationships*

89.   In general, a ternary relationship can be treated as a collection of __binary__ relationships.
Level: *easy*
Section: *Transformation of Entity-Relationship Models into Relational Database Designs*
Subsection: *Representing Ternary and Higher-Order Relationships*

90.   In a(n) __MUST NOT__ constraint, the binary relationship indicates combinations that are not
        allowed to occur in the ternary relationship.
Level: *hard*
Section: *Transformation of Entity-Relationship Models into Relational Database Designs*
Subsection: *Representing Ternary and Higher-Order Relationships*

91.   In a(n) __MUST COVER__ constraint, the binary relationship indicates all combinations that must
        appear in the ternary relationship.
Level: *hard*
Section: *Transformation of Entity-Relationship Models into Relational Database Designs*
Subsection: *Representing Ternary and Higher-Order Relationships*

92.   When transforming an E-R model into a relational model, relationship between the supertype and
        a given subtype is __1:1__ .
Level: *moderate*
Section: *Transformation of Entity-Relationship Models into Relational Database Designs*
Subsection: *Representing Is-A Relationships (Subtypes)*

93.   The key of subtypes is generally the key of the __supertype__ .
Level: *easy*
Section: *Transformation of Entity-Relationship Models into Relational Database Designs*
Subsection: *Representing Is-A Relationships (Subtypes)*

94.   A(n) __tree/hierarchy__ is a data structure in which the elements of the structure have only one-to
        many relationships with one another and each element has only one parent.
Level: *easy*
Section: *Trees, Networks, and Bills of Materials*
Subsection: *Trees*

95.   Each element in a tree is called a(n) __node__ .
Level: *moderate*
Section: *Trees, Networks, and Bills of Materials*
Subsection: *Trees*

96.   Relationships among elements in a tree are called __branches__ .
Level: easy
Section: Trees, Networks, and Bills of Materials
Subsection: Trees

97.   The element at the top of the tree is called the __root__ .
Level: easy
Section: Trees, Networks, and Bills of Materials
Subsection: Trees

98.   Every node of a tree, except the root, has a(n) __parent__ .
Level: easy
Section: Trees, Networks, and Bills of Materials
Subsection: Trees

99.   The descendants of a node in a tree are called __children__ .
Level: easy
Section: Trees, Networks, and Bills of Materials
Subsection: Trees

100.   Nodes having the same parent in a tree are called __twins/siblings__ .
Level: moderate
Section: Trees, Networks, and Bills of Materials
Subsection: Trees

101.   A(n) __simple network__ is a data structure having only 1:N relationships, but permitting elements to have more than one parent, as long as the parents are of different types.
Level: moderate
Section: Trees, Networks, and Bills of Materials
Subsection: Simple Networks

102.   A(n) __complex network__ is a data structure having at least one many-to-many relationship.
Level: easy
Section: Trees, Networks, and Bills of Materials
Subsection: Complex Networks

103.   A complex network requires using at least one __intersection__ relation.
Level: hard
Section: Trees, Networks, and Bills of Materials
Subsection: Complex Networks

104.   A(n) __bill of materials__ is a data structure frequently occurring in manufacturing applications, and is commonly described as a network with recursive M:N relationships.
Level: moderate
Section: Trees, Networks, and Bills of Materials
Subsection: Bills of Materials

105.   A(n) __surrogate__ key is a unique, system-supplied identifier used as the primary key of a relation.
Level: *easy*
Section: *Trees, Networks, and Bills of Materials*
Subsection: *Surrogate Keys*

106.   The values of a(n) __surrogate key__ have no meaning to the users and are usually hidden on forms and reports.
Level: *moderate*
Section: *Trees, Networks, and Bills of Materials*
Subsection: *Surrogate Keys*

107.   A(n) __null value__ is an attribute value that has never been supplied.
Level: *easy*
Section: *Trees, Networks, and Bills of Materials*
Subsection: *Null Values*

Essay Questions

108.   Briefly describe the process of converting an E-R model into a relational model.
To convert an E-R model into a relational model, first a relation must be defined for each entity. The attributes of the entity are represented as the columns of the relation. The relation is then examined according to the normalization criteria. If appropriate, the relations should be normalized to achieve a proper data design. Finally, the relationships between the entities are represented through the creation of foreign keys.
Section: *Transformation of Entity-Relationship Models into Relational Database Designs*
Subsection: *Representing Entities with the Relational Model*

109.   Explain the representation of a many-to-many relationship in a relational model.
Many-to-many relationships cannot be directly represented in a relational model. Therefore, many-to-many relationships are essentially broken into two one-to-many relationships by creating an intersection relation that represents the relationship itself. The intersection relation takes its key as a combination of the keys of the two original, or parent, entities. Each of the parent entities has a one-to-many relationship with the intersection relation that is represented by placing the keys of the parents into the intersection relation.
Section: *Transformation of Entity-Relationship Models into Relational Database Designs*
Subsection: *Representing Has-A Relationships*

110.   Distinguish between trees, simple networks, and complex networks.
Trees, simple networks, and complex networks are all data structures that represent patterns of relationships among entities. A tree structure is composed of nodes that all have one-to-many relationships, with each node having at most one parent. Simple networks expand the tree structure to allow nodes to have more than one parent as long as the parents are different types. Finally, the complex network expands on the simple network by including at least one many-to-many relationship.
Section: *Trees, Networks, and Bills of Materials*

111.   Explain the pragmatic reason for using surrogate keys.
        Primary keys are often duplicated as foreign keys to represent relationships. They are also commonly included in indexes, and are used to identify records to be retrieved by users. When the primary key contains a lengthy text field, this creates a large amount of duplicated data that must be frequently manipulated, thereby degrading database performance. For these reasons, it is often practical to use a surrogate key that is generated by the system and is relatively small and easy to manipulate.
        Section: *Trees, Networks, and Bills of Materials*
        Subsection: *Surrogate Keys*

112.   Explain the negative aspects of null values.
        A null value is an attribute value that has never been supplied. The disadvantage of allowing null values to exist in the database is that they create ambiguity. When an attribute has a null value, it is not possible to determine whether the attribute's value is unknown, inappropriate for a given entity instance, or known to be blank.
        Section: *Trees, Networks, and Bills of Materials*
        Subsection: *Null Values*

CHAPTER 7

Database Design with Semantic Object Models

True-False Questions

1. Normalization problems are more frequent with semantic objects than with E-R models.
    Answer: False   *Level: easy*
    Section: Transformation of Semantic Objects into Relational Database Designs

2. Semantic object modeling usually separates semantic themes into group attributes or objects.
    Answer: True   *Level: easy*
    Section: Transformation of Semantic Objects into Relational Database Designs

3. A simple object can be represented by a single relation in the database.
    Answer: True   *Level: moderate*
    Section: Transformation of Semantic Objects into Relational Database Designs
    Subsection: Simple Objects

4. Any identifier of a simple object can be used as the key of the relation that represents that object.
    Answer: False   *Level: easy*
    Section: Transformation of Semantic Objects into Relational Database Designs
    Subsection: Simple Objects

5. A composite object will require at least three relations in the database.
    Answer: False   *Level: easy*
    Section: Transformation of Semantic Objects into Relational Database Designs
    Subsection: Composite Objects

6. To transform a composite object, a relation is defined for the base object and another relation for each multi-value attribute.
    Answer: True   *Level: hard*
    Section: Transformation of Semantic Objects into Relational Database Designs
    Subsection: Composite Objects

7. When transforming a composite object into a relational model, the key of the relation that represents a multi-value group attribute is a composite of the identifier of the base object and the identifier of the group.
    Answer: True   *Level: easy*
    Section: Transformation of Semantic Objects into Relational Database Designs
    Subsection: Composite Objects

8. When transforming a composite object into a relational model, the minimum cardinality from the group to the base object is the minimum cardinality of the group attribute.
    Answer: False   *Level: easy*
    Section: Transformation of Semantic Objects into Relational Database Designs
    Subsection: Composite Objects

9.   When transforming a composite object into a relational model, the minimum cardinality from the group to the base object is always one.
      Answer: True   *Level: easy*
      Section: Transformation of Semantic Objects into Relational Database Designs
      Subsection: Composite Objects

10.   The key of a relation created to represent a nested group attribute is the composite of the key of the containing group and the identifier of the nested group.
      Answer: True   *Level: moderate*
      Section: Transformation of Semantic Objects into Relational Database Designs
      Subsection: Composite Objects

11.   The representation of compound objects in a relational model is similar to the representation of entities in a relational model.
      Answer: True   *Level: moderate*
      Section: Transformation of Semantic Objects into Relational Database Designs
      Subsection: Compound Objects

12.   Representing one-to-one compound objects in a relational model requires the creation of an intersection relation.
      Answer: False   *Level: moderate*
      Section: Transformation of Semantic Objects into Relational Database Designs
      Subsection: Representing One-to-One Composite Objects

13.   When representing one-to-one compound objects in a relational model, the key of either relation can be placed in the relation of the other object as a foreign key.
      Answer: True   *Level: moderate*
      Section: Transformation of Semantic Objects into Relational Database Designs
      Subsection: Representing One-to-One Composite Objects

14.   When representing one-to-many relationships between compound objects, the key of the relation on the "one" side of the relationship is placed as a foreign key in the relation on the "many" side of the relationship.
      Answer: True   *Level: easy*
      Section: Transformation of Semantic Objects into Relational Database Designs
      Subsection: Representing One-to-Many and Many-to-One Relationships

15.   When representing a one-to-many relationship between compound objects, the minimum cardinality of the object on the "many" side is always one.
      Answer: False   *Level: moderate*
      Section: Transformation of Semantic Objects into Relational Database Designs
      Subsection: Representing One-to-Many and Many-to-One Relationships

16.   When representing a many-to-one relationship between compound objects, the maximum cardinality of the object on the "many" side of the relationship is always one.
      Answer: False   *Level: easy*
      Section: Transformation of Semantic Objects into Relational Database Designs
      Subsection: Representing One-to-Many and Many-to-One Relationships

17.   When representing a one-to-many relationship between compound objects, the minimum cardinality of the object on the "many" side is always zero.
      Answer: False   *Level: moderate*
      Section: Transformation of Semantic Objects into Relational Database Designs
      Subsection: Representing One-to-Many and Many-to-One Relationships

18.   Since semantic objects tend to have a single theme, not all many-to-many relationships between objects require an intersection relation.
      Answer: False   *Level: hard*
      Section: Transformation of Semantic Objects into Relational Database Designs
      Subsection: Representing Many-to-Many Relationships

19.   For many-to-many compound objects, the intersection relation never contains non-key data.
      Answer: True   *Level: moderate*
      Section: Transformation of Semantic Objects into Relational Database Designs
      Subsection: Representing Many-to-Many Relationships

20.   When creating an intersection relation to handle a many-to-many compound object, the minimum cardinalities of the parent relations are always one.
      Answer: True   *Level: moderate*
      Section: Transformation of Semantic Objects into Relational Database Designs
      Subsection: Representing Many-to-Many Relationships

21.   Hybrid objects are represented in a relational model using a combination of the techniques used for representing composite and compound objects.
      Answer: True   *Level: easy*
      Section: Transformation of Semantic Objects into Relational Database Designs
      Subsection: Hybrid Objects

22.   Association objects are a special case of composite objects.
      Answer: False   *Level: moderate*
      Section: Transformation of Semantic Objects into Relational Database Designs
      Subsection: Association Objects

23.   Association objects most often occur in assignment situations.
      Answer: True   *Level: hard*
      Section: Transformation of Semantic Objects into Relational Database Designs
      Subsection: Association Objects

24.   If the relation representing an association object has no unique identifier, the keys from the other relations participating in the relationship are combined to create a key.
      Answer: True   *Level: hard*
      Section: Transformation of Semantic Objects into Relational Database Designs
      Subsection: Association Objects

25.   When representing an association object in a relational model, a relation is defined for each object participating in the relationship except for the association object itself.
      Answer: False   *Level: hard*
      Section: Transformation of Semantic Objects into Relational Database Designs
      Subsection: Association Objects

26.   The key of a subtype object is the key of the parent object.
        Answer: True   *Level: moderate*
        Section: Transformation of Semantic Objects into Relational Database Designs
        Subsection: Parent / Subtype Objects

27.   In considering subtype objects, the performance of the database can be improved by the use of a
        type indicator attribute in the parent relation.
        Answer: True   *Level: easy*
        Section: Transformation of Semantic Objects into Relational Database Designs
        Subsection: Parent / Subtype Objects

28.   When dealing with subtypes that are mutually exclusive, a single type indicator attribute in the
        parent relation is the preferred design.
        Answer: True   *Level: easy*
        Section: Transformation of Semantic Objects into Relational Database Designs
        Subsection: Parent / Subtype Objects

29.   Archetype/version objects are represented by two relations.
        Answer: True   *Level: hard*
        Section: Transformation of Semantic Objects into Relational Database Designs
        Subsection: Archetype / Version Objects

30.   In the child relation formed for a version, the key of the archetype object is both a local and a
        foreign key.
        Answer: True   *Level: moderate*
        Section: Transformation of Semantic Objects into Relational Database Designs
        Subsection: Archetype / Version Objects

Multiple Choice Questions

31.   Creating a relational model from semantic objects:
        a.)   is less prone to normalization problems than when working with E-R models
        b.)   generally produces fewer relations than when working with E-R models
        c.)   requires converting the semantic objects into E-R models first
        d.)   produces fewer business rules than E-R models
        e.)   all of the above

Level: moderate
Section: Transformation of Semantic Objects into Relational Database Designs

32.   The definition of semantic objects:
    a.)   reduces the users' identifiers
    b.)   eliminates normalization errors
    c.)   separates semantic themes into group attributes and objects
    d.)   implements the business rules
    e.)   produces relational keys

Level: hard
Section: Transformation of Semantic Objects into Relational Database Designs

33.   The transformation of a simple object into a relational model:
    a.)   produces a weak relation
    b.)   requires the creation of a subtype relation
    c.)   requires only a single relation
    d.)   produces a relation with no non-key attributes
    e.)   none of the above

Level: moderate
Section: Transformation of Semantic Objects into Relational Database Designs
Subsection: Simple Objects

34.   When transforming a simple object into a relational model, the key of the relation:
    a.)   may be a unique identifier of the object
    b.)   may be a combination of non-unique attributes that collectively create a unique key
    c.)   may be a surrogate key
    d.)   may or may not come from the attributes of the simple object
    e.)   all of the above

Level: easy
Section: Transformation of Semantic Objects into Relational Database Designs

35.   A simple object can be represented in a relational model by a(n):
    a.)   single relation
    b.)   intersection relation
    c.)   relation for the base object and another for each repeating group attribute
    d.)   association relation
    e.)   multi-value relation

Level: easy
Section: Transformation of Semantic Objects into Relational Database Designs
Subsection: Simple Objects

36.   A composite object can be represented in a relational model by a(n):
  a.)   single relation
  b.)   intersection relation
  c.)   relation for the base object and another for each repeating group attribute
  d.)   association relation
  e.)   multi-value relation

Level: *hard*
Section: *Transformation of Semantic Objects into Relational Database Designs*
Subsection: *Composite Objects*

37.   The representation of a composite object in a relational model:
  a.)   involves only a single relation
  b.)   involves at least one 1:N relationship between relations
  c.)   involves at least one M:N relationship between relations
  d.)   involves at least one 1:1 relationship between relations
  e.)   involves at least one association relation

Level: *hard*
Section: *Transformation of Semantic Objects into Relational Database Designs*
Subsection: *Composite Objects*

38.   When a relation is created to represent a multi-value group attribute, the key of the relation:
  a.)   is the key of the base object
  b.)   is the unique identifier of the group attribute
  c.)   is stored in the base object as a foreign key
  d.)   is the combination of the key of the base object and the unique identifier of the group attribute
  e.)   has no meaning to the users

Level: *moderate*
Section: *Transformation of Semantic Objects into Relational Database Designs*
Subsection: *Composite Objects*

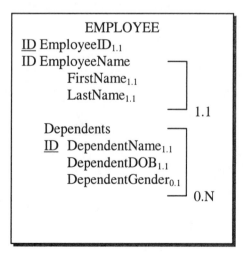

39.   Which of the following would be a correct relation that could be included in the relational model representation of the EMPLOYEE semantic object above
    a.)   DEPENDENT (<u>DependentName</u>, DependentDOB, DependentGender)
    b.)   DEPENDENT (<u>DependentName</u>, DependentDOB, DependentGender, EmployeeID)
    c.)   DEPENDENT (<u>DependentName</u>, DependentDOB, DependentGender, EmployeeName)
    d.)   DEPENDENT (<u>DependentName</u>, <u>EmployeeID</u>, DependentDOB, DependentGender)
    e.)   DEPENDENT (<u>DependentName</u>, <u>EmployeeName</u>, DependentDOB, DependentGender)

Level: hard
Section: Transformation of Semantic Objects into Relational Database Designs
Subsection: Composite Objects

40.   When creating a relation to represent a multi-value group attribute, the minimum cardinality from the group to the object:
    a.)   is 1
    b.)   may be 1
    c.)   is 0
    d.)   may be 0
    e.)   both b and d

Level: moderate
Section: Transformation of Semantic Objects into Relational Database Designs
Subsection: Composite Objects

41.   If a multi-value group (GROUP1) contains another multi-value group (GROUP2), the key
    a.)   of GROUP1 contains the key of GROUP2
    b.)   of GROUP1 and GROUP2 are the same
    c.)   of GROUP2 must be a surrogate key
    d.)   of GROUP2 is not unique
    e.)   of GROUP2 contains the key of GROUP1

Level: moderate
Section: Transformation of Semantic Objects into Relational Database Designs
Subsection: Composite Objects

42.   When representing a 1:1 relationship between two objects in a relational model, we place:
    a.)   the key of the first relation into the second as a foreign key
    b.)   the key of the second relation into the first as a foreign key
    c.)   the key of either relation into the other as a foreign key
    d.)   the key of either relation into the other as a part of the primary key
    e.)   the key of both relations into the other as a part of both primary keys

Level: hard
Section: Transformation of Semantic Objects into Relational Database Designs
Subsection: Representing One-to-One Compound Objects

43.   When representing a 1:N relationship between two semantic objects in a relational model:
  a.)   the key of the parent relation is placed into the child relation as a foreign key
  b.)   the key of the child relation is placed into the parent relation as a foreign key
  c.)   the key of either relation is placed into the other as a foreign key
  d.)   the key of either relation is placed into the other as a part of the primary key
  e.)   the key of each relation is placed into the other as a part of both primary keys

Level: hard
Section: Transformation of Semantic Objects into Relational Database Designs
Subsection: Representing One-to-Many and Many-to-One Relationships

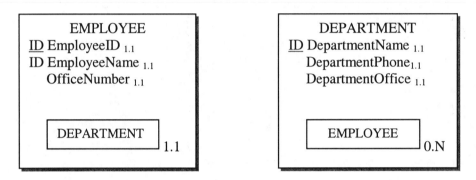

44.   Which of the following would be included after representing the above semantic objects in a relational model:
  a.)   EMPLOYEE (<u>EmployeeID</u>, EmployeeName, OfficeNumber)
  b.)   EMPLOYEE (<u>EmployeeID</u>, EmployeeName, OfficeNumber, DepartmentName)
  c.)   EMPLOYEE (<u>EmployeeID</u>, <u>EmployeeName</u>, OfficeNumber, DepartmentName)
  d.)   DEPARTMENT (<u>DepartmentName</u>, <u>EmployeeID</u>, DepartmentPhone, DepartmentOffice)
  e.)   DEPARTMENT (<u>DepartmentName</u>, DepartmentPhone, DepartmentOffice, EmployeeID)

Level: moderate
Section: Transformation of Semantic Objects into Relational Database Designs
Subsection: Representing One-to-Many and Many-to-One Relationships

45.   When transforming a one-to-many semantic object relationship into a relational model, the minimum cardinality of the relation on the "one" side is:
  a.)   always 0
  b.)   always 1
  c.)   always N
  d.)   dependent on the minimum cardinality of the object attribute located in the semantic object on the "one" side of the relationship
  e.)   dependent on the minimum cardinality of the object attribute located in the semantic object on the "many" side of the relationship

Level: hard
Section: Transformation of Semantic Objects into Relational Database Designs
Subsection: Representing One-to-Many and Many-to-One Relationships

46.   When representing a M:N relationship between two semantic objects in a relational model, we place:
   a.)   the key of the first relation into the second as a foreign key
   b.)   the key of the second relation into the first as a foreign key
   c.)   the key of either relation into the other as a foreign key
   d.)   the key of either relation into the intersection relation as a part of the primary key
   e.)   the key of both relations into the intersection relation as a part of the primary key

Level: *moderate*
Section: *Transformation of Semantic Objects into Relational Database Designs*
Subsection: *Representing Many-to-Many Relationships*

47.   When transforming a many-to-many semantic object relationship into a relational model, the minimum cardinality of the parent relations is:
   a.)   always 0
   b.)   always 1
   c.)   always N
   d.)   dependent on the minimum cardinality of the object attribute located in the semantic object on the "one" side of the relationship
   e.)   dependent on the minimum cardinality of the object attribute located in the semantic object on the "many" side of the relationship

Level: *hard*
Section: *Transformation of Semantic Objects into Relational Database Designs*
Subsection: *Representing Many-to-Many Relationships*

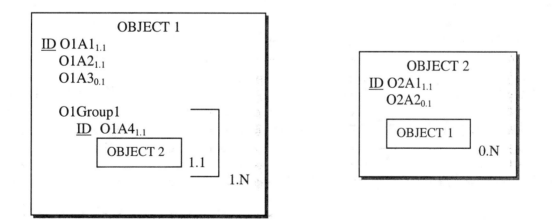

48.   To represent the semantic objects shown above in a relational model, how many relations will be needed?
   a.)   2
   b.)   3
   c.)   4
   d.)   5
   e.)   none of the above

Level: *moderate*

Section: Transformation of Semantic Objects into Relational Database Designs
Subsection: Hybrid Objects

49.   For an association relationship between two objects, we place:
   a.)   the key of the first relation into the second as a foreign key
   b.)   the key of the second relation into the first as a foreign key
   c.)   the key of either relation into the other as a foreign key
   d.)   the key of either relation into the association relation as a part of the primary key
   e.)   the key of both relations into the association relation as a foreign key

Level: moderate
Section: Transformation of Semantic Objects into Relational Database Designs
Subsection: Association Objects

50.   The performance of parent/subtype relationships can be improved by:
   a.)   combining the relations
   b.)   creating an intersection relation
   c.)   creating an association relation
   d.)   adding a type indicator attribute to the parent relation
   e.)   adding a type indicator attribute to the subtype relation

Level: easy
Section: Transformation of Semantic Objects into Relational Database Designs
Subsection: Parent / Subtype Objects

Fill in the Blank Questions

51.   When working with semantic objects, __normalization__ problems are less likely than with E-R models.
Level: easy
Section: Transformation of Semantic Objects into Relational Database Designs

52.   The definition of semantic objects usually separates semantic themes into __group attributes__ and objects.
Level: moderate
Section: Transformation of Semantic Objects into Relational Database Designs

53.   When transforming semantic objects into relations, the relations are generally already close to __domain / key__ normal form.
Level: hard
Section: Transformation of Semantic Objects into Relational Database Designs

54.   A __simple__ object can be transformed into a single relation in the database.
Level: moderate
Section: Transformation of Semantic Objects into Relational Database Designs
Subsection: Simple Objects

55.   Because a key is an attribute that uniquely identifies a row of a table, only __unique identifiers__ can be transformed into keys.
Level: easy
Section: Transformation of Semantic Objects into Relational Database Designs
Subsection: Simple Objects

56.   A __composite__ object is an object that has at least one multi-value attribute and no object attributes.
Level: easy
Section: Transformation of Semantic Objects into Relational Database Designs
Subsection: Composite Objects

57.   A composite object is transformed into a relational model by creating a relation for the object itself and a relation for each __multi-value attribute__.
Level: easy
Section: Transformation of Semantic Objects into Relational Database Designs
Subsection: Composite Objects

58.   When transforming a composite object into a relational model, the minimum cardinality from the group to the object is always __one__.
Level: easy
Section: Transformation of Semantic Objects into Relational Database Designs
Subsection: Composite Objects

59.   When transforming a composite object into a relational model, the key of the object is combined with the identifier of the __group__ to create a key for the relation representing the group.
Level: moderate
Section: Transformation of Semantic Objects into Relational Database Designs
Subsection: Composite Objects

60.   The minimum number of relations needed to represent a composite object in a relational model is __two__.
Level: moderate
Section: Transformation of Semantic Objects into Relational Database Designs
Subsection: Composite Objects

61.   The number of relations needed to represent a one-to-one relationship between two compound objects is __two__.
Level: moderate
Section: Transformation of Semantic Objects into Relational Database Designs
Subsection: Representing One-to-One Compound Objects

62.   When transforming a 1:1 semantic object relationship into a relational model, the foreign key is placed in __either relation__.
Level: hard
Section: Transformation of Semantic Objects into Relational Database Designs
Subsection: Representing One-to-One Compound Objects

63.   When transforming a 1:N semantic object relationship into a relational model, the foreign key is placed in the __child relation__.
Level: hard
Section: Transformation of Semantic Objects into Relational Database Designs
Subsection: Representing One-to-Many and Many-to-One Relationships

64.   When transforming a 1:N semantic object relationship into a relational model, the key of the parent relation is placed in the __child__ relation.
Level: moderate
Section: Transformation of Semantic Objects into Relational Database Designs
Subsection: Representing One-to-Many and Many-to-One Relationships

65.   The minimum number of relations needed to represent a 1:N semantic object relationship is __two__.
Level: easy
Section: Transformation of Semantic Objects into Relational Database Designs
Subsection: Representing One-to-Many and Many-to-One Relationships

66.   The minimum number of relations needed to represent a M:N semantic object relationship is __three__.
Level: hard
Section: Transformation of Semantic Objects into Relational Database Designs
Subsection: Representing Many-to-Many Relationships

67.   To represent a M:N semantic object relationship in a relational model, a relation is created for each of the two objects participating in the relationship and a(n) __intersection__ relation to represent the relationship itself.
Level: hard
Section: Transformation of Semantic Objects into Relational Database Designs
Subsection: Representing Many-to-Many Relationships

68.   An intersection relation consists only of the __keys__ of the two objects involved in the relationship.
Level: moderate
Section: Transformation of Semantic Objects into Relational Database Designs
Subsection: Representing Many-to-Many Relationships

69.   An intersection relation contains no __non-key__ data.
Level: easy
Section: Transformation of Semantic Objects into Relational Database Designs
Subsection: Representing Many-to-Many Relationships

70.   The parents of an intersection relation always have a minimum cardinality of __one__.
Level: easy
Section: Transformation of Semantic Objects into Relational Database Designs
Subsection: Representing Many-to-Many Relationships

71.   __Hybrid__ objects can be transformed into a relational model using a combination of the techniques used for composite and compound objects.

Level: *moderate*
Section: *Transformation of Semantic Objects into Relational Database Designs*
Subsection: *Hybrid Objects*

72.   An association object is a special case of __compound__ objects.

Level: *easy*
Section: *Transformation of Semantic Objects into Relational Database Designs*
Subsection: *Association Objects*

73.   __Association__ objects occur most frequently in assignment situations.

Level: *easy*
Section: *Transformation of Semantic Objects into Relational Database Designs*
Subsection: *Association Objects*

74.   __Association__ relations differ from intersection relations in that they contain non-key data.

Level: *easy*
Section: *Transformation of Semantic Objects into Relational Database Designs*
Subsection: *Association Objects*

75.   The keys of the parent relations appear in the association relation as __foreign keys__.

Level: *easy*
Section: *Transformation of Semantic Objects into Relational Database Designs*
Subsection: *Association Objects*

76.   When transforming subtype objects into a relational model, the key of the subtype relations is the same as the key of the __supertype (parent)__ relation.

Level: *moderate*
Section: *Transformation of Semantic Objects into Relational Database Designs*
Subsection: *Parent / Subtype Objects*

77.   If a supertype object indicates a cardinality of "1.2.3" for a group of subtype objects, then an instance of the supertype object is required to be a member of at least __two__ subtype(s).

Level: *moderate*
Section: *Transformation of Semantic Objects into Relational Database Designs*
Subsection: *Parent / Subtype Objects*

78.   All relationships between the parent and the subtype are __one-to-one__.

Level: *easy*
Section: *Transformation of Semantic Objects into Relational Database Designs*
Subsection: *Parent / Subtype Objects*

79.   When working with relations representing subtype objects, a type indicator may be placed in the __parent__ relation.

Level: *hard*
Section: *Transformation of Semantic Objects into Relational Database Designs*
Subsection: *Parent / Subtype Objects*

80.   The minimum number of relations needed to represent an archetype / version object in a
       relational model is __two__ .
Level: *moderate*
Section: *Transformation of Semantic Objects into Relational Database Designs*
Subsection: *Archetype / Version Objects*

Essay Questions

81.   Explain the process of converting a composite semantic object into a relational model.
       *To transform a composite semantic object into a relational model, first define a relation for the
       base object and a relation for each of the multi-value attributes. The single-value attributes of
       the base object are represented in its relation as columns. If a group attribute is multi-valued,
       then the attributes in the group are placed as columns of the relation representing the multi-value
       group attribute. A multi-value attribute is always on the "many" side of a 1:N relationship with
       the base object. The minimum cardinality of the base object in the relationship is always one.
       The minimum cardinality of the relation of the group attribute is determined by the minimum
       cardinality of the group attribute in the composite object. Since multi-value attributes are always
       ID-dependent on the base object, the key of the base object is placed as a foreign key in the multi-
       value group relation. The key of the multi-value group relation is a composite key composed of
       the key of the base object and the identifier of the group attribute.*
       Section: *Transformation of Semantic Objects into Relational Database Designs*
       Subsection: *Composite Objects*

82.   Briefly explain the process of transforming a Hybrid semantic object into a relational model.
       *A Hybrid object contains a multi-value group attribute that contains an object attribute. First a
       relation is defined for the base object and for the object attribute. Then a relation is defined for
       the multi-value group attribute. A 1:N relationship is defined between the base object and the
       multi-value group relation, just as is done with Composite objects. A relationship is then defined
       between the relation representing the object that was contained in the group and the relation
       representing the group itself. This relationship is either 1:1, 1:N, or M:N as dictated by the
       maximum cardinalities of the paired attributes. The relationship is represented using the same
       rules as for relationships with Compound objects.*
       Section: *Transformation of Semantic Objects into Relational Database Designs*
       Subsection: *Hybrid Objects*

83.   Compare and contrast intersection relations and association relations.
       *Intersection relations and association relations are alike in that they are both relations created to
       represent a relationship between other relations. Both also receive the keys of the relations that
       they are relating together. Intersection relations, however, are simpler than association relations
       are since they represent only the intersection of rows between two tables. Intersection relations
       contain no attributes other than the keys of the two relations that they are relating. These keys
       are used together as the composite key of the intersection relation. Association relations, on the
       other hand, can contain attributes that describe characteristics of the relationship between the
       relations being related. Association relations can also have unique identifiers of their own*
       Section: *Transformation of Semantic Objects into Relational Database Designs*
       Subsection: *Association Objects*

84.   Explain the use of type indicators in Parent / Subtype relations.

Type indicators are an attribute, or group of attributes, added to the Parent relation to improve database performance when retrieving data from a parent / subtype relationship. Without a type indicator, when retrieving data on an instance of the parent object, the database must search each subtype relation to determine if the instance is a member of any subtype. A type indicator attribute in the parent relation can quickly inform the database which, if any, subtype the instance belongs to. If the subtypes are mutually exclusive, a single type indicator attribute is preferred that contains a pointer to whichever subtype the instance belongs to. If the subtypes are not mutually exclusive, a group of Boolean type indicator attributes – one for each subtype – is placed in the parent relation. These Boolean attributes indicate a "yes/no" value indicating if the instance is a member of the subtype that the attribute represents.

Section: Transformation of Semantic Objects into Relational Database Designs
Subsection: Parent/Subtype Objects

85.   Explain the process of transforming Parent / Subtype objects into a relational model.

A relation is defined for the parent object and one for each of the subtype objects. The attributes of the supertype are placed in its relation, and the attributes for each subtype are placed in their respective relations. A 1:1 relationship is then defined between the parent relation and each subtype relation. The key of the parent relation is placed in each subtype as the key of the subtype relation. Type indicator attributes can then be added to the parent relation to improve database performance.

Section: Transformation of Semantic Objects into Relational Database Designs
Subsection: Parent/Subtype Objects

CHAPTER 8

Foundations of Relational Implementation

True-False Questions

1. Some relations allow multiple values in a single cell.
    Answer: False　　　　　　　　　　　*Level: easy*
    Section: Defining Relational Data
    Subsection: Review of Terminology

2. All the entries in a column of a relation are of the same kind.
    Answer: True　　　　　　　　　　　*Level: easy*
    Section: Defining Relational Data
    Subsection: Review of Terminology

3. Every attribute has a *domain*, which is a physical and logical description of allowed values.
    Answer: True　　　　　　　　　　　*Level: easy*
    Section: Defining Relational Data
    Subsection: Review of Terminology

4. Duplicate rows are permitted in some relations.
    Answer: False　　　　　　　　　　　*Level: easy*
    Section: Defining Relational Data
    Subsection: Review of Terminology

5. A "logical key" is a unique identifier.
    Answer: True　　　　　　　　　　　*Level: moderate*
    Section: Defining Relational Data
    Subsection: Review of Terminology

6. A "physical key" is the implementation of a logical key.
    Answer: False　　　　　　　　　　　*Level: hard*
    Section: Defining Relational Data
    Subsection: Review of Terminology

7. Defining an index for an attribute facilitates sorting rows according to the values of that attribute.
    Answer: True　　　　　　　　　　　*Level: moderate*
    Section: Defining Relational Data
    Subsection: Review of Terminology

8. Indexing the rows of a relation facilitates quick access to any given row using the value of the indexed attribute.
    Answer: True　　　　　　　　　　　*Level: moderate*
    Section: Defining Relational Data
    Subsection: Review of Terminology

9.   An index can be used to enforce uniqueness rules.
        Answer: True   *Level: hard*
        Section: Defining Relational Data
        Subsection: Review of Terminology

10.   A database designed using the relational model can be directly implemented using any DBMS
        product.
        Answer: False   *Level: hard*
        Section: Defining Relational Data
        Subsection: Implementing a Relational Database

11.   The structure of a database is generally defined graphically on personal computer DBMS
        products.
        Answer: True   *Level: easy*
        Section: Defining Relational Data
        Subsection: Implementing a Relational Database

12.   All DBMS products allocate physical media storage space automatically.
        Answer: False   *Level: hard*
        Section: Defining Relational Data
        Subsection: Implementing a Relational Database

13.   The best case scenario for filling the database with existing data is for all of the data to already be
        in a format that the DBMS can import directly.
        Answer: True   *Level: easy*
        Section: Defining Relational Data
        Subsection: Implementing a Relational Database

14.   Relational algebra requires the user to know what is wanted but not how to get it.
        Answer: False   *Level: hard*
        Section: Relational Data Manipulation
        Subsection: Categories of Relational Data Manipulation Language

15.   Relational calculus does not require the user to know how to get the desired results.
        Answer: True   *Level: moderate*
        Section: Relational Data Manipulation
        Subsection: Categories of Relational Data Manipulation Language

16.   Transform-oriented languages require the user to know how to get the desired results.
        Answer: False   *Level: moderate*
        Section: Relational Data Manipulation
        Subsection: Categories of Relational Data Manipulation Language

17.   Query-By-Example and Query-By-Form are examples of transform-oriented languages.
        Answer: False   *Level: hard*
        Section: Relational Data Manipulation
        Subsection: Categories of Relational Data Manipulation Language

18.   Most default forms created automatically by a DBMS as a DML interface are comprised of two
        relations.
        Answer: False   *Level: moderate*
        Section: Relational Data Manipulation
        Subsection: DML Interfaces to the DBMS

19.   Most query languages can be used to perform updates as well as carry out queries.
        Answer: True   *Level: easy*
        Section: Relational Data Manipulation
        Subsection: DML Interfaces to the DBMS

20.   A "trigger" is a special type of stored procedure that the user can activate when necessary.
        Answer: False   *Level: hard*
        Section: Relational Data Manipulation
        Subsection: DML Interfaces to the DBMS

21.   A database cannot be accessed from traditional file-processing programming languages.
        Answer: False   *Level: easy*
        Section: Relational Data Manipulation
        Subsection: DML Interfaces to the DBMS

22.   In relational algebra, the variables are relations.
        Answer: True   *Level: moderate*
        Section: Relational Algebra

23.   Any two relations can be combined using the *union* operator.
        Answer: False   *Level: easy*
        Section: Relational Algebra
        Subsection: Relational Operators

24.   The *difference* of two relations is a third relation containing tuples that occur in the second
        relation but not in the first.
        Answer: False   *Level: moderate*
        Section: Relational Algebra
        Subsection: Relational Operators

25.   The *intersection* of two relations is a third relation containing the tuples that appear in both the
        first and second relations.
        Answer: True   *Level: moderate*
        Section: Relational Algebra
        Subsection: Relational Operators

26.   The *product* of two relations is the concatenation of every tuple of one relation with every tuple
        of the second relation.
        Answer: True   *Level: moderate*
        Section: Relational Algebra
        Subsection: Relational Operators

27.   *Projection* is an operation that selects specified rows from a relation.
        Answer: False   *Level: moderate*
        Section: Relational Algebra
        Subsection: Relational Operators

28.   *Selection* is an operation that selects specified rows from a relation.
        Answer: True   *Level: moderate*
        Section: Relational Algebra
        Subsection: Relational Operators

29.   The *join* operation is a combination of the product, selection, and optionally the projection
        operations.
        Answer: True   *Level: moderate*
        Section: Relational Algebra
        Subsection: Relational Operators

30.   The number of columns resulting from an *equijoin* is greater than the number of columns
        resulting from a *natural join*.
        Answer: True   *Level: hard*
        Section: Relational Algebra
        Subsection: Relational Operators

Multiple Choice Questions

31.   Which of the following is not true about keys?
        a.)   can be a composite of every column in the relation
        b.)   usually composed of one or two attributes
        c.)   can be logical
        d.)   can physical
        e.)   all of the above <u>are</u> true about keys

Level: moderate
Section: Defining Relational Data
Subsection: Review of Terminology

32.   The domain of an attribute includes:
        a.)   only the description of physical values allowed
        b.)   only the description of logical values allowed
        c.)   the description of physical and logical values allowed
        d.)   the description of its functional dependencies
        e.)   the description of its index

Level: easy
Section: Defining Relational Data
Subsection: Review of Terminology

33.   The relation structure plus the allowable constraints on data values is called the:
    a.)   data definition language
    b.)   data manipulation language
    c.)   transform-oriented language
    d.)   relational schema
    e.)   domain

Level: hard
Section: Defining Relational Data
Subsection: Review of Terminology

34.   A group of one or more attributes that uniquely identifies a tuple in a relation is called a:
    a.)   logical key
    b.)   physical key
    c.)   functional dependency
    d.)   relational schema
    e.)   domain

Level: easy
Section: Defining Relational Data
Subsection: Review of Terminology

35.   Which of the following is not true about physical keys?
    a.)   must be unique
    b.)   facilitates quick access of rows based on the value of an attribute
    c.)   can be an index
    d.)   can be a data structure other than an index
    e.)   constructed to improve performance

Level: hard
Section: Defining Relational Data
Subsection: Review of Terminology

36.   An index may be defined to:
    a.)   facilitate sorting rows by an attribute's values
    b.)   represent a functional dependency
    c.)   express a physical domain
    d.)   implement a relation
    e.)   all of the above

Level: easy
Section: Defining Relational Data
Subsection: Review of Terminology

37.   "Index" is commonly used as another name for a:
      a.)   logical key
      b.)   physical key
      c.)   functional dependency
      d.)   relational schema
      e.)   domain

Level: easy
Section: *Defining Relational Data*
Subsection: *Review of Terminology*

38.   An index:
      a.)   must be unique
      b.)   cannot be unique
      c.)   may be unique, as specified by the developers
      d.)   may be unique, as determined by the DBMS
      e.)   may be unique, depending on the functional dependency

Level: hard
Section: *Defining Relational Data*
Subsection: *Review of Terminology*

39.   When a relational design is to be implemented using a relational DBMS:
      a.)   the design must first be converted into a semantic object model design
      b.)   the design must first be converted into a hierarchical model design
      c.)   the design must first be converted into relational algebra
      d.)   the design must first be converted into a transform-oriented language
      e.)   the design can be directly defined to the relational DBMS without being converted

Level: moderate
Section: *Defining Relational Data*
Subsection: *Implementing a Relational Database*

40.   DBMS products on personal computers typically allow the structure of the database to be
      described _____.
      a.)   using a DL/I
      b.)   textually
      c.)   graphically
      d.)   semantically
      e.)   using DB2

Level: easy
Section: *Defining Relational Data*
Subsection: *Implementing a Relational Database*

41.   A text file used to describe the structure of the database to the DBMS is written using:
     a.)   data definition language
     b.)   data manipulation language
     c.)   transform-oriented language
     d.)   relational algebra
     e.)   relational calculus

Level: moderate
Section: Defining Relational Data
Subsection: Implementing a Relational Database

42.   When allocating media space for a database on a server or mainframe:
     a.)   all tables should be stored on the same disk
     b.)   each table should be stored on a different disk
     c.)   the developer must determine the best place to locate the data
     d.)   the DBMS determines the best place to locate the data
     e.)   the user determines the best place to locate the data

Level: moderate
Section: Defining Relational Data
Subsection: Implementing a Relational Database

43.   The easiest way to add existing data to the database is to:
     a.)   manually key in the data from original source documents
     b.)   manually key in the data from printouts of the data in traditional computer files
     c.)   scan the data from original source documents
     d.)   scan the data from printouts of the data in traditional files
     e.)   import the data from traditional computer files

Level: easy
Section: Defining Relational Data
Subsection: Implementing a Relational Database

44.   A "procedural" language:
     a.)   requires you to know what you want but not how to get it
     b.)   requires you to know what you want and how to get it
     c.)   requires you to be able to express what you want graphically using a form
     d.)   requires you to be able to express what you want graphically using a spreadsheet
     e.)   requires you to be able to express what you want semantically

Level: easy
Section: Relational Data Manipulation
Subsection: Categories of Relational Data Manipulation Language

45. _____ is a procedural data manipulation language that uses operators that work on relations.
    a.)   A transform-oriented language
    b.)   Query-By-Example
    c.)   Query-By-Form
    d.)   Relational algebra
    e.)   Relational calculus

Level: *moderate*
Section: *Relational Data Manipulation*
Subsection: *Categories of Relational Data Manipulation Language*

46. _____ is a nonprocedural data manipulation language that uses relations as input and produces a single relation as the result.
    a.)   A transform-oriented language
    b.)   Query-By-Example
    c.)   Query-By-Form
    d.)   Relational algebra
    e.)   Relational calculus

Level: *moderate*
Section: *Relational Data Manipulation*
Subsection: *Categories of Relational Data Manipulation Language*

47. _____ is a nonprocedural data manipulation language that is used largely for theoretical rather than practical purposes.
    a.)   A transform-oriented language
    b.)   Query-By-Example
    c.)   Query-By-Form
    d.)   Relational algebra
    e.)   Relational calculus

Level: *moderate*
Section: *Relational Data Manipulation*
Subsection: *Categories of Relational Data Manipulation Language*

48. The single most important query language is:
    a.)   Query-By-Example
    b.)   Query-By-Form
    c.)   Relational algebra
    d.)   Relational calculus
    e.)   SQL

Level: *easy*
Section: *Relational Data Manipulation*
Subsection: *DML Interfaces to the DBMS*

49.   A common data manipulation language interface that lets the user see multiple rows at a time or shows each row as an independent entity is a(n):

      a.)   application program interface
      b.)   form
      c.)   precompiler
      d.)   query language
      e.)   stored program interface

Level: easy
Section: Relational Data Manipulation
Subsection: DML Interfaces to the DBMS

50.   A common data manipulation language interface that lets the user enter commands that specify the desired actions is a(n):

      a.)   application program interface
      b.)   form
      c.)   precompiler
      d.)   query language
      e.)   stored program interface

Level: moderate
Section: Relational Data Manipulation
Subsection: DML Interfaces to the DBMS

51.   A common data manipulation language interface that uses a collection of SQL statements stored as a file that can be invoked by a single command is a(n):

      a.)   application program interface
      b.)   form
      c.)   precompiler
      d.)   query language
      e.)   stored procedure

Level: easy
Section: Relational Data Manipulation
Subsection: DML Interfaces to the DBMS

52.   A _____ is a special type of stored procedure that the DBMS invokes when a certain condition occurs.

      a.)   precompiler
      b.)   query
      c.)   form
      d.)   trigger
      e.)   auto-spec

Level: easy
Section: Relational Data Manipulation
Subsection: DML Interfaces to the DBMS

53.   Relational algebra is said to be _____, meaning that the results of one or more relational operations are always a relation.
         a.)   procedural
         b.)   nonprocedural
         c.)   closed
         d.)   open
         e.)   transform-oriented

Level: hard
Section: Relational Algebra

54.   In relational algebra, which relational operator adds the tuples from one relation to those of a second relation to produce a third relation?
         a.)   difference
         b.)   intersection
         c.)   join
         d.)   product
         e.)   union

Level: moderate
Section: Relational Algebra
Subsection: Relational Operators

55.   In relational algebra, which relational operator takes two relations and produces a third relation containing tuples that occur in the first relation but not in the second?
         a.)   difference
         b.)   intersection
         c.)   join
         d.)   product
         e.)   union

Level: moderate
Section: Relational Algebra
Subsection: Relational Operators

56.   In relational algebra, which relational operator takes two relations and produces a third relation containing only the tuples that the first and second relations had in common?
         a.)   difference
         b.)   intersection
         c.)   join
         d.)   product
         e.)   union

Level: moderate
Section: Relational Algebra
Subsection: Relational Operators

57.   Which of the following relational operators does <u>not</u> require the relations to be union-compatible?
       a.)   union
       b.)   difference
       c.)   product
       d.)   intersection
       e.)   All of the above <u>do</u> require relations to be union-compatible.

Level: hard
Section: Relational Algebra
Subsection: Relational Operators

58.   In relational algebra, which relational operator takes two relations and produces a third relation that contains the concatenation of every tuple of the first relation with every tuple of the second relation?
       a.)   difference
       b.)   intersection
       c.)   join
       d.)   product
       e.)   union

Level: moderate
Section: Relational Algebra
Subsection: Relational Operators

59.   In relational algebra, which relational operator involves a combination of the product, selection, and (possibly) projection operations?
       a.)   difference
       b.)   intersection
       c.)   join
       d.)   product
       e.)   union

Level: easy
Section: Relational Algebra
Subsection: Relational Operators

60.   In relational algebra, to create a vertical subset of a relation, which operator would be used?
       a.)   Cartesian product
       b.)   difference
       c.)   selection
       d.)   projection
       e.)   subsetting

Level: moderate
Section: Relational Algebra
Subsection: Relational Operators

61.   In relational algebra, the _____ operator takes tuples meeting specified criteria and
        places them into the result relation.
        a.)   Cartesian product
        b.)   Difference
        c.)   selection
        d.)   projection
        e.)   subsetting

Level: moderate
Section: Relational Algebra
Subsection: Relational Operators

Fill in the Blank Questions

62.   The physical and logical description of values an attribute can have is called the __domain__ of the
        attribute.
Level: easy
Section: Defining Relational Data
Subsection: Review of Terminology

63.   The relation structure plus constraints on allowable data values is called the __relational schema__ .
Level: hard
Section: Defining Relational Data
Subsection: Review of Terminology

64.   A(n) __logical key__ is a group of one or more attributes that uniquely identifies a tuple in a
        relation.
Level: easy
Section: Defining Relational Data
Subsection: Review of Terminology

65.   In terms of relational implementation, a(n) __physical key__ is a column on which the DBMS
        builds an index or other data structure.
Level: easy
Section: Defining Relational Data
Subsection: Review of Terminology

66   A physical key is also called a(n) __index__ .
Level: easy
Section: Defining Relational Data
Subsection: Review of Terminology

67.   One reason to build an index is to enforce __uniqueness__ .
Level: moderate
Section: Defining Relational Data
Subsection: Review of Terminology

68.   The language used to describe the structure of a database is called __data definition language (DDL)__ .

Level: *hard*
Section: *Defining Relational Data*
Subsection: *Implementing a Relational Database*

69.   DBMS products on personal computers generally use __graphical__ means to define the structure of the database.

Level: *moderate*
Section: *Defining Relational Data*
Subsection: *Implementing a Relational Database*

70.   A(n) __maintenance plan__ is a schedule of activities, such as backing up the database and optimizing disk space, that are performed on a recurring basis.

Level: *hard*
Section: *Defining Relational Data*
Subsection: *Implementing a Relational Database*

71.   __Relational algebra__ is a procedural DML that defines operators that work on relations.

Level: *moderate*
Section: *Relational Data Manipulation*
Subsection: *Categories of Relational Data Manipulation Language*

72.   __Relational calculus__ was the first nonprocedural DML and is used largely for theoretical rather than practical purposes.

Level: *easy*
Section: *Relational Data Manipulation*
Subsection: *Categories of Relational Data Manipulation Language*

73.   __Transform-oriented languages__ are a class of nonprocedural data manipulation languages that transform input data expressed as relations into results expressed as a single relation.

Level: *moderate*
Section: *Relational Data Manipulation*
Subsection: *Categories of Relational Data Manipulation Language*

74.   __Procedural__ data manipulation techniques, such as relational algebra, require you to know not only what you want but also how to get it.

Level: *easy*
Section: *Relational Data Manipulation*
Subsection: *Categories of Relational Data Manipulation Language*

75.   With a(n) __graphical__ DML, such as Query-By-Example, the DBMS maps the materialization to the underlying relation and constructs queries on behalf of the user.

Level: *moderate*
Section: *Relational Data Manipulation*
Subsection: *Categories of Relational Data Manipulation Language*

76.   A(n) __form__ is a type of data manipulation interface for the user that may be tabular.
Level: *moderate*
Section: *Relational Data Manipulation*
Subsection: *DML Interfaces to the DBMS*

77.   Although commonly referred to as "query" languages, query languages can also perform
__updates__ to the database as well.
Level: *moderate*
Section: *Relational Data Manipulation*
Subsection: *DML Interfaces to the DBMS*

78.   __SQL__ is the single most important query language.
Level: *moderate*
Section: *Relational Data Manipulation*
Subsection: *DML Interfaces to the DBMS*

79.   __Stored procedures__ is a DLM interface composed of a collection of SQL statements stored as a
file that can be invoked with a single command.
Level: *moderate*
Section: *Relational Data Manipulation*
Subsection: *DML Interfaces to the DBMS*

80.   A special type of stored procedure, called a(n) __trigger__, is invoked by the DBMS whenever a
given condition occurs.
Level: *moderate*
Section: *Relational Data Manipulation*
Subsection: *DML Interfaces to the DBMS*

81.   The type of DML interface to the DBMS that requires the use of a precompiler is the
__application program interface__.
Level: *hard*
Section: *Relational Data Manipulation*
Subsection: *DML Interfaces to the DBMS*

82.   The __union__ of two relations is formed by adding the tuples from one relation to those of the
second relation to produce a third relation.
Level: *moderate*
Section: *Relational Algebra*
Subsection: *Relational Operators*

83.   In relational algebra terms, if two relations have the same number of attributes, and the attributes
in corresponding columns come from the same domain, then the relations are said to be __union
compatible__.
Level: *moderate*
Section: *Relational Algebra*
Subsection: *Relational Operators*

84.   The   difference   of two relations is a third relation containing tuples that occur in the first relation but not in the second.
Level: *moderate*
Section: *Relational Algebra*
Subsection: *Relational Operators*

85.   The   intersection   of two relations is a third relation containing the tuples that appear in both the first and second relations.
Level: *moderate*
Section: *Relational Algebra*
Subsection: *Relational Operators*

86.   The   (Cartesian) product   is the concatenation of every tuple of one relation with every tuple of a second relation.
Level: *moderate*
Section: *Relational Algebra*
Subsection: *Relational Operators*

87.   Projection   is an operation that selects specified attributes from a relation.
Level: *moderate*
Section: *Relational Algebra*
Subsection: *Relational Operators*

88.   Selection   is a relational operation that creates a horizontal subset by taking tuples that meet specified criteria and placing them into the result relation.
Level: *moderate*
Section: *Relational Algebra*
Subsection: *Relational Operators*

89.   The   join   operation is a combination of the product, selection, and (possibly) projection operations.
Level: *moderate*
Section: *Relational Algebra*
Subsection: *Relational Operators*

90.   A(n)   natural   join is similar to an equijoin, except the redundant attribute from the equality condition is removed.
Level: *hard*
Section: *Relational Algebra*
Subsection: *Relational Operators*

91.   A(n)   left outer   join is used to retrieve all tuples from the first relation and the matching tuples, when they exist, from the second relation.
Level: *hard*
Section: *Relational Algebra*
Subsection: *Relational Operators*

Essay Questions

92. Discuss the confusion that exists around the meaning of the term "key".
     The reason there is confusion regarding the meaning of the term "key" is because it has a different meaning in terms of design than it does in terms of implementation. In design, "key" means "logical key", which is an attribute or group of attributes that uniquely identify tuples in a relation. In implementation, "key" means "physical key", which is a column of a table on which the DBMS has created an index or other data structure to improve the performance of the database. A logical key must be unique, but a physical key may or may not be unique.
     Section: *Defining Relational Data*
     Subsection: *Review of Terminology*

93. Briefly describe the steps in implementing a relational model into a relational database.
     The first step in implementing a relational database is to describe the structure of the database to the DBMS using either a textual or graphical data definition language. In addition, the developer may need to make decisions regarding the allocation of storage space on the physical storage media to the database structures. Further, the allocation of space for growth of the database may also need to be specified. Often, a maintenance plan will be created at this time to specify procedures and schedules for recurring tasks such as backing up the database. Finally, the database must be populated with any existing data that needs to fill the database. While the data may be entered into the database in any number of ways, including manual re-keying or importing electronic data, once the data has been moved to the database, it must be verified to ensure accuracy of the data transfer.
     Section: *Defining Relational Data*
     Subsection: *Implementing a Relational Database*

94. Distinguish among the four categories of data manipulation languages.
     The first category of DML is relational algebra. Relational algebra is the only procedural DML, which means that it requires users to know what they want and how to get it. Relational calculus developed as the first non-procedural DML. While relational calculus is difficult to use and is not of practical value, it set an important trend for the use of non-procedural data manipulation languages. Transform-oriented languages next developed to provide a non-procedural DML that was easier to use than relational calculus. This class of languages takes relations as input and produces a single relation as a result. The fourth class of DML is the graphical DML. Graphical data manipulation languages continue the trend of improving ease-of-use and are typified by techniques such as query-by-example and query-by-form, which remove the need to know the underlying language.
     Section: *Relational Data Manipulation*
     Subsection: *Categories of Relational Data Manipulation Language*

95.   Explain the problem with embedding SQL within traditional programming languages and how
        that problem is addressed.
        The problem with embedding SQL within traditional programming languages is one of
        orientation. SQL is a transform-oriented data manipulation language, therefore it takes relations
        as input and produces a relation as a result. SQL is oriented to work with a whole table of data
        at one time. Traditional programming languages were developed to work with file-processing
        systems. These languages are oriented to deal with data only one record at a time. In order to
        address the problem, the results of an embedded SQL command are treated as a sequential file
        and processed one record at a time sequentially.
        Section: *Relational Data Manipulation*
        Subsection: *DML Interfaces to the DBMS*

96.   Explain the difference between "inner joins" and "outer joins".
        An inner join returns the product of two relations selected to only the records that have columns
        meeting given criteria. With an inner join, only records that match the criteria are returned. An
        outer join returns every record in one relation and only the records in the other relation that
        match the criteria.
        Section: *Relational Algebra*
        Subsection: *Relational Operators*

CHAPTER 9

Structured Query Language

True-False Questions

1. SQL stands for *Standard Query Language.*
    Answer: False   *Level: easy*
    Section: Chapter Introduction

2. SQL has become the standard language for information exchange among computers.
    Answer: True   *Level: easy*
    Section: Chapter Introduction

3. SQL is generally available only on microcomputer products.
    Answer: False   *Level: moderate*
    Section: Chapter Introduction

4. In addition to being a data sublanguage, SQL is also a programming language, like COBOL.
    Answer: False   *Level: moderate*
    Section: Chapter Introduction

5. SQL commands can be embedded in application programs.
    Answer: True   *Level: hard*
    Section: Chapter Introduction

6. SQL is not considered a *closed* language.
    Answer: False   *Level: hard*
    Section: Chapter Introduction

7. SQL can only query a single table.
    Answer: False   *Level: easy*
    Section: Querying a Single Table

8. The SQL language is case sensitive.
    Answer: False   *Level: hard*
    Section: Querying a Single Table

9. The SQL keyword *PROJECT* is used to perform the equivalent of the relational algebra operation "projection."
    Answer: False   *Level: moderate*
    Section: Querying a Single Table
    Subsection: Projections Using SQL

10. The SQL keyword *SELECT* is equivalent to the relational algebra operator *selection.*
    Answer: False   *Level: hard*
    Section: Querying a Single Table

Subsection: Projections Using SQL

11.   The SQL keyword *FROM* is used to specify the table to be used.
        Answer: True   *Level: easy*
        Section: Querying a Single Table
        Subsection: Projections Using SQL

12.   The columns to be obtained by an SQL command are listed after the *FROM* keyword.
        Answer: False   *Level: moderate*
        Section: Querying a Single Table
        Subsection: Projections Using SQL

13.   The result of an SQL *SELECT* operation can contain duplicate rows.
        Answer: True   *Level: moderate*
        Section: Querying a Single Table
        Subsection: Projections Using SQL

14.   To have SQL automatically eliminate duplicate rows from a result, use the qualifier *DISTINCT* with the FROM keyword.
        Answer: False   *Level: hard*
        Section: Querying a Single Table
        Subsection: Projections Using SQL

15.   An asterisk (*) following the *SELECT* verb means that all columns are to be obtained.
        Answer: True   *Level: moderate*
        Section: Querying a Single Table
        Subsection: Selections Using SQL

16.   The *WHERE* clause contains the condition that specifies which columns are to be selected.
        Answer: False   *Level: moderate*
        Section: Querying a Single Table
        Subsection: Selections Using SQL

17.   A *WHERE* clause can contain only one condition.
        Answer: False   *Level: easy*
        Section: Querying a Single Table
        Subsection: Selections Using SQL

18.   The condition in *WHERE* clauses can refer to a set of values by using the *IN* keyword.
        Answer: True   *Level: moderate*
        Section: Querying a Single Table
        Subsection: Selections Using SQL

19.   ANSI standard SQL uses the symbol "%" to represent a series of one or more unspecified characters.
        Answer: True   *Level: hard*
        Section: Querying a Single Table
        Subsection: Selections Using SQL

20.   The rows of the result relation can be sorted by the values in one or more columns.
       Answer: True   *Level: easy*
       Section: Querying a Single Table
       Subsection: Sorting

21.   Sorting is specified by the use of the *SORT BY* phrase.
       Answer: False   *Level: moderate*
       Section: Querying a Single Table
       Subsection: Sorting

22.   The clause *SELECT COUNT (*)* results in a table with a single row and a single column.
       Answer: True   *Level: moderate*
       Section: Querying a Single Table
       Subsection: SQL Built-in Functions

23.   The built-in function *SUM* can be used with any column.
       Answer: False   *Level: hard*
       Section: Querying a Single Table
       Subsection: SQL Built-in Functions

24.   The SQL keyword *GROUP BY* instructs the DBMS to group together those rows that have the
       same value in a column.
       Answer: True   *Level: easy*
       Section: Querying a Single Table
       Subsection: Built-in Functions and Grouping

25.   A *WHERE* clause can contain a subquery.
       Answer: True   *Level: easy*
       Section: Querying Multiple Tables
       Subsection: Retrieval Using Subquery

26.   A subquery is not appropriate when the results to be displayed include attributes from two tables.
       Answer: True   *Level: moderate*
       Section: Querying Multiple Tables
       Subsection: Retrieval Using Subquery

27.   Two or more tables can be joined by giving the table names in the *FROM* clause and specifying
       the equality of the respective column names as a condition in the *WHERE* clause.
       Answer: True   *Level: hard*
       Section: Querying Multiple Tables
       Subsection: Joining with SQL

28.   Every subquery can be alternatively expressed by a join.
       Answer: False   *Level: moderate*
       Section: Querying Multiple Tables
       Subsection: Comparison of SQL Subquery and Join

29.   ANSI standard SQL uses the keyword *LEFT JOIN* to implement outer joins.
       Answer: False   *Level: hard*
       Section: Querying Multiple Tables

Subsection: Outer Join

30.   *EXISTS* and *NOT EXISTS* are logical operators whose value is either true or false depending on the presence or absence of rows that fit the qualifying conditions.
      Answer: *True*   Level: *hard*
      Section: *Exists and Not Exists*

31.   The *INSERT* clause can be used to insert only a single row into a table.
      Answer: *False*   Level: *moderate*
      Section: *Changing Data*
      Subsection: *Inserting Data*

32.   The *ERASE* command is used to delete a single row from one table.
      Answer: *False*   Level: *moderate*
      Section: *Changing Data*
      Subsection: *Deleting Data*

33.   The keyword *MODIFY* is used to change a column value.
      Answer: *False*   Level: *hard*
      Section: *Changing Data*
      Subsection: *Modifying Data*

Multiple Choice Questions

34.   SQL is a(n):
      a.)   interactive query language
      b.)   transform-oriented language
      c.)   data access language
      d.)   data sublanguage
      e.)   all of the above

Level: *moderate*
Section: *Chapter Introduction*

35.   Which SQL keyword must be used to remove duplicate rows from the result relation?
      a.)   DELETE
      b.)   DISTINCT
      c.)   NOT EXISTS
      d.)   UNIQUE
      e.)   KEY

Level: *hard*
Section: *Querying a Single Table*
Subsection: *Projections Using SQL*

36.   Which SQL keyword is used to state the condition that specifies which rows are to be selected?
        a.)   EXISTS
        b.)   FROM
        c.)   SELECT
        d.)   SET
        e.)   WHERE

Level: easy
Section: Querying a Single Table
Subsection: Selections Using SQL

37.   Which SQL keyword is used to specify the table(s) to be used?
        a.)   EXISTS
        b.)   FROM
        c.)   SELECT
        d.)   SET
        e.)   WHERE

Level: easy
Section: Querying a Single Table
Subsection: Selections Using SQL

38.   Which SQL keyword is used to join two conditions that both must be true for the rows to be selected?
        a.)   AND
        b.)   EXISTS
        c.)   HAVING
        d.)   IN
        e.)   OR

Level: easy
Section: Querying a Single Table
Subsection: Selections Using SQL

39.   Which keyword is used to determine if a column value is equal to any one of a set of values?
        a.)   AND
        b.)   EXISTS
        c.)   HAVING
        d.)   IN
        e.)   OR

Level: moderate
Section: Querying a Single Table
Subsection: Selections Using SQL

40.   Given a relation with the structure: EMPLOYEE (EmpNo, Name, Salary, HireDate), which of the
        following would find all employees whose name begins with the letter "S?"
        a.)   SELECT * FROM EMPLOYEE WHERE Name IN ['S']
        b.)   SELECT EmpNo FROM EMPLOYEE WHERE Name LIKE 'S'
        c.)   SELECT * FROM Name WHERE EMPLOYEE LIKE 'S*'
        d.)   SELECT * FROM EMPLOYEE WHERE Name LIKE 'S%'
        e.)   none of the above

Level: hard
Section: Querying a Single Table
Subsection: Selections Using SQL

41.   Which of the following symbols is used by ANSI SQL to represent a single unspecified
        character?
        a.)   _ (underscore)
        b.)   ? (question mark)
        c.)   * (asterisk)
        d.)   % (percent)
        e.)   # (pound)

Level: hard
Section: Querying a Single Table
Subsection: Selections Using SQL

42.   Given a relation with the structure: EMPLOYEE (EmpNo, Name, Salary, HireDate), which of the
        following is <u>not</u> a valid ANSI SQL command?
        a.)   SELECT * FROM EMPLOYEE WHERE Name LIKE 'Ja%'
        b.)   SELECT COUNT (*) FROM EMPLOYEE WHERE Salary < 30000
        c.)   SELECT COUNT (EmpNo) FROM EMPLOYEE
        d.)   SELECT HireDate, COUNT (*) FROM EMPLOYEE WHERE Salary < 30000
        e.)   SELECT HireDate, COUNT (*) FROM EMPLOYEE GROUP BY HireDate

Level: hard
Section: Querying a Single Table
Subsection: Selections Using SQL

43.   Which keyword is used to sort the result relation by the values in one or more columns?
        a.)   GROUP BY
        b.)   ORDER BY
        c.)   SELECT
        d.)   SORT BY
        e.)   WHERE

Level: moderate
Section: Querying a Single Table
Subsection: Sorting

44.   Which built-in function is used to compute the number of rows in a table?
        a.)   AVG
        b.)   COUNT
        c.)   MAX
        d.)   MIN
        e.)   MEAN

Level: *easy*
Section: *Querying a Single Table*
Subsection: *SQL Built-in Functions*

45.   Which built-in function is used to total numeric columns?
        a.)   AVG
        b.)   COUNT
        c.)   MAX
        d.)   MEAN
        e.)   SUM

Level: *easy*
Section: *Querying a Single Table*
Subsection: *SQL Built-in Functions*

46.   Which built-in function is used to compute the average value of numeric columns?
        a.)   AVG
        b.)   MEAN
        c.)   MAX
        d.)   MIN
        e.)   SUM

Level: *easy*
Section: *Querying a Single Table*
Subsection: *SQL Built-in Functions*

47.   Which built-in function is used to obtain the largest value of numeric columns?
        a.)   AVG
        b.)   COUNT
        c.)   MAX
        d.)   MIN
        e.)   SUM

Level: *easy*
Section: *Querying a Single Table*
Subsection: *SQL Built-in Functions*

48.   Which built-in function is used to obtain the smallest value of numeric columns?
   a.)   AVG
   b.)   COUNT
   c.)   MAX
   d.)   MIN
   e.)   SUM

Level: easy
Section: Querying a Single Table
Subsection: SQL Built-in Functions

SALESREP

SalesRepNo	RepName	HireDate
654	Jones	01/02/1999
734	Smith	02/03/2000
345	Chen	01/25/1998
434	Johnson	11/23/1998

CUSTOMER

CustNo	CustName	Balance	SalesRepNo
9870	Winston	500	345
8590	Gonzales	350	434
7840	Harris	800	654
4870	Miles	100	345

49.   Based on the tables above, which of the following ANSI SQL commands would return the average customer balance grouped by SalesRepNo?
   a.)   SELECT AVG (Balance)
           FROM CUSTOMER
           WHERE SalesRepNo
   b.)   SELECT AVG (Balance)
           FROM CUSTOMER
           GROUP BY SalesRepNo
   c.)   SELECT AVG (Balance)
           FROM CUSTOMER, SALESREP
           WHERE SALESREP.SalesRepNo = CUSTOMER.SalesRepNo
   d.)   SELECT AVG (Balance)
           FROM CUSTOMER
           ORDER BY SalesRepNo
   e.)   SELECT AVG (Balance)
           FROM CUSTOMER, SALESREP
           WHERE CUSTOMER.SalesRepNo = CUSTOMER.SalesRepNo
           HAVING SalesRepNo

Level: hard
Section: Querying a Single Table
Subsection: Built-in Functions and Grouping

50.   Which SQL keyword is used with built-in functions to group together rows that have the same value in a specified column?
   a.)   GROUP BY
   b.)   ORDER BY
   c.)   SELECT
   d.)   SORT BY
   e.)   DISTINCT SET

Level: easy
Section: Querying a Single Table
Subsection: Built-in Functions and Grouping

51.   Which keyword is used with *GROUP BY* to select groups meeting specified criteria?
   a.)   AND
   b.)   EXISTS
   c.)   HAVING
   d.)   IN
   e.)   WHERE

Level: moderate
Section: Querying a Single Table
Subsection: Built-in Functions and Grouping

52.   Which keyword is used to implement a subquery?
   a.)   GROUP BY
   b.)   HAVING
   c.)   ORDER BY
   d.)   SELECT
   e.)   SORT BY

Level: hard
Section: Querying Multiple Tables
Subsection: Retrieval Using Subquery

53.   When one query is embedded in the WHERE clause of another query, this is referred to as a
   _____.
   a.)   subset
   b.)   join
   c.)   WHERE Query
   d.)   subquery
   e.)   set query

Level: moderate
Section: Querying Multiple Tables
Subsection: Retrieval Using Subquery

54.   Which keyword is used to specify the names of tables to be joined?
  a.)   FROM
  b.)   HAVING
  c.)   JOIN
  d.)   SELECT
  e.)   WHERE

Level: *easy*
Section: *Querying Multiple Tables*
Subsection: *Joining with SQL*

55.   Which keyword is used to specify the condition(s) for a join operation?
  a.)   FROM
  b.)   HAVING
  c.)   JOIN
  d.)   SELECT
  e.)   WHERE

Level: *moderate*
Section: *Querying Multiple Tables*
Subsection: *Joining with SQL*

56.   Regarding the interchangeability of subqueries and joins:
  a.)   A join can always be used as an alternative to a subquery, and a subquery can always be used as an alternative to a join.
  b.)   A join can sometimes be used as an alternative to a subquery, and a subquery can sometimes be used as an alternative to a join.
  c.)   A join can always be used as an alternative to a subquery, and a subquery can sometimes be used as an alternative to a join.
  d.)   A join can sometimes be used as an alternative to a subquery, and a subquery can always be used as an alternative to a join.
  e.)   A join can never be used as an alternative to a subquery, and a subquery can never be used as an alternative to a join.

Level: *moderate*
Section: *Querying Multiple Tables*
Subsection: *Comparison of SQL Subquery and Join*

SALESREP

SalesRepNo	RepName	HireDate
654	Jones	01/02/1999
734	Smith	02/03/2000
345	Chen	01/25/1998
434	Johnson	11/23/1998

CUSTOMER

CustNo	CustName	Balance	SalesRepNo
9870	Winston	500	345
8590	Gonzales	350	434
7840	Harris	800	654
4870	Miles	100	345

57. Based on the tables above, which of the following commands in ANSI SQL would return only the name of the sales representative and name of the customer for each customer that has a balance greater than 400?

a.) SELECT *
FROM SALESREP, CUSTOMER
WHERE Balance > 400

b.) SELECT DISTINCT RepName, CustName
FROM SALESREP, CUSTOMER
WHERE Balance > 400

c.) SELECT *
FROM SALESREP, CUSTOMER
WHERE SALESREP.SalesRepNo = CUSTOMER.SalesRepNo
AND Balance > 400

**d.) SELECT RepName, CustName
FROM SALESREP, CUSTOMER
WHERE SALESREP.SalesRepNo = CUSTOMER.SalesRepNo
AND Balance > 400**

e.) SELECT RepName, CustName
FROM SALESREP, CUSTOMER
WHERE Balance > 400
GROUP BY SalesRepNo

Level: hard
Section: Querying Multiple Tables
Subsection: Joining with SQL

58.   Which of the following is <u>not</u> an ANSI SQL keyword(s)?
    a.)   EXISTS
    b.)   ORDER BY
    c.)   LEFT JOIN
    d.)   HAVING
    e.)   DISTINCT

Level: hard
Section: Querying Multiple Tables
Subsection: Outer Join

59.   Which keyword is a logical operator whose value is either true or false depending on the presence or absence of rows that meet the qualifying conditions?
    a.)   AND
    b.)   EXISTS
    c.)   HAVING
    d.)   IN
    e.)   OR

Level: moderate
Section: Exists and Not Exists

60.   Rows in the same table can be compared to each other by:
    a.)   joining the table to itself
    b.)   sorting the table on the column to be compared
    c.)   grouping the table on the column to be compared
    d.)   assigning two different names to the table
    e.)   removing duplicate rows

Level: hard
Section: Exists and Not Exists

61.   Which keyword is used to add one or more rows to a table?
    a.)   DELETE
    b.)   INSERT
    c.)   SELECT
    d.)   SET
    e.)   UPDATE

Level: easy
Section: Changing Data
Subsection: Inserting Data

62.   Which keyword is used to remove one or more rows from a table?
    a.)   DELETE
    b.)   INSERT
    c.)   ERASE
    d.)   SET
    e.)   UPDATE

Level: moderate
Section: Changing Data
Subsection: Deleting Data

63.   Which keyword is used to change one or more rows in a table?
    a.)   MODIFY
    b.)   INSERT
    c.)   SELECT
    d.)   CHANGE
    e.)   UPDATE

Level: moderate
Section: Changing Data
Subsection: Modifying Data

64.   Which keyword is used to change a column value?
    a.)   CHANGE
    b.)   INSERT
    c.)   SELECT
    d.)   SET
    e.)   MODIFY

Level: hard
Section: Changing Data
Subsection: Modifying Data

Fill in the Blank Questions

65.   SQL stands for ___Structured Query Language___ .
Level: easy
Section: Chapter Introduction

66.   The ___American National Standards Institute (ANSI)___ maintains the standards for SQL.
Level: hard
Section: Chapter Introduction

67.   The keyword ___SELECT___ is used to specify the columns to be obtained.
Level: easy
Section: Querying a Single Table
Subsection: Projections Using SQL

68.   The keyword __FROM__ is used to specify the table(s) that contains the data to be retrieved.
Level: *easy*
Section: *Querying a Single Table*
Subsection: *Projections Using SQL*

69.   To remove duplicate rows from the result of a query, specify the qualifier __DISTINCT__ .
Level: *hard*
Section: *Querying a Single Table*
Subsection: *Projections Using SQL*

70.   To obtain all columns, use a(n) __asterisk (*)__ instead of listing all the column names.
Level: *easy*
Section: *Querying a Single Table*
Subsection: *Selections Using SQL*

71.   The __WHERE__ clause contains the condition that specifies which rows are to be selected.
Level: *easy*
Section: *Querying a Single Table*
Subsection: *Selections Using SQL*

72.   When two conditions must both be true for the rows to be selected, the conditions are separated by the keyword __AND__ .
Level: *easy*
Section: *Querying a Single Table*
Subsection: *Selections Using SQL*

73.   To refer to a set of values in a condition, the values are placed inside __square brackets [ ]__ and separated by commas.
Level: *hard*
Section: *Querying a Single Table*
Subsection: *Selections Using SQL*

74.   Including multiple values in a set as part of a condition has the same effect as using multiple conditions separated by the __OR__ logical operator.
Level: *moderate*
Section: *Querying a Single Table*
Subsection: *Selections Using SQL*

75.   To exclude one or more values using a condition, the keyword __NOT__ must be used.
Level: *hard*
Section: *Querying a Single Table*
Subsection: *Selections Using SQL*

76.   The __LIKE__ keyword is used in SQL expressions to select on partial values.
Level: *moderate*
Section: *Querying a Single Table*
Subsection: *Selections Using SQL*

77.   To sort the rows of the result relation, the __ORDER BY__ clause is specified.
Level: *moderate*
Section: *Querying a Single Table*
Subsection: *Sorting*

78.   Columns can be sorted in descending sequence by using the keyword __DESC__ .
Level: *moderate*
Section: *Querying a Single Table*
Subsection: *Sorting*

79.   The built-in function __COUNT__ computes the number of rows in a table.
Level: *easy*
Section: *Querying a Single Table*
Subsection: *SQL Built-in Functions*

80.   The built-in function __SUM__ totals values in numeric columns.
Level: *easy*
Section: *Querying a Single Table*
Subsection: *SQL Built-in Functions*

81.   The built-in function __AVG__ computes the average of values in numeric columns.
Level: *easy*
Section: *Querying a Single Table*
Subsection: *SQL Built-in Functions*

82.   The built-in function __MAX__ obtains the largest value in a numeric column.
Level: *easy*
Section: *Querying a Single Table*
Subsection: *SQL Built-in Functions*

83.   The built-in function __MIN__ obtains the smallest value in a numeric column.
Level: *easy*
Section: *Querying a Single Table*
Subsection: *SQL Built-in Functions*

84.   The SQL keyword __GROUP BY__ is used to collect those rows that have the same value in a specified column.
Level: *moderate*
Section: *Querying a Single Table*
Subsection: *Built-in Functions and Grouping*

85.   A nested SELECT statement (one that appears within the WHERE clause of another SQL statement) is called a __subquery__ , and must be enclosed in parentheses.
Level: *moderate*
Section: *Querying Multiple Tables*
Subsection: *Retrieval Using Subquery*

86.   The names of tables to be joined are listed in the __FROM__ clause.
Level: easy
Section: *Querying Multiple Tables*
Subsection: *Joining with SQL*

87.   A join operation is achieved by specifying the equality of the respective column names as a condition in the __WHERE__ clause.
Level: moderate
Section: *Querying Multiple Tables*
Subsection: *Joining with SQL*

88.   The keyword __EXISTS__ is a logical operator whose value is either true or false depending on the presence or absence of rows that fit the qualifying conditions.
Level: moderate
Section: *Exists and Not Exists*

89.   One or more rows can be added to a table by using the __INSERT__ statement.
Level: moderate
Section: *Changing Data*
Subsection: *Inserting Data*

90.   When a row is added to a table but the value for a column is not known, the DBMS places a __null__ value for the column in the new row.
Level: hard
Section: *Changing Data*
Subsection: *Inserting Data*

91.   Rows can be copied from one table to another by the use of a __SELECT__ statement to specify the rows to be copied.
Level: hard
Section: *Changing Data*
Subsection: *Inserting Data*

92.   Rows can be removed from a table by using the __DELETE__ statement.
Level: moderate
Section: *Changing Data*
Subsection: *Deleting Data*

93.   Rows in a table can be changed by using the __UPDATE__ statement.
Level: moderate
Section: *Changing Data*
Subsection: *Modifying Data*

94.   The keyword __SET__ is used to specify a new value when changing a column value.
Level: hard
Section: *Changing Data*
Subsection: *Modifying Data*

Essay Questions

95.   Explain what SQL is.
SQL is a transform-oriented data manipulation language. It has become the standard for data interchange among computer systems because it has been implemented in a variety of database management systems across most computing platforms. It is a closed language, meaning that it accepts relations as input and produces a single relation as output. It is a data sublanguage that is used to access data both interactively and as an embedded data access language within traditional programming languages.
Section: *Chapter Introduction*

96.   Distinguish between the SQL "SELECT" statement and the relational operator "Selection."
The relational operator "Selection" serves a very specific function – it is used to create a horizontal subset of a relation. The SELECT keyword is much more versatile. SELECT is an SQL verb that is not only used in creating a horizontal subset of a relation but also projections and others operations.
Section: *Querying a Single Table*
Subsection: *Projections Using SQL*

97.   Explain the use of the LIKE keyword in SQL.
The LIKE keyword is used in SQL to select rows based on partial values. Through the use of wildcard characters that can represent one or more unspecified characters, the LIKE operator can search for a given string of characters within a column value. The ANSI wildcards "%" can represent one or more unspecified characters, and the wildcard "_ " (underscore) can represent any single unspecified character. These wildcards are used with the LIKE operator as a condition in the WHERE clause of an SQL statement to find records that have column values that contain the given partial value.
Section: *Querying a Single Table*
Subsection: *Selections Using SQL*

98.   Briefly describe subqueries and joins and when each is not an acceptable alternative for the other.
Subqueries and joins are both methods for retrieving data from multiple tables. Subqueries involve nesting one SELECT statement within another. The nested SELECT is used as part of a condition in the WHERE clause of the first SELECT statement. The nested SELECT statement can return a set of records from one table, which are then used in a logical operator within the parent SELECT query. A join combines records from each table into concatenated records containing the fields of both tables. The records are concatenated based on matching values in similar columns in the two tables. Joins cannot be used in situations that require the use of the EXISTS or NOT EXISTS operators. Subqueries cannot be used in situations where the results to be displayed include attributes from more than one table.
Section: *Querying Multiple Tables*
Subsection: *Comparison of SQL Subquery and Join*

99.   Explain the use of the GROUP BY keyword.
       The GROUP BY keyword is used in conjunction with the built-in functions of SQL. The GROUP BY keyword is given a column that records are to be grouped on. Records in the result relation are then collected into groups based on the value of the grouping column. The built-in function is then performed on the records of each group separately.
       Section: *Querying a Single Table*
       Subsection: *Built-in Functions and Grouping*

CHAPTER 10

Database Application Design

True-False Questions

1. One fundamental purpose of a database application is to create, read, update, and delete views.
    Answer: True   *Level: easy*
    Section: Functions of a Database Application

2. Materializing a view means adding a row to a relation.
    Answer: False   *Level: moderate*
    Section: Functions of a Database Application

3. An application view must be constructed from rows in a single table.
    Answer: False   *Level: moderate*
    Section: Functions of a Database Application

4. A view is a structured list of data items from the entities or semantic objects defined in the data model.
    Answer: True   *Level: easy*
    Section: Creating, Reading, Updating, and Deleting View Instances

5. A view instance is a view that is populated with data for one instance of an entity or semantic object.
    Answer: True   *Level: moderate*
    Section: Creating, Reading, Updating, and Deleting View Instances

6. There is only one way to materialize a given view in an application.
    Answer: False   *Level: hard*
    Section: Creating, Reading, Updating, and Deleting View Instances

7. Table data can be added using the *INSERT* SQL statement.
    Answer: True   *Level: moderate*
    Section: Creating, Reading, Updating, and Deleting View Instances
    Subsection: Creating View Instances

8. When a DBMS supports cascading deletions, they are performed manually by the user.
    Answer: False   *Level: hard*
    Section: Creating, Reading, Updating, and Deleting View Instances
    Subsection: Deleting View Instances

9. "Cascading deletions" is a function provided by some DBMS products that removes dependent rows when parent row is deleted.
    Answer: True   *Level: moderate*
    Section: Creating, Reading, Updating, and Deleting View Instances
    Subsection: Deleting View Instances

10. A *form* is a screen display used only to present data to the user.
    Answer: False   *Level: moderate*
    Section: Form Design

11. The structure of a form should reflect the structure of the view that it materializes.
    Answer: True   *Level: easy*
    Section: Form Design
    Subsection: The Form Structure Should Reflect the View Structure

12. Attributes in the base relation of a view are sometimes <u>not</u> placed contiguously on a form.
    Answer: True   *Level: hard*
    Section: Form Design
    Subsection: The Form Structure Should Reflect the View Structure

13. Data that are semantically related should not be placed graphically close to one another on a form.
    Answer: False   *Level: easy*
    Section: Form Design
    Subsection: The Semantics of the Data Should Be Graphically Evident

14. A drop-down list box on a form can be designed such that users cannot add data to it.
    Answer: True   *Level: easy*
    Section: Form Design
    Subsection: Forms in a GUI Environment

15. One advantage of drop-down list boxes over data entry boxes is that the drop-down list boxes only require the user to *recollect* the data value instead of having to *recognize* it.
    Answer: False   *Level: hard*
    Section: Form Design
    Subsection: Forms in a GUI Environment

16. The alternatives in a group of option buttons are mutually exclusive.
    Answer: True   *Level: easy*
    Section: Form Design
    Subsection: Forms in a GUI Environment

17. The alternatives in a group of check boxes are mutually exclusive.
    Answer: False   *Level: moderate*
    Section: Form Design
    Subsection: Forms in a GUI Environment

18. Web forms that appear in a browser are not considered GUI forms and therefore have a very different set of rules for design than traditional Windows forms.
    Answer: False   *Level: hard*
    Section: Form Design
    Subsection: Forms in a GUI Environment

19. Special-purpose keys such as *ESC* should have different, customized actions on each form.
    Answer: False   *Level: moderate*
    Section: Form Design
    Subsection: Cursor Movement and Pervasive Keys

20. The principles of effective report design are similar to those for form design.
    Answer: True   *Level: easy*
    Section: Report Design
    Subsection: Report Structure

21. A report often has calculated data attributes that are not part of the underlying view and are not stored in the database.
    Answer: True   *Level: hard*
    Section: Report Design
    Subsection: Report Structure

22. The structure of a report should reflect the structure of the underlying object.
    Answer: True   *Level: easy*
    Section: Report Design
    Subsection: Report Structure

23. A report may be based on a *set of objects*, rather than a single object.
    Answer: True   *Level: hard*
    Section: Report Design
    Subsection: Implied Objects

24. It is better to enforce constraints in the DBMS instead of the application program because the DBMS is a central point that all data changes must pass through.
    Answer: True   *Level: easy*
    Section: Enforcing Constraints

25. In general, it is not possible to enforce constraints on the semantic component of an attribute domain.
    Answer: True   *Level: moderate*
    Section: Enforcing Constraints
    Subsection: Domain Constraints

26. Uniqueness constraints are best enforced by the DBMS.
    Answer: True   *Level: easy*
    Section: Enforcing Constraints
    Subsection: Uniqueness Constraints

27. Referential integrity constraints occur because of the values of minimum and maximum cardinality on relationships.
    Answer: False   *Level: hard*
    Section: Enforcing Constraints
    Subsection: Relationship Constraints

28.   Referential integrity constraints are considered a type of domain constraint.
        Answer: False   *Level: moderate*
        Section: Enforcing Constraints
        Subsection: Relationship Constraints

29.   A row that exists inappropriately without a required parent or child is called an orphan.
        Answer: False   *Level: moderate*
        Section: Enforcing Constraints
        Subsection: Relationship Constraints

30.   A parent row of a Mandatory-Optional relationship can always be deleted without violating
        relationship constraints.
        Answer: False   *Level: hard*
        Section: Enforcing Constraints
        Subsection: Relationship Constraints

31.   A child row of a Mandatory-Mandatory relationship can only be deleted if another suitable child
        row exists or is created.
        Answer: True   *Level: moderate*
        Section: Enforcing Constraints
        Subsection: Relationship Constraints

32.   There are no generic features of DBMS products to automatically enforce business rule
        constraints.
        Answer: True   *Level: moderate*
        Section: Enforcing Constraints
        Subsection: Business Rule Constraints

33.   Modern DBMS products automatically enforce all constraints.
        Answer: False   *Level: moderate*
        Section: Enforcing Constraints
        Subsection: Business Rule Constraints

34.   Most DBMS products have built-in support for horizontal security.
        Answer: False   *Level: hard*
        Section: Security and Control
        Subsection: Security

35.   Vertical security can be used to limit access to specified rows.
        Answer: False   *Level: hard*
        Section: Security and Control
        Subsection: Security

Multiple Choice Questions

36.   Which of the following is <u>not</u> a function of a database application?
    a.)   enforce constraints
    b.)   materialize views
    c.)   execute application logic
    d.)   process views
    e.)   all of the above <u>are</u> functions of database applications

Level: *moderate*
Section: *Functions of a Database Application*

37.   Which of the following is not a basic processing function?
    a.)   read
    b.)   transaction
    c.)   update
    d.)   delete
    e.)   create

Level: *easy*
Section: *Functions of a Database Application*

38.   A view that has been formatted is called a:
    a.)   child
    b.)   materialization
    c.)   subtype
    d.)   table
    e.)   representation

Level: *moderate*
Section: *Functions of a Database Application*

39.   A structured list of data items from the entities or semantic objects defined in the data model is called a(n):
    a.)   child
    b.)   materialization
    c.)   subtype
    d.)   table
    e.)   view

Level: *easy*
Section: *Creating, Reading, Updating, and Deleting View Instances*

40.   In the context of application development, the result of an SQL statement is called a:
      a.)   form
      b.)   query
      c.)   recordset
      d.)   table
      e.)   view

Level: hard
Section: Creating, Reading, Updating, and Deleting View Instances
Subsection: Reading View Instances

41.   Which SQL statement is used to retrieve view instances?
      a.)   CREATE
      b.)   DELETE
      c.)   INSERT
      d.)   SELECT
      e.)   UPDATE

Level: easy
Section: Creating, Reading, Updating, and Deleting View Instances
Subsection: Reading View Instances

42.   Which SQL statement is used to create view instances?
      a.)   CREATE
      b.)   DELETE
      c.)   INSERT
      d.)   SELECT
      e.)   UPDATE

Level: moderate
Section: Creating, Reading, Updating, and Deleting View Instances
Subsection: Creating View Instances

43.   Which SQL statement is used to modify values in view instances?
      a.)   CREATE
      b.)   DELETE
      c.)   INSERT
      d.)   SELECT
      e.)   UPDATE

Level: moderate
Section: Creating, Reading, Updating, and Deleting View Instances
Subsection: Updating View Instances

44.   Which SQL statement is used to delete view instances?
      a.)   CREATE
      b.)   DELETE
      c.)   INSERT
      d.)   SELECT
      e.)   UPDATE

Level: easy
Section: Creating, Reading, Updating, and Deleting View Instances
Subsection: Deleting View Instances

45.   A _____ is a screen display used for data entry and edit.
      a.)   form
      b.)   query
      c.)   relation
      d.)   report
      e.)   table

Level: easy
Section: Form Design

46.   The structure of a form should reflect the underlying:
      a.)   view structure
      b.)   CRUD
      c.)   materialization
      d.)   report structure
      e.)   table structure

Level: moderate
Section: Form Design
Subsection: The Form Structure Should Reflect the View Structure

47.   Which of the following is a characteristic of a well-designed form?
      a.)   The form should be vertically oriented.
      b.)   The form should be horizontally oriented.
      c.)   The GUI controls should be vertically oriented.
      d.)   The semantics of the data should be graphically evident.
      e.)   The view of the materialization should be actionable.

Level: hard
Section: Form Design
Subsection: The Semantics of the Data Should Be Graphically Evident

48.   A GUI form feature that presents a list of items from which the user can choose is called a(n):
       a.)   check box
       b.)   drop-down list box
       c.)   hyperlink
       d.)   option or radio button
       e.)   text box

Level: easy
Section: Form Design
Subsection: Forms in a GUI Environment

49.   A GUI form feature that enables the user to select one alternative condition or state from a sequence of mutually exclusive possibilities is called a(n):
       a.)   check box
       b.)   hyperlink
       c.)   text box
       d.)   option or radio button
       e.)   none of the above

Level: easy
Section: Form Design
Subsection: Forms in a GUI Environment

50.   A GUI form feature that enables the user to select one or more alternative conditions from a set of possibilities is called a(n):
       a.)   check box
       b.)   drop-down list box
       c.)   menu
       d.)   option or radio button
       e.)   text box

Level: easy
Section: Form Design
Subsection: Forms in a GUI Environment

51.   What feature is available with web forms using a browser that is not available with traditional Windows forms?
       a.)   option or radio button
       b.)   hyperlink
       c.)   text box
       d.)   drop-down list box
       e.)   check box

Level: easy
Section: Form Design
Subsection: Forms in a GUI Environment

52.   In designing forms for database applications, the actions of special-purpose keys such as *ESC*:
         a.)   should not be utilized
         b.)   should be customized differently on each form in the application
         c.)   should be customizable by each user of the form
         d.)   should be the same on all forms in the application
         e.)   are determined by the DBMS

Level: hard
Section: *Form Design*
Subsection: *Cursor Movement and Pervasive Keys*

53.   The structure of a report should reflect the underlying:
         a.)   forms
         b.)   view
         c.)   queries
         d.)   relations
         e.)   tables

Level: moderate
Section: *Report Design*
Subsection: *Report Structure*

54.   An *implied object* is based on:
         a.)   an instance of an object type
         b.)   an instance of more than one object type
         c.)   a request by a developer
         d.)   a request by a user
         e.)   the most frequently used objects

Level: hard
Section: *Report Design*
Subsection: *Implied Objects*

55.   One way the change from a base object to an implied object is signified is when _____.
         a.)   the developer normalizes the data model
         b.)   a view is constructed
         c.)   sorting by an object identifier
         d.)   a view has no objects
         e.)   all of the above

Level: hard
Section: *Report Design*
Subsection: *Implied Objects*

56.   Which of the following is <u>not</u> a type of constraint that must be enforced?
    a.)   transaction boundaries
    b.)   referential integrity
    c.)   business rules
    d.)   domains
    e.)   uniqueness

Level: moderate
Section: Enforcing Constraints

57.   The part of an attribute's domain that often can be automatically enforced by the DBMS is called the _____ component:
    a.)   business rule
    b.)   format
    c.)   implied
    d.)   physical
    e.)   semantic

Level: moderate
Section: Enforcing Constraints
Subsection: Domain Constraints

58.   A row that exists inappropriately without a required parent or child is called a(n):
    a.)   fragment
    b.)   implied object
    c.)   orphan
    d.)   subtype
    e.)   supertype

Level: moderate
Section: Enforcing Constraints
Subsection: Relationship Constraints

59.   A child row that exists without a mandatory parent is called a(n):
    a.)   fragment
    b.)   implied object
    c.)   orphan
    d.)   subtype
    e.)   supertype

Level: moderate
Section: Enforcing Constraints
Subsection: Relationship Constraints

60.   A parent of a(n) _____ relationship can be inserted only if at least one child
        is created.
        a.)   Mandatory-Mandatory
        b.)   Mandatory-Optional
        c.)   Optional-Mandatory
        d.)   Optional-Optional
        e.)   Conditional

Level: hard
Section: *Enforcing Constraints*
Subsection: *Relationship Constraints*

61.   The only restriction on modifying the key of a child of a(n) _____
        relationship is that a sibling must exist.
        a.)   Mandatory-Mandatory
        b.)   Mandatory-Optional
        c.)   Optional-Mandatory
        d.)   Optional-Optional
        e.)   Conditional

Level: hard
Section: *Enforcing Constraints*
Subsection: *Relationship Constraints*

62.   A parent of a(n) _____ relationship can be inserted only if at least one child
        is created or an appropriate child already exists.
        a.)   Mandatory-Mandatory
        b.)   Mandatory-Optional
        c.)   Optional-Mandatory
        d.)   Optional-Optional
        e.)   Conditional

Level: hard
Section: *Enforcing Constraints*
Subsection: *Relationship Constraints*

63.   The key of a parent or of a child of a(n) _____ relationship can be modified
        without restriction.
        a.)   Mandatory-Mandatory
        b.)   Mandatory-Optional
        c.)   Optional-Mandatory
        d.)   Optional-Optional
        e.)   Conditional

Level: hard
Section: *Enforcing Constraints*
Subsection: *Relationship Constraints*

64.   There are no generic DBMS features to automatically enforce which type of constraint?
      a.)   domain
      b.)   implied object
      c.)   **business rule**
      d.)   security
      e.)   referential integrity

Level: moderate
Section: Enforcing Constraints
Subsection: Business Rule Constraints

65.   Which type of security is used to limit access to specified rows of a table?
      a.)   **horizontal**
      b.)   password
      c.)   user name
      d.)   transaction boundary
      e.)   vertical

Level: moderate
Section: Security and Control

Fill in the Blank Questions

66.   The acronym commonly used to refer to the four basic processing functions is   CRUD .
Level: easy
Section: Functions of a Database Application

67.   One function of a database application is to format, or   materialize , the views that are being processed.
Level: moderate
Section: Functions of a Database Application

68.   A(n)   view   is a structured list of data items from the entities or semantic objects defined in the data model.
Level: moderate
Section: Creating, Reading, Updating, and Deleting View Instances

69.   A(n)   view instance   is a view that is populated with data for one entity or semantic object.
Level: hard
Section: Creating, Reading, Updating, and Deleting View Instances

70.   In the context of application development, the result of an SQL statement is called a(n)   recordset .
Level: hard
Section: Creating, Reading, Updating, and Deleting View Instances
Subsection: Reading View Instances

71.   View instances can be added using the __INSERT__ SQL statement.
Level: moderate
Section: *Creating, Reading, Updating, and Deleting View Instances*
Subsection: *Reading View Instances*

72.   Data in a view instance can be modified using the __UPDATE__ SQL statement.
Level: moderate
Section: *Creating, Reading, Updating, and Deleting View Instances*
Subsection: *Updating View Instances*

73.   View instances can be removed using the __DELETE__ SQL statement.
Level: easy
Section: *Creating, Reading, Updating, and Deleting View Instances*
Subsection: *Deleting View Instances*

74.   Some DBMS products support __cascading deletions__, which remove *dependent* rows when the parent row is removed.
Level: moderate
Section: *Creating, Reading, Updating, and Deleting View Instances*
Subsection: *Deleting View Instances*

75.   A(n) __form__ is a screen display used for data entry and edit.
Level: easy
Section: *Form Design*

76.   The structure of a form should reflect the structure of the __view__.
Level: moderate
Section: *Form Design*
Subsection: *The Form Structure Should Reflect the View Structure*

77.   One characteristic of a well-designed form is that the __semantics__ of the data should be graphically evident.
Level: hard
Section: *Form Design*
Subsection: *The Semantics of the Data Should Be Graphically Evident*

78.   A(n) __drop-down list box__ is a GUI control that presents a list of items from which the user can choose.
Level: easy
Section: *Form Design*
Subsection: *Forms in a GUI Environment*

79.   A(n) __option button/radio button__ is a display device that enables users to select one alternative condition or state from a set of mutually exclusive possibilities.
Level: easy
Section: *Form Design*
Subsection: *Forms in a GUI Environment*

80.   A(n) __check box__ is a display device that enables users to select one *or more* alternative conditions or states from a set of possibilities.
Level: *easy*
Section: *Form Design*
Subsection: *Forms in a GUI Environment*

81.   Web forms used in a browser have one feature, __hyperlinks__, that traditional Windows forms do not have.
Level: *moderate*
Section: *Form Design*
Subsection: *Forms in a GUI Environment*

82.   The actions of special-purpose keys such as *ESC* should be __consistent/pervasive__ throughout an application.
Level: *hard*
Section: *Form Design*
Subsection: *Cursor Movement and Pervasive Keys*

83.   A(n) __implied__ object is generally created by sorting a set of objects.
Level: *hard*
Section: *Report Design*
Subsection: *Implied Objects*

84.   In general, it is not possible to enforce the __semantic__ component of an attribute domain through automated processes.
Level: *moderate*
Section: *Enforcing Constraints*
Subsection: *Domain Constraints*

85.   Required value constraints are important because they eliminate the possibility of __null values__.
Level: *hard*
Section: *Enforcing Constraints*
Subsection: *Domain Constraints*

86.   All referential integrity constraints are limitations on __foreign key__ values.
Level: *hard*
Section: *Enforcing Constraints*
Subsection: *Relationship Constraints*

87.   A child row that exists without a mandatory parent is called a(n) __orphan__ .
Level: *moderate*
Section: *Enforcing Constraints*
Subsection: *Relationship Constraints*

88.   A(n) __Mandatory-Mandatory/M-M__ constraint means that neither the parent or child can exist without the other.
Level: *moderate*
Section: *Enforcing Constraints*
Subsection: *Relationship Constraints*

89.   A(n)   Mandatory-Optional/M-O   constraint means that a parent can exist without a child, but a child cannot exist without a parent.
Level: *moderate*
Section: *Enforcing Constraints*
Subsection: *Relationship Constraints*

90.   The only restriction on modifying the key of a child of a(n)   Optional-Mandatory/O-M   relationship is that a sibling must exist.
Level: *hard*
Section: *Enforcing Constraints*
Subsection: *Relationship Constraints*

91.   A parent of a(n)   Optional-Mandatory/O-M   relationship can be inserted only if at least one child is created or an appropriate child already exists.
Level: *hard*
Section: *Enforcing Constraints*
Subsection: *Relationship Constraints*

92.   A(n)   trigger   is a stored procedure that is invoked when a specified event occurs in the database.
Level: *easy*
Section: *Enforcing Constraints*
Subsection: *Business Rule Constraints*

93.   Triggers are used by some DBMS products to support trapping events to help enforce   business rule   constraints.
Level: *hard*
Section: *Enforcing Constraints*
Subsection: *Business Rule Constraints*

94.   Vertical   security limits access to specified columns.
Level: *moderate*
Section: *Security and Control*
Subsection: *Security*

95.   Horizontal   security limits access to specified rows.
Level: *moderate*
Section: *Security and Control*
Subsection: *Security*

96.   Transaction   boundaries identify work that must be completed as a unit.
Level: *moderate*
Section: *Security and Control*
Subsection: *Security*

Essay Questions

97.   Explain the difference between a view and a materialization.
       *A view is simply a structured list of data items. It has no specified format and has not been
       organized to support readability and comprehension. A materialization is a view that has been
       formatted to meet a specific purpose. A view can be formatted several different ways for different
       purposes; therefore a view can have many materializations.*
       Section: *Functions of a Database Application*

98.   Explain the principle that the form structure should encourage appropriate action.
       *The structure of the form should make it easy to perform correct actions and difficult to perform
       inappropriate actions. This can be done through the choice of controls on the form and by
       manipulating the properties of the controls. An example would be making data entry boxes
       uneditable if they contain data that should not be changed from the given view, or using controls
       that limit a user's choices to allow only appropriate values.*
       Section: *Form Design*
       Subsection: *The Form Structure Should Encourage Appropriate Action*

99.   Discuss appropriate cursor movement within a form.
       *The cursor should move easily and naturally through the form. If the user is performing data
       entry from source documents, the cursor should move in a pattern that reflects the order of
       processing the source document. If the input for data entry is through telephone conversations,
       the flow of the cursor should match the structure of the conversation. This is especially true after
       an error, or exception, condition that requires the user to re-enter data. The cursor should be
       placed logically to simplify the re-entry of data with appropriate values.*
       Section: *Form Design*
       Subsection: *Cursor Movement and Pervasive Keys*

100.   Explain the concept of implied objects.
       *Often when structuring a report, a report may be based on a set of objects instead of a single
       object instance. For example, instead of a report being based on Object A, it may be based on
       the Set of All Object A's. This change from focusing on a specific object to focusing on a set of
       objects is usually signaled by a request for a report that sorts the objects on an attribute.*
       Section: *Report Design*
       Subsection: *Implied Objects*

101.   Distinguish between horizontal and vertical security.
       *Horizontal security means restricting individual users to a view of only a horizontal subset, or
       selection, of records. Users are allowed to view all attributes of a relation, but they can see those
       attributes only for specific records within the relation. Vertical security means restricting users
       to a view of only a vertical subset, or projection, of records. Users are allowed to see only
       certain attributes of a relation, but they can see those attributes for all records in the relation.*
       Section: *Security and Control*
       Subsection: *Security*

CHAPTER 11

Managing Multi-User Databases

True-False Questions

1. Database administration tasks have to be performed for single-user, personal databases.
    Answer: True   *Level: hard*
    Section: Database Administration

2. Database administration is more important but less difficult in multi-user database systems than in single-user database systems.
    Answer: False   *Level: moderate*
    Section: Database Administration

3. In general, the overall responsibility of the DBA is to facilitate the development and use of the database system.
    Answer: True   *Level: easy*
    Section: Database Administration

4. The DBA has to find a balance between the conflicting goals of maximizing availability of the database to users and protecting the database.
    Answer: True   *Level: moderate*
    Section: Database Administration

5. The DBA is responsible for managing changes to the database structure, but is rarely involved in the original design of the structure.
    Answer: False   *Level: moderate*
    Section: Database Administration
    Subsection: Managing the Database Structure

6. Changes in the database structure usually involve only one application.
    Answer: False   *Level: hard*
    Section: Database Administration
    Subsection: Managing the Database Structure

7. One important reason for documenting changes to the database structure is for diagnosing errors.
    Answer: True   *Level: easy*
    Section: Database Administration
    Subsection: Managing the Database Structure

8. Concurrency control measures are taken to ensure that one user's work has absolutely no influence on another user's work.
    Answer: False   *Level: moderate*
    Section: Concurrency Control

9.   A transaction is a group of alternative database actions from which the database can choose to perform only one of them.
      Answer: False   *Level: easy*
      Section: Concurrency Control
      Subsection: The Need for Atomic Transactions

10.   "Resource locking" is one remedy to the lost update problem.
      Answer: True   *Level: moderate*
      Section: Concurrency Control
      Subsection: The Need for Atomic Transactions

11.   "Explicit locks" are locks that are placed automatically by the DBMS.
      Answer: False   *Level: easy*
      Section: Concurrency Control
      Subsection: Resource Locking

12.   Locks with large granularity are easy for the DBMS to administer but frequently cause conflicts.
      Answer: True   *Level: moderate*
      Section: Concurrency Control
      Subsection: Resource Locking

13.   In general, the boundaries of a transaction should correspond to the definition of the database view it is processing.
      Answer: True   *Level: hard*
      Section: Concurrency Control
      Subsection: Resource Locking

14.   Resource locking must be carefully planned because most DBMS products cannot detect a deadlock condition.
      Answer: False   *Level: moderate*
      Section: Concurrency Control
      Subsection: Resource Locking

15.   Resources are locked for a shorter amount of time with pessimistic locking because the transaction is pre-processed.
      Answer: False   *Level: easy*
      Section: Concurrency Control
      Subsection: Optimistic vs. Pessimistic Locking

16.   In general, optimistic locking is the preferred technique for Internet databases.
      Answer: True   *Level: hard*
      Section: Concurrency Control
      Subsection: Optimistic vs. Pessimistic Locking

17.   Transaction isolation is achieved through the use of locks.
      Answer: True   *Level: hard*
      Section: Concurrency Control
      Subsection: Transaction Isolation Level

18. "Repeatable Reads" isolation is the most restrictive level of isolation.
     Answer: False   *Level: moderate*
     Section: Concurrency Control
     Subsection: Transaction Isolation Level

19. The goal of database security is to ensure that only authorized users can perform authorized activities at authorized times.
     Answer: True   *Level: easy*
     Section: Database Security

20. In regard to database security, neither the DBMS nor the database applications can enforce processing responsibilities.
     Answer: True   *Level: moderate*
     Section: Database Security
     Subsection: Processing Rights and Responsibilities

21. Processing responsibilities should be documented and encoded into manual procedures.
     Answer: True   *Level: easy*
     Section: Database Security
     Subsection: Processing Rights and Responsibilities

22. Processing rights may be implemented at the DBMS level.
     Answer: True   *Level: easy*
     Section: Database Security
     Subsection: Processing Rights and Responsibilities

23. All commercial DBMS products use some version of "username and password" as part of their security features.
     Answer: True   *Level: easy*
     Section: Database Security
     Subsection: DBMS Security

24. The security provided by the DBMS often has to be augmented by additional security features within the application program.
     Answer: True   *Level: moderate*
     Section: Database Security
     Subsection: Application Security

25. A "database save" is used to mark the end of a transaction.
     Answer: False   *Level: moderate*
     Section: Database Recovery

26. Reprocessing is normally the most convenient method for recovery after a system failure.
     Answer: False   *Level: easy*
     Section: Database Recovery

27. Rollforward and reprocessing are two different names for the same technique.
     Answer: False   *Level: hard*
     Section: Database Recovery

28.   Both rollforward and rollback require the use of a log of transaction results.
        Answer: True   *Level: easy*
        Section: Database Recovery

29.   The DBA should periodically analyze run-time statistics of database performance to help manage
        the DBMS.
        Answer: True   *Level: easy*
        Section: Managing the DBMS

30.   A passive repository is preferred over an active repository because it requires less human
        intervention.
        Answer: False   *Level: moderate*
        Section: Maintaining the Data Repository

Multiple Choice Questions

31.   Which of the following is <u>not</u> a database administration responsibility of a DBA?
        a.)   managing the database structure
        b.)   managing data activity
        c.)   managing the DBMS
        d.)   maintaining the data repository
        e.)   all of the above <u>are</u> database administration responsibilities of a DBA

Level: easy
Section: Database Administration

32.   Which of the following is true about making changes to the database structure?
        a.)   The DBA need not get input from users on the issue because it is a technical decision.
        b.)   Formal policies and procedures for requesting a change are not used because they are too
                limiting.
        **c.)   Documentation of when the change was made, how it was made, and why it was
                made must be created.**
        d.)   Changes do not produce unexpected results because the DBA will have investigated the
                change thoroughly before implementing it.
        e.)   If the database is properly designed, changes should not be necessary throughout the
                system's lifetime.

Level: hard
Section: Database Administration
Subsection: Managing the Database Structure

33.   The task of diagnosing errors due to changes in the database structure is eased by:
    a.)   formal policies for requesting changes
    b.)   database structure change documentation
    c.)   rollback analysis
    d.)   configuration control
    e.)   none of the above

Level: moderate
Section: Database Administration
Subsection: Managing the Database Structure

34.   Measures that are taken to prevent one user's work from inappropriately influencing another user's work are called:
    a.)   concurrency control
    b.)   checkpoint
    c.)   database recovery
    d.)   database logging
    e.)   interleaving

Level: easy
Section: Concurrency Control

35.   A series of actions to be taken on the database such that either all actions are completed successfully, or none of them can be completed, is known as a(n):
    a.)   checkpoint
    b.)   log
    c.)   lock
    d.)   transaction
    e.)   concurrent

Level: easy
Section: Concurrency Control
Subsection: The Need for Atomic Transactions

36.   When two transactions are being processed against the database at the same time,
    a.)   they are called concurrent transactions
    b.)   they are usually interleaved
    c.)   they always result in a lost update problem
    d.)   one must be rolled back
    e.)   both a and b

Level: easy
Section: Concurrency Control
Subsection: The Need for Atomic Transactions

37.   The situation that occurs when one user's changes to the database are lost by a second user's changes to the database is known as the:
   a.)   concurrent update problem
   b.)   deadly embrace problem
   c.)   inconsistent read problem
   d.)   inconsistent write problem
   e.)   deadlock problem

Level: hard
Section: Concurrency Control
Subsection: The Need for Atomic Transactions

38.   One remedy for the inconsistencies caused by concurrent processing is _____.
   a.)   lost updates
   b.)   checkpointing
   c.)   rollback
   d.)   resource locking
   e.)   concurrency

Level: easy
Section: Concurrency Control
Subsection: The Need for Atomic Transactions

39.   A lock placed automatically by the DBMS is called a(n) _____ lock.
   a.)   exclusive
   b.)   explicit
   c.)   granular
   d.)   implicit
   e.)   shared

Level: moderate
Section: Concurrency Control
Subsection: Resource Locking

40.   Which of the following is not true about locks?
   a.)   Locks with large granularity are easier for the DBMS to administer.
   b.)   Locks with small granularity cause more conflicts.
   c.)   Locks with large granularity produce fewer details for the DBMS to track.
   d.)   Locks may have a table level granularity.
   e.)   Locks may have a database level granularity.

Level: hard
Section: Concurrency Control
Subsection: Resource Locking

41.   Which type of lock prevents all types of access to the locked resource?
     a.)   **exclusive lock**
     b.)   shared lock
     c.)   two-phased lock
     d.)   explicit lock
     e.)   implicit lock

Level: *easy*
Section: *Concurrency Control*
Subsection: *Resource Locking*

42.   Which type of lock still allows other transactions to have read-only access to the locked resource?
     a.)   exclusive lock
     b.)   **shared lock**
     c.)   two-phased lock
     d.)   explicit lock
     e.)   implicit lock

Level: *easy*
Section: *Concurrency Control*
Subsection: *Resource Locking*

43.   Which of the following is <u>not</u> true about two-phased locking?
     a.)   can make transactions serializable
     b.)   **uses only shared locks**
     c.)   has a growing phase
     d.)   has a shrinking phase
     e.)   cannot obtain a new lock once a lock has been released

Level: *hard*
Section: *Concurrency Control*
Subsection: *Resource Locking*

44.   The situation that occurs when two users are each waiting for a resource that the other person has locked is known as a(n):
     a.)   lost update problem
     b.)   **deadlock**
     c.)   inconsistent read problem
     d.)   inconsistent write problem
     e.)   checkpoint

Level: *moderate*
Section: *Concurrency Control*
Subsection: *Resource Locking*

45.   Requiring all application programs to lock resources in the same order is a technique for preventing what problem?
  a.) concurrent update
  b.) lost update
  c.) deadlock
  d.) exclusive locks
  e.) growing phase locking

Level: hard
Section: Concurrency Control
Subsection: Resource Locking

46.   Locks that are placed assuming that a conflict will occur are called:
  a.) dynamic locks
  b.) explicit locks
  c.) implicit locks
  d.) optimistic locks
  e.) pessimistic locks

Level: moderate
Section: Concurrency Control
Subsection: Optimistic vs. Pessimistic Locking

47.   Locks that are placed assuming that a conflict will <u>not</u> occur are called:
  a.) dynamic
  b.) explicit
  c.) implicit
  d.) optimistic
  e.) pessimistic

Level: moderate
Section: Concurrency Control
Subsection: Optimistic vs. Pessimistic Locking

48.   Ensuring that all rows impacted by the actions of a transaction are protected from changes until the entire transaction is completed is called:
  a.) statement level consistency
  b.) optimistic locking
  c.) transaction level consistency
  d.) durable transactions
  e.) ARID transactions

Level: hard
Section: Concurrency Control
Subsection: Consistent Transactions

49.   Which of the following is allowed by "Read Committed Isolation?"
    a.)   non-repeatable reads
    b.)   dirty reads
    c.)   serial reads
    d.)   phantom reads
    e.)   all of the above

Level: hard
Section: Concurrency Control
Subsection: Transaction Isolation Level

50.   Which of the following is true of forward only cursors?
    a.)   Current values for each row are retrieved when the application accesses a row.
    b.)   All changes of any type from any source are visible.
    c.)   Changes made by the transaction are visible only if they occur on rows ahead of the cursor.
    d.)   Applications may scroll backward in the record set.
    e.)   It requires the greatest overhead of any cursor type.

Level: moderate
Section: Concurrency Control
Subsection: Cursor Type

51.   Which of the following cannot be enforced in the DBMS or application programs?
    a.)   processing rights
    b.)   security
    c.)   processing responsibilities
    d.)   cursors
    e.)   transaction isolation

Level: moderate
Section: Database Security
Subsection: Processing Rights and Responsibilities

52.   Once processing rights have been defined, they may be implemented at any of these levels <u>except</u>:
    a.)   network
    b.)   operating system
    c.)   data
    d.)   DBMS
    e.)   application

Level: hard
Section: Database Security
Subsection: Processing Rights and Responsibilities

53.   Which of the following is <u>not</u> true of DBMS security features?
    a.)   Users may be assigned to one or more roles.
    b.)   A role may be assigned to only one user.
    c.)   Both users and roles can have many permissions.
    d.)   Objects have many permissions.
    e.)   Each permission pertains to one user or role and one object.

Level: moderate
Section: Database Security
Subsection: DBMS Security

54.   Recovering a database via reprocessing involves:
    a.)   restoring the database from the save and reprocessing all the transactions since the save.
    b.)   restoring the database from the save and reapplying all the changes made by transactions since the save.
    c.)   undoing the changes made by erroneous or partially processed transactions, and restarting the valid transactions that were in process at the time of the failure.
    d.)   recreating the database by reentering all of the data from the beginning, and then reprocessing all of the transactions.
    e.)   synchronizing the database and the transaction log by checkpointing.

Level: easy
Section: Database Recovery

55.   Recovering a database via rollforward involves:
    a.)   restoring the database from the save and reprocessing all the transactions since the save.
    b.)   restoring the database from the save and reapplying all the changes made by transactions since the save.
    c.)   undoing the changes made by erroneous or partially processed transactions, and restarting the valid transactions that were in process at the time of the failure.
    d.)   recreating the database by reentering all of the data from the beginning, and then reprocessing all of the transactions.
    e.)   synchronizing the database and the transaction log by checkpointing.

Level: easy
Section: Database Recovery

56.   Recovering a database via rollback involves:
    a.)   restoring the database from the save and reprocessing all the transactions since the save.
    b.)   restoring the database from the save and reapplying all the changes made by transactions since the save.
    c.)   undoing the changes made by erroneous or partially processed transactions, and restarting the valid transactions that were in process at the time of the failure.
    d.)   recreating the database by reentering all of the data from the beginning and, then reprocessing all of the transactions.
    e.)   synchronizing the database and the transaction log by checkpointing.

Level: easy
Section: Database Recovery

57.   Which of the following would <u>not</u> be contained in a transaction log?
     a.)   before-images
     b.)   type of operation
     c.)   pointers
     d.)   time of the action
     e.)   permissions

Level: moderate
Section: Database Recovery

58.   Which of the following would a DBA do in managing the DBMS?
     a.)   analyze system performance statistics
     b.)   investigate user complaints
     c.)   evaluate new DBMS product features
     d.)   tune DBMS product options to accommodate other software in use
     e.)   all of the above

Level: easy
Section: Managing the DBMS

59.   Which of the following is <u>not</u> true of data repositories?
     a.)   They are usually created after the database has been implemented and optimized for performance.
     b.)   They may be virtual.
     c.)   They may contain metadata about database applications.
     d.)   They may contain metadata about users.
     e.)   They may contain metadata about web pages.

Level: moderate
Section: Maintaining the Data Repository

60.   Which type of data repository is composed of metadata that is created automatically as the system components are created?
     a.)   passive
     b.)   dynamic
     c.)   active
     d.)   automatic
     e.)   summary

Level: moderate
Section: Maintaining the Data Repository

Fill in the Blank Questions

61.   The overall responsibility of the __DBA__ is to facilitate the development and use of the database.
Level: easy
Section: Database Administration

62.   The database is most vulnerable to failure after a change to its __structure__ .
Level: *hard*
Section: *Database Administration*
Subsection: *Managing the Database Structure*

63.   A(n) __transaction__ is a series of actions to be taken on the database such that either all of them are performed successfully or none of them is performed at all.
Level: *easy*
Section: *Concurrency Control*

64.   A transaction is sometimes called __atomic__ , since it is performed as a unit.
Level: *easy*
Section: *Concurrency Control*

65.   Locks placed automatically by the DBMS are called __implicit__ locks.
Level: *moderate*
Section: *Concurrency Control*
Subsection: *Resource Locking*

66.   Locks placed by a command issued to the DBMS from the application program are called __explicit__ locks.
Level: *moderate*
Section: *Concurrency Control*
Subsection: *Resource Locking*

67.   The size of a lock is referred to as the lock __granularity__ .
Level: *hard*
Section: *Concurrency Control*
Subsection: *Resource Locking*

68.   A(n) __exclusive__ lock locks the item from access of any type.
Level: *easy*
Section: *Concurrency Control*
Subsection: *Resource Locking*

69.   A(n) __shared__ lock locks the item from change but not from read access.
Level: *easy*
Section: *Concurrency Control*
Subsection: *Resource Locking*

70.   Two-phased locking is a scheme for achieving __serializability__ of transactions.
Level: *hard*
Section: *Concurrency Control*
Subsection: *Resource Locking*

71.   In two-phase locking, all locks are obtained during the __growing__ phase.
Level: *moderate*
Section: *Concurrency Control*
Subsection: *Resource Locking*

72.   In two-phase locking, all locks are released during the   shrinking   phase.
Level: *moderate*
Section: *Concurrency Control*
Subsection: *Resource Locking*

73.   Requiring all application programs to lock resources in the same order is one way of preventing a   deadlock   condition.
Level: *hard*
Section: *Concurrency Control*
Subsection: *Resource Locking*

74.   With   optimistic   locking, the assumption is made that no conflict will occur.
Level: *easy*
Section: *Concurrency Control*
Subsection: *Optimistic vs. Pessimistic Locking*

75.   With   pessimistic   locking, the assumption is made that a conflict will occur.
Level: *easy*
Section: *Concurrency Control*
Subsection: *Optimistic vs. Pessimistic Locking*

76.   The transaction   boundaries   are the essential information that the DBMS needs from the application programs to enforce different locking strategies.
Level: *hard*
Section: *Concurrency Control*
Subsection: *Declaring Lock Characteristics*

77.   A(n)   durable   transaction is one for which all committed changes are permanent.
Level: *hard*
Section: *Concurrency Control*
Subsection: *Consistent Transactions*

78.   Transaction level   consistency   means that all rows impacted by any actions in a transaction are protected from change during the entire transaction.
Level: *moderate*
Section: *Concurrency Control*
Subsection: *Consistent Transactions*

79.   A(n)   dirty read   occurs when one transaction reads a changed record that has not been committed to the database.
Level: *hard*
Section: *Concurrency Control*
Subsection: *Transaction Isolation Levels*

80.   Non-repeatable reads   occur when a transaction rereads data it has previously read and finds modifications or deletions caused by a committed transaction.
Level: *hard*
Section: *Concurrency Control*
Subsection: *Transaction Isolation Levels*

81.   According to ANSI SQL, the __serializable__ isolation level will prevent phantom reads, dirty reads, and non-repeatable reads.
Level: hard
Section: Concurrency Control
Subsection: Transaction Isolation Levels

82.   A(n) __static__ cursor processes a snapshot of the relation that was taken when the cursor was opened.
Level: moderate
Section: Concurrency Control
Subsection: Cursor Type

83.   A(n) __keyset__ cursor saves primary key values when the cursor is opened and retrieves the values for each row as the application program accesses it.
Level: moderate
Section: Concurrency Control
Subsection: Cursor Type

84.   __Rollforward__ is a method of database recovery that restores the database save and all valid transactions since the save was reapplied.
Level: easy
Section: Database Recovery

85.   To support rollforward and rollback recovery, transactions must be written to a(n) __log__ before they are applied to the database.
Level: easy
Section: Database Recovery

86.   Copies of each database record or page before it was changed by a transaction that are saved for use in database recovery are called __before-images__.
Level: easy
Section: Database Recovery

87.   Copies of each database record or page after it was changed by a transaction that are saved for use in database recovery are called __after-images__.
Level: easy
Section: Database Recovery

88.   A(n) __checkpoint__ is a point of synchronization between the database and the transaction log.
Level: moderate
Section: Database Recovery

89.   A(n) __active__ data repository is one in which the metadata is automatically created as the system components are created.
Level: easy
Section: Maintaining the Data Repository

90.   A(n) __passive__ data repository is one which requires a person to generate the metadata and place it in the repository.
Level: easy

Section: *Maintaining the Data Repository*

Essay Questions

91.   Explain the importance of documenting changes in database structure.
      Changes in database structure may introduce errors that do not become apparent for long
      periods of time. Documentation provides a record of changes to assist the investigation into the
      cause of database errors. Further, documentation of database changes can be used to determine
      the structure of the database at some point in the past. This is necessary for proper
      interpretation of any historical records that may need to be retrieved. Finally, documentation
      can assist in recovering the database from a previous copy in case of database failure. Not only
      do transactions have to be restored to the recovered database, but also any structural changes
      since the backup was created will have to be reapplied.
      Section: *Database Administration*
      Subsection: *Managing the Database Structure*

92.   Explain the concept of serializable transactions.
      Concurrent transactions are two or more transactions that are processed against the database at
      the same time. It is desirable for concurrent transactions to be serializable; that is, the results of
      the concurrent transactions should be logically consistent with the results that would be obtained
      if the transactions were not processed concurrently but rather in an arbitrary serial order.
      Section: *Concurrency Control*
      Subsection: *Resource Locking*

93.   Which are more commonly used – implicit or explicit locks? Why?
      Implicit locks are more commonly used than explicit locks. Concurrency control involves many
      complex factors that influence the performance of the system. The impact of some of these factors
      can only be determined through trial and error. Changing explicit locks to tune system
      performance can require making changes throughout the program code to obtain and release
      locks at various places in the transactions. Implicit locks are much easier to change since a
      locking strategy can be specified in a system parameter or lock declaration area and then the
      DBMS will place the locks implicitly wherever they are needed to implement that strategy.
      Section: *Concurrency Control*
      Subsection: *Declaring Lock Characteristics*

94.   Distinguish among the four cursor types.
      Forward only cursors are the simplest type of cursor, and only allow the application program to
      move forward through the record set. The three other types of cursors are all scrollable cursors,
      meaning that the application program can move forward and backward through the record set.
      Static cursors take a snapshot of the relation at the point in time when the cursor was opened.
      Keyset cursors save a copy of the primary key value for each record in the cursor. This key value
      is then used to retrieve the values of each record as the application program accesses that
      record. Dynamic cursors are fully functional cursors and can see any changes made to the
      records by any committed transactions.
      Section: *Concurrency Control*
      Subsection: *Cursor Types*

95.   Explain the purpose of transaction logs and checkpoints.
Transaction logs are created to facilitate the recovery of the database. All transactions that make changes to the database are recorded in the transaction log before they are applied to the database. In the event that the database fails, the transactions in the log can be used to undo changes made by transactions that were not committed, and to redo changes that were committed since the database was last saved. Checkpoints are used in conjunction with transaction logs. A checkpoint is a marker for when the last time the database and the transaction log were synchronized. If the database must be restored, only after-images for transactions that began after the last checkpoint have to be applied.
Section: *Database Security*

CHAPTER 12

Managing Databases with Oracle

True-False Questions

1. Oracle provides only one method for creating an Oracle database.
    Answer: False   *Level: moderate*
    Section: Creating an Oracle Database

2. When creating a new database in Oracle, two new accounts are automatically created in the database.
    Answer: False   *Level: moderate*
    Section: Creating an Oracle Database

3. When creating a new database, Oracle will automatically create default files for transaction logs.
    Answer: True   *Level: easy*
    Section: Creating an Oracle Database

4. To sign on to an Oracle database, the network name of the computer the database resides on must be entered as the "Host String."
    Answer: False   *Level: easy*
    Section: Creating an Oracle Database
    Subsection: Using SQL Plus

5. Among its many functions, SQL Plus is also a text editor.
    Answer: True   *Level: moderate*
    Section: Creating an Oracle Database
    Subsection: Using SQL Plus

6. To see the contents of the SQL Plus buffer, use the *VIEW* command.
    Answer: False   *Level: hard*
    Section: Creating an Oracle Database
    Subsection: Using SQL Plus

7. Oracle commands, table names, and column names are case insensitive.
    Answer: True   *Level: easy*
    Section: Creating an Oracle Database
    Subsection: Using SQL Plus

8. With Oracle, a single attribute primary key can be defined either when the table is created or after it is created.
    Answer: True   *Level: moderate*
    Section: Creating an Oracle Database
    Subsection: Creating Tables

9.   With Oracle, if a table has a composite primary key, then the key must be defined within the
        CREATE TABLE command.
        Answer: False   *Level: hard*
        Section: Creating an Oracle Database
        Subsection: Creating Tables

10.   It is possible to view the structure of a table in Oracle by using the *DESCRIBE* command.
        Answer: True   *Level: easy*
        Section: Creating an Oracle Database
        Subsection: Creating Tables

11.   When creating a table, Oracle automatically changes the ANSI SQL standard data type *varchar*
        into *varchar2*.
        Answer: True   *Level: moderate*
        Section: Creating an Oracle Database
        Subsection: Creating Tables

12.   When using Oracle, a *sequence* is an object that generates a sequential series of unique numbers.
        Answer: True   *Level: easy*
        Section: Creating an Oracle Database
        Subsection: Creating Tables

13.   With Oracle, using a *sequence* does not guarantee valid surrogate key values.
        Answer: True   *Level: hard*
        Section: Creating an Oracle Database
        Subsection: Creating Tables

14.   With Oracle, relationships between tables must be created by defining foreign key constraints
        when the table is created.
        Answer: False   *Level: moderate*
        Section: Creating an Oracle Database
        Subsection: Creating Relationships

15.   The ON DELETE CASCADE phrase used when defining foreign keys indicates that if a row is
        deleted from the child table, the corresponding row in the parent table should also be deleted.
        Answer: False   *Level: moderate*
        Section: Creating an Oracle Database
        Subsection: Creating Relationships

16.   In Oracle, indexes are created using the *ALTER* command.
        Answer: False   *Level: easy*
        Section: Creating an Oracle Database
        Subsection: Creating Indexes

17.   Care must be taken when using the *ALTER TABLE* command to change the structure of a table in
        Oracle because data may be lost.
        Answer: True   *Level: easy*
        Section: Creating an Oracle Database
        Subsection: Changing Table Structure

18. With Oracle, you can only drop a column from a table if that column contains no data values.
    Answer: False   *Level: easy*
    Section: Creating an Oracle Database
    Subsection: Changing Table Structure

19. With Oracle, you can only change a column's data type if the column contains only null values.
    Answer: True   *Level: moderate*
    Section: Creating an Oracle Database
    Subsection: Changing Table Structure

20. With Oracle, check constraints containing sequences are used to enforce valid surrogate key values.
    Answer: False   *Level: hard*
    Section: Creating an Oracle Database
    Subsection: Check Constraints

21. An SQL view in Oracle can contain only one multi-value path.
    Answer: True   *Level: easy*
    Section: Creating an Oracle Database
    Subsection: Views

22. In general, it is not possible to update data from a join view.
    Answer: True   *Level: hard*
    Section: Creating an Oracle Database
    Subsection: Views

23. With Oracle, stored procedures can be invoked remotely.
    Answer: True   *Level: easy*
    Section: Application Logic
    Subsection: Stored Procedures

24. Oracle triggers are PL/SQL or Java procedures that are invoked when specified database activity occurs.
    Answer: True   *Level: easy*
    Section: Application Logic
    Subsection: Triggers

25. All Oracle triggers work at the row level.
    Answer: False   *Level: moderate*
    Section: Application Logic
    Subsection: Triggers

26. A common use of triggers in Oracle is to roll back transactions.
    Answer: False   *Level: hard*
    Section: Application Logic
    Subsection: Triggers

27. Oracle uses a system change number to identify before-images in rollback segments to prevent dirty reads.
     Answer: True   *Level: hard*
     Section: Concurrency Control

28. Oracle only reads committed changes; hence dirty reads are not possible.
     Answer: True   *Level: moderate*
     Section: Concurrency Control

29. The default isolation level in Oracle is Read Committed, which provides statement level isolation.
     Answer: True   *Level: moderate*
     Section: Concurrency Control
     Subsection: Read Committed Transaction Isolation Level

30. With Oracle, system privileges concern actions on particular database element constructs like tables, views, and sequences.
     Answer: False   *Level: hard*
     Section: Oracle Security

31. Control files, as used by Oracle's backup and recovery features, contain records of database changes.
     Answer: False   *Level: easy*
     Section: Oracle Backup and Recovery
     Subsection: Oracle Recovery Facilities

32. In the event of an application failure, Oracle uses the in-memory rollback segments and OnLine ReDo files to recover.
     Answer: True   *Level: moderate*
     Section: Oracle Backup and Recovery
     Subsection: Types of Failure

33. To performance recovery from an instance failure, Oracle requires the use of Archive ReDo files.
     Answer: True   *Level: moderate*
     Section: Oracle Backup and Recovery
     Subsection: Types of Failure

Multiple Choice Questions

34. Which of the following is the method for creating a database with Oracle?
     a.)   the SQL CREATE TABLE command
     b.)   the Oracle Database Configuration Assistant
     c.)   the Oracle Database Wizard
     d.)   the Oracle Database Administration Guide
     e.)   all of the above

Level: *easy*
Section: *Creating an Oracle Database*

35.   Which of the following is an account name and password that Oracle creates automatically when a new database is created?
      a.)   ORACLE with password ACCOUNT
      b.)   SYS with password ACCOUNT
      c.)   SYSTEM with password MANAGER
      d.)   MANAGER with password CHANGE_ON_INSTALL
      e.)   INTERNAL with password SYSTEM

Level: hard
Section: Creating an Oracle Database

36.   To have SQL Plus finish a statement and execute it, type which key and press <ENTER>?
      a.)   # (pound)
      b.)   / (right-leaning slash)
      c.)   % (percent)
      d.)   : (colon)
      e.)   ; (semi-colon)

Level: easy
Section: Creating an Oracle Database
Subsection: Using SQL Plus

37.   Which command is issued to have SQL Plus display the contents of the buffer?
      a.)   LIST
      b.)   / (right-leaning slash)
      c.)   *VIEW*
      d.)   *DESCRIBE*
      e.)   *DISPLAY*

Level: moderate
Section: Creating an Oracle Database
Subsection: Using SQL Plus

38.   To modify the contents of the current line in the SQL Plus buffer such that *oldstring* is replaced by *newstring*, which of the following commands would be issued?
      a.)   change:newstring:oldstring
      b.)   modify/oldstring/newstring
      c.)   change/newstring/oldstring
      d.)   set:oldstring:newstring
      e.)   change/oldstring/newstring

Level: hard
Section: Creating an Oracle Database
Subsection: Using SQL Plus

39.   Which command is issued to have SQL Plus execute the statement in the buffer?
        a.)   # (pound)
        b.)   / (right-leaning slash)
        c.)   % (percent)
        d.)   : (colon)
        e.)   ; (semi-colon)

Level: easy
Section: Creating an Oracle Database
Subsection: Using SQL Plus

40.   Which of the following commands would be issued in SQL Plus to invoke the external text editor?
        a.)   EDIT
        b.)   MODIFY
        c.)   UPDATE
        d.)   EXTERNAL
        e.)   EDITOR

Level: easy
Section: Creating an Oracle Database
Subsection: Using SQL Plus

41.   To define a composite primary key for a table using Oracle, which SQL command must be used?
        a.)   CREATE TABLE
        b.)   CREATE CONSTRAINT
        c.)   ALTER TABLE
        d.)   ALTER KEY
        e.)   CREATE KEY

Level: moderate
Section: Creating an Oracle Database
Subsection: Creating Tables

42.   Which of the following commands is used in SQL Plus to display the structure of a table?
        a.)   ASC
        b.)   STRUCT
        c.)   DESC
        d.)   LIST
        e.)   DISP

Level: easy
Section: Creating an Oracle Database
Subsection: Creating Tables

43.   When creating tables, Oracle automatically converts the SQL standard data type "int" into:
      a.)   **number (38)**
      b.)   integer (32)
      c.)   number (5)
      d.)   integer (16)
      e.)   number (64)

Level: hard
Section: *Creating an Oracle Database*
Subsection: *Creating Tables*

44.   Which method returns the next value in a sequence?
      a.)   CountVal
      b.)   Next
      c.)   UpVal
      d.)   **NextVal**
      e.)   Append

Level: easy
Section: *Creating an Oracle Database*
Subsection: *Creating Tables*

45.   Which of the following would be the proper statement to have SQL Plus remove a column named C2 from a table named T2?
      a.)   DROP T2 COLUMN C2;
      b.)   DROP TABLE T2 COLUMN C2;
      c.)   ALTER TABLE T2 REMOVE COLUMN C2;
      d.)   **ALTER TABLE T2 DROP COLUMN C2;**
      e.)   DROP COLUMN C2 ALTER TABLE T2;

Level: hard
Section: *Creating an Oracle Database*
Subsection: *Creating Tables*

46.   With Oracle, relationships are created among tables by defining what?
      a.)   deletion cascades
      b.)   primary key sequences
      c.)   referential constraints
      d.)   cascading constraints
      e.)   **foreign key constraints**

Level: easy
Section: *Creating an Oracle Database*
Subsection: *Creating Relationships*

47.   Based on the SQL statement
            SELECT column1, column2, column3
            FROM table1
            WHERE column2 = "SMITH";
      which column(s) should be considered for indexing?
      a.)   column1 only
      b.)   column2 only
      c.)   column3 only
      d.)   column1, column2, and column3
      e.)   none of the above

Level: easy
Section: *Creating an Oracle Database*
Subsection: *Creating Indexes*

48.   Which of the following statements would cause Oracle to include a new column named C5, which is a two-digit whole number, to a table named T2?
      a.)   UPDATE TABLE T2 ADD COLUMN C5 NUMBER (2);
      b.)   ALTER TABLE T2 ADD COLUMN C5 NUMBER (2);
      c.)   UPDATE TABLE T2 INSERT C5 NUMBER (2,0);
      d.)   ALTER TABLE T2 INSERT COLUMN C5 NUMBER (2,0);
      e.)   ALTER TABLE T2 ADD C5 NUMBER (2);

Level: hard
Section: *Creating an Oracle Database*
Subsection: *Changing Table Structure*

49.   Which of the following is a change to database structure that Oracle will allow you to make to a table only when all rows of a given column contain null values?
      a.)   increase the number of decimal places for numeric data
      b.)   decrease the width of numeric data
      c.)   increase the width of numeric data
      d.)   decrease the number of decimal places for numeric data
      e.)   increase the width of character data

Level: hard
Section: *Creating an Oracle Database*
Subsection: *Changing Table Structure*

50.   Which of the following is not true about check constraints?
      a.)   can contain sequences
      b.)   must evaluate to true or false
      c.)   cannot contain a subquery
      d.)   cannot refer to the SysDate function
      e.)   cannot use values from other rows in the same table

Level: hard
Section: *Creating an Oracle Database*
Subsection: *Check Constraints*

51.   Which of the following is <u>not</u> a reason for using SQL views?
    a.)   improve security
    b.)   present users with two multi-value paths
    c.)   hide selected columns or records in a table
    d.)   perform a join for a user
    e.)   hide the table structure from users

Level: moderate
Section: Creating an Oracle Database
Subsection: Views

52.   Which of the following is <u>not</u> true of stored procedures in Oracle?
    a.)   They are programs.
    b.)   They can have parameters.
    c.)   They can be invoked remotely.
    d.)   They can return values.
    e.)   They can be written in C++.

Level: easy
Section: Application Logic
Subsection: Stored Procedures

53.   Which of the following is true about stored procedures in Oracle?
    a.)   They can be written using C++.
    b.)   They must include the data type and length of parameters.
    c.)   They can raise exceptions.
    d.)   They do not contain variables.
    e.)   They cannot invoke other procedures.

Level: easy
Section: Application Logic
Subsection: Stored Procedures

54.   Which of the following can Oracle <u>not</u> support?
    a.)   Triggers that are fired when SQL commands create new database structures.
    b.)   Triggers that are fired before each row change in a table.
    c.)   Triggers that are fired once when changes are made to rows in a table.
    d.)   Triggers that are fired after each row change in a table.
    e.)   All of the above <u>are</u> supported.

Level: moderate
Section: Application Logic
Subsection: Triggers

55.   In Oracle, which of the following prefixes is only available to triggers?
      a.)   :current
      b.)   := same
      c.)   :new
      d.)   := current
      e.)   :insert

Level: hard
Section: Application Logic
Subsection: Triggers

56.   Which type of trigger is commonly used to update views?
      a.)   BEFORE triggers
      b.)   UPDATE triggers
      c.)   SELECT triggers
      d.)   INSTEAD OF triggers
      e.)   VIEW triggers

Level: easy
Section: Application Logic
Subsection: Triggers

57.   In Oracle, which table contains metadata about the data dictionary itself?
      a.)   DICT
      b.)   DATA
      c.)   META
      d.)   DD
      e.)   DATA_DICT

Level: hard
Section: Data Dictionary

58.   Which of the following is <u>not</u> a transaction isolation level supported by Oracle?
      a.)   Read Committed
      b.)   Serializable
      c.)   Repeatable Read
      d.)   Read-only
      e.)   all of the above <u>are</u> supported

Level: hard
Section: Concurrency Control

59.   Which of the following is the default transaction isolation level offered by Oracle?
    a.)   **Read Committed**
    b.)   Serializable
    c.)   Repeatable Read
    d.)   Read-only
    e.)   Read Uncommitted

Level: moderate
Section: Concurrency Control
Subsection: Read Committed Transaction Isolation Level

60.   In Oracle, to achieve transaction level consistency, which level of transaction isolation must be used?
    a.)   Read Committed
    b.)   **Serializable**
    c.)   Repeatable Read
    d.)   Read-only
    e.)   Read Uncommitted

Level: moderate
Section: Concurrency Control
Subsection: Read Committed Transaction Isolation Level

61.   Which of the following is true of Oracle when the isolation level is set to Serializable?
    a.)   It will update any row having a SCN greater than the Transaction SCN.
    b.)   It will delete any row having a SCN greater than the Transaction SCN.
    c.)   It will read any row having a SCN greater than the Transaction SCN.
    d.)   **It will wait for a blocking transaction to release an exclusive lock.**
    e.)   It will not generate an error if the transaction must be rolled back.

Level: moderate
Section: Concurrency Control
Subsection: Serializable Transaction Isolation Level

62.   Which of the following is <u>not</u> a type of file in Oracle backup and recovery features?
    a.)   OnLine ReDo files
    b.)   **Rollback Segments**
    c.)   Archive ReDo files
    d.)   Datafiles
    e.)   Control files

Level: moderate
Section: Oracle Backup and Recovery
Subsection: Oracle Recovery Facilities

63.   For which of the following types of failure would Oracle use Offline ReDo files as part of a recovery effort?
   a.)   Instance failure
   b.)   Administrative failure
   c.)   Media failure
   d.)   Logic failure
   e.)   Application failure

Level: moderate
Section: Oracle Backup and Recovery
Subsection: Types of Failure

Fill in the Blank Questions

64.   __PL/SQL__ is a programming language provided with Oracle that adds programming constructs to the SQL language.
Level: easy
Section: Chapter Introduction

65.   In SQL Plus, typing a(n) __; (semi-colon)__ and pressing <ENTER> will cause SQL Plus to finish the statement and then execute it.
Level: easy
Section: Creating an Oracle Database
Subsection: Using SQL Plus

66.   The basic syntax for the CREATE TABLE SQL statement is the CREATE TABLE expression followed by the table name, followed by a list of column names, __data types__, and properties enclosed in parenthesis.
Level: moderate
Section: Creating an Oracle Database
Subsection: Creating Tables

67.   If a table has a composite primary key, then the key must be defined using the __ALTER TABLE__ method.
Level: moderate
Section: Creating an Oracle Database
Subsection: Creating Tables

68.   When creating a table, Oracle will automatically convert the SQL standard data type *varchar* into __varchar2__.
Level: hard
Section: Creating an Oracle Database
Subsection: Creating Tables

69.   A(n) __sequence__ is an object that generates a sequential series of unique numbers.
Level: easy
Section: Creating an Oracle Database
Subsection: Creating Tables

70.   Sequences are most often used to provide values for __surrogate__ keys.
Level: *moderate*
Section: *Creating an Oracle Database*
Subsection: *Creating Tables*

71.   The __NextVal__ method provides the next value in a sequence.
Level: *easy*
Section: *Creating an Oracle Database*
Subsection: *Creating Tables*

72.   The __CurrVal__ method provides the current value in a sequence.
Level: *easy*
Section: *Creating an Oracle Database*
Subsection: *Creating Tables*

73.   With Oracle, you create relationships among tables by defining __foreign key__ constraints.
Level: *moderate*
Section: *Creating an Oracle Database*
Subsection: *Creating Relationships*

74.   When defining a foreign key constraint in Oracle, the phrase __ON DELETE CASCADE__
        specifies that child rows should be deleted when a parent row is deleted.
Level: *moderate*
Section: *Creating an Oracle Database*
Subsection: *Creating Relationships*

75.   In Oracle data type notation, a data type specified as __number (5,2)__ would mean a numeric data
        type that has 3 digits to the left of the decimal and two digits to the right of the decimal.
Level: *hard*
Section: *Creating an Oracle Database*
Subsection: *Creating Relationships*

76.   When creating an index in Oracle, to make the index unique add the keyword UNIQUE before
        the keyword __INDEX__ .
Level: *easy*
Section: *Creating an Oracle Database*
Subsection: *Creating Indexes*

77.   In Oracle, you can change the data type of an existing column in a table only if the value of the
        column for all rows is __NULL__ .
Level: *easy*
Section: *Creating an Oracle Database*
Subsection: *Changing Table Structure*

78.   __Check__ constraints are used to constrain the values that columns may have in Oracle.
Level: *moderate*
Section: *Creating an Oracle Database*
Subsection: *Check Constraints*

79.   Check constraints cannot contain __subqueries__, sequences, or references to the SysDate function.
Level: hard
Section: Creating an Oracle Database
Subsection: Check Constraints

80.   The important limitation of SQL views is that they cannot contain more than one __multi-value__ path.
Level: hard
Section: Creating an Oracle Database
Subsection: Views

81.   When creating an Oracle stored procedure using SQL Plus, issue the __show errors__ command to see any reported compilation errors.
Level: moderate
Section: Application Logic
Subsection: Stored Procedures

82.   When writing stored procedures in Oracle, the assignment operator is __:=__ .
Level: hard
Section: Application Logic
Subsection: Stored Procedures

83.   In Oracle, triggers that are fired once for each row that is changed in a table are called __row triggers__.
Level: easy
Section: Application Logic
Subsection: Triggers

84.   __INSTEAD OF__ triggers are used to update views.
Level: easy
Section: Application Logic
Subsection: Triggers

85.   The __Read-only__ transaction isolation level is unique to Oracle.
Level: moderate
Section: Concurrency Control

86.   In Oracle security, __system__ privileges are rights to general tasks such as SELECT ANY TABLE.
Level: hard
Section: Oracle Security

87.   In Oracle security, __object__ privileges concern actions on particular database element constructs like tables, views, and sequences.
Level: hard
Section: Oracle Security

88.   In Oracle security, a(n) __GRANT__ statement may be used to give a privilege to another user.
Level: moderate
Section: Oracle Security

89.   In Oracle recovery facilities, __control__ files are small files that describe the name, contents, and locations of various files used by Oracle.
Level: easy
Section: Oracle Backup and Recovery
Subsection: Oracle Recovery Facilities

90.   In Oracle recovery facilities, __OnLine ReDo__ files are maintained on disk and contain the rollback segments from recent database changes.
Level: easy
Section: Oracle Backup and Recovery
Subsection: Oracle Recovery Facilities

91.   The type of failure that occurs when Oracle itself fails due to an operating system or computer hardware failure is called a(n) __instance__ failure.
Level: moderate
Section: Oracle Backup and Recovery
Subsection: Types of Failure

92.   The type of failure that occurs when Oracle is unable to write to a physical file is called a(n) __media__ failure.
Level: moderate
Section: Oracle Backup and Recovery
Subsection: Types of Failure

93.   In Oracle backup and recovery facilities, a(n) __consistent__ backup is one in which all uncommitted changes have been removed from the database.
Level: hard
Section: Oracle Backup and Recovery
Subsection: Types of Failure

Essay Questions

94.   Explain the potential problems with using a sequence to generate surrogate keys.
A sequence generates a sequential series of unique numbers. However, the sequence is defined for the entire database and is not tied to a particular field or table within the database. This means that a developer can use a defined sequence for tasks other than the surrogate key it was created for. This produces surrogate keys that skip values that have been used for other purposes. Also, there is nothing that forces the surrogate key field to use the numbers generated by the sequence, therefore a record may be inserted that does not follow the sequence. Finally, if a database has multiple sequences defined, it is possible for someone to enter a record using the wrong sequence.
Section: Creating an Oracle Database
Subsection: Creating Tables

95.   Explain the restrictions on modifying a column in the structure of an existing table.
        A column may be dropped from a table at any time. However, any data in the column will be lost.
        A NULL column may be added to a table at any time. The number of characters in character
        columns or the number of digits in a numeric column may be increased at any time. Also, the
        number of digits to the right of the decimal in numeric columns can be increased or decreased at
        any time. A column's data type may be changed, the number of characters in a character column
        may be decreased, or the number of digits in a numeric column may be decreased only if the
        column contains NULL values for all rows.
        Section: *Creating an Oracle Database*
        Subsection: *Changing Table Structure*

96.   What are some of the uses of SQL views?
        A SQL view can be used to support database security by giving users with different privileges
        different views of a table. A SQL view can also be used to shield a user from seeing columns or
        records that are not pertinent to that user. A view can also be used to perform a join for a user
        so that the user does not have to know how to create the join. Finally, a view can be used to hide
        table structures from the users.
        Section: *Creating an Oracle Database*
        Subsection: *Views*

97.   Briefly describe how Oracle implements serializable transaction isolation.
        Whenever a transaction begins, Oracle records a System Change Number (SCN), which is a
        database-wide value that is incremented every time a change is made to the database. As a
        transaction proceeds, for each record the transaction reads, Oracle retrieves the committed
        values that the record contained when its SCN was less than or equal to the SCN of the current
        transaction. This prevents any dirty reads, non-repeatable reads, or phantom reads. As long as
        the transaction does not attempt to update or delete a record that has a committed change with a
        SCN greater than the SCN of the current transaction, the transaction will proceed normally. If
        the transaction does attempt to change a record with a greater SCN, then an error is produced
        that must be handled by the application program.
        Section: *Concurrency Control*
        Subsection: *Serialized Transaction Isolation Level*

98.   Briefly explain the different types of files used by the Oracle recovery facilities.
        The first type of file is the Datafile. Datafiles contain the user and system data. Because Oracle
        writes data from its buffers to disk at arbitrary times, the datafiles often contain uncommitted
        changes to the database that will eventually either be committed or removed. OnLine ReDo files
        are backups of the rollback segments that Oracle keeps in memory. The rollback segments
        contain information about changes made to the database. These changes are periodically written
        to the OnLine ReDo files. Offline or Archive ReDo files are historical copies of the OnLine ReDo
        files that have been created as the OnLine ReDo files become full. Control files are small files
        that tell Oracle the names, contents, and locations of files that Oracle needs to operate. These
        control files are updated frequently by Oracle.
        Section: *Oracle Backup and Recovery*
        Subsection: *Oracle Recovery Facilities*

CHAPTER 13

Managing Databases with SQL Server 2000

True-False Questions

1. The SQL Server default when creating a new database is to create two data files and one log file for each database.
   Answer: False   *Level: moderate*
   Section: Creating a SQL Server 2000 Database

2. When viewing the SQL Server list of tables in a database, *dbo* means "domain base object" and indicates a system table.
   Answer: False   *Level: easy*
   Section: Creating a SQL Server 2000 Database

3. SQL Server 2000 provides two ways to create tables – graphically and through SQL code.
   Answer: True   *Level: easy*
   Section: Creating a SQL Server 2000 Database
   Subsection: Creating Tables

4. With SQL Server, database structures cannot be defined programmatically.
   Answer: False   *Level: easy*
   Section: Creating a SQL Server 2000 Database
   Subsection: Creating Tables

5. To use a SQL Server reserved word as a user identifier, it must be enclosed in square brackets [ ].
   Answer: True   *Level: hard*
   Section: Creating a SQL Server 2000 Database
   Subsection: Creating Tables

6. When defining a table using the CREATE TABLE method in SQL Server, if a column is not specified as NULL or NOT NULL then SQL Server makes it NOT NULL by default.
   Answer: False   *Level: hard*
   Section: Creating a SQL Server 2000 Database
   Subsection: Creating Tables

7. SQL Server's Query Analyzer tool will report syntax errors in SQL statements.
   Answer: True   *Level: easy*
   Section: Creating a SQL Server 2000 Database
   Subsection: Creating Tables

8. When viewing a table in the table design window in SQL Server, the primary key is indicated by a block arrow.
   Answer: False   *Level: moderate*
   Section: Creating a SQL Server 2000 Database
   Subsection: Creating Tables

9. When using the graphical table creation window to indicate that SQL Server should supply the values for a surrogate key, set the *identity* property of that column to "Yes."
    Answer: True   *Level: easy*
    Section: Creating a SQL Server 2000 Database
    Subsection: Creating Tables

10. Only one column in a table can be an identity column.
    Answer: True   *Level: moderate*
    Section: Creating a SQL Server 2000 Database
    Subsection: Creating Tables

11. User-Defined Data Types in SQL Server are useful in representing domains.
    Answer: True   *Level: easy*
    Section: Creating a SQL Server 2000 Database
    Subsection: Creating Tables

12. Rules cannot be combined with User-Defined Data Types.
    Answer: False   *Level: moderate*
    Section: Creating a SQL Server 2000 Database
    Subsection: Creating Tables

13. In SQL Server, rules serve the same purpose as *CHECK* clauses in SQL.
    Answer: True   *Level: hard*
    Section: Creating a SQL Server 2000 Database
    Subsection: Creating Tables

14. With SQL Server, the length of char and varchar data types can only be changed if the column contains only NULL values.
    Answer: False   *Level: hard*
    Section: Creating a SQL Server 2000 Database
    Subsection: Creating Tables

15. SQL Server will allow you to change a column's data type even if the column contains data values that are incompatible with the new data type.
    Answer: True   *Level: hard*
    Section: Creating a SQL Server 2000 Database
    Subsection: Creating Tables

16. Stored procedures in SQL Server will not work on a table named *TRANSACTION*, even if it is enclosed in square brackets [ ].
    Answer: True   *Level: moderate*
    Section: Creating a SQL Server 2000 Database
    Subsection: Creating Tables

17. To define a relationship in SQL Server using the database diagram, the primary key of one table is dragged and dropped anywhere in the second table.
    Answer: False   *Level: moderate*
    Section: Creating a SQL Server 2000 Database
    Subsection: Defining Relationships

18.   When defining a relationship in SQL Server using the database diagram, referential integrity constraints only apply to new data that will be entered and cannot be applied to existing data already in the tables.
      Answer: False   *Level: moderate*
      Section: Creating a SQL Server 2000 Database
      Subsection: Defining Relationships

19.   Database views can only be created in SQL Server through the use of SQL commands.
      Answer: False   *Level: easy*
      Section: Creating a SQL Server 2000 Database
      Subsection: Views

20.   In SQL Server when referring to a table name, by default the table name has a user name appended to it.
      Answer: True   *Level: hard*
      Section: Creating a SQL Server 2000 Database
      Subsection: Views

21.   Without using triggers in SQL Server, some views can be used for updating data and some cannot.
      Answer: True   *Level: easy*
      Section: Creating a SQL Server 2000 Database
      Subsection: Views

22.   SQL Server automatically creates an index on primary key fields only.
      Answer: False   *Level: hard*
      Section: Creating a SQL Server 2000 Database
      Subsection: Indexes

23.   PL-SQL is a programming language for SQL Server that adds programming constructs to the SQL language.
      Answer: False   *Level: moderate*
      Section: Application Logic

24.   With the advent of the Internet, it is becoming more common to distribute stored procedures onto users' computers rather than store them in the database.
      Answer: False   *Level: hard*
      Section: Application Logic
      Subsection: Stored Procedures

25.   SQL Server supports AFTER and INSTEAD OF triggers, but not BEFORE triggers.
      Answer: True   *Level: moderate*
      Section: Application Logic
      Subsection: Triggers

26.   In SQL Server, if a statement causes an AFTER trigger to be executed, the trigger is executed before any cascading updates or deletes are performed.
      Answer: False   *Level: hard*
      Section: Application Logic
      Subsection: Triggers

27.   SQL Server automatically makes determinations of whether or not to promote or demote a lock.
        Answer: True   *Level: hard*
        Section: Concurrency Control

28.   In SQL Server, it is not possible to make *dirty reads*.
        Answer: False   *Level: moderate*
        Section: Concurrency Control
        Subsection: Transaction Isolation Level

29.   The default cursor concurrency for a dynamic cursor in SQL Server is optimistic.
        Answer: True   *Level: hard*
        Section: Concurrency Control
        Subsection: Cursor Concurrency

30.   Locking hints included in a SQL statement will override locking behavior based on explicit transaction isolation level statements.
        Answer: True   *Level: moderate*
        Section: Concurrency Control
        Subsection: Locking Hints

31.   The simple recovery model is sufficient for most organizational databases.
        Answer: False   *Level: easy*
        Section: Backup and Recovery
        Subsection: SQL Server Recovery Models

Multiple Choice Questions

32.   Anytime you want to use a SQL Server reserved word as a user identifier enclose it in:
        a.)   { }
        b.)   [ ]
        c.)   ( )
        d.)   " "
        e.)   < >

Level: easy
Section: Creating a SQL Server Database
Subsection: Creating Tables

33.   SQL statements can be passed to SQL Server using the:
    a.)   Enterprise Manager
    b.)   SQL Activator
    c.)   Query Analyzer
    d.)   SQL Reader
    e.)   user file

Level: easy
Section: Creating a SQL Server Database
Subsection: Creating Tables

34.   Which of the following is <u>not</u> a system supplied data type in SQL Server?
    a.)   char
    b.)   decimal
    c.)   numeric
    d.)   money
    e.)   varchar2

Level: hard
Section: Creating a SQL Server Database
Subsection: Creating Tables

35.   When creating a table in SQL Server, setting which property to "Yes" indicates that the column is a surrogate key for which SQL Server should automatically supply values?
    a.)   Identity
    b.)   Surrogate
    c.)   AutoIncrement
    d.)   AutoNumber
    e.)   Sequence

Level: moderate
Section: Creating a SQL Server Database
Subsection: Creating Tables

36.   Although "rules" in SQL Server are graphically created, they serve the same purpose as what type of SQL clause?
    a.)   CREATE
    b.)   UPDATE
    c.)   ON DELETE CASCADE
    d.)   PURGE
    e.)   CHECK

Level: hard
Section: Creating a SQL Server Database
Subsection: Creating Tables

37.   Which of the following changes in table structure will SQL Server <u>not</u> allow you to perform?
   a.)   change data type from Int to Decimal for columns containing data
   b.)   increase the length of a column with data type Char for a column containing data
   c.)   reduce the length of a column with data type Char for a column containing data
   d.)   change data type from Char to Int for columns containing data
   e.)   All of the above <u>are</u> allowed by SQL Server

Level: hard
Section: Creating a SQL Server Database
Subsection: Creating Tables

38.   What name is so special to SQL Server that no stored procedure will work on a table with that name, not even if it is enclosed in brackets?
   a.)   *Name*
   b.)   *Update*
   c.)   *Transaction*
   d.)   *SQL*
   e.)   *Key*

Level: moderate
Section: Creating a SQL Server Database
Subsection: Creating Tables

39.   Which of the following <u>cannot</u> be specified while defining a relationship using SQL Server's graphical tools?
   a.)   cascade update related fields
   b.)   check referential integrity in existing data
   c.)   check constraints for relationship domain
   d.)   enforce referential integrity on INSERTS and DELETES
   e.)   cascade delete related fields

Level: moderate
Section: Creating a SQL Server Database
Subsection: Defining Relationships

40.   Which of the following is true about updating views in SQL Server without triggers?
   a.)   All views can be used for updating data.
   b.)   A view based on a single table may be used for inserts if it contains all NULL columns.
   c.)   Any view based on a single table may be used for delete operations.
   d.)   A view based on a single table may be used to update values if it contains no aggregate functions or derived columns.
   e.)   A view based on a single table may be used for inserting data if it contains no aggregate functions and contains all columns that can contain NULL values.

Level: hard
Section: Creating a SQL Server Database
Subsection: Views

41.　　Which of the following is true about updating views based on joins without triggers?
　　　a.)　　They cannot be used for deletions.
　　　b.)　　They can be used for deletions if they include no aggregate functions or derived columns.
　　　c.)　　They can accept updates as long as they include no aggregate functions or derived columns.
　　　d.)　　They cannot be used for inserts.
　　　e.)　　They can accept inserts under any circumstances.

Level: hard
Section: Creating a SQL Server Database
Subsection: Views

42.　　Which of the following is true about indexes in SQL Server?
　　　a.)　　SQL Server automatically creates indexes for columns appearing in WHERE clauses in queries.
　　　b.)　　SQL Server pads all indexes.
　　　c.)　　SQL Server supports filling up to a limit of 70 percent.
　　　d.)　　SQL Server automatically creates indexes for foreign keys.
　　　e.)　　All of the above.

Level: moderate
Section: Creating a SQL Server Database
Subsection: Indexes

43.　　Which type of index in SQL Server has a bottom level that does not contain data but has pointers to the data?
　　　a.)　　free
　　　b.)　　padded
　　　c.)　　baseline
　　　d.)　　non-clustered
　　　e.)　　blank

Level: moderate
Section: Creating a SQL Server Database
Subsection: Indexes

44.　　Which of the following is true of clustered indexes?
　　　a.)　　They are normally slower than non-clustered indexes for retrieving data.
　　　b.)　　Only one is allowed per table.
　　　c.)　　They are normally slower than non-clustered indexes for updating data.
　　　d.)　　They do not have data in the bottom level.
　　　e.)　　Both a and c

Level: moderate
Section: Creating a SQL Server Database
Subsection: Indexes

45.   The language available in SQL Server that adds programming constructs to the SQL language is
       known as:
       a.)   PL/SQL
       b.)   SQLP
       c.)   C++
       d.)   INTERACT-SQL
       e.)   TRANSACT-SQL

Level: easy
Section: Application Logic

46.   Which of the following is <u>not</u> be used to submit TRANSACT-SQL programs to the DBMS?
       a.)   JDBC
       b.)   stored procedures
       c.)   embedded in web script programs
       d.)   triggers
       e.)   SQL Query Analyzer

Level: hard
Section: Application Logic

47.   Which of the following is known to be true if the command *abcCust @Cost = 5* is used to invoke
       a stored procedure?
       a.)   *Cost = 5* is a CHECK constraint.
       b.)   The name of the stored procedure is *abcCust*.
       c.)   The name of the stored procedure is *abc*.
       d.)   *Cust* is given the value 5.
       e.)   *abcCust* is the name of a table or view in the database.

Level: hard
Section: Application Logic
Subsection: Stored Procedures

48.   A stored procedure can:
       a.)   invoke other stored procedures
       b.)   process many databases
       c.)   have arbitrarily complicated logic
       d.)   invoke functions
       e.)   all of the above

Level: moderate
Section: Application Logic
Subsection: Stored Procedures

49.   Which of the following is <u>not</u> a type of trigger supported by SQL Server?
  a.) BEFORE
  b.) INSTEAD OF
  c.) CONCURRENT
  d.) AFTER
  e.) both a and c

Level: easy
Section: Application Logic
Subsection: Triggers

50.   A view that is otherwise not updateable in SQL Server can be made updateable through the use of what type of what?
  a.) BEFORE triggers
  b.) CONCURRENT triggers
  c.) Remote procedures
  d.) INSTEAD OF triggers
  e.) AFTER triggers

Level: easy
Section: Application Logic
Subsection: Triggers

51.   Which of the following is <u>not</u> a lock granularity supported by SQL Server?
  a.) row
  b.) key
  c.) table
  d.) page
  e.) all of the above <u>are</u> supported

Level: easy
Section: Concurrency Control

52.   Which of the following is <u>not</u> a transaction isolation level supported by SQL Server?
  a.) Pessimistic
  b.) Read Committed
  c.) Serializable
  d.) Read Uncommitted
  e.) Repeatable Read

Level: moderate
Section: Concurrency Control
Subsection: Transaction Isolation Level

53.   Which of the following is the default transaction isolation level for SQL Server?
    a.)   Pessimistic
    b.)   Read Committed
    c.)   Serializable
    d.)   Read Uncommitted
    e.)   Repeatable Read

Level: moderate
Section: Concurrency Control
Subsection: Transaction Isolation Level

54.   Which of the following is the most restrictive transaction isolation level supported by SQL Server?
    a.)   Pessimistic
    b.)   Read Committed
    c.)   Serializable
    d.)   Read Uncommitted
    e.)   Repeatable Read

Level: easy
Section: Concurrency Control
Subsection: Transaction Isolation Level

55.   Which of the following is a type of cursor concurrency that causes SQL Server to place an update lock on a row when the row is read?
    a.)   SCROLL_LOCK
    b.)   Optimistic
    c.)   Serializable
    d.)   Read-only
    e.)   Forward-only

Level: hard
Section: Concurrency Control
Subsection: Cursor Concurrency

56.   The default cursor concurrency setting for a static cursor in SQL Server is:
    a.)   SCROLL_LOCK
    b.)   Optimistic
    c.)   Serializable
    d.)   Read-only
    e.)   Pessimistic

Level: moderate
Section: Concurrency Control
Subsection: Cursor Concurrency

57.   The default cursor concurrency setting for a keyset cursor in SQL Server is:
        a.)   SCROLL_LOCK
        b.)   Optimistic
        c.)   Serializable
        d.)   Read-only
        e.)   Pessimistic

Level: moderate
Section: Concurrency Control
Subsection: Cursor Concurrency

58.   Specifying locking hints in which parameter in a SQL clause can modify locking behavior in SQL Server?
        a.)   SELECT
        b.)   WITH
        c.)   LOCK
        d.)   TRANS
        e.)   HINT

Level: moderate
Section: Concurrency Control
Subsection: Locking Hints

59.   Which type of backup in SQL Server will create a backup of the entire database?
        a.)   Full backup
        b.)   Transaction backup
        c.)   Database backup
        d.)   Complete backup
        e.)   DBMS backup

Level: easy
Section: Backup and Recovery
Subsection: Types of Backup

60.   Which type of backup in SQL Server will make a copy of changes that have been made to the database since the last time a backup was made of the entire database?
        a.)   Rollback backup
        b.)   Differential backup
        c.)   Transaction backup
        d.)   Partial backup
        e.)   Image backup

Level: easy
Section: Backup and Recovery
Subsection: Types of Backup

61.   Which of the following is a type of recovery model supported in SQL Server in which all
        database changes are logged?
        a.)   Logged
        b.)   Bulk-logged
        c.)   Full
        d.)   Simple
        e.)   Complete

Level: moderate
Section: Backup and Recovery
Subsection: SQL Server Recovery Models

Fill in the Blank Questions

62.   In SQL Server, the term *dbo* stands for   database owner   .
Level: easy
Section: Creating a SQL Server 2000 Database

63.   To use a SQL Server reserved word, such as NAME, as a user identifier it must be enclosed in
         [ ] square brackets   .
Level: easy
Section: Creating a SQL Server 2000 Database
Subsection: Creating Tables

64.   The starting value for a field that has been set as an *identity* in SQL Server is set in the   Identity
        Seed   property.
Level: hard
Section: Creating a SQL Server 2000 Database
Subsection: Creating Tables

65.   In SQL Server, the amount to add to the surrogate key value when adding a new row is specified
        by the   Identity Increment   property.
Level: hard
Section: Creating a SQL Server 2000 Database
Subsection: Creating Tables

66.   One of the important benefits of User-Defined Data Types in SQL Server is that they can be used
        to enforce   domains   .
Level: moderate
Section: Creating a SQL Server 2000 Database
Subsection: Creating Tables

67.   Rules   are declarative expressions that limit data values in SQL Server.
Level: moderate
Section: Creating a SQL Server 2000 Database
Subsection: Creating Tables

68.   Rules in SQL Server serve the same purpose as __CHECK__ clauses of CREATE and ALTER
        statements in SQL.
Level: *hard*
Section: *Creating a SQL Server 2000 Database*
Subsection: *Creating Tables*

69.   The name __TRANSACTION__ is so special to SQL Server that no stored procedures will work
        on a table with that name.
Level: *moderate*
Section: *Creating a SQL Server 2000 Database*
Subsection: *Creating Tables*

70.   __Referential integrity__ constraints ensure that a key value in a child table exists in a related
parent table.
Level: *easy*
Section: *Creating a SQL Server 2000 Database*
Subsection: *Defining Relationships*

71.   SQL Server allows enforcing relationships for __replication__ , which deals with distributed
        processing.
Level: *hard*
Section: *Creating a SQL Server 2000 Database*
Subsection: *Defining Relationships*

72.   In general, any view that is based on a(n) __single table__ can be used for update and delete
        operations as long as it does not contain any aggregate functions or derived columns in its
        SELECT clause.
Level: *moderate*
Section: *Creating a SQL Server 2000 Database*
Subsection: *Views*

73.   Views based on a single table can be used for update and delete operations if they contain no
        __aggregate functions__ or derived columns in its SELECT clause.
Level: *moderate*
Section: *Creating a SQL Server 2000 Database*
Subsection: *Views*

74.   A view based on a single table that can be used for update and delete operations can also be used
        for inserting data if it contains all of the table's __NOT NULL__ columns.
Level: *moderate*
Section: *Creating a SQL Server 2000 Database*
Subsection: *Views*

75.   With SQL Server, no view that has more than one table in its FROM clause can be used for
        __delete__ operations.
Level: *moderate*
Section: *Creating a SQL Server 2000 Database*
Subsection: *Views*

76.   SQL Server automatically creates indexes on all primary and __foreign__ keys.
Level: easy
Section: Creating a SQL Server 2000 Database
Subsection: Indexes

77.   When creating an index in SQL Server, __padding__ causes space to be left open for inserts in all levels of the index except the bottom one.
Level: hard
Section: Creating a SQL Server 2000 Database
Subsection: Indexes

78.   When creating an index in SQL Server, __filling__ refers to the amount of empty space left in the bottom level of the index.
Level: hard
Section: Creating a SQL Server 2000 Database
Subsection: Indexes

79.   With SQL Server, a(n) __clustered__ index has the data with and in the same order as the bottom level of the index.
Level: hard
Section: Creating a SQL Server 2000 Database
Subsection: Indexes

80.   With SQL Server, a(n) __nonclustered__ index at the bottom level of the index does not contain data but has pointers to the data.
Level: hard
Section: Creating a SQL Server 2000 Database
Subsection: Indexes

81.   A SQL Server database may be processed by a procedure written in __TRANSACT-SQL__, which is a language that adds programming elements to the basic capabilities of SQL.
Level: moderate
Section: Application Logic

82.   Parameters and variables in TRANSACT-SQL are preceded by __@__ signs.
Level: hard
Section: Application Logic
Subsection: Stored Procedures

83.   SQL Server does not support __BEFORE__ triggers as Oracle does.
Level: easy
Section: Application Logic
Subsection: Triggers

84.   In SQL Server, SCROLL_LOCK is a version of __pessimistic__ locking.
Level: easy
Section: Concurrency Control
Subsection: Cursor Concurrency

85.   In SQL Server, locking behavior can be modified by providing locking hints in the __WITH__ parameter of the FROM clause in SELECT statements.
Level: moderate
Section: Concurrency Control
Subsection: Locking Hints

86.   When recovering a database in SQL Server, it is possible to process the log to a particular point in time or to a __transaction mark__ .
Level: hard
Section: Backup and Recovery

87.   In SQL Server, a(n) __complete__ backup makes a copy of the entire database.
Level: moderate
Section: Backup and Recovery
Subsection: Types of Backup

88.   In SQL Server, a(n) __differential__ backup makes a copy of the changes that have been made since the last time a backup of the entire database was made.
Level: easy
Section: Backup and Recovery
Subsection: Types of Backup

89.   In SQL Server, the __bulk-logged__ recovery model creates a log for all changes except those that cause large log entries.
Level: easy
Section: Backup and Recovery
Subsection: SQL Server Recovery Models

90.   In SQL Server, the __full__ recovery model creates a log for every change to the database.
Level: easy
Section: Backup and Recovery
Subsection: SQL Server Recovery Models

91.   In SQL Server, the __simple__ recovery model does not create any logs.
Level: moderate
Section: Backup and Recovery
Subsection: SQL Server Recovery Models

Essay Questions

92. Explain the potential problems with changing a column's length and data type in SQL Server.
Making changes to the structure of a column in a SQL Server table is dangerous because SQL Server will allow the user to make changes without restriction. Unfortunately, some changes have negative consequences. Reducing the length of text data types, such as char or varchar, may result in data being truncated. This truncation may cause duplicate values. Data types can also be changed; however, changing a field that contains text data into a numeric data type can result in a loss of data.
Section: *Creating a SQL Server 2000 Database*
Subsection: *Creating Tables*

93. What options concerning referential integrity are available when defining a relationship in SQL Server?
With SQL Server, there is an option to check existing data for compliance with the referential integrity constraints of the relationship. It is also possible to have SQL Server enforce the referential integrity constraints for the relationship when the database is replicated. Finally, the user can select to have the referential integrity constraints checked when inserts or updates are performed on the data.
Section: *Creating a SQL Server 2000 Database*
Subsection: *Defining Relationships*

94. What are the restrictions in SQL Server on updating data from a view without the use of triggers?
In general, any view that is based on a single table can support update and delete operations as long as the view does not contain any aggregate functions or any derived columns in its SELECT clause. Such a view may also be used for inserting data if it contains all of the columns of the table that are defined as NOT NULL. Views based on joins cannot support delete operations. Multi-table joins can support insert and update operations as long as the inserts and updates are made to a single table within the view that meets the requirements for making inserts and updates to a single-table view.
Section: *Creating a SQL Server 2000 Database*
Subsection: *Views*

95. Briefly describe how a developer defines the type of locking behavior to be used with SQL Server.
Locking behavior in SQL Server is determined by the interaction of transaction isolation level, cursor concurrency setting, and locking hints. Transaction isolation level can be defined to be Read Uncommitted, Read Committed, Repeatable Read, or Serializable. Read Committed is the default setting. Cursor concurrency can be set to Read-only, Optimistic, or Scroll_Lock. Scroll_Lock is a type of pessimistic locking. The cursor type determines the default type of cursor concurrency. Locking hints can be used by experienced developers to modify locking behavior. Locking hints can override transaction isolation level for a given transaction, or influence the types of locks that SQL Server uses for a given transaction. Locking hints are specified by the WITH parameter of the FROM clause in SELECT SQL statements.
Section: *Concurrency Control*

96.   Briefly explain the different SQL Server recovery models.
        SQL Server supports three recovery models: simple, full, and bulk-logged. The simple recovery model does not create logs of any changes to the database. This recovery method relies only on complete database backups in the event that the database must be recovered. The full recovery model logs all changes that are made to the database. The bulk-logged recovery model logs all changes to the database except for changes that would result in large log entries.
        Section: *Backup and Recovery*
        Subsection: *SQL Server Recovery Models*

CHAPTER 14

Networks, Multi-tier Architectures, and XML

True-False Questions

1. Networks that use standardized protocols are considered "public" networks.
    Answer: False   *Level: moderate*
    Section: Network Environments

2. HTTP is poll-oriented.
    Answer: False   *Level: easy*
    Section: Network Environments
    Subsection: The Internet

3. HTTP applications are *stateless*.
    Answer: True   *Level: easy*
    Section: Network Environments
    Subsection: The Internet

4. Database applications require HTTP to be augmented to provide a state-oriented environment.
    Answer: True   *Level: moderate*
    Section: Network Environments
    Subsection: The Internet

5. Firewalls serve as security gateways between Intranets and the Internet.
    Answer: True   *Level: easy*
    Section: Network Environments
    Subsection: Intranets

6. One major difference between Intranets and the Internet is the use of stateless connections on the Internet.
    Answer: False   *Level: moderate*
    Section: Network Environments
    Subsection: Intranets

7. More of the application processing can be performed on a client using the Internet than on a client using an Intranet.
    Answer: False   *Level: moderate*
    Section: Network Environments
    Subsection: Intranets

8. A three-tier architecture is common for most Internet-technology database applications.
    Answer: True   *Level: hard*
    Section: Multi-Tier Architecture

9. With three-tier architecture, the database server creates forms and reports, but not menus.
    Answer: False   *Level: moderate*
    Section: Multi-Tier Architecture

10. One responsibility of the Web server in three-tier database application architecture is to create, read, update, and delete view instances.
    Answer: True   *Level: easy*
    Section: Multi-Tier Architecture

11. In three-tier database application architecture, both the Web server and the client host scripting environments.
    Answer: True   *Level: moderate*
    Section: Multi-Tier Architecture

12. In a Windows 2000 Web server environment, the HTTP server will almost always be Apache.
    Answer: False   *Level: hard*
    Section: Multi-Tier Architecture
    Subsection: Windows 2000 Web Server Environment

13. ASP pages can only be used with Microsoft Web servers.
    Answer: False   *Level: hard*
    Section: Multi-Tier Architecture
    Subsection: Unix and Linux Web Server Environment

14. One problem database applications had with the original HTML specification was that view data and view materialization were mixed.
    Answer: True   *Level: easy*
    Section: Markup Languages: HTML and DHTML
    Subsection: Problems with HTML

15. One important feature of DHTML is the Common Object Model (COM), which exposes the page elements as objects that can be manipulated by scripts.
    Answer: False   *Level: moderate*
    Section: Markup Languages: HTML and DHTML
    Subsection: DHTML

16. One important feature of HTML 4.0 and DHTML is support for Cascading Style Sheets (CSS), which enables the definition of formats for types of elements.
    Answer: True   *Level: easy*
    Section: Markup Languages: HTML and DHTML
    Subsection: DHTML

17. XML still allows document structure, data content, and materialization to be mixed just as HTML does.
    Answer: False   *Level: moderate*
    Section: XML – Extensible Markup Language
    Subsection: XML as a Markup Language

18. XML documents accurately represent the semantics of their data.
     Answer: True   *Level: easy*
     Section: XML – Extensible Markup Language
     Subsection: XML as a Markup Language

19. All type-valid XML documents are required to have a DTD.
     Answer: True   *Level: easy*
     Section: XML – Extensible Markup Language
     Subsection: XML Document Type Declarations

20. XSLT is a robust and powerful transformation language that can be used to materialize XML documents into HTML.
     Answer: True   *Level: hard*
     Section: XML – Extensible Markup Language
     Subsection: Materializing XML Documents

21. The structure of an XSL stylesheet is of the form *{loop, action}*.
     Answer: False   *Level: hard*
     Section: XML – Extensible Markup Language
     Subsection: Materializing XML Documents

22. XSL processors are context oriented; that is, each statement is evaluated within the context of the match that has already been made.
     Answer: True   *Level: hard*
     Section: XML – Extensible Markup Language
     Subsection: Materializing XML Documents

23. XML Schema is a synonym for Document Type Declaration (DTD).
     Answer: False   *Level: moderate*
     Section: XML – Extensible Markup Language
     Subsection: XML Schema

24. XML documents that conform to an XML Schema are called *type-valid*.
     Answer: False   *Level: easy*
     Section: XML – Extensible Markup Language
     Subsection: XML Schema

25. The most important improvement of XML Schema over DTDs is that XML Schemas are themselves XML documents.
     Answer: True   *Level: moderate*
     Section: XML – Extensible Markup Language
     Subsection: XML Schema

26. In XML Schema there are two types of elements, simple and composite.
     Answer: False   *Level: hard*
     Section: XML – Extensible Markup Language
     Subsection: XML Schema

27.   In XML Schema, the default cardinality of elements is 0.1.
        Answer: False   *Level: hard*
        Section: XML – Extensible Markup Language
        Subsection: XML Schema

28.   In XML Schema, the default cardinalities can be overridden using the minoccurs and maxoccurs attributes.
        Answer: True   *Level: moderate*
        Section: XML – Extensible Markup Language
        Subsection: XML Schema

29.   An XML document's default namespace must be the same as the target namespace.
        Answer: False   *Level: moderate*
        Section: XML – Extensible Markup Language
        Subsection: XML Schema

30.   The names of XML namespaces must be unique anywhere the XML Schema will ever be used.
        Answer: True   *Level: easy*
        Section: XML – Extensible Markup Language
        Subsection: XML Schema

31.   WAP has been defined to facilitate the use of Internet technology on wireless devices.
        Answer: True   *Level: easy*
        Section: XML – Extensible Markup Language
        Subsection: Wireless Application Protocol

32.   Mini browsers are ultra thin applications that process WML on wireless devices.
        Answer: False   *Level: moderate*
        Section: XML – Extensible Markup Language
        Subsection: Wireless Application Protocol

Multiple Choice Questions

33.   Which of the following is true about HTTP?
        a.)   It is state oriented.
        b.)   It is request oriented.
        c.)   It is a superset of TCP/IP.
        d.)   It is supported only by Microsoft products.
        e.)   All of the above

Level: *easy*
Section: *Network Environments*
Subsection: *The Internet*

34.   A firewall is used _____.
       a.)   to connect wireless devices to the Internet
       b.)   to improve Intranet speed
       c.)   as a security gateway between public and private networks
       d.)   as a HTTP server
       e.)   as a database server in a three-tier architecture

Level: easy
Section: Network Environments
Subsection: Intranets

35.   One distinguishing difference between the Internet and Intranets is that:
       a.)   Intranets are private networks and the Internet is not.
       b.)   The Internet uses HTTP and Intranets do not.
       c.)   Intranets use TCP/IP and the Internet does not.
       d.)   The Internet is a WAN and Intranets are always a LAN.
       e.)   Internet users connect at faster speeds than Intranet users.

Level: easy
Section: Network Environments
Subsection: Intranets

36.   Which of the following is <u>not</u> true about the database server in a three-tier architecture?
       a.)   processes SQL statements
       b.)   performs database management tasks
       c.)   serves data
       d.)   creates menus
       e.)   does not create reports

Level: moderate
Section: Multi-Tier Architecture

37.   Which of the following is <u>not</u> true about the Web server in three-tier database application architecture?
       a.)   processes the HTTP protocol
       b.)   materializes view instances
       c.)   hosts scripting environments
       d.)   receives requests and generates responses in HTTP format
       e.)   creates, reads, updates, and deletes view instances

Level: hard
Section: Multi-Tier Architecture

38.   Which of the following is <u>not</u> true of Web servers running Windows 2000 in three-tier database application architecture?
    a.)   The HTTP server is usually IIS.
    b.)   They support processing ASP pages through the ISAPI interface.
    c.)   The data access standard used will usually be ODBC, ADO, or OLE DB.
    d.)   They support embedded ActiveX controls in ASP pages.
    e.)   They support JSP pages through the use of Tomcat.

Level: moderate
Section: Multi-Tier Architecture
Subsection: Windows 2000 Web Server Environment

39.   The world's most common web server is _____.
    a.)   *Apache*
    b.)   *Tomcat*
    c.)   *IIS*
    d.)   *Netscape Server*
    e.)   *Java*

Level: easy
Section: Multi-Tier Architecture
Subsection: Unix and Linux Web Server Environment

40.   Which of the following was not a problem with the original HTML specification?
    a.)   Content, layout, and format of pages were confounded.
    b.)   There was a lack of style definitions to facilitate consistent styles within and across pages.
    c.)   It was not accessible to the general computing public.
    d.)   Web page elements were not accessible to scripts or other programs.
    e.)   There were no constructs to facilitate data manipulation on the client.

Level: easy
Section: Markup Languages: HTML and DHTML
Subsection: Problems with HTML

41.   The facility in HTML 4.0 and DHTML that allows formats to be defined for the types of elements in a page is _____.
    a.)   DOM
    b.)   COM
    c.)   CSS
    d.)   WML
    e.)   XML

Level: easy
Section: Markup Languages: HTML and DHTML
Subsection: DHTML

42.   Which of the following is **not** true of cascading style sheets?
    a.)   An element can have two conflicting styles.
    b.)   Style sheets can be contained within the page.
    c.)   They allow content and materialization to be separated.
    d.)   Style sheets can be obtained externally from other files that contain the style definitions.
    e.)   Style sheets expose all page elements as objects that can be manipulated from scripts.

Level: moderate
Section: Markup Languages: HTML and DHTML
Subsection: DHTML

43.   Which of the following is true about XML?
    a.)   It allows the confounding of document structure, content, and format.
    b.)   It is non-standardized to allow for extension by developers.
    c.)   The structure of documents is formally defined.
    d.)   XML documents do not represent the semantics of the data they contain.
    e.)   None of the above.

Level: easy
Section: XML – Extensible Markup Language
Subsection: XML as a Markup Language

44.   The document type declaration for an XML document begins with the keyword _____.
    a.)   XML
    b.)   DTD
    c.)   TYPE
    d.)   DOCTYPE
    e.)   TYPEDECL

Level: hard
Section: XML – Extensible Markup Language
Subsection: XML Document Type Declarations

45.   XML documents that conform to their DTD are said to be _____.
    a.)   DTD-valid
    b.)   XML-valid
    c.)   DTD-compliant
    d.)   document-valid
    e.)   type-valid

Level: easy
Section: XML – Extensible Markup Language
Subsection: XML Document Type Declarations

46.   Which of the following is <u>not</u> true about document type declarations for XML documents?
  a.)   They are not required.
  b.)   They are required for type-valid documents.
  c.)   They cannot be contained inside the XML document.
  d.)   Storing the DTD externally allows many documents to be validated against the same DTD.
  e.)   The DTD can be extended by the developer with any elements he or she wants to include.

Level: moderate
Section: XML – Extensible Markup Language
Subsection: XML Document Type Declarations

47.   Which of the following is <u>not</u> true about XSLT?
  a.)   It is declarative.
  b.)   It is a transformation language.
  c.)   It can materialize XML documents into HTML.
  d.)   It can transform an XML document into another XML document with a different structure.
  e.)   It requires the use of CSS.

Level: moderate
Section: XML – Extensible Markup Language
Subsection: Materializing XML Documents

48.   Which of the following is true about XSL stylesheets?
  a.)   They have the same format as cascading stylesheets.
  b.)   They are context oriented.
  c.)   They may be used instead of XSLT.
  d.)   Their structure is of the form *{style, loop}*.
  e.)   The output stream must match the input stream in terms of the order of the elements.

Level: hard
Section: XML – Extensible Markup Language
Subsection: Materializing XML Documents

49.   The standard for addressing elements within documents, such as <xsl:value-of-select="name/lastname"> is called _____.
  a.)   XML
  b.)   XSL
  c.)   SAX
  d.)   XPath
  e.)   DOM

Level: hard
Section: XML – Extensible Markup Language
Subsection: XML Terminology and Standards

50.   One difference between SAX and DOM is that:
      a.)   DOM-compliant parsers can parse XML documents
      b.)   SAX-compliant parsers interact with an XSLT processor
      c.)   **DOM-compliant parsers process the entire document at one time**
      d.)   SAX-compliant parsers create a tree representation of a document
      e.)   SAX-compliant parsers can validate XML documents against DTDs

Level: hard
Section: XML – Extensible Markup Language
Subsection: XML Terminology and Standards

51.   XML Schema is a standard for constraining _____.
      a.)   **XML documents**
      b.)   XQL queries
      c.)   DOM-compliant parsers
      d.)   DTDs
      e.)   XPath searches

Level: easy
Section: XML – Extensible Markup Language
Subsection: XML Schema

52.   The most important improvement of XML Schema over DTDs is that:
      a.)   XML Schema can be stored external to the document
      b.)   XML Schema support XQL queries
      c.)   **XML Schema are XML documents**
      d.)   XML Schema are not required
      e.)   XML Schema can validate XML documents

Level: easy
Section: XML – Extensible Markup Language
Subsection: XML Schema

53.   Which of the following is a type of element in an XML Schema?
      a.)   simple
      b.)   composite
      c.)   compound
      d.)   complex
      e.)   **both a and d**

Level: moderate
Section: XML – Extensible Markup Language
Subsection: XML Schema

54.   In an XML Schema, if an element has the domain *prev:date*, then:
  a.)   the element is constrained by the *prev* definition in the *date* namespace
  b.)   the element is referenced by the *prev* constraint in the *date* namespace
  c.)   the element is constrained by the *date* definition in the *prev* namespace
  d.)   the element is referenced by the *date* constraint in the *prev* namespace
  e.)   none of the above

Level: hard
Section: XML – Extensible Markup Language
Subsection: XML Schema

55.   The default cardinality for elements in a XML Schema is _____.
  a.)   0.1
  b.)   1.1
  c.)   1.N
  d.)   N.1
  e.)   M.N

Level: moderate
Section: XML – Extensible Markup Language
Subsection: XML Schema

56.   The expression xmlns="http://www.anydomain.org/docs/schema" indicates that:
  a.)   the default schema is named http://www.anydomain.org/docs/schema
  b.)   a labeled namespace called "schema" should be used
  c.)   the target namespace is named http://www.anydomain.org/docs/schema
  d.)   the default namespace is named http://www.anydomain.org/docs/schema
  e.)   the schema located at http://www.anydomain.org/docs/schema should be created by the parser

Level: hard
Section: XML – Extensible Markup Language
Subsection: XML Schema

57.   The expression xmlns:partial="http://www.freespace.org/domain" indicates that:
  a.)   the default namespace is labeled "partial"
  b.)   a namespace labeled "partial" is created and named http://www.freespace.org/domain
  c.)   the default namespace is named http://www.freespace.org/domain
  d.)   there is no target namespace
  e.)   the target namespace is named http://www.freespace.org/domain

Level: hard
Section: XML – Extensible Markup Language
Subsection: XML Schema

58.　　The names of namespaces:
　　　a.)　　must be assigned to a labeled namespace
　　　b.)　　must be a URL
　　　c.)　　must be the same for target and default namespaces
　　　d.)　　must be unique everywhere the XML Schema will ever be used
　　　e.)　　all of the above

Level: moderate
Section: XML – Extensible Markup Language
Subsection: XML Schema

59.　　The XML Schema standard will allow elements to be constrained:
　　　a.)　　to certain values
　　　b.)　　to certain ranges of numbers
　　　c.)　　to be constant
　　　d.)　　to have default values
　　　e.)　　all of the above

Level: moderate
Section: XML – Extensible Markup Language
Subsection: XML Schema

60.　　Which of the following is not true about WML?
　　　a.)　　WML is a subset of XML.
　　　b.)　　WML documents can be validated against XML Schema but not against DTDs.
　　　c.)　　WML documents can be transformed into XML using XSLT.
　　　d.)　　The WML standard includes the WML Script scripting language.
　　　e.)　　WML is compressed into WMLC by the Web Gateway.

Level: moderate
Section: XML – Extensible Markup Language
Subsection: Wireless Application Protocol

61.　　The individual sections of a WML document that can be displayed on a wireless device at one time are called _____.
　　　a.)　　segments
　　　b.)　　cards
　　　c.)　　decks
　　　d.)　　fragments
　　　e.)　　micro documents

Level: moderate
Section: XML – Extensible Markup Language
Subsection: Wireless Application Protocol

62.   Which of the following is <u>not</u> an important contribution of XML to database applications?
   a.)   It provides a standard means of expressing the structure of database views.
   b.)   It cleanly separates structure, content, and materialization.
   c.)   It provides for standardized document validity checking.
   d.)   It allows industry groups to develop industry-wide DTDs and XML Schemas.
   e.)   All of the above <u>are</u> important contributions.

Level: moderate
Section: XML – Extensible Markup Language
Subsection: The Importance of XML to Database Applications

Fill in the Blank Questions

63.   A(n) __network__ is a collection of computers that communicate with one another using a standardized protocol.
Level: easy
Section: Network Environments

64.   __Hypertext transfer protocol (HTTP)__ is a TCP/IP-based protocol that enables the sharing of documents with embedded links with other documents over TCP/IP networks.
Level: easy
Section: Network Environments
Subsection: The Internet

65.   HTTP applications are __stateless__, meaning that no attempt is made to conduct a continuing session with a given client.
Level: moderate
Section: Network Environments
Subsection: The Internet

66.   A(n) __Intranet__ is a private network that uses Internet technologies.
Level: easy
Section: Network Environments
Subsection: Intranets

67.   A(n) __firewall__ is a computer that serves as a security gateway connecting a private network to a public network.
Level: easy
Section: Network Environments
Subsection: Intranets

68.   __Wireless Application Protocol (WAP)__ has been developed to create a standard for network access from wireless devices.
Level: easy
Section: Network Environments
Subsection: Wireless Network Access

69.   A variant of XML, called __wireless markup language (WML)__ , has been defined to enable web pages to be displayed on wireless devices.
Level: *moderate*
Section: *Network Environments*
Subsection: *Wireless Network Access*

70.   The IIS web server provides an interface called __Internet Server Application Program Interface (ISAPI)__ that allows other programs to trap and process HTTP requests.
Level: *hard*
Section: *Multi-Tier Architecture*
Subsection: *Windows 2000 Web Server Environment*

71.   __Apache__ is the world's most common web server.
Level: *easy*
Section: *Multi-Tier Architecture*
Subsection: *Unix and Linux Web Server Environment*

72.   With JSP, all coding is written in the __Java__ programming language.
Level: *moderate*
Section: *Multi-Tier Architecture*
Subsection: *Unix and Linux Web Server Environment*

73.   __Markup__ languages are used to specify the appearance and behavior of a Web page.
Level: *easy*
Section: *Markup Languages: HTML and DHTML*

74.   __DHTML__ is a Microsoft implementation of HTML 4.0 that includes all the features of that standard plus additional features and functions.
Level: *moderate*
Section: *Markup Languages: HTML and DHTML*
Subsection: *DHTML*

75.   DHTML provides an object model called __Document Object Model (DOM)__ that exposes all page elements as object that can be manipulated by scripts.
Level: *moderate*
Section: *Markup Languages: HTML and DHTML*
Subsection: *DHTML*

76.   A key feature of HTML 4.0 and DHTML is support for __Cascading Style Sheets (CSS)__ that enable formats to be defined for the types of elements in a page.
Level: *easy*
Section: *Markup Languages: HTML and DHTML*
Subsection: *DHTML*

77.   __Simple Object Access Protocol (SOAP)__ is a means of transmitting remote procedure calls as small XML documents using HTTP.
Level: *hard*
Section: *XML – Extensible Markup Language*

78.   XML creates a clear separation between document structure, content, and __materialization__ .
Level: moderate
Section: XML – Extensible Markup Language
Subsection: XML as a Markup Language

79.   XML documents are said to accurately represent the __semantics__ of their data.
Level: hard
Section: XML – Extensible Markup Language
Subsection: XML as a Markup Language

80.   In an XML document type declaration, if an element is defined as __#PCDATA__ that means it is a string of character data.
Level: hard
Section: XML – Extensible Markup Language
Subsection: XML Document Type Declarations

81.   XML documents that conform to their DTD are said to be __type-valid__ XML documents.
Level: moderate
Section: XML – Extensible Markup Language
Subsection: XML Document Type Declarations

82.   __Extensible Style Language: Transformations (XSLT)__ is a declarative, transformation language that can be used to materialize XML documents into DHTML or HTML.
Level: easy
Section: XML – Extensible Markup Language
Subsection: Materializing XML Documents

83.   __XPath__ is a standard for addressing elements with documents, such as <xsl:value-of-select="name/lastname">.
Level: hard
Section: XML – Extensible Markup Language
Subsection: XML Terminology and Standards

84.   __XQL__ is an emerging standard for expressing queries in terms of XML.
Level: hard
Section: XML – Extensible Markup Language
Subsection: XML Terminology and Standards

85.   To override the default minimum cardinality of elements in a XML Schema use the __minoccurs__ attribute.
Level: hard
Section: XML – Extensible Markup Language
Subsection: XML Schema

86.   To allow an unlimited number of occurrences of an element in a XML Schema, set maxoccurs equal to __"unbounded"__ .
Level: hard
Section: XML – Extensible Markup Language
Subsection: XML Schema

87.   __XSLT__   can be used to transform XML documents into WML for processing on wireless
           devices.
Level: *easy*
Section: *XML – Extensible Markup Language*
Subsection: *Wireless Application Protocol*

88.   The WML standard includes a scripting language called __WML Script__ .
Level: *easy*
Section: *XML – Extensible Markup Language*
Subsection: *Wireless Application Protocol*

89.   WML is transformed by a Web Gateway into a compressed form called __WMLC__ .
Level: *easy*
Section: *XML – Extensible Markup Language*
Subsection: *Wireless Application Protocol*

90.   __Micro__ browsers are ultra thin applications that process WML.
Level: *moderate*
Section: *XML – Extensible Markup Language*
Subsection: *Wireless Application Protocol*

91.   When using WML, documents are divided into sections called __cards__ that are small enough to
           be displayed on wireless devices.
Level: *moderate*
Section: *XML – Extensible Markup Language*
Subsection: *Wireless Application Protocol*

92.   One important contribution of XML is that it provides a standardized means of expressing the
           structure of a(n) __database view__ that has more than one multi-value path through the schema.
Level: *moderate*
Section: *XML – Extensible Markup Language*
Subsection: *The Importance of XML to Database Applications*

Essay Questions

93.   What does it mean to say that HTTP applications are *stateless*?
           A stateless application is one that does not maintain an identity with the server. When an HTTP
           server receives a request, it processes the request, and transmits an appropriate response. There
           is no attempt made to conduct a continuing session or conversation with the client that made the
           request. Once the request is handled, the client is forgotten.
           Section: *Network Environments*
           Subsection: *The Internet*

94.   Contrast Intranets and the Internet.
      *The first major distinguishing characteristic between Intranets and the Internet is that Intranets
      are private networks and the Internet is a public network. Security on private networks like
      Intranets is less problematic than it is on public networks since the computers on the private
      network are known and managed by the organization that owns the Intranet. The second major
      difference between Intranets and the Internet is speed. Users connecting to an Intranet generally
      connect at much higher speeds than users connecting to the Internet.*
      Section: *Network Environments*
      Subsection: *Intranets*

95.   Briefly describe the responsibilities of the different tiers in three-tier database application
      architecture.
      *In a three-tier database application architecture, the database server is responsible for receiving
      SQL requests, processing the SQL requests, serving data in response to those requests, and
      performing database administration tasks. The web server is responsible for handling HTTP
      requests and generating responses to those requests. This includes managing connections to the
      database server, accumulating SQL responses from the database server into database views,
      processing database views (CRUD), executing business logic, and enforcing business rules. The
      web server also provides a host environment for scripting languages. The client or browser is
      responsible for transforming user actions and requests into HTTP requests to be sent to the web
      server. It provides a host environment for scripting languages to execute on the client computer.
      Finally, the client materializes views by transforming HTML and other markup languages into
      appropriate displays for the user.*
      Section: *Multi-Tier Architecture*

96.   What problems existed in the original specification of HTML?
      *The original specification of HTML confounded the definition of content, layout, and format so
      that it was impossible to separate a view from the materialization of the view. Another problem
      was the lack of a means of defining style definitions that would allow the developer to specify a
      format for all instances of a type of element. Further, there was no means to access the
      individual elements of a web page from scripts or other programs. This meant that any changes
      to the format or content of a page required the delivery of a new page from the web server.
      Finally, there were no facilities to cache or manipulate data on the client.*
      Section: *Markup Languages: HTML and DHTML*
      Subsection: *Problems with HTML*

97.   Briefly explain the major contributions that makes XML important to database applications.
      *XML is important to database applications for several reasons. First, XML provides a
      standardized means for expressing database views, including views that contain more than one
      multi-value path through the schema. Second, XML provides a clean break between document
      structure, content, and materialization. This simplifies the creation of multiple materializations
      of the content. Third, it allows for standardized document validity checking. Finally, it enables
      organizations and industry groups to create common, industry-wide schema.*
      Section: *XML – Extensible Markup Language*
      Subsection: *The Importance of XML to Database Applications*

CHAPTER 15

ODBC, OLE DB, ADO, and ASP

True-False Questions

1. ODBC has not had practical success, but has shown great potential for future development.
    Answer: False   *Level: moderate*
    Section: The Web Server Data Environment

2. ODBC works with table-like data sources such as relational databases and spreadsheets.
    Answer: True   *Level: easy*
    Section: The Web Server Data Environment

3. ODBC acts as a wrapper for OLE DB.
    Answer: False   *Level: easy*
    Section: The Web Server Data Environment

4. ODBC is an object-oriented interface to access ADO objects.
    Answer: False   *Level: easy*
    Section: The Web Server Data Environment

5. OLE DB can be used to access ODBC data sources.
    Answer: True   *Level: moderate*
    Section: The Web Server Data Environment

6. OLE DB is an object-oriented interface.
    Answer: True   *Level: easy*
    Section: The Web Server Data Environment

7. ADO provides access to ODBC functionality to programming languages that ordinarily could not access ODBC functions.
    Answer: False   *Level: hard*
    Section: The Web Server Data Environment

8. ADO is accessible from languages such as C++ and C#, but not Visual Basic or scripting languages.
    Answer: False   *Level: moderate*
    Section: The Web Server Data Environment

9. With ODBC, the driver manager serves as an intermediary between the application and the DBMS drivers.
    Answer: True   *Level: easy*
    Section: Open Database Connectivity (ODBC) Standard
    Subsection: ODBC Architecture

10. With ODBC, only a single *driver* is needed to handle all data source types, such as Oracle, DB2, and Access.
Answer: False   *Level: hard*
Section: Open Database Connectivity (ODBC) Standard
Subsection: ODBC Architecture

11. In ODBC, the amount of work that the *driver* must do is largely determined by the degree of SQL-compliance of the data source.
Answer: True   *Level: moderate*
Section: Open Database Connectivity (ODBC) Standard
Subsection: ODBC Architecture

12. A multiple-tier ODBC driver may reformat an SQL request, but it does not actually process the SQL statement.
Answer: True   *Level: hard*
Section: Open Database Connectivity (ODBC) Standard
Subsection: ODBC Architecture

13. With ODBC, a database and the DBMS that processes it are identified by the *data source*.
Answer: True   *Level: easy*
Section: Open Database Connectivity (ODBC) Standard
Subsection: ODBC Architecture

14. With ODBC, a *file data source* is available only to the user that created it.
Answer: False   *Level: hard*
Section: Open Database Connectivity (ODBC) Standard
Subsection: Establishing an ODBC Source Name

15. In general, the best type of ODBC data source to define for a web application is a *system data source*.
Answer: True   *Level: hard*
Section: Open Database Connectivity (ODBC) Standard
Subsection: Establishing an ODBC Source Name

16. OLE DB objects are COM objects.
Answer: True   *Level: moderate*
Section: OLE DB

17. In OLE DB, a *recordset* is a more abstract representation of a *rowset*.
Answer: False   *Level: moderate*
Section: OLE DB

18. Objects have properties that represent characteristics of the object.
Answer: True   *Level: easy*
Section: OLE DB

19. One of the properties of all collections is Count, which is the number of objects in the collection.
Answer: True   *Level: moderate*
Section: OLE DB

20.   One important result of OLE DB is that data does not have to be moved or converted from one
        form to another.
        Answer: True   *Level: easy*
        Section: OLE DB
        Subsection: Goals of OLE DB

21.   In OLE DB, all of an object's properties must be exposed in all interfaces, but not all methods
        have to be exposed.
        Answer: False   *Level: easy*
        Section: OLE DB
        Subsection: Goals of OLE DB

22.   An OLE DB service provider accepts data from an OLE DB tabular data provider.
        Answer: True   *Level: easy*
        Section: OLE DB
        Subsection: OLE DB Basic Constructs

23.   ADO is a simple object model that can be used by data consumers to process any OLE DB data.
        Answer: True   *Level: easy*
        Section: ADO (Active Data Objects)

24.   The ADO object model and interfaces are the same regardless of the type of data processed.
        Answer: True   *Level: moderate*
        Section: ADO (Active Data Objects)

25.   When invoking ADO from ASP, the first object that must be created is a Recordset object.
        Answer: False   *Level: easy*
        Section: ADO (Active Data Objects)
        Subsection: ADO Object Model

26.   When invoking ADO from ASP, cursor type and lock type must be specified when creating the
        connection object.
        Answer: False   *Level: moderate*
        Section: ADO (Active Data Objects)
        Subsection: ADO Object Model

27.   With ADO, program code to explicitly create the Errors collection must precede the code to
        create the Recordset object since errors may occur during the creation of the Recordset.
        Answer: False   *Level: hard*
        Section: ADO (Active Data Objects)
        Subsection: ADO Object Model

28.   A Recordset object is used in ADO to execute queries and stored procedures that are stored in the
        database.
        Answer: False   *Level: easy*
        Section: ADO (Active Data Objects)
        Subsection: ADO Object Model

29.   With ADO, parameters are passed in a Command object using the Parameters collection.
        Answer: True   *Level: moderate*
        Section: ADO (Active Data Objects)
        Subsection: ADO Object Model

30.   The ASP processor maintains transaction state through the use of session variables.
        Answer: True   *Level: easy*
        Section: ADO Examples

Multiple Choice Questions

31.   Which of the following can only interact with relational database and table-like data structures?
        a.)   OLE DB
        b.)   ODBC
        c.)   ASP
        d.)   ADO
        e.)   all of the above

Level: easy
Section: The Web Server Data Environment

32.   Which of the following is true about ODBC?
        a.)   ODBC has experienced little practical success.
        b.)   ODBC requires developers to have a thorough knowledge of many DBMS native libraries.
        c.)   ODBC can be used to access data from spreadsheets.
        d.)   ODBC has an object-oriented interface.
        e.)   ODBC does not include facilities to return error messages.

Level: moderate
Section: The Web Server Data Environment

33.   Which of the following is not true about OLE DB?
        a.)   Scripting languages cannot access OLE DB.
        b.)   OLE DB is object-oriented.
        c.)   OLE DB can access ODBC data sources.
        d.)   OLE DB can access non-relational data sources.
        e.)   OLE DB is used as a wrapper for ADO objects.

Level: easy
Section: The Web Server Data Environment

34.   According to the ODBC standard, which of the following is <u>not</u> part of the specification of a *data source*?
    a.)   the associated DBMS
    b.)   the database
    c.)   the driver
    d.)   the operating system
    e.)   the network platform

Level: moderate
Section: Open Database Connectivity (ODBC) Standard
Subsection: ODBC Architecture

35.   The ODBC standard defines a means of doing which of the following?
    a.)   start transactions
    b.)   rollback transactions
    c.)   create a connection
    d.)   issue SQL commands
    e.)   all of the above

Level: easy
Section: Open Database Connectivity (ODBC) Standard
Subsection: ODBC Architecture

36.   Which of the following is a function performed by the *driver manager* in ODBC?
    a.)   submit SQL statements to the data source
    b.)   determine the type of DBMS that processes a given ODBC data source
    c.)   load the appropriate ODBC driver into memory
    d.)   convert data source error codes into ODBC error codes
    e.)   both b and c

Level: easy
Section: Open Database Connectivity (ODBC) Standard
Subsection: ODBC Architecture

37.   The intermediary between the application and the DBMS drivers in the ODBC architecture is the _____.
    a.)   driver manager
    b.)   OLE DB interface
    c.)   ODBC driver
    d.)   data source
    e.)   database connector

Level: easy
Section: Open Database Connectivity (ODBC) Standard
Subsection: ODBC Architecture

38.   Which of the following is a task performed by the *driver* according to the ODBC standard?
    a.)   determines the appropriate DBMS
    b.)   validates the format of the ODBC command received from the application
    c.)   converts data source error codes into ODBC standard error codes
    d.)   verifies the application to the data source
    e.)   converts the data source into an SQL-compliant data structure

Level: moderate
Section: Open Database Connectivity (ODBC) Standard
Subsection: ODBC Architecture

39.   The _____ processes ODBC requests and submits specific SQL statements to a given type of data source.
    a.)   driver manager
    b.)   ADO
    c.)   driver
    d.)   source converter
    e.)   ODBC translator

Level: easy
Section: Open Database Connectivity (ODBC) Standard
Subsection: ODBC Architecture

40.   A data source that is fully SQL-compliant would use what type of DBMS driver?
    a.)   single-tier
    b.)   multiple-tier
    c.)   SQL transform
    d.)   text-based
    e.)   conformance

Level: hard
Section: Open Database Connectivity (ODBC) Standard
Subsection: ODBC Architecture

41.   How does an application determine the level of ODBC conformance available from a driver?
    a.)   The application makes a call to the driver manager.
    b.)   The application makes a call to the data source.
    c.)   The application makes a call to the driver.
    d.)   The developer must determine the level of conformance before the application is written.
    e.)   It does not have to determine ODBC conformance since all ODBC drivers have the same functionality by definition.

Level: hard
Section: Open Database Connectivity (ODBC) Standard
Subsection: ODBC Architecture

42.   Support for a scrollable cursor is a sign of what type of conformance in a DBMS driver?
    a.)   Level 1 API
    b.)   Extended SQL Grammar
    c.)   Core API
    d.)   Level 2 API
    e.)   Core SQL Grammar

Level: hard
Section: Open Database Connectivity (ODBC) Standard

43.   Support for subqueries and creating indexes is a sign of what type of conformance in a DBMS driver?
    a.)   Level 2 API
    b.)   Minimum SQL Grammar
    c.)   Core API
    d.)   Extended SQL Grammar
    e.)   Core SQL Grammar

Level: hard
Section: Open Database Connectivity (ODBC) Standard

44.   A _____ data source can be shared among database users as long as they have the same DBMS driver and privilege to access the database.
    a.)   file
    b.)   common
    c.)   shared
    d.)   system
    e.)   user

Level: easy
Section: Open Database Connectivity (ODBC) Standard
Subsection: Establishing an ODBC Data Source Name

45.   A data source that is local to a single computer and can be used by the operating system and any user on that computer is called a(n) _____ data source.
    a.)   file
    b.)   common
    c.)   shared
    d.)   system
    e.)   user

Level: easy
Section: Open Database Connectivity (ODBC) Standard
Subsection: Establishing an ODBC Data Source Name

46.   In general, for web applications it is best to create what type of data source on the web server?
        a.)   file
        b.)   common
        c.)   shared
        d.)   system
        e.)   user

Level: *moderate*
Section: *Open Database Connectivity (ODBC) Standard*
Subsection: *Establishing an ODBC Data Source Name*

47.   OLE DB breaks the features and functions of a DBMS into what type of objects?
        a.)   COM
        b.)   DBMS
        c.)   MTS
        d.)   ODBC
        e.)   ASP

Level: *moderate*
Section: *OLE DB*

48.   ODBC interfaces are abstractions of:
        a.)   OLE objects
        b.)   native DBMS access methods
        c.)   driver managers
        d.)   DBMS data sources
        e.)   recordsets

Level: *moderate*
Section: *OLE DB*

49.   The characteristics of an object are called:
        a.)   classes
        b.)   collections
        c.)   methods
        d.)   properties
        e.)   procedures

Level: *easy*
Section: *OLE DB*

50.   The actions that an object can perform are called:
        a.)   classes
        b.)   collections
        c.)   methods
        d.)   properties
        e.)   procedures

Level: *easy*
Section: *OLE DB*

51.   An important method of a collection is a(n) _____, which can be used to pass through or otherwise identify the items in the collection.
    a.)   iterator
    b.)   identifier
    c.)   converter
    d.)   transformer
    e.)   signal

Level: hard
Section: OLE DB

52.   A set of objects and the properties and methods that they expose are known as a(n) _____.
    a.)   provider
    b.)   data consumer
    c.)   implementation
    d.)   instantiation
    e.)   interface

Level: easy
Section: OLE DB
Subsection: Goals of OLE DB

53.   Which of the following is a type of OLE DB data provider?
    a.)   relational data provider
    b.)   method provider
    c.)   sequential data provider
    d.)   tabular data provider
    e.)   implementation provider

Level: moderate
Section: OLE DB
Subsection: OLE DB Basic Constructs

54.   Which standard interface in OLE DB is invoked to declare a forward-only cursor?
    a.)   IRowSet
    b.)   IAccessor
    c.)   IColumnsInfo
    d.)   adXact
    e.)   ADODB

Level: hard
Section: OLE DB
Subsection: OLE DB Basic Constructs

55.   Which of the following is <u>not</u> true of ADO?
      a.)   ADO is a simple object model for OLE DB data consumers.
      b.)   ADO can be used from VBScript and JavaScript.
      c.)   ADO is less abstract than OLE DB.
      d.)   Data access objects in ADO are the same for all types of OLE DB data.
      e.)   All of the above <u>are</u> true of ADO.

Level: hard
Section: ADO (Active Data Objects)

56.   In ASP, any programming language statements that are to be processed on the server must be enclosed in _____.
      a.)   <!-- .... --!>
      b.)   [ ]
      c.)   ( )
      d.)   <% .... %>
      e.)

Level: moderate
Section: ADO (Active Data Objects)
Subsection: Invoking ADO from Active Server Pages

57.   The first ADO element to be created is the:
      a.)   command object
      b.)   connection object
      c.)   errors collection
      d.)   parameters collection
      e.)   recordset object

Level: moderate
Section: ADO (Active Data Objects)
Subsection: ADO Object Model

58.   An ADO automatically instantiates a(n) _____ when it is needed.
      a.)   command object
      b.)   connection object
      c.)   errors collection
      d.)   parameters collection
      e.)   recordset object

Level: moderate
Section: ADO (Active Data Objects)
Subsection: ADO Object Model

59.   Each _____ has a *fields collection.*
        a.)   command object
        b.)   connection object
        c.)   errors collection
        d.)   parameters collection
        e.)   recordset object

Level: *moderate*
Section: *ADO (Active Data Objects)*
Subsection: *ADO Object Model*

60.   Each _____ has a *parameters collection.*
        a.)   command object
        b.)   connection object
        c.)   errors collection
        d.)   field object
        e.)   recordset object

Level: *moderate*
Section: *ADO (Active Data Objects)*
Subsection: *ADO Object Model*

Fill in the Blank Questions

61.   The open database connectivity (ODBC) standard is an interface by which application
        programs can access and process SQL databases in a DBMS-independent manner.
Level: *easy*
Section: *Open Database Connectivity (ODBC) Standard*

62.   According to the ODBC standard, a(n) data source is a database, its associated DBMS,
        operating system, and network platform.
Level: *easy*
Section: *Open Database Connectivity (ODBC) Standard*
Subsection: *ODBC Architecture*

63.   With ODBC, the driver manager serves as an intermediary between the application and the
        DBMS drivers.
Level: *moderate*
Section: *Open Database Connectivity (ODBC) Standard*
Subsection: *ODBC Architecture*

64.   A(n) driver processes ODBC requests and submits specific SQL statements to a given type of
        data source.
Level: *moderate*
Section: *Open Database Connectivity (ODBC) Standard*
Subsection: *ODBC Architecture*

65.   Within the ODBC architecture, if a data source is itself not SQL-compliant, the __driver__ may perform processing to fill in for a lack of capability at the data source.
Level: hard
Section: Open Database Connectivity (ODBC) Standard
Subsection: ODBC Architecture

66.   A(n) __single-tier__ driver processes both ODBC calls and SQL statements.
Level: moderate
Section: Open Database Connectivity (ODBC) Standard
Subsection: ODBC Architecture

67.   A(n) __multiple-tier__ driver processes ODBC calls but passes the SQL requests directly to the database server.
Level: moderate
Section: Open Database Connectivity (ODBC) Standard
Subsection: ODBC Architecture

68.   __ODBC conformance__ levels concern the features and functions that are made available through the driver's application program interface.
Level: moderate
Section: Open Database Connectivity (ODBC) Standard
Subsection: Conformance Levels

69.   A driver __API__ is a set of functions that the application can call to receive services.
Level: hard
Section: Open Database Connectivity (ODBC) Standard
Subsection: Conformance Levels

70.   __Level 2 API__ conformance level is necessary for a driver to support scrollable cursors.
Level: hard
Section: Open Database Connectivity (ODBC) Standard
Subsection: Conformance Levels

71.   __SQL conformance__ levels specify which SQL statements, expressions, and data types a driver can process.
Level: easy
Section: Open Database Connectivity (ODBC) Standard
Subsection: Conformance Levels

72.   A(n) __file__ data source can be shared among database users that have the same DBMS driver and privileges to access the database.
Level: moderate
Section: Open Database Connectivity (ODBC) Standard
Subsection: Establishing an ODBC Data Source Name

73.   A(n) __system__ data source is one that is local to a single computer.
Level: moderate
Section: Open Database Connectivity (ODBC) Standard
Subsection: Establishing an ODBC Data Source Name

74.   A(n) __user__ data source is only available to the user who created it.
Level: easy
Section: Open Database Connectivity (ODBC) Standard
Subsection: Establishing an ODBC Data Source Name

75.   In general, the best choice of ODBC data sources for a web application is to create a(n) __system__ data source on the web server.
Level: hard
Section: Open Database Connectivity (ODBC) Standard
Subsection: Establishing an ODBC Data Source Name

76.   __OLE DB__ is the foundation of data access in the Microsoft world.
Level: hard
Section: OLE DB

77.   Abstraction involves the loss of __detail__ for the sake of gaining the ability to work with a broader range of types.
Level: easy
Section: OLE DB

78.   A(n) __rowset__ is the OLE DB abstraction of a recordset.
Level: moderate
Section: OLE DB

79.   The characteristics of an object are called __properties__.
Level: easy
Section: OLE DB

80.   The actions an object can perform are called __methods__.
Level: easy
Section: OLE DB

81.   A(n) __collection__ is an object that contains a group of other objects.
Level: easy
Section: OLE DB

82.   Data __consumers__ are users of OLE DB functionality.
Level: moderate
Section: OLE DB
Subsection: Goals of OLE DB

83.   A(n) __interface__ is specified by a set of objects and the properties and methods that they expose.
Level: moderate
Section: OLE DB
Subsection: Goals of OLE DB

84.   A(n) __service provider__ accepts OLE DB data from an OLE DB tabular data provider and transforms it in some way.
Level: *hard*
Section: *OLE DB*
Subsection: *OLE DB Basic Constructs*

85.   The __rowset__ object is the OLE DB equivalent to a cursor.
Level: *moderate*
Section: *OLE DB*
Subsection: *OLE DB Basic Constructs*

86.   The __IRowSet__ interface is invoked to declare a forward-only cursor in OLE DB.
Level: *hard*
Section: *OLE DB*
Subsection: *OLE DB Basic Constructs*

87.   The __IColumnInfo__ interface has methods for obtaining information about the columns of a rowset.
Level: *hard*
Section: *OLE DB*
Subsection: *OLE DB Basic Constructs*

88.   __Active Data Objects (ADO)__ is a simple object model that can be used to process any OLE DB data.
Level: *easy*
Section: *ADO (Active Data Objects)*

89.   With ADO, every Recordset object has a(n) __Fields__ collection.
Level: *moderate*
Section: *ADO (Active Data Objects)*
Subsection: *ADO Object Model*

90.   The ADO __Command__ object is used to execute queries or stored procedures that are stored within the database.
Level: *hard*
Section: *ADO (Active Data Objects)*
Subsection: *ADO Object Model*

Essay Questions

91. Explain the relationships among native DBMS libraries, ODBC, OLE DB, and ADO, and why each led to the development of the next.

All of these provide means of data access. Native DBMS libraries are the least abstract and are DBMS-specific access methods. Due to the large numbers of data sources that developers have to deal with, learning that many DBMS libraries was cumbersome. ODBC developed as a more abstract means of data access that shielded developers from having to learn multiple native DBMS libraries. One shortcoming of ODBC, however, was that it can only access data from sources that have a table-like structure. Therefore, OLE DB was developed as a means of accessing data from a much broader range of data source types. OLE DB is an object-oriented interface that is suitable for use by many object-oriented languages. Many developers, however, use languages such as Visual Basic and scripting languages that cannot access OLE DB. ADO was therefore developed to further abstract OLE DB and provide access to OLE DB functionality to programming languages that cannot directly access OLE DB.
Section: *The Web Server Data Environment*

92. Briefly describe the components of the ODBC architecture.

In the ODBC architecture, the application program, driver manager, and DBMS drivers reside on the web server, and the database and DBMS reside on the database server. The combination of the database and its associated DBMS comprise the data source. The data source contains the data used by the application. The application program talks to the driver manager. When the application requests a connection, the driver manager checks to see which DBMS the data source uses and loads the appropriate DBMS driver into memory. The driver manager also checks the format of the ODBC requests coming from the application program. The DBMS driver processes the ODBC requests and submits the SQL statements to the data source. The driver also ensures that the responses coming from the data source are in appropriate ODBC format.
Section: *Open Database Connectivity (ODBC) Standard*
Subsection: *ODBC Architecture*

93. What are the different types of conformance levels within the ODBC standard, and why do they exist?

There are two types of conformance levels within the ODBC standard – ODBC conformance, and SQL conformance. ODBC conformance deals with the features and functions that are available to the application program through the DBMS driver API. The SQL conformance standard deals with the SQL statements, expressions, and data types that the driver can process. The reason for these levels is to accommodate the varying ability of different vendors to comply with the power and expressiveness of the ODBC standard and the SQL language. Without these different levels of compliance, the ODBC standard would either be too simple to very useful, or too rigorous for many vendors to comply with.
Section: *Open Database Connectivity (ODBC) Standard*
Subsection: *Conformance Levels*

94.   Why is the decomposition of the features and functions of a DBMS into different objects an advantage for OLE DB?

First, by breaking the features of the DBMS into different objects, vendors have the option of implementing only a portion of their product in OLE DB. This is significant since the all-or-nothing approach required with ODBC was a major disincentive to vendors because of the large investment necessary to achieve ODBC compliance. OLE DB allows the vendor to increase their OLE DB participation in a piecemeal fashion. Second, it allows vendors to create multiple interfaces to their products that have different properties and methods exposed. This improves flexibility for data consumers since they can select an interface that only provides the methods they need, and it is more flexible for data providers since they can change the implementation of an interface without negatively impacting their data consumers.
Section: *OLE DB*
Subsection: *Goals of OLE DB*

95.   Briefly describe the ADO object model.

The ADO object model is built on top of the OLE DB object model. The ADO object model contains a Connection object. The Connection object includes Recordset objects. All Recordset objects contain a Fields collection. The Fields collection contains every field in the recordset. The Connection object can also contain one or more Command objects. The Command object is used to execute queries and stored procedures stored in the database. Every Command object contains a Parameters collection. The Parameters collection contains any parameters that are passed to the DBMS driver and the data source. Finally, the Connection object can contain an Errors collection. The ADO will automatically create the Errors collection and place any errors into it when an error occurs.
Section: *ADO (Active Data Objects)*
Subsection: *ADO Object Model*

CHAPTER 16

JDBC, Java Server Pages, and MySQL

True-False Questions

1.   Only open source products may be used in conjunction with JDBC.
      Answer: False   *Level: moderate*
      Section: Chapter Introduction

2.   To use JDBC, programs must be written in Java.
      Answer: True   *Level: easy*
      Section: Chapter Introduction

3.   JDBC drivers only exist for a limited number of DBMS products at this time.
      Answer: False   *Level: moderate*
      Section: JDBC

4.   JDBC-ODBC bridge drivers resolve inconsistencies between Java and C/C++ to allow Java
      access to ODBC data sources.
      Answer: True   *Level: easy*
      Section: JDBC
      Subsection: Driver Types

5.   Type 2 JDBC drivers access ODBC data sources over a network.
      Answer: False   *Level: moderate*
      Section: JDBC
      Subsection: Driver Types

6.   Type 4 JDBC drivers translate JDBC calls into a DBMS-independent network protocol.
      Answer: False   *Level: hard*
      Section: JDBC
      Subsection: Driver Types

7.   Java programs are compiled into machine-independent bytecode.
      Answer: True   *Level: easy*
      Section: JDBC
      Subsection: Driver Types

8.   Java programs tend to execute faster than programs compiled into machine-dependent code
      because the Java virtual machine only has to interpret the bytecode.
      Answer: False   *Level: moderate*
      Section: JDBC
      Subsection: Driver Types

9.   An applet is a Java bytecode program that executes on the web server.
      Answer: False   *Level: easy*

Section: JDBC
Subsection: Driver Types

10. Applet bytecode is sent to the user's computer and is invoked using the HTTP protocol.
     Answer: True   *Level: moderate*
     Section: JDBC
     Subsection: Driver Types

11. Java programs that access a database from an applet must use a Type 2 JDBC driver.
     Answer: False   *Level: hard*
     Section: JDBC
     Subsection: Driver Types

12. The first step in using a JDBC driver is to establish a connection.
     Answer: False   *Level: moderate*
     Section: JDBC
     Subsection: Using JDBC

13. Developers must manually register new JDBC drivers with the *DriverManager* class so they will
     be available for use.
     Answer: False   *Level: hard*
     Section: JDBC
     Subsection: Using JDBC

14. The *openConnection* method is used with the *DriverManager* class to establish a connection to a
     JDBC data source.
     Answer: False   *Level: hard*
     Section: JDBC
     Subsection: Using JDBC

15. When establishing a connection with a JDBC data source, the first parameter passed to the
     DriverManager is always "jdbc.".
     Answer: True   *Level: moderate*
     Section: JDBC
     Subsection: Using JDBC

16. After creating a connection, the next step in using JDBC is to create a Statement.
     Answer: True   *Level: easy*
     Section: JDBC
     Subsection: Using JDBC

17. Creating a Statement in JDBC is similar to creating a Command object in ADO.
     Answer: True   *Level: easy*
     Section: JDBC
     Subsection: Using JDBC

18. Invoking the executeUpdate method of a JDBC statement returns a result set that can be
     processed like a cursor.
     Answer: False   *Level: moderate*
     Section: JDBC

Subsection: Using JDBC

19.   With JDBC, the getMetaData method is used to help find out the names of columns in a result set.
        Answer: True   *Level: hard*
        Section: JDBC
        Subsection: Using JDBC

20.   While the JDBC standard could support stored procedures, no implementation of JDBC currently
        supports them.
        Answer: False   *Level: hard*
        Section: JDBC
        Subsection: Using JDBC

21.   With JDBC, a Callable statement can be used to run stored procedures.
        Answer: True   *Level: moderate*
        Section: JDBC
        Subsection: Using JDBC

22.   Java applications written to use JDBC should not attempt to import the JDBC drivers.
        Answer: True   *Level: easy*
        Section: JDBC
        Subsection: JDBC Examples

23.   In Java, a multi-line comment is started with <!--.
        Answer: False   *Level: moderate*
        Section: JDBC
        Subsection: JDBC Examples

24.   JSP and ASP look similar because the underlying technology is almost identical.
        Answer: False   *Level: moderate*
        Section: Java Server Pages

25.   JSP can be coded only in Java and JavaScript.
        Answer: False   *Level: moderate*
        Section: Java Server Pages

26.   Since JSP are automatically converted into servlets, you do not have to code in complete classes
        or methods.
        Answer: True   *Level: moderate*
        Section: Java Server Pages
        Subsection: JSP Pages and Servlets

27.   JSP pages are automatically re-compiled if the uncompiled JSP page is newer than the compiled
        version of the page.
        Answer: True   *Level: easy*
        Section: Java Server Pages
        Subsection: Setting Up Tomcat for JSP Processing

28.   Like CGI files, there can be many copies of a given JSP page in memory at one time.
        Answer: False   *Level: moderate*

29.   A Java bean has no more than one public instance variable.
       Answer: False   *Level: hard*
       Section: Java Server Pages
       Subsection: JSP Examples

30.   MySQL is an open source DBMS that only runs on Unix and Linux operating systems.
       Answer: False   *Level: easy*
       Section: MySQL

31.   MySQL has limited transaction management and logging capabilities.
       Answer: True   *Level: easy*
       Section: MySQL

32.   MySQL can properly parse foreign key constraints, but does not execute them.
       Answer: True   *Level: moderate*
       Section: MySQL
       Subsection: MySQL Limitations

33.   MySQL is missing many of the features and functions of a modern DBMS product.
       Answer: True   *Level: easy*
       Section: MySQL
       Subsection: MySQL Summary

Multiple Choice Questions

34.   Which of the following is true of JDBC?
       a.)   Programs must be written in Java.
       b.)   JDBC only works with open-source products.
       c.)   JDBC is only available for Unix-like operating systems, such as Linux.
       d.)   JDBC is actually a DBMS.
       e.)   both b and c

Level: *easy*
Section: *Chapter Introduction*

35.   What type of JDBC driver is known as a JDBC-ODBC bridge?
       a.)   type 1 driver
       b.)   type 4 driver
       c.)   type J-O driver
       d.)   type 2 driver
       e.)   Java driver

Level: *moderate*
Section: *JDBC*
Subsection: *Driver Types*

36.   What type of JDBC driver connects to the native-API of the DBMS?
       a.)   type J-O driver
       b.)   type 1 driver
       c.)   type 2 driver
       d.)   type 3 driver
       e.)   type 4 driver

Level: moderate
Section: JDBC
Subsection: Driver Types

37.   What type of JDBC driver translates JDBC calls into DBMS-independent network protocols?
       a.)   type J-O driver
       b.)   type 1 driver
       c.)   type 2 driver
       d.)   type 3 driver
       e.)   type 4 driver

Level: hard
Section: JDBC
Subsection: Driver Types

38.   What type of JDBC driver translates JDBC calls in DBMS-specific network protocols?
       a.)   type J-O driver
       b.)   type 1 driver
       c.)   type 2 driver
       d.)   type 3 driver
       e.)   type 4 driver

Level: hard
Section: JDBC
Subsection: Driver Types

39.   A Java virtual machine is actually a _____.
       a.)   program compiler
       b.)   JDBC data source
       c.)   bytecode interpreter
       d.)   JDBC driver
       e.)   servlet

Level: easy
Section: JDBC
Subsection: Driver Types

40.   Which of the following is true about bytecode interpretation?
         a.)   It may be performed on the client.
         b.)   It may be performed on the server.
         c.)   It is slower than running a program compiled into machine code.
         d.)   It increases portability.
         e.)   all of the above

Level: easy
Section: JDBC
Subsection: Driver Types

41.   Applet bytecode is transmitted to the user's computer via _____.
         a.)   the JDBC driver
         b.)   the Java virtual machine
         c.)   HTTP
         d.)   SQL
         e.)   the bytecode interpreter

Level: moderate
Section: JDBC
Subsection: Driver Types

42.   A(n) _____ is a Java program that is interpreted and executed by a bytecode interpreter on the web server.
         a.)   applet
         b.)   Java virtual machine
         c.)   servlet
         d.)   HTTP
         e.)   JDBC translator

Level: easy
Section: JDBC
Subsection: Driver Types

43.   Which type of JDBC driver can be used if the DBMS and the web server are running on the same computer?
         a.)   type 1 driver
         b.)   type 2 driver
         c.)   type 3 driver
         d.)   type 4 driver
         e.)   all of the above

Level: hard
Section: JDBC
Subsection: Driver Types

44.   The first step in using a JDBC driver is:
        a.)   establish a connection to the database
        b.)   load the driver
        c.)   create a statement
        d.)   call the DriverManager object
        e.)   invoke the executeQuery method

Level: moderate
Section: JDBC
Subsection: Using JDBC

45.   To load a JDBC driver, the driver library must be located in a directory that is in the _____
        for the Java compiler and the Java virtual machine.
        a.)   API
        b.)   SQL
        c.)   CLASS method
        d.)   CLASSPATH
        e.)   Class library

Level: hard
Section: JDBC
Subsection: Using JDBC

46.   Which of the following would load the JDBC driver identified by *org.gjt.mm.msql.Driver*?
        a.)   Class.getDriver("org.gjt.mm.msql.Driver").newInstance( )
        b.)   Driver.loadInstance("org.gjt.mm.msql.Driver")
        c.)   Name.getClass("org.gjt.mm.msql.Driver").newInstance
        d.)   Object.newInstance("org.gjt.mm.msql.Driver")
        e.)   Class.forName("org.gjt.mm.msql.Driver").newInstance( )

Level: hard
Section: JDBC
Subsection: Using JDBC

47.   The first part of the string parameter passed to getConnection is always:
        a.)   *jdbc*
        b.)   *new*
        c.)   *open*
        d.)   *connect*
        e.)   *name*

Level: moderate
Section: JDBC
Subsection: Using JDBC

48.   Which method can be used with JDBC to obtain the column names in a result set?
        a.)   IColumnInfo
        b.)   getColumnInfo
        c.)   getDataName
        d.)   getMetaData
        e.)   IRowSet

Level: *moderate*
Section: *JDBC*
Subsection: *Using JDBC*

49.   Compiled queries are invoked in JDBC by using:
        a.)   callable statements
        b.)   stored procedures
        c.)   compilation statements
        d.)   prepared statements
        e.)   remote object statements

Level: *hard*
Section: *JDBC*
Subsection: *Using JDBC*

50.   Stored procedures are invoked in JDBC by using:
        a.)   callable statements
        b.)   prepared queries
        c.)   compilation statements
        d.)   prepared statements
        e.)   remote object statements

Level: *hard*
Section: *JDBC*
Subsection: *Using JDBC*

51.   Which of the following would return a result set that can be used like a cursor?
        a.)   executeUpdate
        b.)   executeQuery
        c.)   processUpdate
        d.)   runStmt
        e.)   none of the above

Level: *moderate*
Section: *JDBC*
Subsection: *Using JDBC*

52.   Calls from the ResultSet JDBC component are routed via _____ to the proper driver.
        a.)   the library
        b.)   the collection
        c.)   the DriverManager
        d.)   Statement
        e.)   getMetaData

Level: moderate
Section: JDBC
Subsection: Using JDBC

53.   Many JDBC methods are programmed inside of _____ blocks because they generate exceptions.
        a.)   if-then-else
        b.)   On Error Resume Next
        c.)   try:catch
        d.)   error:handler
        e.)   Statement

Level: easy
Section: JDBC
Subsection: JDBC Examples

54.   The coding for Java Server Pages may be written in _____.
        a.)   Java
        b.)   JavaScript
        c.)   C++
        d.)   Visual Basic
        e.)   all of the above

Level: easy
Section: Java Server Pages

55.   Which of the following is true about JSP code?
        a.)   It must be written in Java or JavaScript.
        b.)   It does not have access to HTTP functionality.
        c.)   It must be coded as complete Java classes and methods.
        d.)   It is automatically converted into Java servlets.
        e.)   all of the above

Level: moderate
Section: Java Server Pages
Subsection: JSP Pages and Servlets

56. Which of the following is <u>not</u> true about Tomcat?
    a.) It is a servlet processor.
    b.) It can be used as a standalone web server.
    c.) It is often used in conjunction with Apache.
    d.) It is an applet processor.
    e.) It has limited web server facilities.

Level: moderate
Section: Java Server Pages
Subsection: Apache Tomcat

57. JSP pages are:
    a.) automatically compiled by the servlet processor as needed
    b.) required to be compiled by the developer before being made public
    c.) automatically checked for syntax errors by the servlet as they are written
    d.) slower to execute but more memory efficient than CGI files
    e.) both a and d

Level: hard
Section: Java Server Pages
Subsection: Setting Up Tomcat for JSP Processing

58. As compared to CGI files, JSP pages:
    a.) are less memory efficient
    b.) require more processor time
    c.) execute faster
    d.) keep more copies of a given page in memory
    e.) none of the above

Level: hard
Section: Java Server Pages
Subsection: Setting Up Tomcat for JSP Processing

59. The ability of JSP pages to invoke precompiled objects is useful because:
    a.) it separates writing program logic from generating HTML
    b.) it allows logic to be encapsulated into reusable modules
    c.) it reduces the complexity of the program logic
    d.) it makes program execution faster
    e.) both a and b

Level: moderate
Section: Java Server Pages
Subsection: JSP Examples

60.   Which of the following is <u>not</u> true about a Java bean?
        a.)   It has no public instance variables.
        b.)   It is a Java class.
        c.)   All persistent values are accessed using methods named getxxx and setxxx, where xxx is the name of the persistent value.
        d.)   If it has any constructors, it can only have one explicitly defined zero-argument constructor.
        e.)   It has only one global persistent variable.

Level: hard
Section: Java Server Pages
Subsection: JSP Examples

61.   MySQL is particularly good for:
        a.)   database logging
        b.)   transaction management
        c.)   query applications
        d.)   concurrency control
        e.)   stored procedures

Level: moderate
Section: MySQL

62.   MySQL maintains metadata in a database named _____.
        a.)   metadata
        b.)   dataobject
        c.)   SQLdata
        d.)   querydata
        e.)   mysql

Level: moderate
Section: MySQL
Subsection: Setting Access Permissions for JDBC Use

63.   What lock granularity does MySQL support?
        a.)   table level
        b.)   row level
        c.)   field level
        d.)   database level
        e.)   MySQL does not support locks.

Level: easy
Section: MySQL
Subsection: Concurrency Control

Fill in the Blank Questions

64.   According to Sun Microsystems, the inventor of Java, JDBC stands for __JDBC__ .
Level: easy
Section: JDBC

65.   In regard to JDBC drivers, Type 1 drivers are __JDBC-ODBC__ bridge drivers.
Level: easy
Section: JDBC
Subsection: Driver Types

66.   Bridge drivers resolve inconsistencies between __Java__ and C/C++.
Level: easy
Section: JDBC
Subsection: Driver Types

67.   Type 2 JDBC drivers connect to the __native-API__ of the DBMS.
Level: hard
Section: JDBC
Subsection: Driver Types

68.   A Type 3 JDBC driver translates JDBC calls into a(n) __DBMS-independent__ network protocol.
Level: hard
Section: JDBC
Subsection: Driver Types

69.   Type __4__ JDBC drivers translate JDBC calls into DBMS-specific network protocols.
Level: moderate
Section: JDBC
Subsection: Driver Types

70.   To accomplish goals for Java portability, Java programs are compiled into machine-independent __bytecode__ .
Level: moderate
Section: JDBC
Subsection: Driver Types

71.   Bytecode interpreters are referred to as Java __virtual machines__ .
Level: easy
Section: JDBC
Subsection: Driver Types

72.   A(n) __applet__ is a Java bytecode program that runs on the application user's computer.
Level: easy
Section: JDBC
Subsection: Driver Types

73.   A(n) __servlet__ is a Java bytecode program that runs on the web server computer.
Level: easy
Section: JDBC
Subsection: Driver Types

74.   With JDBC, all of the work to define a connection is done in Java code via the JDBC __driver__.
Level: moderate
Section: JDBC
Subsection: Using JDBC

75.   JDBC drivers must register themselves with the __DriverManager__ class.
Level: hard
Section: JDBC
Subsection: Using JDBC

76.   The first part of the string parameter passed to getConnection is always __jdbc__.
Level: hard
Section: JDBC
Subsection: Using JDBC

77.   The content of the second and third parts of the string parameter passed to getConnection are determined by the __JDBC driver__ being used.
Level: moderate
Section: JDBC
Subsection: Using JDBC

78.   __Prepared Statement__ objects can be used with JDBC to invoke compiled queries.
Level: hard
Section: JDBC
Subsection: Using JDBC

79.   __Callable Statement__ objects can be used with JDBC to invoke stored procedures.
Level: hard
Section: JDBC
Subsection: Using JDBC

80.   Many JDBC methods are programmed inside of __try:catch__ blocks because they generate exceptions.
Level: moderate
Section: JDBC
Subsection: JDBC Examples

81.   A Java multi-line comment is started with __/*__.
Level: easy
Section: JDBC
Subsection: JDBC Examples

82.   A Java single line comment starts with   // .
Level: *easy*
Section: *JDBC*
Subsection: *JDBC Examples*

83.   The metadata for a result set can be placed in a(n)   ResultSetMetaData   object.
Level: *hard*
Section: *JDBC*
Subsection: *JDBC Examples*

84.   JSP and ASP look similar because they both blend   HTML   with program code.
Level: *moderate*
Section: *Java Server Pages*

85.   With JSP, all programming must be done in the   Java   language.
Level: *easy*
Section: *Java Server Pages*

86.   Tomcat   is a servlet processor that can work in conjunction with Apache.
Level: *easy*
Section: *Java Server Pages*
Subsection: *Apache Tomcat*

87.   MySQL   is an open source DBMS that runs on Unix, Linux, and Windows.
Level: *easy*
Section: *MySQL*

88.   Because of its limited transaction management and logging capabilities, MySQL is very fast for
        pure query applications.
Level: *moderate*
Section: *MySQL*

89.   While MySQL will correctly parse   foreign key   constraints, it will not execute them.
Level: *hard*
Section: *MySQL*
Subsection: *MySQL Limitations*

90.   In MySQL, surrogate keys that use a sequence maintained by MySQL should be given a data type
        of   AUTO_INCREMENT   .
Level: *hard*
Section: *MySQL*
Subsection: *Using MySQL*

91.   MySQL maintains metadata in the database named   mysql .
Level: *moderate*
Section: *MySQL*
Subsection: *Setting Access Permissions for JDBC Use*

92.   MySQL uses read and write locks at the __table__ level.
Level: *moderate*
Section: *MySQL*
Subsection: *Concurrency Control*

93.   With MySQL transaction rollback must be performed by the __application__.
Level: *hard*
Section: *MySQL*
Subsection: *Concurrency Control*

Essay Questions

94.   Distinguish among the four types of JDBC drivers.
Type 1 drivers are JDBC-ODBC bridge drivers that resolve some of the inconsistencies between Java and C/C++ to provide access to ODBC data sources from Java. Type 2 drivers are written wholly in Java, and they connect to the native-API of the DBMS. Type 3 and Type 4 drivers have network capabilities. Type 3 drivers transform JDBC calls into a DBMS-independent network protocol. Type 4 drivers transform JDBC calls into DBMS-specific network protocols.
Section: *JDBC*
Subsection: *Driver Types*

95.   Compare and contrast *servlets* and *applets*.
Servlets and applets are both Java programs compiled into machine-independent bytecode. Both are interpreted and executed by bytecode interpreters called Java virtual machines. Both are invoked using the HTTP protocol. Servlets, however, are interpreted and executed on the web server computer. It then sends its results to the user's computer via the response capabilities of HTTP. Applets, on the other hand, are interpreted and executed on the user's computer. The bytecode for the applet is transmitted via HTTP to the user's computer, where the Java virtual machine will interpret and execute it locally.
Section: *Open Database Connectivity (ODBC) Standard*
Subsection: *ODBC Architecture*

96.   Explain the process by which JSP pages are compiled.
All JSP pages are compiled into servlets. When a JSP page is requested, the servlet processor checks to see if the uncompiled version of the JSP page is older or newer than the compiled servlet. If the servlet is older than the uncompiled version of the JSP page, then the JSP page is parsed into standard Java source code and is recompiled into a new version of the servlet. This new version of the servlet is then loaded into memory. If the uncompiled version of the JSP page was created at or before the time of the current servlet, the servlet processor checks to see if the current servlet is already loaded into memory. If it is not, then the servlet is loaded. In either case, the servlet is then ready to be executed by the servlet processor.
Section: *Java Server Pages*
Subsection: *Setting Up Tomcat for JSP Processing*

97.   What is a Java bean?

A Java bean is a Java class that meets certain requirements. First, a Java bean has no public instance variables. Second, all persistent values are accessed through methods named getxxx and setxxx, where xxx is the name of the persistent value. The getxxx method is used to retrieve a persistent value, and the setxxx method is used to set the persistent value. Finally, the Java bean either has no constructor, or if it does have a constructor, the constructor is an explicitly defined zero-argument constructor.

Section: *Java Server Pages*
Subsection: *JSP Examples*

98.   What are some of the limitations of MySQL?

MySQL has limited support for transaction management and logging. It does not support views, stored procedures, or triggers. Although MySQL does correctly parse foreign key constraints, it does not execute those constraints. MySQL also has limited support for concurrency control. It does not support transactions, and therefore ca not rollback transactions or provide transaction isolation support. Finally, MySQL only issues locks at the table level, and requires an application to place all of its locks at once. This increases the amount of time during update transactions that the tables will effectively be single-user tables.

Section: *MySQL*
Subsection: *MySQL Limitations*

CHAPTER 17

Sharing Enterprise Data

True-False Questions

1. Teleprocessing systems split all processing between the server and the user's computer.
    Answer: False   *Level: moderate*
    Section: Enterprise Database Processing Architectures
    Subsection: Teleprocessing Systems

2. Teleprocessing systems generally have a graphical user interface.
    Answer: False   *Level: easy*
    Section: Enterprise Database Processing Architectures
    Subsection: Teleprocessing Systems

3. In a client-server system, there may be many database servers but each one processes a separate database.
    Answer: True   *Level: moderate*
    Section: Enterprise Database Processing Architectures
    Subsection: Client-Server Systems

4. In a client-server system, the server processes the application programs.
    Answer: False   *Level: moderate*
    Section: Enterprise Database Processing Architectures
    Subsection: Client-Server Systems

5. With a file-sharing system, each user's computer contains the DBMS.
    Answer: True   *Level: moderate*
    Section: Enterprise Database Processing Architectures
    Subsection: File-Sharing Systems

6. A file-sharing system generates more traffic on the network than does a client-server system.
    Answer: True   *Level: easy*
    Section: Enterprise Database Processing Architectures
    Subsection: File-Sharing Systems

7. In a partitioned, distributed database system, a vertical fragment refers to a table that is broken into two or more sets of columns.
    Answer: True   *Level: hard*
    Section: Enterprise Database Processing Architectures
    Subsection: Distributed Database Systems

8. A distributed database may be broken into vertical or horizontal partitions, but not both.
    Answer: False   *Level: hard*
    Section: Enterprise Database Processing Architectures

Subsection: Distributed Database Systems

9.   Of the different types of distributed database systems, the partitioned, replicated distributed
      database tends to offer the greatest flexibility.
      Answer: True   *Level: moderate*
      Section: Enterprise Database Processing Architectures
      Subsection: Distributed Database Systems

10.   The simplest type of distributed database processing is to allow multiple computers to update the
      data but designate one computer to resolve any conflicts.
      Answer: True   *Level: hard*
      Section: Enterprise Database Processing Architectures
      Subsection: Distributed Database Systems

11.   Downloaded data are typically downloaded, updated, and uploaded back to the database.
      Answer: False   *Level: moderate*
      Section: Downloading Data

12.   One potential problem with downloaded data is providing control against inconsistencies
      resulting from local updates.
      Answer: True   *Level: easy*
      Section: Downloading Data
      Subsection: Potential Problems in Processing Downloaded Databases

13.   An OLAP cube is limited to three dimensions.
      Answer: False   *Level: moderate*
      Section: On Line Analytic Processing (OLAP)

14.   OLAP uses extensions to SQL to define and process its data structures.
      Answer: True   *Level: hard*
      Section: On Line Analytic Processing (OLAP)

15.   In OLAP processing, a snowflake schema is faster but requires more storage space than a star
      schema.
      Answer: False   *Level: hard*
      Section: On Line Analytic Processing (OLAP)

16.   *MOLAP* is the term for the Microsoft solution to OLAP storage available in SQL Server.
      Answer: False   *Level: moderate*
      Section: On Line Analytic Processing (OLAP)

17.   The role of the data warehouse is to store extracts of operational data and make them available to
      users.
      Answer: True   *Level: easy*
      Section: Data Warehouses

18.   Some of the data in a data warehouse could have been purchased from other organizations.
      Answer: True   *Level: moderate*
      Section: Data Warehouses

19.   It is not necessary to store any metadata in the data warehouse.
        Answer: False   *Level: easy*
        Section: Data Warehouses
        Subsection: Components of a Data Warehouse

20.   The term *drill down* refers to the capability of seeing the data in smaller and smaller units.
        Answer: True   *Level: moderate*
        Section: Data Warehouses
        Subsection: Requirements for a Data Warehouse

21.   All data in the data warehouse are made consistent in timing and domain in the process of extraction.
        Answer: False   *Level: moderate*
        Section: Data Warehouses
        Subsection: Challenges for Data Warehouses

22.   Users generally want the capability of graphical output from a data warehouse.
        Answer: True   *Level: easy*
        Section: Data Warehouses
        Subsection: Challenges for Data Warehouses

23.   The term *data mart* is another name for the term *data warehouse*.
        Answer: False   *Level: moderate*
        Section: Data Warehouses
        Subsection: Data Marts

24.   A *data mart* may contain several data warehouses.
        Answer: False   *Level: easy*
        Section: Data Warehouses
        Subsection: Data Marts

25.   Data are an organizational asset, as are plant, equipment, and financial assets.
        Answer: True   *Level: easy*
        Section: Data Administration

26.   Organizational data consists only of text and numeric data.
        Answer: False   *Level: moderate*
        Section: Data Administration
        Subsection: Challenges for Data Administration

27.   The scope of data administration is the same as that of database administration.
        Answer: False   *Level: hard*
        Section: Data Administration
        Subsection: Challenges for Data Administration

28.   The data administration group is usually responsible for defining and maintaining the official organizational standard for all data items in the organization.
        Answer: False   *Level: moderate*
        Section: Data Administration
        Subsection: Functions of Data Administration

29.   Data administration is responsible for defining data security policies.
        Answer: True   *Level: easy*
        Section: Data Administration
        Subsection: Functions of Data Administration

30.   In general, data administration has the responsibility to resolve conflicts between user groups
        concerning data needs.
        Answer: True   *Level: easy*
        Section: Data Administration
        Subsection: Functions of Data Administration

Multiple Choice Questions

31.   Which of the following is <u>not</u> a type of multi-user database architecture?
        a.)   teleprocessing
        b.)   data warehouse
        c.)   file-server
        d.)   client-server
        e.)   distributed database

Level: hard
Section: *Enterprise Database Processing Architectures*

32.   A *teleprocessing system* is a multi-user database architecture in which:
        a.)   dumb terminals transmit data to a centralized computer
        b.)   one computer processes the database, and other computers in the network process
                application programs
        c.)   the DBMS as well as the application programs are stored on the users' computers
        d.)   part or all of the database is duplicated on more than one computer
        e.)   parts of the database are stored on more than one computer

Level: moderate
Section: *Enterprise Database Processing Architectures*
Subsection: *Teleprocessing Systems*

33.   Which of the following is characteristic of *teleprocessing systems*?
        a.)   interactive graphical user interfaces
        b.)   all processing performed on a single computer
        c.)   the DBMS is on a local computer
        d.)   different columns of a table may reside on different computers
        e.)   all of the above

Level: easy
Section: *Enterprise Database Processing Architectures*
Subsection: *Teleprocessing Systems*

34.   A *client-server system* is a multi-user database architecture in which:

      a.)   dumb terminals transmit data to a centralized computer

      b.)   one computer processes the database, and other computers in the network process application programs

      c.)   the DBMS as well as the application programs are stored on the users' computers

      d.)   part or all of the database is duplicated on more than one computer

      e.)   parts of the database are stored on more than one computer

Level: moderate
Section: Enterprise Database Processing Architectures
Subsection: Client-Server Systems

35.   Which of the following is true of client-server systems?

      a.)   Client-server systems make extensive use of dumb terminals.

      b.)   Client-server systems only request file-level services from the server.

      c.)   Client-server systems execute applications on the server.

      d.)   Client-server systems may have multiple database processing servers but each one processes a different database.

      e.)   All of the above are true of client-server systems.

Level: hard
Section: Enterprise Database Processing Architectures
Subsection: Client-Server Systems

36.   A *file-sharing system* is a multi-user database architecture in which:

      a.)   dumb terminals transmit data to a centralized computer

      b.)   one computer processes the database, and other computers in the network process application programs

      c.)   the DBMS as well as the application programs are stored on the users' computers

      d.)   part or all of the database is duplicated on more than one computer

      e.)   parts of the database are stored on more than one computer

Level: moderate
Section: Enterprise Database Processing Architectures
Subsection: File-Sharing Systems

37.   A partitioned system is a multi-user database architecture in which:

      a.)   dumb terminals transmit data to a centralized computer

      b.)   one computer processes the database, and other computers in the network process application programs

      c.)   the DBMS as well as the application programs are stored on the users' computers

      d.)   part or all of the database is duplicated on more than one computer

      e.)   parts of the database are stored on more than one computer

Level: moderate
Section: Enterprise Database Processing Architectures
Subsection: Distributed Database Systems

38.   A *vertical fragment* or *partition* refers to:
       a.)   the rows of a table when they are divided into pieces
       b.)   a table that is broken into two or more sets of columns
       c.)   a database downloaded in a file-sharing system
       d.)   the data measures held constant in a data cube
       e.)   the data elements sliced in a data cube

Level: easy
Section: Enterprise Database Processing Architectures
Subsection: Distributed Database Systems

39.   A *horizontal fragment* or *partition* refers to:
       a.)   the rows of a table when they are divided into pieces
       b.)   a table that is broken into two or more sets of columns
       c.)   a database downloaded in a file-sharing system
       d.)   the data measures held constant in a data cube
       e.)   the data elements sliced in a data cube

Level: easy
Section: Enterprise Database Processing Architectures
Subsection: Distributed Database Systems

40.   The greatest disadvantage of distributed databases is the:
       a.)   availability
       b.)   security risk
       c.)   cost/complexity
       d.)   difficulty of control and possible integrity problems
       e.)   flexibility

Level: moderate
Section: Enterprise Database Processing Architectures
Subsection: Distributed Database Systems

41.   The greatest advantage of distributed databases is the:
       a.)   availability
       b.)   security risk
       c.)   cost/complexity
       d.)   difficulty of control and possible integrity problems
       e.)   flexibility

Level: moderate
Section: Enterprise Database Processing Architectures
Subsection: Distributed Database Systems

42.   Which of the following is the simplest type of distributed database processing?
    a.)   **downloading read-only data**
    b.)   distributed update conflict
    c.)   teleprocessing
    d.)   allow updates on multiple computers with a single computer for conflict resolution
    e.)   allow updates on multiple computers with multiple computers for conflict resolution

Level: moderate
Section: Enterprise Database Processing Architectures
Subsection: Distributed Database Systems

43.   Read-only data downloaded from a distributed database processing system is called a(n) _____ in Oracle.
    a.)   distributed read
    b.)   snapshot
    c.)   distributed view
    d.)   read view
    e.)   **materialized view**

Level: hard
Section: Enterprise Database Processing Architectures
Subsection: Distributed Database Systems

44.   Read-only data downloaded from a distributed database processing system is called a(n) _____ in SQL Server.
    a.)   distributed read
    b.)   **snapshot**
    c.)   distributed view
    d.)   read view
    e.)   materialized view

Level: hard
Section: Enterprise Database Processing Architectures
Subsection: Distributed Database Systems

45.   Which of the following is an advantage of downloaded data?
    a.)   data consistency is improved
    b.)   coordination of updating and downloading data is improved
    c.)   **data is closer to the user**
    d.)   less opportunity for computer crimes
    e.)   easier to control access to data

Level: easy
Section: Downloading Data
Subsection: Potential Problems in Processing Downloaded Databases

46.   If downloading data occurs in the morning, which of the following is most likely to be true in the afternoon?
    a.)   the organizational database is current and downloaded data are current
    b.)   the organizational database is current and downloaded data are out of date
    c.)   the organizational database is out of date and downloaded data are current
    d.)   the organizational database is out of date and downloaded data are out of date
    e.)   it depends on the method used for downloading

Level: moderate
Section: Downloading Data
Subsection: Potential Problems in Processing Downloaded Databases

47.   In an OLAP cube, the attributes on an axis are called:
    a.)   levels
    b.)   dimensions
    c.)   measures
    d.)   members
    e.)   slices

Level: hard
Section: On Line Analytic Processing (OLAP)

48.   The dimension(s) that are held constant in an OLAP cube are called:
    a.)   axes
    b.)   levels
    c.)   measures
    d.)   members
    e.)   slices

Level: hard
Section: On Line Analytic Processing (OLAP)

49.   The values of a dimension in an OLAP cube are called:
    a.)   axes
    b.)   levels
    c.)   measures
    d.)   members
    e.)   slices

Level: hard
Section: On Line Analytic Processing (OLAP)

50.   The OLAP schema in which every dimension table is adjacent to the table storing the measure
        values and the tables may or may not be normalized is called a(n) _____.
        a.)   snowflake
        b.)   network
        c.)   star
        d.)   tree
        e.)   ring

Level: *moderate*
Section: *On Line Analytic Processing (OLAP)*

51.   Which of the following is an OLAP storage alternative that advocates the use of both relational
        DBMS products and specialized OLAP engines?
        a.)   HOLAP
        b.)   COLAP
        c.)   MOLAP
        d.)   ROLAP
        e.)   TOLAP

Level: *moderate*
Section: *On Line Analytic Processing (OLAP)*

52.   Which of the following OLAP storage alternatives provides the fastest performance?
        a.)   HOLAP
        b.)   COLAP
        c.)   MOLAP
        d.)   ROLAP
        e.)   TOLAP

Level: *moderate*
Section: *On Line Analytic Processing (OLAP)*

53.   A data warehouse is a store of enterprise data designed to:
        a.)   support transaction processing
        b.)   facilitate management decision making
        c.)   hold backup files in case the system needs to be recovered
        d.)   hold test data for developers to use when creating new applications
        e.)   hold old data that may be used for long-term analysis

Level: *easy*
Section: *Data Warehouses*

54.   The term *drill down* means the user wants to:
        a.)   summarize data
        b.)   get older data
        c.)   sort
        d.)   get more details
        e.)   aggregate data

Level: easy
Section: Data Warehouses
Subsection: Requirements for a Data Warehouse

55.   Data in a data warehouse may be inconsistent because of differences in the:
        a.)   attributes
        b.)   domains
        c.)   indexes
        d.)   rows
        e.)   tables

Level: moderate
Section: Data Warehouses
Subsection: Challenges for Data Warehouses

55.   A *data mart* differs from a data warehouse in that the:
        a.)   data mart has a smaller scope
        b.)   data mart may be restricted to a particular type of data
        c.)   data mart may be restricted to a particular business function
        d.)   data mart may be restricted to a particular business unit or location
        e.)   all of the above

Level: easy
Section: Data Warehouses
Subsection: Data Marts

56.   Protecting and ensuring effective use of the entire organization's data is the responsibility of the:
        a.)   office of data administration
        b.)   database administrator
        c.)   developers
        d.)   end users
        e.)   vendors

Level: easy
Section: Data Administration

57. Which of the following is <u>not</u> within the function of data administration?
    a.)   conflict resolution
    b.)   data policies
    c.)   data standards
    d.)   marketing data administration services
    e.)   all of the above <u>are</u> within the function of data administration

Level: *moderate*
Section: *Data Administration*
Subsection: *Functions of Data Administration*

58. A *data proponent* is in charge of:
    a.)   developers
    b.)   data administration
    c.)   data items
    d.)   the database
    e.)   the database administrator

Level: *moderate*
Section: *Data Administration*
Subsection: *Functions of Data Administration*

59. Resolving conflicts among user groups about data is the responsibility of:
    a.)   developers
    b.)   data administration
    c.)   data items
    d.)   users
    e.)   database administrator

Level: *easy*
Section: *Data Administration*
Subsection: *Functions of Data Administration*

60. Data administration should have a(n) _____ attitude towards information managemer
    a.)   ad hoc
    b.)   authoritative
    c.)   managerial
    d.)   proactive
    e.)   reactive

Level: *easy*
Section: *Data Administration*
Subsection: *Functions of Data Administration*

Fill in the Blank Questions

61.   A(n) __teleprocessing__ system is a multi-user database system that uses one computer and one CPU.
Level: moderate
Section: Enterprise Database Processing Architectures
Subsection: Teleprocessing Systems

62.   A system in which one computer processes the database and other computers in the network process application programs is called a(n) __client-server__ system.
Level: moderate
Section: Enterprise Database Processing Architectures
Subsection: Client-Server Systems

63.   A system in which the DBMS as well as the application programs are stored on the users' computers is called a(n) __file-sharing__ system.
Level: moderate
Section: Enterprise Database Processing Architectures
Subsection: File-Sharing Systems

64.   A system in which part or all of the database is duplicated on more than one computer is known as a(n) __replicated__ distributed database system.
Level: hard
Section: Enterprise Database Processing Architectures
Subsection: Distributed Database Systems

65.   A system in which parts of the database are stored on more than one computer is known as a(n) __partitioned__ distributed database system.
Level: hard
Section: Enterprise Database Processing Architectures
Subsection: Distributed Database Systems

66.   A(n) __vertical fragment__ refers to a table that is broken into two or more sets of columns.
Level: moderate
Section: Enterprise Database Processing Architectures
Subsection: Distributed Database Systems

67.   A(n) __horizontal fragment__ refers to the rows of a table when they are divided into pieces.
Level: moderate
Section: Enterprise Database Processing Architectures
Subsection: Distributed Database Systems

68.   SQL Server uses the term __snapshot__ to refer to read-only data that has been downloaded.
Level: hard
Section: Enterprise Database Processing Architectures
Subsection: Distributed Database Systems

69.   Downloaded read-only data that is sent to multiple computers for processing is referred to as
        __materialized views__ by Oracle.
Level: hard
Section: Enterprise Database Processing Architectures
Subsection: Distributed Database Systems

70.   To address the problem of providing atomic transactions in a distributed environment, an
        algorithm called __two-phased commit__ is used to provisionally commit updates pending
        notification from the distributed transaction manager.
Level: moderate
Section: Enterprise Database Processing Architectures
Subsection: Distributed Database Systems

71.   Downloaded data typically cannot be updated because once they are removed from the
        operational database they are no longer subject to __concurrency control__.
Level: easy
Section: Downloading Data

72.   When a user changes downloaded data, the data is no longer __consistent__ with the corporate
        database and also with other users who have downloaded the data.
Level: easy
Section: Downloading Data
Subsection: Potential Problems in Processing Downloaded Databases

73.   Downloading creates problems with __access control__, meaning it necessitates placing
        restrictions on which data each employee may create, delete, read, or update.
Level: moderate
Section: Downloading Data
Subsection: Potential Problems in Processing Downloaded Databases

74.   Since OLAP places no limits on the number of axes an OLAP cube can have, the term OLAP
        __hypercube__ is sometimes used instead of "cube."
Level: easy
Section: On Line Analytic Processing (OLAP)

75.   Both the columns and the rows of an OLAP cube are called __axes__.
Level: moderate
Section: On Line Analytic Processing (OLAP)

76.   The attributes that appear on an axis of an OLAP cube are called __dimensions__ of the cube.
Level: hard
Section: On Line Analytic Processing (OLAP)

77.   The cells of an OLAP cube represent the __measures__ of the cube, which are the data values to
        be displayed.
Level: moderate
Section: On Line Analytic Processing (OLAP)

78.   The values of a dimension of an OLAP cube are called __members__ .
Level: *hard*
Section: *On Line Analytic Processing (OLAP)*

79.   The position of a dimension in its hierarchy is called its __level__ .
Level: *moderate*
Section: *On Line Analytic Processing (OLAP)*

80.   An OLAP __star__ schema has every dimension table adjacent to the table storing the measure values and the tables may or may not be normalized.
Level: *hard*
Section: *On Line Analytic Processing (OLAP)*

81.   An OLAP __snowflake__ schema can have multi-levels of tables and all the tables will be normalized.
Level: *hard*
Section: *On Line Analytic Processing (OLAP)*

82.   __ROLAP__ is an OLAP storage alternative that uses relational DBMS products.
Level: *easy*
Section: *On Line Analytic Processing (OLAP)*

83.   A(n) __data warehouse__ is a store of enterprise data that is designed to facilitate management decision making.
Level: *easy*
Section: *Data Warehouses*

84.   Getting more detailed information, or disaggregating, from a data warehouse is called __drilling down__ .
Level: *easy*
Section: *Data Warehouses*
Subsection: *Requirements for a Data Warehouse*

85.   Summarizing or grouping data is known as data __aggregation__ .
Level: *easy*
Section: *Data Warehouses*
Subsection: *Requirements for a Data Warehouse*

86.   __Ad hoc__ queries are those that are not of a regular, recurring, pre-planned nature.
Level: *moderate*
Section: *Data Warehouses*
Subsection: *Challenges for Data Warehouses*

87.   A(n) __data mart__ is a facility like a data warehouse but for a much smaller domain.
Level: *easy*
Section: *Data Warehouses*
Subsection: *Data Marts*

88.   __Data__ are an important organizational asset, as are plant, equipment, and financial assets.
Level: *easy*
Section: *Data Administration*
Subsection: *Challenges for Data Warehouses*

89.   The scope of the office of data administration is the __entire organization__ .
Level: *moderate*
Section: *Data Administration*
Subsection: *Challenges for Data Administration*

90.   A(n) __data proponent__ is the organizational unit in charge of managing the standard for a specific data item.
Level: *moderate*
Section: *Data Administration*
Subsection: *Functions of Data Administration*

91.   The office of data administration must have a(n) __proactive__ attitude toward information management.
Level: *moderate*
Section: *Data Administration*
Subsection: *Functions of Data Administration*

Essay Questions

92.   Distinguish among teleprocessing systems, file-sharing systems, client-server systems, and distributed database systems.
Teleprocessing systems perform all database and application processing on a single computer with the use of a dumb terminal to display results to the user. File-sharing systems place the database on a shared storage device, but all database and application processing take place on the user's computer. Client-server systems split the processing between the client and the server. In this architecture, the server processes the database and the client processes the application. Finally, the distributed database system processes the application on the client computer, and distributes the processing of a single database among a number of different database servers.
Section: *Enterprise Database Processing Architectures*

93.   Briefly describe the different types of distributed database systems and the continuum of advantages and disadvantages.
The different types of systems - nonpartitioned nonreplicated databases, partitioned nonreplicated databases, nonpartitioned replicated databases, and partitioned replicated databases – create a continuum. A partitioned database has tables or parts of tables split up across a number of different sites. A replicated database has copies of tables or parts of tables spread across a number of different sites. Along the continuum of distributed databases, systems toward the nonpartitioned nonreplicated databases end are the least flexible, provide the least data availability, and the least independence. Systems on the partitioned replicated databases end have the highest cost, pose the greatest security risks, and are the most difficult to control.
Section: *Enterprise Database Processing Architectures*
Subsection: *Distributed Database Systems*

94.   Briefly describe the three distributed processing techniques.
        The simplest type of distributed processing is the download of read-only data. This downloaded data can be used for queries and reports only. The next type of distributed processing is to allow multiple computers to make requests to update data, but a single computer within the system performs all of the actual update processing. With this technique, updated data is periodically forwarded back to all of the distributed systems to synchronize the databases. Finally, a distributed processing alternative is to allow multiple computers to handle the update processing. In this case, a single computer is designated to resolve conflicts that may arise.
        Section: *Enterprise Database Processing Architectures*
        Subsection: *Distributed Database Systems*

95.   Distinguish among ROLAP, MOLAP, and HOLAP.
        ROLAP, MOLAP, and HOLAP describe alternative methods for OLAP storage. ROLAP, or relational OLAP, is the application of traditional relational DBMS technology to OLAP storage. MOLAP, or multidimensional OLAP, is the development of specially designed engines to handle the specific requirements of OLAP. HOLAP, or hybrid OLAP, is the use of both relational DBMS products and specially designed OLAP engines. ROLAP takes advantage of existing technologies and uses the least storage, but provides the slowest performance. MOLAP provides the fastest performance but requires the most storage. HOLAP is a compromise between ROLAP and MOLAP and provides fast performance for high-level processing but is slower on detail processing.
        Section: *On Line Analytic Processing (OLAP)*

96.   Distinguish between data warehouses and data marts.
        The primary difference between data warehouses and data marts is one of scope. Data warehouses have an organization-wide scope. Data marts are more restrictive. Data marts can be restricted to a specific type of data, a specific business function, or a specific business unit or geographic location. The smaller scope of data marts simplifies several issues regarding data inconsistencies and management.
        Section: *Data Warehouses*
        Subsection: *Data Marts*

CHAPTER 18

Object-Oriented Database Processing

True-False Questions

1.   Object-oriented programming is almost identical to traditional programming.
Answer: False   *Level: easy*
Section: A Sketch of Object-Oriented Programming

2.   *Object-oriented programming* is organized around data first and logic second.
Answer: True   *Level: moderate*
Section: A Sketch of Object-Oriented Programming

3.   With OOP, an object needs to know the structure of all the other objects.
Answer: False   *Level: easy*
Section: A Sketch of Object-Oriented Programming
Subsection: OOP Terminology

4.   The external appearance of an object is known as its *interface*.
Answer: True   *Level: moderate*
Section: A Sketch of Object-Oriented Programming
Subsection: OOP Terminology

5.   The encapsulated internals of an object are referred to as its *polymorphism*.
Answer: False   *Level: moderate*
Section: A Sketch of Object-Oriented Programming
Subsection: OOP Terminology

6.   An OOP object can invoke methods of other objects but can execute only the methods it contains.
Answer: True   *Level: moderate*
Section: A Sketch of Object-Oriented Programming
Subsection: OOP Terminology

7.   OOP objects interact by setting each other's attributes.
Answer: False   *Level: easy*
Section: A Sketch of Object-Oriented Programming
Subsection: OOP Terminology

8.   A class is said to *inherit* all the properties of its subclass.
Answer: False   *Level: easy*
Section: A Sketch of Object-Oriented Programming
Subsection: OOP Terminology

9.   The characteristic that allows different objects and subclass objects to have methods of the same name but perform differently is called *polymorphism*.

Answer: True   Level: hard
Section: A Sketch of Object-Oriented Programming
Subsection: OOP Terminology

10.   The logical structure of an object is called an *object class*.
       Answer: True   Level: easy
       Section: A Sketch of Object-Oriented Programming
       Subsection: OOP Terminology

11.   A *transient object* is one that can be passed from one program to another.
       Answer: False   Level: hard
       Section: A Sketch of Object-Oriented Programming
       Subsection: OOP Terminology

12.   A *persistent object* is one that survives the end of execution of a program, and is saved to
       permanent storage.
       Answer: True   Level: easy
       Section: A Sketch of Object-Oriented Programming
       Subsection: OOP Terminology

13.   The methods for a persistent object class are stored in each object instance.
       Answer: False   Level: hard
       Section: A Sketch of Object-Oriented Programming
       Subsection: OOP Terminology

14.   The purpose of an ODBMS is to provide persistent object storage.
       Answer: True   Level: easy
       Section: A Sketch of Object-Oriented Programming
       Subsection: OOP Terminology

15.   A subclass object can have a method that overrides the method of the same name in the base
       class.
       Answer: True   Level: hard
       Section: A Sketch of Object-Oriented Programming
       Subsection: OOP Terminology

16.   A *callback* is an OOP statement in which an object gives a pointer to itself to another object.
       Answer: True   Level: moderate
       Section: OOP Example

17.   The process of transforming permanent object identifiers into in-memory addresses is called
       swizzling.
       Answer: True   Level: moderate
       Section: Object Persistence

18.   In most OOP languages, a pointer is some form of disk storage media location.
       Answer: False   Level: moderate
       Section: Object Persistence

19.   An object cannot be made persistent using traditional file storage techniques.

Answer: False   *Level: easy*
Section: Object Persistence

20.   Traditional file storage is viable for storing persistent objects only if there are just a few objects
      and those objects have a simple, stable structure.
      Answer: True   *Level: moderate*
      Section: Object Persistence
      Subsection: Object Persistence Using Traditional File Storage

21.   An object method can be stored as a memo field in a table of a relational DBMS.
      Answer: True   *Level: moderate*
      Section: Object Persistence
      Subsection: Object Persistence Using Relational DBMS

22.   When using a relational DBMS to make an object persistent, it is possible to delete one side of a
      many-to-many relationship without deleting the other side.
      Answer: True   *Level: hard*
      Section: Object Persistence
      Subsection: Object Persistence Using Relational DBMS

23.   ODBMS automatically create file and data structures to store objects.
      Answer: True   *Level: moderate*
      Section: Object Persistence
      Subsection: Object Persistence Using ODBMS

24.   With ODBMS, the programmer must ensure that an object is located in memory before
      attempting to access its attributes so that swizzling can be completed first.
      Answer: False   *Level: moderate*
      Section: Object Persistence
      Subsection: Object Persistence Using ODBMS

25.   Relational databases that have been extended to include support for persistent objects are referred
      to as *relational-object* databases.
      Answer: False   *Level: hard*
      Section: Object Persistence Using Oracle

26.   Currently, Oracle supports the use of object types as table columns, but support for object
      collections is still missing.
      Answer: False   *Level: moderate*
      Section: Object Persistence Using Oracle
      Subsection: Object Types and Collections

27.   With Oracle, UPDATE and DELETE statements can be used to manipulate rows in a *variable
      length array*.
      Answer: False   *Level: moderate*
      Section: Object Persistence Using Oracle
      Subsection: Object Types and Collections

28.   With Oracle, nested table data is stored in a table separate from the table in which it is defined.
      Answer: True   *Level: hard*

Section: Object Persistence Using Oracle
Subsection: Object Types and Collections

29.   In the proposed SQL3 standard, users can define an *abstract data type* that is equivalent to an
      OOP object.
      Answer: True   *Level: moderate*
      Section: ODBMS Standards
      Subsection: SQL3

30.   The proposed SQL3 standard supports inheritance of columns in tables.
      Answer: True   *Level: hard*
      Section: ODBMS Standards
      Subsection: SQL3

31.   One advantage of the ODMG-93 standard is that all objects are mutable, that is, they can be
      changed.
      Answer: False   *Level: moderate*
      Section: ODBMS Standards
      Subsection: ODMG-93

32.   The proposed ODMG-93 standard arises out of the context of object programming.
      Answer: True   *Level: easy*
      Section: ODBMS Standards
      Subsection: ODMG-93

Multiple Choice Questions

33.   Object-oriented programming is organized around:
      a.)   data only
      b.)   logic only
      c.)   data first and logic second
      d.)   logic first and data second
      e.)   depends on the application

Level: moderate
Section: A Sketch of Object-Oriented Programming

34.   When developing an object-oriented program, the first step is to:
      a.)   develop a flowchart of the logic
      b.)   develop pseudocode for the logic
      c.)   select the data elements involved
      d.)   identify the objects involved
      e.)   determine the relationships involved

Level: easy
Section: A Sketch of Object-Oriented Programming

35.   The *external* appearance of an object is known as its:
    a.)   attributes
    b.)   encapsulated structure
    c.)   implementation
    d.)   interface
    e.)   methods

Level: *moderate*
Section: *A Sketch of Object-Oriented Programming*
Subsection: *OOP Terminology*

36.   The *internals* of an object are known as its:
    a.)   attributes
    b.)   encapsulated structure
    c.)   implementation
    d.)   interface
    e.)   methods

Level: *moderate*
Section: *A Sketch of Object-Oriented Programming*
Subsection: *OOP Terminology*

37.   Which characteristic of an OOP object deals with the fact that it is complete in itself?
    a.)   implementation
    b.)   interface
    c.)   polymorphism
    d.)   encapsulation
    e.)   inheritance

Level: *easy*
Section: *A Sketch of Object-Oriented Programming*
Subsection: *OOP Terminology*

38.   The sequences of instructions an object executes are known as its:
    a.)   attributes
    b.)   encapsulated structure
    c.)   implementation
    d.)   interface
    e.)   methods

Level: *easy*
Section: *A Sketch of Object-Oriented Programming*
Subsection: *OOP Terminology*

39.   The *logical structure* of an object is known as its:
       a.)   attributes
       b.)   implementation
       c.)   methods
       d.)   object class
       e.)   object instance

Level: easy
Section: A Sketch of Object-Oriented Programming
Subsection: OOP Terminology

40.   The characteristic when a subclass object contains the attributes and methods of its base class
       object is known as:
       a.)   encapsulation
       b.)   inheritance
       c.)   persistence
       d.)   polymorphism
       e.)   transience

Level: easy
Section: A Sketch of Object-Oriented Programming
Subsection: OOP Terminology

41.   The characteristic when a subclass object has a method that overrides the method of the same
       name in its base class object is known as:
       a.)   encapsulation
       b.)   inheritance
       c.)   persistence
       d.)   polymorphism
       e.)   transience

Level: moderate
Section: A Sketch of Object-Oriented Programming
Subsection: OOP Terminology

42.   An object that exists only in volatile memory during the execution of a program and is lost at the
       end of execution is called:
       a.)   encapsulated
       b.)   inherited
       c.)   persistent
       d.)   polymorphic
       e.)   transient

Level: moderate
Section: A Sketch of Object-Oriented Programming
Subsection: OOP Terminology

43.   An object that survives after the execution of a program is called:
        a.)   encapsulated
        b.)   inherited
        c.)   persistent
        d.)   polymorphic
        e.)   transient

Level: *easy*
Section: *A Sketch of Object-Oriented Programming*
Subsection: *OOP Terminology*

44.   In most OOP languages, objects may contain pointers, which are:
        a.)   an in-memory address
        b.)   persistent methods
        c.)   transient attributes
        d.)   encapsulated structures
        e.)   swizzles

Level: *moderate*
Section: *Object Persistence*

45.   The process of transforming permanent identifiers into in-memory addresses is called:
        a.)   calling back
        b.)   inheritance
        c.)   persistence
        d.)   swizzling
        e.)   transience

Level: *easy*
Section: *Object Persistence*

46.   Which technique for implementing object persistence places the greatest burden on the
        programmer?
        a.)   ODBMS
        b.)   relational DBMS
        c.)   traditional file storage
        d.)   direct pointers
        e.)   indirect pointers

Level: *easy*
Section: *Object Persistence*
Subsection: *Object Persistence Using Traditional File Storage*

47.   Which of the following is <u>not</u> a problem with object persistence in traditional file storage?
        a.)   implementing swizzling algorithms
        b.)   implementing de-swizzling algorithms
        c.)   creating data structures
        d.)   manipulating foreign keys to create relationships
        e.)   bootstrapping read methods

Level: hard
Section: Object Persistence
Subsection: Object Persistence Using Traditional File Storage

48.   Which technique for implementing object persistence stores methods as memo type fields?
        a.)   ODBMS
        b.)   relational DBMS
        c.)   traditional file storage
        d.)   direct pointers
        e.)   indirect pointers

Level: moderate
Section: Object Persistence
Subsection: Object Persistence Using Relational DBMS

49.   Which of the following is <u>not</u> a task that must be performed by the developer when using a
        relational DBMS for object persistence?
        a.)   swizzling
        b.)   create SQL code
        c.)   define relational data structures
        d.)   manage file space
        e.)   embed SQL in programs

Level: hard
Section: Object Persistence
Subsection: Object Persistence Using Relational DBMS

50.   Which technique for implementing object persistence makes it unnecessary for the program and
        the programmer to know whether an object is in volatile or permanent memory?
        a.)   ODBMS
        b.)   relational DBMS
        c.)   traditional file storage
        d.)   direct pointers
        e.)   indirect pointers

Level: moderate
Section: Object Persistence
Subsection: Object Persistence Using Relational DBMS

51.   Which of the following is a task that must be handled by the developer when using ODBM to handle object persistence?
        a.)   define data structures
        b.)   find objects on demand
        c.)   invoke ODBMS Save methods
        d.)   pack and unpack objects into file structures
        e.)   all of the above

Level: moderate
Section: Object Persistence
Subsection: Object Persistence Using Relational DBMS

52.   In Oracle, a TYPE created to represent an object can be used in any of the following ways except:
        a.)   nested tables
        b.)   variable length arrays
        c.)   semantic objects
        d.)   column objects
        e.)   row objects

Level: moderate
Section: Object Persistence Using Oracle
Subsection: Object Types and Collections

53.   The use of an Oracle object type to define a table column is called a:
        a.)   column array
        b.)   variable length array
        c.)   column object
        d.)   nested table
        e.)   none of the above

Level: easy
Section: Object Persistence Using Oracle
Subsection: Object Types and Collections

54.   When working with objects in Oracle, which of the following is true of a REF data type?
        a.)   REF is the same as a foreign key.
        b.)   REF points to an object not a table row.
        c.)   REFs require cascade updates.
        d.)   REFs represent a two-way relationship.
        e.)   all of the above

Level: hard
Section: Object Persistence Using Oracle
Subsection: Oracle Objects

55.   Which of the following is <u>not</u> an advantage of ODBMS for object persistence?
  a.)   ODBMS automatically create persistent object Ids.
  b.)   Method storage and management are automatic.
  c.)   Relationships are defined outside of context.
  d.)   ODBMS provide single-level memory.
  e.)   ODBMS are integrated in object-oriented programming languages.

Level: hard
Section: Object Persistence Using Oracle

56.   In the proposed SQL3 standard, users can define a(n) _____ that is equivalent to an OOP
        object.
  a.)   abstract data type
  b.)   column
  c.)   OID
  d.)   row identifier
  e.)   subtable

Level: moderate
Section: ODBMS Standards
Subsection: SQL3

57.   Which of the following is <u>not</u> true of ADTs in SQL3?
  a.)   ADTs have methods.
  b.)   ADTs are always persistent.
  c.)   ADTs can be used in SQL expressions.
  d.)   ADTs can be stored in a table.
  e.)   ADTs can be subtypes of other ADTs.

Level: moderate
Section: ODBMS Standards
Subsection: SQL3

58.   Which of the following is true of Value ADTs in SQL3?
  a.)   They are assigned an OID.
  b.)   They cannot exist except in the context in which they are created.
  c.)   They cannot be created as a column in a table.
  d.)   They cannot be created in a function.
  e.)   All of the above are true.

Level: hard
Section: ODBMS Standards
Subsection: SQL3

59.   Which type of SQL3 table has no duplicate rows?
        a.)   OID
        b.)   Set
        c.)   Multiset
        d.)   Identity
        e.)   ADT

Level: hard
Section: ODBMS Standards
Subsection: SQL3

60.   In the proposed SQL3 standard, a subtable inherits all of the _____ of its supertable.
        a.)   abstract data types
        b.)   columns
        c.)   extents
        d.)   OIDs
        e.)   row identifiers

Level: moderate
Section: ODBMS Standards
Subsection: SQL3

61.   In the proposed ODMG-93 standard, a(n) _____ object can be changed.
        a.)   extensible
        b.)   immutable
        c.)   mutable
        d.)   subtable
        e.)   supertable

Level: moderate
Section: ODBMS Standards
Subsection: ODMG-93

62.   In the proposed ODMG-93 standard, all of the instances of an object class are called the object's
        _____ .
        a.)   abstract data types
        b.)   attributes
        c.)   extent
        d.)   OID
        e.)   subtables

Level: hard
Section: ODBMS Standards
Subsection: ODMG-93

Fill in the Blank Questions

63.   __Object-oriented programming (OOP)__ is organized around data first and logic second.
Level: easy
Section: A Sketch of Object-Oriented Programming

64.   An OOP object is an __encapsulated__ structure.
Level: easy
Section: A Sketch of Object-Oriented Programming
Subsection: OOP Terminology

65.   An OOP object contains __methods__ , which are sequences of instructions the object executes.
Level: easy
Section: A Sketch of Object-Oriented Programming
Subsection: OOP Terminology

66.   The external appearance of an object is referred to as its __interface__ .
Level: moderate
Section: A Sketch of Object-Oriented Programming
Subsection: OOP Terminology

67.   The encapsulated internals of an object are referred to as its __implementation__ .
Level: moderate
Section: A Sketch of Object-Oriented Programming
Subsection: OOP Terminology

68.   A subclass __inherits__ all the attributes and methods of its general class.
Level: easy
Section: A Sketch of Object-Oriented Programming
Subsection: OOP Terminology

69.   __Polymorphism__ is the name for the characteristic where a subclass object has a method that overrides the method of the same name in the base class.
Level: hard
Section: A Sketch of Object-Oriented Programming
Subsection: OOP Terminology

70.   The logical structure of an object is called a(n) __object class__ .
Level: easy
Section: A Sketch of Object-Oriented Programming
Subsection: OOP Terminology

71.   A(n) __transient__ object exists only in volatile memory during the execution of a program.
Level: moderate
Section: A Sketch of Object-Oriented Programming
Subsection: OOP Terminology

72.   A(n) __persistent__ object is an object that has been saved to permanent storage, such as disk media.
Level: easy
Section: A Sketch of Object-Oriented Programming
Subsection: OOP Terminology

73.   A(n) __callback__ is an OOP statement in which an object gives the pointer to itself to another object.
Level: hard
Section: OOP Example

74.   The process of transforming permanent identifiers into in-memory addresses is called __swizzling__.
Level: easy
Section: Object Persistence

75.   Objects can be saved using traditional file storage, but doing so places a large burden on the __programmer__.
Level: moderate
Section: Object Persistence
Subsection: Object Persistence Using Traditional File Storage

76.   An object method can be stored as a(n) __memo__ type field in a table of a relational database.
Level: moderate
Section: Object Persistence
Subsection: Object Persistence Using Relational DBMS

77.   When saving persistent objects in a relational DBMS, the most common way of using foreign keys to make persistent relationships is to code the creation of unique IDs in the object's __constructor__ method.
Level: hard
Section: Object Persistence
Subsection: Object Persistence Using Relational DBMS

78.   The characteristic of some ODBMS products that makes it unnecessary for the program and the programmer to know whether an object is in volatile or permanent memory is called __single-level__ memory.
Level: hard
Section: Object Persistence
Subsection: Object Persistence Using ODBMS

79.   Relational DBMS that have been extended to include support for persistent objects are often called __object-relational__ databases.
Level: moderate
Section: Object Persistence Using Oracle

80.   To develop persistent storage for objects in Oracle you first create a(n) __Type__ that represents the object.
Level: moderate
Section: Object Persistence Using Oracle
Subsection: Object Types and Collections

81.   The simplest way to use an object type in Oracle is as a(n) __column object__, which is to use the object type to define a table column.
Level: moderate
Section: Object Persistence Using Oracle
Subsection: Object Types and Collections

82.   In Oracle, to update or delete individual rows in a(n) __variable length array__ you have to write a PL/SQL procedure to loop through it.
Level: hard
Section: Object Persistence Using Oracle
Subsection: Object Types and Collections

83.   In Oracle, a(n) __nested table__ is similar to a variable length array except the data is stored in a separate table.
Level: hard
Section: Object Persistence Using Oracle
Subsection: Object Types and Collections

84.   In Oracle, a(n) __row object__ is simply a table that contains only objects.
Level: moderate
Section: Object Persistence Using Oracle
Subsection: Object Types and Collections

85.   One advantage to using ODBMS for object persistence is that the developer defines relationships in __context__ and the ODBMS creates the appropriate data structures to store it.
Level: moderate
Section: Object Persistence Using Oracle

86.   In the proposed SQL3 standard, users can define a(n) __abstract data type__ that is equivalent to an OOP object.
Level: moderate
Section: ODBMS Standards
Subsection: SQL3

87.   In the proposed SQL3 standard, every object definition is assigned an identifier called a(n) __OID__.
Level: moderate
Section: ODBMS Standards
Subsection: SQL3

88.   In the proposed SQL3 standard, a(n) __value__ ADT does not have an OID and cannot exist other than in the context in which it was created.
Level: moderate
Section: ODBMS Standards
Subsection: SQL3

89.   In the proposed SQL3 standard, every row in a table has a(n) __row identifier__ automatically.
Level: hard
Section: ODBMS Standards
Subsection: SQL3

90.   In the proposed SQL3 standard, a subtable inherits all of the __columns__ of its supertable.
Level: moderate
Section: ODBMS Standards
Subsection: SQL3

91.   In the proposed ODMG-93 standard, a(n) __mutable__ object can be changed.
Level: moderate
Section: ODBMS Standards
Subsection: ODMG-93

92.   In the proposed ODMG-93 standard, all of the instances of an object class are called the object's __extent__ .
Level: hard
Section: ODBMS Standards
Subsection: ODMG-93

Essay Questions

93.   Distinguish among an object class, an object class library, and an object instance.
An object class library, an object class, and an object instance create a hierarchy of object structures. The logical structure of an object, its attributes and methods, is the object class. A group of object classes are called an object class library. A particular instance of an object class is an object instance. Therefore, an object class library contains object classes, and object classes contain object instances.
Section: *A Sketch of Object-Oriented Programming*
Subsection: *OOP Terminology*

94.   What is *swizzling*, and why is it done?
Swizzling is the process of transforming permanent identifiers into in-memory addresses. Swizzling is necessary as a part of making objects persistent. Objects can contain pointers to other objects. These pointers are references to in-memory locations that may be different each time an object is loaded into memory. In saving a persistent object, these pointers must be changed to references to a permanent object identifier. When loading the persistent object from storage back into memory, swizzling is the process of changing these references to the permanent object identifiers into references to the correct in-memory address for the current location of the object in memory.
Section: *Object Persistence*

95.   Describe how object persistence is implemented using traditional file storage, a relational DBMS, and an ODBMS.

Using traditional file storage for object persistence places the greatest burden on the programmer. With file storage, the programmer must create the data structures, write code to save and load objects, perform swizzling, find objects, and manage unused space. Using a relational DBMS product for object persistence requires the developer to create relational structures that will hold the object structures, perform swizzling, and write and embed SQL commands to store and retrieve objects. Using an ODBMS places the lightest burden on the developer. Since ODBMS are integrated with OOP languages, data structures are created automatically and swizzling is done automatically. The developer merely has to invoke the ODBMS to save and retrieve objects.
***Section:** Object Persistence*

96.   What are the four ways that an object type can be used in an Oracle relation?

An object type can be used in a relation in Oracle in four different ways. First, it can be used as a column object. A column object uses an object type to define a column in a table. Second, it can be used as a variable length array. Third, it can be used as a nested table. The only difference between a variable length array and a nested table is that with a variable length array the data is stored with the table in which it is defined. A nested tables stores the data in a separate table. Finally, an object type can be used as a row object. A row object table is a table that contains only objects.
***Section:** Object Persistence Using Oracle*

97.   Explain the difference in perspective between SQL3 and ODMG-93.

SQL3 is developed as an extension to the SQL92 database standard. As such, SQL3 starts from the perspective of a relational database, and attempts to extend that idea to include support for object structures and OOP processes. Therefore, SQL3 starts with database thinking and moves toward object thinking. ODMG-93 is developed from the base of the Common Object Model. As such, ODMG-93 starts from the perspective of object structures and object processing. ODMG-93 considers the object to be the fundamental building block, whereas SQL3 starts with a relation as the fundamental building block.
***Section:** ODBMS Standards*